Counterterrorism:
Bridging Operations and Theory

A TERRORISM RESEARCH CENTER BOOK

Robert J. Bunker, John P. Sullivan, Brian Michael Jenkins,
Matthew G. Devost, and James T. Kirkhope

Editors

COUNTERTERRORISM:
BRIDGING OPERATIONS AND THEORY
A TERRORISM RESEARCH CENTER BOOK

iUniverse books may be ordered through booksellers or by contacting:

iUniverse
1663 Liberty Drive
Bloomington, IN 47403
www.iuniverse.com
1-800-Authors (1-800-288-4677)

ISBN: 978-1-4917-5977-6 (sc)
ISBN: 978-1-4917-5978-3 (e)

Printed in the United States of America.

iUniverse rev. date: 02/06/2015

Acknowledgements

This book is the product of the long-term collaboration, both formal and informal, of many of the editors and contributors. During the early phases of the project, we received sponsorship from the Memorial Institute for the Prevention of Terrorism in Oklahoma City. Accordingly we would like to thank General Dennis Reimer, former director of that center for his support. We also benefited from the support of the Terrorism Research Center (TRC) throughout the course of assembling this text. This, like many projects, grew beyond that initial phase in scope and timetable, and this work is the responsibility of the editors alone. Several people have directly provided editorial support for this text. During the early phases of production, Andre DeMarce and Betty O'Hearn at the TRC provided editorial and administrative support, respectively. They were joined by Adam Elkus, then a student at Occidental College, who also provided early editorial support. Pamela Ligouri Bunker provided the last round of editorial support for this project. Finally, the editors would like to acknowledge all of the contributors for their insights and advice. —*The Editors*

Dedication

This text is dedicated to the men and women of all disciplines who work to combat terrorism. Specifically, however, we dedicate this book to our colleague Scott Gerwehr. Scott was a pioneer in understanding deception and counter-deception in the fight against terrorism. He tragically lost his life in a motorcycle accident in May 2008 while this text was still early in production. His wise counsel and energy will continue to inspire those of us who had the honor to work with him. We also recognize two additional contributors who died prior to publication: James P. Denney, Los Angeles City Fire Department retired, and William C. Patrick III, influential bioweaponeer and biodefense specialist. Their work has contributed to the understanding of terrorism response. —*The Editors*

About the Terrorism Research Center

The Terrorism Research Center (TRC) is non-profit think tank focused on investigating and researching global terrorism issues through multi-disciplinary collaboration amongst a group of international experts. Originally founded as a commercial entity in 1996, the TRC was an independent institute dedicated to the research of terrorism, information warfare and security, critical infrastructure protection, homeland security, and other issues of low-intensity political violence and gray-area phenomena. Over the course of 15 years, the TRC has conducted research, analysis, and training on a wide range of counterterrorism and homeland security issues.

First established on April 19, 1996, the year anniversary of the Oklahoma City terrorist bombing, the TRC operated for 15 years as a commercial entity providing research, analysis, and training on issues of terrorism and international security. The three original co-founders, Matthew Devost, Brian Houghton, and Neal Pollard, are reconstituting a new board of directors, comprised of researchers, first responders, and academic and professional experts. "The TRC had an incredible legacy as a commercial company," says Matthew Devost. "We believe there is still a strong need to continue the research and collaboration on such critical topics in the public's best interest."

From 1996 through 2010, the TRC contributed to international counterterrorism and homeland security initiatives such as Project Responder and the Responder Knowledge Base, Terrorism Early Warning Groups, Project Pediatric Preparedness, Global Fusion Center, and the "Mirror Image" training program. These long-standing programs leveraged an international network of specialists from government, industry, and academia. Reconstituting TRC as a non-profit will help establish the next generation of programs, research, and training to combat the emerging international security issues.

"Thousands of researchers utilized the TRC knowledge base on a daily basis, says Brian Houghton, "Our intent is to open the dialogue, provide valuable counterterrorism resources, and advance the latest thinking in counterterrorism for the public good."

"We want to put the 15-year legacy and goodwill of TRC to continuing benefit for the public, rather than focus on a specific business model," says Neal Pollard. "TRC was founded in the wake of the 1995 Oklahoma City bombing and made its most significant contributions to the nation and the world after the attacks of September 11, 2001. Now that the War on Terrorism has evolved and the United States is entering a new era of transnational threats, the TRC will maintain its familiar role as the vanguard of next-generation research into these emerging threats."

For more information visit www.terrorism.org

Contents

Preface

The original imperative for this book was identified over a decade ago as the editors recognized a need to inform concerned individuals on foundational issues in counterterrorism. One need only look at the headlines to understand that terrorism is one of the most persistent threats that global citizens face regardless of their location, system of government, or heritage.

Early in the development of this book, John Sullivan, James Kirkhope, Neal Pollard, Brian Jenkins, and myself collected a series of topical essays on counterterrorism to be published in a volume sponsored by the National Memorial Institute for the Prevention of Terrorism (MIPT) in Oklahoma City. However, as priorities re-aligned, funding for the book was dropped and the initial effort stalled.

I was very pleased when Robert Bunker offered to dust-off the original collection of essays and led the editorial effort to collect new essays in order to publish this volume through the Terrorism Research Center. Without his efforts, this publication would not exist.

We also made a decision to slightly change the original intent of the book and focus on bridging the gap between counterterrorism operations and theory. As we learned through the formation of a National Terrorism Early Warning Network prior to, and in the aftermath of, the attacks of September 11th there is a requirement to provide both communities with a baseline understanding of the other. For example, if you asked a counterterrorism operations specialist what ten essays a counterterrorism academic should read and vice versa, our hope was that this volume would fulfill both requirements. It is required reading for both communities by design.

Some of the essays in this book are timely given current headlines, but they are also intended to be timeless and address issues like radicalization, homegrown extremism, force protection, deception, counterinsurgency, and cyberwarfare. These are concepts that will endure for generations in the counterterrorism and international security communities. Other essays serve as case studies of important persons or groups that not only inform current counterterrorism experts but serve as a vital historical foundation for future practitioners.

While a volume such as this one will greatly contribute to our counterterrorism efforts, it can only do so much. Future success requires continued community engagement and the exchange of ideas, lessons learned, and institutional knowledge. We invite you to visit www. terrorism.org to continue the dialogue.

Matthew G. Devost
Co-Founder
Terrorism Research Center
mgd@terrorism.org

Introduction

This book, *Counterterrorism: Bridging Operations and Theory*, is meant to help facilitate spanning the gulf between those engaging in applied aspects of counterterrorism—essentially early warning, pre-emption response, mitigation, and consequence management—and those who are studying the underlying components of terrorism itself—e.g. how to define it, its causation, radicalization processes, group evolutionary patterns, and incident lessons learned—in order to better understand this phenomena for counterterrorism research purposes. Often such a diverse grouping of professionals and scholars are not found together in a project such as this because their paths do not normally cross.

A basic typology of the differences between such operators and theorists can be seen in *Figure 1. Counterterrorism Operators and Theorists.* Counterterrorism operators are training and unit focused, valuing physical outcomes in real world settings where time is a crucial component to tactical actions and missions and failure means that people can easily die. These individuals follow strict procedural and oversight requirements and defined chains of command in their activities. The downside to operators, however, is that they can be myopic in their vision and even rigid in their approach and, at times, do not have a handle on the larger context of their actions.

Theorists, even counterterrorism ones, on other hand, are more academically focused and quite typically operate individually or, at times, in small collaborative research groups. They tend to contemplate a problem—rather than having to immediately act—and value their autonomy of approach, creativity, and ability to engage in debate (and the consideration of different perspectives) when analyzing an issue or interaction. Methodology, models, replication, and validation of an approach or simulation can take precedent over the physical, and when conducting research, timeliness is not always considered a critical component. Theorist downsides are that they can become detached from day-to-day realities and lose sight of the 'so what' factor of how their work translates into meaningful counterterrorism applications.[1]

Figure 1: Counterterrorism Operations and Theorists

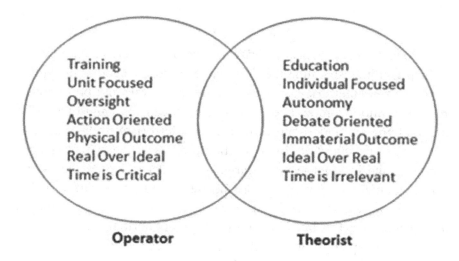

Training
Unit Focused
Oversight
Action Oriented
Physical Outcome
Real Over Ideal
Time is Critical

Education
Individual Focused
Autonomy
Debate Oriented
Immaterial Outcome
Ideal Over Real
Time is Irrelevant

Operator   **Theorist**

While some individuals do exist in the gray area of these extremes that have the essential operational and theoretical skills to approach counterterrorism from both perspectives, including a quite a few of the contributors to this volume, this is by far the exception rather than the norm. As a result, a gulf exists between the physical (e.g. trigger pullers and beat cops) and the analytical (e.g. intelligence and subject matter specialists) which has often been commented upon in the past regarding various elements of counterterrorism activities.[2] The level of divergence with operators is even greater when terrorism studies academics not specifically involved with policy response are factored into this equation. Many of the applied theorists in counterterrorism (and counterinsurgency) are police and military officers with advanced graduate level training, and are keenly aware of such polarization and have been actively involved in efforts to overcome this deficiency.

Hence, this situation is changing, albeit slowly, in our national capabilities; an example is the implementation of the FBI intelligence analysts program which pairs these specialists with special agents for intelligence led policing purposes. Years prior to this FBI program, the intent behind the Terrorism Early Warning Groups network was the leveraging of operators and theorists across both jurisdictional (local, state, federal and private) and disciplinary (fire, health, law, military and academic) boundaries to improve both proactive and incident specific response capabilities.[3]

With these thoughts in mind, the sixty-five essays in this book contributed by some fifty-four contributors range along a continuum from the operational through the theoretically focused, including many in the gray areas of the spectrum. At the same time, they also represent works ranging from the internationally through the U.S. domestically focused. The positioning of some of these essays along these axes can be viewed in *Figure 2. Counterterrorism Essays in Context*. Each contributor is writing to their professional and research expertise and strengths with many internationally recognizable names—Arquilla, van Creveld, Gunaratna, Hammes, Jenkins, Kilcullen, and Ronfeldt, to list but a few—participating in this project.

Figure 2: Counterterrorism Essays in Context

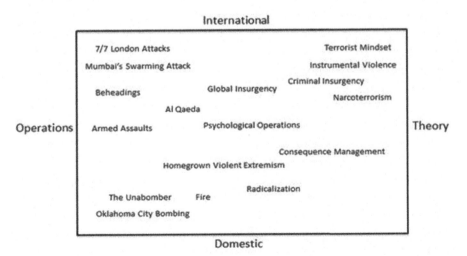

All of the quadrants of *Figure 2.* are pretty much covered within the pages of this book except for that of domestically focused theory because it represents a more specialized subset of writings on counterterrorism. Still, we believe that the various essays contained within this book will appeal to the operator, theorist, and hybrid (applied theorist) counterterrorism communities and allow them to gain an appreciation for each other's areas of focus as a bridging mechanism. The numerous contributors to this collection of essays run the gambit from police and military officers, national security professionals and even appointees, through university and think tank academics, those with private security consulting backgrounds, along with many individuals who have been held multiple counterterrorism positions during their careers. Hopefully, the dialogue created in this work amongst these many contributors will provide interested readers useful insights and lessons learned in support of furthering their knowledge and understanding of both counterterrorism operations and theory and our need to more effectively integrate these disciplines in order to better respond to ever evolving forms of 21st century terrorism.

The Editors
Counterterrorism:
Bridging Operations
and Theory

Notes

1. This dichotomy was readily evident in a Terrorism Research Center (TRC) Mirror Image Training rotation many years ago in which some of the operators initially refused to wear the keffiyeh as part of their terrorist garb for roleplaying purposes (they loathed the opposing force) and some of the terrorism subject matter experts (SMEs) didn't have the skill sets to properly engage in tactical actions (lack of small unit training).

2. For a counterterrorism red teaming example, see Robert J. Bunker, "Force Protection and Suicide Bombers: The Necessity for Two Types of Canadian Military Red Teams." *Canadian Military Journal.* Vol. 12, No. 4. (Autumn 2012): 35-43.

3. John P. Sullivan and Alain Bauer, Eds., *Terrorism Early Warning: 10 Years of Achievement in Fighting Crime and Terrorism.* Los Angeles: Los Angeles County Sheriff's Department, 2008.

Abu Nidal Organization

Jennifer Hardwick

The Abu Nidal Organization (ANO), which was active primarily in the 1980s but still remains on the U.S. Foreign Terrorist Organizations list to this day, targeted Western interests, along with Palestinian negotiators, Arab states (specifically, moderates like Jordan, Egypt, and the Gulf states), and representatives of the Israeli government. Their two goals were to disrupt the Palestinian Liberation Organization's (PLO) talks with the West—which it saw as compromising with Israel over Palestinian statehood—and the outright elimination of Israel (the Zionist enemy).

The ANO, which is known by various other names (Fatah al-Qiyadah al-Thawriyyah; Arab Revolutionary Brigades; Arab Revolutionary Council; Fatah Revolutionary Council; Revolutionary Organization of Socialist Muslims), split from the PLO in 1974 over its more radical ideology in facilitating a violent Arab revolution to liberate occupied Palestine. This resulted in the targeting of moderate Palestinians, Yassir Arafat supporters and allies, countries holding ANO operatives in prison, and Jewish entities.

Sabri al-Banna, also known as Abu Nidal, was the leader of this terrorist organization which was named after him. His father died in 1945 and his mother was deported to Syria, leaving him with 11 half-siblings and forcing him to abandon his education at about a third grade level. Al-Banna, the group's leader, was deeply impacted by the 1947 UN resolution to create two states in Palestine and the ensuing violent land grab, especially that in his hometown of Jaffa. From 1947-1949, al-Banna and his affluent family were forced into a refugee camp in Gaza and into poverty which was, as he perceived it, due to Israel's existence. By the 1960s, he was working in Saudi Arabia and attending secret meetings and recruiting for the politico-militant struggle for

Palestine. This got him arrested and then expelled from the Kingdom. The 1967 Arab-Israeli War—including the seizure of the Arab West Bank, Abu Nidal's homeland—galvanized the Palestinian liberation movement, writ large, and Abu Nidal, specifically. At first aligned with Fatah, the PLO umbrella group, and their leader Yassir Arafat, around 1974 Abu Nidal and his followers turned away from their willingness to negotiate and compromise with Israel and toward a more violent mantra, including hijacking an airplane in Iraq. Abu Nidal became radically anti-Israel, calling for the elimination of Israel, and the creation of a pan-Arab, secular, democratic homeland: Palestine.

Although a secular, nationalist group, ANO was funded by and found safe haven in Lebanon, Syria, Libya, and Iraq and supplied fighters for these countries. Additional funding may have come from corrupt practices, including blackmail. However, through diplomatic pressures, each country expelled ANO, so its access to materiel and funding are unclear.

The ANO launched attacks in some 20 countries with nearly 900 casualties. Many ANO attacks were targeted assassinations of Israeli political leaders (or allied nations' leaders) involved with discussions on Palestinian statehood. Abu Nidal knew the Israeli government was too powerful and secure; instead, he targeted Israeli diplomats and government officials on travel outside of Israel. They failed in an assassination attempt in 1982 against Shlomo Argov, the Israeli Ambassador to the UK, who was left paralyzed after the attack. This incident was the impetus to Israel's invading Lebanon in search of the PLO (and by extension, all of Palestine) and led to war. ANO also targeted representatives of Israel.

In 1984, ANO assassinated both a British diplomat in Athens and a British High Commissioner in Bombay. The following year, they kidnapped and killed a British journalist working for the UN in Beirut. The group is best known for its December 1985 simultaneous attack on El Al airline ticket counters at Vienna and Rome airports, resulting in 18 deaths and 111 injuries, and for hijacking various airplanes (PanAm 73 in 1986, EgyptAir 648 in 1985). The former attack was responsible for the introduction of military security forces at airports around the world. As can be seen, ANO also targeted allies of Israel. Italy and

Austria were nations friendly to Israel. In 1982, a café popular with Jews in France was bombed, leaving 40 people injured. Analysts believe that Abu Nidal colluded with Libya's Muammar Qaddafi to attack U.S.—also an Israel ally—targets in Beirut.

In a move that alienated many of the pan-Arab movement, Abu Nidal in 1973 began targeting Arab nations aligned with the PLO's strategy to negotiate with Israel. The first such attack was in Paris and targeted the Saudi Arabian Embassy. The group that claimed responsibility was al-Aqab, a known moniker of Abu Nidal. Just a year later, Abu Nidal plotted to assassinate Arafat, who sentenced Abu Nidal to death in absentia. This emboldened Abu Nidal, who then plotted attacks not only against PLO representatives in Kuwait City (Kuwait), London (UK), and Paris (France) but also against Arab newspapers he thought sided with Israel and against countries willing to negotiate with Israel. All of this culminated with the 1986 attack against Pakistani Gulf Air over the UAE, killing all 122 passengers aboard.

In sum, between 1973-1984, the organization, with approximately 200-500 fighters, was responsible for upward of 72 attacks in 20 countries that killed over 300 and wounded over 600 people. Thereafter, the group became less focused and began attacking on behalf of other causes. ANO assassinated the Ambassador of the UAE in Paris in 1984. The group also killed a number of anti-Qaddafi advocates. In 1988, they attacked a Greek ferry, killing 9 and injuring 100 passengers. In 1994, Abu Nidal assassinated a Jordanian diplomat in Lebanon.

Their cell structures were progressive for the time. Cells were often 3-5 members who rarely knew each other so that, under interrogation, members could not identify others. Many sleepers across numerous countries waited for orders to be activated. The group also used many names as a way to fool authorities and maintain some anonymity; conversely, they also claimed credit for attacks they were not involved in. For example, one ANO aide contends the group was behind the Lockerbie Pan Am 103 downing.

Between 1981-1984, Abu Nidal's family—his estranged wife Hiyam al-Bitar and two children, Badia and Nidal—may have been in hiding in Poland. After Abu Nidal hired a hitman to kill his wife's brother-in-law, Hiyam and Abu Nidal never reconciled, but their sizable coffers remained intertwined.

Between 1988 and 2002, Abu Nidal activities were fairly obscure. He may have been hiding in Iraq. Despite an arrest in 2008 of an ANO operative who allegedly was plotting attacks in Jordan, the group has been inactive since Sabri al-Banna (the group's leader) died in Baghdad in 2002 (rumors of his death began circulating in 1984). It remains unknown who killed Abu Nidal—whether himself (i.e. suicide), Mossad, Palestinians, or Hussein sympathizers. Many of his victims' families were upset that he escaped justice. No official successor has been named, likely because al-Banna was highly paranoid and systematically purged his inner circle, including a mass purge in 1982 in which he slaughtered 150 of his own aides and followers. There may still be sympathizers in Iraq, in Palestinian refugee camps in Lebanon, and possibly in Pakistan.

Further Reading

Yossi Melman, *The Master Terrorist: The True Story behind Abu Nidal.* New York: Adama Books, 1986.

Patrick Seale, *Abu Nidal: A Gun for Hire: The Secret Life of the World's Most Notorious Arab Terrorist.* New York: Random House, 1992.

Adaptation

Teaching an Old Dog New Tricks

Donald E. Vandergriff

Adaptability is a buzzword in today's military and homeland security culture. Everyone is seeking to build sleek, "networked" organizations that can deal with the stresses of increasingly complex terrorism and peace operation missions. Organizational change, however, can sometimes occur at the margins and leave the underlying culture largely untouched. The contemporary operating environment (COE) and the future environment may demand more. Recent history provides little encouragement.

The U.S. Army's own problems with adaptability illustrate several important lessons for those seeking to transform organizations to be more effective in asymmetric warfare: change is usually superficial and powerful interests will always resist deeper shifts in an organization's purpose and structure. The Army's evolution to AirLand Battle is one example of the trend of most information age organizations, and it was arguably one of the most important change periods of the post-Vietnam era. Yet, as with most organizations today, changes implemented in the 1982 Field Manual 100-5, *Operations*, largely focused on doctrine and hardware, and left the personnel system intact.

One might argue that change is endemic to Army culture. Several examples include a rapid mechanization of maneuver-oriented forces that occurred during World War II, racial integration in the 1940s and 50s, changing to an all-volunteer force in 1973, and expanded opportunities for women that began in the 1980s and continue today. Nevertheless, while change is arguably a way of life within the Army, so too is inertia, especially at the institutional level. Like most organizations, people at all levels resist change, especially when their definition of success depends on preserving the status-quo. As Edgar H. Schlein notes:

> If an organization has had a long history of success based on certain assumptions about itself and its environment, it is unlikely to want to challenge or reexamine those assumptions. Even if the assumptions are brought to consciousness, the members of the organization are likely to want to hold on to them because they justify the past and are the source of their pride and self esteem.

As the Army moved forward with technological and doctrinal changes, it left key variables untouched—personnel management laws, policies and beliefs—that contributed to management practices of the Army during the Vietnam War. This was highlighted in the Army Training and Leadership Development Panel (ATLDP) report in 2001 and it echoes findings of the Study on Military Professionalism conducted thirty years prior. This trend is also similar in non-military organizations, corporations, and police forces as well.

The ATLDP stated that "micromanagement has become part of the Army culture." Other sources have found that despite being engaged in some type of conflict since 9-11, this has not changed except in selected command environments. In 2003, an Army War College research project observed that "Today's organizational and individual level systems, however, are insufficient to ensure positive command climate is universally-established and sustained across the U.S. Army." The author, Colonel Steven Jones, established a link between climate and adaptability, "The persistence of serious climate problems today and throughout the past thirty years demonstrates convincingly that the organizational mindset and ability to retain aggressive, innovative junior leaders are in jeopardy."

The Army achieved unparalleled tactical success against the Iraqi Army in Operation Desert Storm and the opening combat phases of Operation Iraqi Freedom (OIF) and Operation Enduring Freedom (OEF). One could argue that the Army has been a victim of its own successful deployments validating what has become the ultimate conventional warfighting organization. At the heart of this Industrial Age organization is its commitment to conventional large unit maneuver warfare, as well as a centralized, top-down command style which stands in contrast to public proclamations of adaptability.

The system of promotion and selection is a potent social control mechanism. Promotion and selection laws and policies, as well as popularly espoused criteria of success "have the greatest impact on demonstrating and teaching the values of the organization." In most organizations, promotion and selection as well as evaluation tools provide the primary "power levers for changing or maintaining culture." These critical tools, presented as inherently fair, determine awards and control access to positions of influence and control. Industrial age organizations seeking to avoid error and maximize predictability tend to provide detailed instructions when tasking subordinates and strive for an unreasonable level of certainty. The individual as well as the system carefully monitor the execution of instructions and track all activities and outcomes with the finest attention to detail.

In their book *Embracing Uncertainty: The Essence of Leadership*, Phillip Clampitt and Robert DeKoch are critical of traditional leadership approaches that tend to suppress the acknowledgment of uncertainty that is inherent in today's environment. They argue that our demand for clear direction and confident leadership drives those in authoritative positions to pretend to know what they do not to avoid perceptions of weakness or indecisiveness. They suggest that a desire to control events, the quest for efficiency, emphasis on social cohesion, inertia of success, underdeveloped leadership skills, arrogance, and unrealistic expectations combine to drive organizations away from adaptivity.

Adaptive organizations require "transformation of employees' mind-sets and organizational processes." If any organization is to become a true adaptive learning organization, systems should support and not retard the move to an evolved organization that can solve problems presented in its operating environment. A culture must be in place to support and nurture the adaptability any organization needs in its structure and personnel. This places significant responsibility upon leaders who have the power and authority to identify and change systems and process that impede creativity, innovation, and adaptability.

Evolutionary Adaptability

A culture of adaptability is one that accepts a lack of absolute control over events on and off the operating environment. Implementation requires revisiting "mission orders" or "trust tactics." It necessitates raising the bar in the education, training, and coaching of leaders and employees. It seems trite to suggest that an adaptive institution will reward those who, when the need arises, act without waiting for orders, but this also necessitates a climate that is supportive of those who act and fail to achieve stellar results. Instead of seeking perfection or optimum solutions, operators will find a solution that works locally and then exploit those results as a continual evolution facilitated by an organization adept at receiving and communicating such information.

Past reliance on technically rational approaches will not suffice in the future. Instead of creating longer lists of false independent variables—knowledge, skills and attributes—that leaders must master and professional military education institutions must teach, it may be better to address a few key values and attributes such as fast learning, adaptability, and ethical reasoning. The teaching of 'fewer' earlier, will allow teachers and curriculum to be evolutionary; open to experimentation with up to date lessons learned. The Adaptive Leader's Methodology (ALM) model serves as an example. ALM involves innovative leader development concepts and the latest advances in education—applied at the Georgetown University ROTC detachment and recently implemented by instructors in the Basic Officer Leader Course (BOLC) II, a six-week course for all newly commissioned lieutenants. The application of ALM also translates well to non-military leader development programs. The ALM constantly puts students in difficult, unexpected situations, and then requires them to decide and act under pressure. ALM takes students out of their "comfort zones." Stress—mental and moral as well as physical—is a constant. Wargames, map exercises, tactical decision games and free-play force on force field exercises constitute the bulk of ALM curriculum. But the ALM is more than just a series of key events.

The Adaptive Leader's Methodology holds to the idea that every moment and event offers an opportunity to develop adaptability. Every action taken by a student in the classroom or in the field training is important to the process of inculcating a preference for new solutions. If a student errs while acting in good faith, they do not suffer anything more than corrective coaching. Constructive critiques of solutions are the norm, but more important are the results of actions, and the reasons for those actions. The role of coaching and 360-degree assessment is to develop the student so their future actions will make a positive contribution to their unit's success, no matter what the mission. This idea is based on the premise that one learns more from a well-meaning mistake reviewed critically and constructively than from applying an established and memorized process.

ALM teachers will be very concerned with why the students do what they do—an action-learning approach. The emphasis of the course will be on ensuring that the students gain and maintain a willingness to act. During numerous after action reviews and mentoring sessions—occurring during and after numerous scenarios with different conditions—the teacher will analyze why the students acted as they did and the effect the action had on the overall operation.

The ALM curriculum and leader evaluation system will use two criteria to judge whether students did well: the timeliness of their decisions, and their justification for actions taken. The first criterion will impress on the student the need to act in a timely manner, while the second requires the student to reflect on their actions and gain insights into their own thought processes. Since the student must justify their decision in their own mind before implementing it, imprudent decisions and reckless actions will be less likely. During the course, student decisions in terms of a "school solution" will be relatively unimportant. The emphasis will be on the effect of the students' actions, not on the methods they may have chosen. This encourages a learning environment where there will be few formulas, or processes to achieve optimum solutions. This environment will solicit creative solutions.

The learning evaluation system in the ALM is based on the philosophy that feedback should be given in a way that encourages a willingness to act and then reflect on actions in a manner that maximizes learning. Unconstructive critiques destroy the student leader's willingness to act and can lead to withholding of adverse information or false reporting. The course will avoid formulaic solutions and provide room for innovative solutions in its program of instruction (POI). This begins at the entry level to achieve transformation over a generation of leaders, teaching new dogs new tricks.

Stewards of the profession are responsible for identifying those with future potential. This makes the teachers at the ALM particularly important. When selecting or promoting subordinates the evaluator should ask, "Would I want this person to serve in my department?" Throughout, the teacher instills in students the importance of accurate reporting and to act when the situation demands it. The culture of any organization that wants to evolve as its environment evolves should not tolerate inaction, but it should be tolerant of failed attempts provided that learning occurs. The inability to act becomes the cardinal sin.

Summation

To cultivate a culture of adaptability throughout any complex mature organization will require effort—from the "top-down" as well as "bottom-up." Adaptability is so central to the success of organizations that it applies equally to section leaders and strategic level leaders and managers. It requires an organization that embraces uncertainty, and leaders who are action-learning oriented and risk tolerant. In such an environment future leaders would have to make reckless or negligent errors to reflect negatively on their efficiency reports. Learning and adaptation require exploration and experimentation, and most experiments initially fail.

Moving any organization toward the ideal of a "learning organization"—as an organization-in-action, where its institutions create conditions for adaptive and creative organizing, could bring the collective creativity of the future organization to bear in solving problems at the tactical, operational and strategic levels of its operating environment. It requires senior leaders who encourage, teach, trust, and support innovative subordinates.

Adaptable soldiers and processes are keys to the future organization, especially in an era of unprecedented and accelerating change. Emerging forms of terrorism and insurgency require the creation of innovative solution sets based on new and novel approaches. The understanding and application of adaptability will come through rigorous education and tough training early on and require reinforcement throughout the system of professional military education. The move to adaptability will take more than using the term in PowerPoint presentations or repackaging curricula and personnel policies with adaptive sounding names. Substantive change begins with the use of innovative learning models such as that used in the Adaptive Leader Methodology and with the selection of qualified teachers to implement and carry out the curriculum. Simple recitation of canned lesson plans and implementing "turnkey" curricula will not suffice to prepare our leaders to be action learners in full spectrum operations as those operations emerge. The institutional as well as the operational Army must be prepared to support, encourage, and reinforce adaptability.

Further Reading

Phillip G. Clampitt and Robert J. DeKoch, *Embracing Uncertainty: The Essence of Leadership*. New York: M.E. Sharpe, Inc., 2001.

Williamson Murray, *Military Adaptation in War: With Fear of Change*. New York: Cambridge University Press, 2011.

Donald Vandergriff, *Raising the Bar: Creating and Nurturing Adaptability to Deal With the Changing Face of War*. Washington, DC: Center for Defense Information Press, 2006.

Al Qaeda

Qaedat al-Jihad

Rohan Gunaratna

Today, transnational and national Muslim insurgent and terrorist groups pose the greatest global threat. The genesis of the current wave of terrorism goes back to the Soviet invasion of Afghanistan on Christmas Day 1979. To fight the Soviets, the Pakistani, Saudi, U.S. and British intelligence services collaborated with Muslim youth who gathered in Pakistan. Compared to the Afghan fighters, the Arab contingent was a small component. The Arabs were coordinated by Maktab Khadamāt al-Mujāhidīn al-'Arab (MaKAfghan Service Bureau) founded by the Palestinian-Jordanian Abdullah Azzam in Pakistan in 1984. Azzam's deputy and financier was Osama bin Laden, the unofficial representative of the House of Saud to the anti-Soviet multinational Afghan campaign (1979-1989).

Six months before the Soviets withdrew from Afghanistan, MaK evolved into al Qaeda (The Base). Created by Osama bin Laden in Peshawar, Pakistan on August 11, 1988, the group drew from the vision of Azzam, considered the Father of Jihad. Azzam conceptualized al Qaeda as the "pioneering vanguard of the Islamic movements." After Azzam was killed by the rival Egyptian leaders, the Egyptian Islamic Jihad (EIJ) leader Dr. Ayman al Zawahiri served as bin Laden's advisor. Zawahiri collaborated with al Qaeda from the very inception and later EIJ merged with al Qaeda, renaming it as Qaedat al-Jihad.

The success of the anti-Soviet Multinational Afghan Mujahidin campaign emboldened the Muslim fighters. They planned to assist their Muslim brethren in other conflict zones—Kashmir, Chechnya, Bosnia, Algeria, Palestine, etc. However, bin Laden fell out with the Kingdom following the Iraqi invasion of Kuwait of August 1990s. Bin Laden's offer to bring the mujahidin to defend the Kingdom was rejected by the Saudi royal family. With the Saudis preferring the presence of Western forces, and together with other activists and clerics, bin Laden protested and was placed under house arrest. After intervention by his family, bin Laden left Saudi Arabia. As the Saudi and the Pakistani security services collaborated, he feared for his safety and wanted to leave the country. He accepted an invitation from the National Islamic Front leader Hassan al Turabi to relocated to Khartoum, Sudan in April 1991. In addition to supporting African insurgent and terrorist groups, al Qaeda deepened its network in the Balkans, the Caucuses and the Middle East. Since bin Laden's relocation from the Sudan to Afghanistan in May 1996, the Afghan Taliban collaborated with al Qaeda. The leader of the Islamic Emirate of Afghanistan, Mullah Mohammad Omar, designated the Amir al-Mumineen (Commander of the Faithful), gave al Qaeda the mandate to train fighters worldwide. By providing ideology, training, finance, and weapons in Afghanistan and in other theaters, al Qaeda empowered insurgent and terrorist groups in Asia Africa, the Middle East, the Caucuses, and the Balkans. To attack the distant and far enemies, al Qaeda built an umbrella group—the World Islamic Front for Jihad against Jews and Crusaders in 1998. Al Qaeda attacked the U.S. embassies in Kenya and Tanzania in August 1998 and the U.S.S. Cole in Yemen in October 2000. Nonetheless, the U.S. response was weak and al Qaeda continued to plan a major terrorist attack on U.S. soil.

By staging 9/11, al Qaeda conducted an exhibition attack against America's most iconic economic, military and political landmarks. The attack inspired and instigated 30 associated groups to mount attacks in the global south against Western targets in their own countries as well as against their own governments. Al Qaeda urged their associates to hit both "the US, the head of the poisonous snake shielding corrupt Muslim rulers and ungodly regimes at home." In October 2001, when the U.S. intervened in Afghanistan, al Qaeda leaders relocated either to Pakistan and Iran. A determined and ruthless threat group, al Qaeda worked with the Taliban to attack U.S. and Afghan forces on Afghan soil. Al Qaeda also planned several attacks on Western soil. Richard Reid planned to blow up a U.S. plane using a shoe bomb, Dhiren Barot alias Issa al Hindi alias Issa al Britani planned attacks both on British and U.S. soil, and Rashid Rauf planned the airline liquid plot.

Al Qaeda suffered severely due to Pakistani and U.S. operations. The 9-11 mastermind, Khalid Sheikh Mohamed was captured in Rawalpindi by the Inter-Services-Intelligence of Pakistan on March 1, 2003 and Osama bin Laden was killed in Abbottabad by U.S. Special Operations Forces working with the Central Intelligence Agency on May 2, 2011. Afterwards, Dr. Ayman al Zawahiri, his then deputy, was appointed as the temporary leader. After the Consultative Council of al Qaeda met, al Zawahiri was confirmed as the leader. The former Secretary of bin Laden, Nasir Abdel Karim al-Wuhayshi alias Abu Basir, the leader of al Qaeda in the Arabian Peninsula (AQAP) was appointed as the deputy. As Zawahiri was cautious of his security, he failed to conduct operations outside Pakistan. As the U.S. focused on eliminating al Qaeda in tribal Pakistan, its associate groups in Asia, Africa and the Middle East grew several times stronger than al Qaeda. Al Qaeda itself evolved from an operational group to an ideological and a training organization. Due to their immense wealth and access to weaponry, the al Qaeda associated groups today present a formidable threat. Despite its losses, al Qaeda emerged as a force multiplier by collaboration with its partners. Until al Qaeda disowned Islamic State of Iraq and Syria (ISIS), the al Qaeda movement consisted of five organizations: (1) the Islamic State of Iraq, (2) Jabat al Nusra, (3) al Shabab, (4) al Qaeda in the Islamic Maghreb and (5) al Qaeda in the Arabian Peninsula. As it wished to guide and control the group, al Qaeda was selective. Nonetheless, several groups from the Philippines to Indonesia, Pakistan to Lebanon, and Nigeria to Mali, seek to follow al Qaeda. Rather than enlisting every group that wished to join al Qaeda, both Osama bin Laden and Ayman al Zawahiri chose and embraced likeminded groups very cautiously and carefully. The expansion of al Qaeda from a group into a movement with leaders drawn from Asia and the Middle East makes it resilient.

With the pending U.S.-led coalition withdrawal from Afghanistan, the reconstitution of the Afghan sanctuary by al Qaeda, Taliban, and their associated groups is imminent. Like the earlier generation of Soviet forces, Western forces failed to sustain and succeed in a long drawn out insurgency. Despite the growing threat of terrorism to the

U.S., its allies, and friends, the lack of U.S. public will to commit forces in conflict zones over the long term led to the drawdown. The U.S. intentions are to maintain a smaller footprint of Special Operations Forces, its enablers, and withdraw the bulk of the general purpose forces. In addition to mounting intelligence led counter-terrorism and insurgency operations, the U.S. will provide trainers and advisors to support Afghan capacity to fight and develop a range of capabilities. In contemporary times, they checkmated the Soviets, leading to their withdrawal and collapse as a superpower. From tribal Pakistan, they stage operations into Afghanistan, especially in its southeast and in the capital of Kabul. However, the Afghan security forces without international support cannot sustain themselves against a persistent and a relentless adversary. They are no match against 20,000 highly motivated and battle hardened Taliban fighters. The Afghan Taliban derives its strength from Tehrik-e-Taliban Pakistan (TTP), a conglomerate of groups. As followers of Deobandism—a puritanical sect of Sunni Islam, several hundred foreign fighters, notably al Qaeda, support the Taliban. With news of the U.S. drawdown, they wait to re-enter Afghanistan. As the border is porous, they move back and forth from Pakistan to Afghanistan, capturing bordering towns and villages. Located in tribal Pakistan, these experienced fighters—inspired and instigated by al Qaeda—wage an intergenerational war. Their invincible warrior spirit reflects the deep belief that Afghanistan is the graveyard of empires. Al Qaeda's global aim is to fight "until every spot of the lands of Islam are liberated; and until the flag of victory and jihad is raised high and fluttering over Grozny, Kashgar, Bukhara, Samarkand, Kabul, Manila, Jakarta, Baghdad, Damascus, Mecca, Madina, Sana'a, Mogadishu, Cairo, Algeria, and Ceuta and Melilla; and until the Islamic conquests return, then it will liberate the usurped Andalusia and the stolen Aqsa and restore them and the rest of all the usurped countries of the Muslims to the coming State of the Caliphate, Allah permitting."

Due to operations by the Pakistani security forces and U.S. drones strikes, al Qaeda depleted the strength of its Arab fighters. With below 200 foreign fighters, al Qaeda recruited several South Asian Muslims, mostly Pakistanis to create a new organization. On 3 September 2014, the al Qaeda leader Dr. Zawahiri announced the establishment of al Qaeda in the Indian Subcontinent (AQIS). Jamā'at Qā'idat al-Jihād fī Shibh al-Qārrah al-Hindīyah or the Organisation of the Base of Jihad in the Indian Subcontinent is led by Asim Umar, a former commander of TTP. The recruits included several Pakistani military officers. Those who joined AQIS claimed responsibility for assassinating Brigadier Fazal Zahoor of the Pakistani Army on September 2, 2014. On September 6, 2014, AQIS attacked Karachi Naval dockyard and attempted to hijack a frigate with the intention of attacking a U.S. aircraft carrier. Three attackers were killed and seven were arrested by Pakistani forces.

The single biggest blow to al Qaeda was when one of its associated groups, the Islamic State of Iraq and Syria (ISIS) disobeyed an instruction by Zawahiri not to operate in Syria but to confine its operations to Iraq. The rise of ISIS, ISIS-al Nusra discord, al Qaeda's rejection of ISIS, and the ISIS leader Abu Bakr al Baghdadi proclaiming a Caliphate eroded the power and prestige of al Qaeda in the eyes of the Muslim World. Denying reports of its waning influence and strength, al Qaeda launched an intense media campaign claiming that al Qaeda was not on the decline. In September 2014, al Qaeda official Hossam Abdul Raouf said: "So how then can al-Qaida have shrunken greatly and lost many of its senior leaders at a time when it is expanding horizontally and opening new fronts dependent on it? And it goes without saying that these new branches require a number of senior leaders, and that constant communication must be maintained with them for purposes of coordination, consultation, support, and so on." After the transformation of al Qaeda from a group to a movement, al Qaeda as a structure and an ideology is likely to survive. Although the U.S. weakened several threat groups during the last 15 years, it failed to eliminate a single group belonging to the al Qaeda family. Furthermore, with the diversion of counterterrorism resources worldwide, the fight is likely to last many years.

The ISIS-al Qaeda discord widened after Abu Bakr al Baghdadi declared an Islamic Caliphate in May 2014. Although Zawahiri himself advocated an Islamic Caliphate, he did not agree with the process Abu Bakr followed. An al Qaeda official Muhammad bin Mahmoud Rabie al-Bahtiyti alias Abu Dujana al-Basha issued an audio speech warning Muslims against following the Islamic Caliphate and urging fighters in

Syria to "rescue the ship of jihad, and reach it before it deviates from its course and settles on the path of the people of desires". Reflecting al Qaeda's disappointment with ISIS, he added: "We call to restore the rightly-guided Caliphate on the prophetic method, and not on the method of deviation, lying, breaking promises, and abrogating allegiances—a Caliphate that stands with justice, consultation, and coming together, and not with oppression, infidel-branding the Muslims, killing the monotheists, and dispersing the rank of the mujahideen."

The Arab Spring created opportunities for insurgent, terrorist, and extremist groups to emerge throughout the Middle East and in North Africa. The new environment, a by-product of the Arab Spring, enabled old groups that survived a decade of counter-insurgency and counter-terrorism operations to return to life. Like the local threat groups that embraced al Qaeda in the past, ISIS successes in Iraq and Syria prompted new and old groups worldwide to pledge allegiance to the ISIS leadership of "Caliph" Abu Bakr al Baghdadi. Many of them such as the Bangsamoro Islamic Freedom Fighters and Abu Sayyaf Group in the (Philippines), Jamaat Asharut Tawheed (Indonesia) Sons of the Call for Tawhid and Jihad (Jordan), Jamaat Ansar Bayt al-Maqdis (Sinai) and the Majlis Shura al-Mujahedeen (Gaza) hitherto supported al Qaeda. Although they were not operationally associated with al Qaeda, they were ideologically affiliated with al Qaeda. Despite the ISIS and al Qaeda leadership's clash, the members of ISIS admire al Qaeda and members of al Qaeda admire ISIS. The Caliphate galvanized the imagination of Muslims spurring a segment of Muslim communities to support it, including Muslims from Australia to the UK and Canada and movements in the Muslim World. Support for ISIS split several groups. In North Africa, Jund al-Khilafa split from al Qaeda in the Islamic Maghreb and pledged allegiance to ISIS. In the Middle East, Ansar Al-Dawlah Islamiyah split from al Qaeda in the Arabian Peninsula and went over to ISIS. In South Asia, Tehreek-e-Kalifat split with Tehrik-i-Taliban Pakistan and now supports ISIS. Although others did not split, the membership within a dozen other groups are divided, including al Jamaah al Islamiyah in Southeast Asia, Boko Haram in Nigeria, al Shabab in Somalia and other ideologically affiliated groups of al Qaeda.

Al Qaeda flourished in ungoverned spaces or in conflict zones. The international community's attempts to change the regimes in Iraq, Libya and now Syria and support for pro-democracy movements in the Arab World destabilized the Levant, Maghreb, and Sahel. The cascading chaos has been exploited by the al Qaeda inspired insurgent, terrorist and extremist groups growing in strength, size and influence by expanding territorial control and spreading their ideology. The post-9/11 environment witnessed Western interventions in Afghanistan and Iraq, the Arab Spring turning into an Arab nightmare, and a steadfast deterioration in Shia-Sunni relations. These developments challenged the legitimacy of Muslim leaders and their governments and inflicted suffering on ordinary citizens. Until the rise of ISIS, the al Qaeda movement presented the only security threat to the West. Despite their leaders being at conflict, al Qaeda fighters, operatives, supporters, and followers are a model for ISIS. ISIS is following in the footsteps of al Qaeda. Like al Qaeda at the turn of the century, ISIS today poses a global threat.

In many ways, ISIS is al Qaeda's most virulent strain. An al Qaeda 2.0, ISIS will produce several permutations. With a fledgling external wing, ISIS is likely to support several groups, operational cells, and individuals worldwide that will pose a long-term strategic threat to global stability and security. In retaliation to coalition operations, the Islamic Caliphate's worldwide support network of groups, supporters, and sympathizers are likely to attack the U.S., their allies, and friends. As ISIS is one of the world's largest insurgent-terrorist groups, with 20,000-30,000 fighters straddling Iraq, Syria and a global network, the conflict is likely to last several years. Although the al Qaeda threat is manageable, the ISIS threat is formidable. Unlike al Qaeda, ISIS poses an existential threat to the Muslim World, at least in the Levant. The timely intervention by the U.S.-led coalition in September 2014 prevented ISIS from expanding its territory and threatening the entire region. In the eyes of ISIS supporters and followers, their corrupt regimes and ungodly rulers have failed them and the pious pray for change. Defeating the new Iraqi Army and capturing large swathes of territory straddling Iraq and Syria offer hope to a segment of the Sunni Muslims challenged for centuries by the West as well as threatened by a

Shia Iran. Islamic nationalists see the Caliphate as the height of Islam's glory, especially after centuries of Western dominance of the Muslim World.

After the U.S. led international coalition intervened in Iraq and Syria in September 2014, ISIS is replacing al Qaeda as the global leader of radical and violent movements. The old cast of leaders have been decapitated, incarcerated, or disappeared. A new cast of leaders are struggling to be born. The global strategy is needed to contain, isolate, and eliminate ISIS, Jabat al Nusra, and other players. To be effective, the effort should be very similar to the model that contained and isolated al Qaeda. A multipronged, multidimensional, multiagency, multinational, and multijurisdictional response is needed. Today, the world's most ruthless insurgent group is not al Qaeda but ISIS. Just as al Qaeda could not be disrupted, degraded, and destroyed by air power, ISIS too will survive. A much smaller al Qaeda could not be destroyed after a decade of drone and air strikes and special operations missions. Although airpower can slow down the lightening advances of ISIS, the group will survive the current campaign and revive with a vengeance. Without highly trained specially equipped ground forces with real time intelligence and air assets, ISIS cannot be fought effectively. The collateral damage and destruction will expand recruitment and global support. Exploiting civilian deaths and injuries from air strikes, ISIS is likely to sustain sympathy and support from the affected and beyond. Like al Qaeda ideology penetrated territorial, diaspora and migrant communities, the ISIS virus too will infect Muslims, creating a global network of groups, homegrown cells, and individuals willing to kill and die.

The successes and failures of fighting al Qaeda can be applied to the campaign to defeat ISIS. The international coalition seeking to degrade and destroy ISIS in Iraq will succeed only if the international community can first restore stability in Syria. Like al Qaeda moved in to tribal Pakistan, ISIS will exploit the chaos in Syria. As the border between Iraq and Syria is virtually non-existent, when ISIS is attacked in Iraq it will seek sanctuary in Syria. Likewise, in order to dismantle Jabat al Nusra and the Khorasan Group (an al Qaeda operational group in Syria), the international coalition will need the support of the Syrian regime. Due to the heightened threat posed by ISIS and Jabat al Nursa, the international community may be compelled to work with Russia, Iran, and Syria.

The greatest challenge for the U.S., their allies, and friends in the early 21st century is to fight al Qaeda, its associated and affiliated groups, and its home grown cells. It is not states but such non-state actors that present the greatest threat. Considering the extensive use of social media by such groups, the fight will have to be kinetic and non kinetic. To be successful, the fight against this new generation of groups will have to be in both real and cyber space. In addition to fighting threat groups on the battlefield, governments—in partnership with their community organizations—should counter extremist ideologies and promote moderation. Mainstream Muslim leaders must maintain vigilance against attempts by misguided leaders who, for their personal and political advantage, seek to spread propaganda to recruit Muslim youth to extremism and violence. In addition to criminalizing by law those nationals advocating, supporting, or participating in fighting overseas, governments should pass harmony acts making it illegal to incite religious hatred. To ensure Muslims are not attracted to violent and extremist groups such as al Qaeda, the Taliban, ISIS, Jabat al Nusra, al Shabab and Boko Haram, Muslim community and religious leaders must rise to the occasion by exposing their large scale cruel massacres. Through schools, youth organizations, and strategic communications platforms, they must promote coexistence, moderation, and tolerance within local and other communities. To fight prejudice and suspicion propagated by extremist and violent groups, governments should take the lead and work together with Muslim community organizations. To counter the extremist message both in real and cyber space, they must train, groom, and mentor a new generation of champions of harmony. Understanding al Qaeda, the prototype, is the key to defeating the al Qaeda Movement.

Further Reading

Rohan Gunaratna, *Inside al Qaeda: The Global Network of Terror.* New York: Columbia University Press, 2002.

Ali Soufan, *The Black Banners: The Inside Story of 9/11 and the War Against al-Qaeda.* New York: W. W. Norton & Company, 2011.

Lawrence Wright, *The Looming Tower: Al-Qaeda and the Road to 9/11.* New York: Alfred A. Knopf, 2006.

Anthrax

The Anthrax Letters: Six Months Later

William C. Patrick III

Editors' Note: This analysis of the 2002 anthrax letters was written in late June 2002. We have included it, despite its age, because it deviates from the usual analysis of the attacks. William C. Patrick III, a former member of the U.S. bioweapons program (before it was dismantled), has unique insight on the nature and effect of the attacks. In late 2014, the further reading section of this essay was updated with current works on this topical area.

It has been about six months since this nation experienced the anthrax letters. I refer not to the hoax letters but letters that contained, if not weapons grade powder, a high quality anthrax powder. What has been our response to these acts of bioterrorism? From my perspective, the response has not been particularly effective. Probably less than 10 grams of agent have caused 22 infections with five deaths. We kill and maim more people each day in car accidents, yet the anthrax event has shut down two important Federal buildings, caused widespread panic among our people, and has literally changed our national lifestyle. At last count, 42,000 people have been administered antibiotics. The economic cost, although high, is difficult to estimate. The manner in which large and small companies open their mail has changed in response to anthrax letters. The Hart Office Building, which houses our highest elected officials, was closed for about three months. The Brentwood Postal Facility, a very large building in which millions of letters were processed daily, has yet to be decontaminated and reoccupied.

It is a cliché to say that the "terrorists will win" if we don't continue our everyday lives, but in this case I cannot agree more. Our collective response has more than likely exceeded the wildest objectives of the perpetrator(s). Who would ever have anticipated the opening of a letter, a very poor and inefficient method for producing a small-particle, infectious aerosol, would have caused significant modification to our way of life? I do not believe that even the perpetrator(s) anticipated that high-speed processing equipment of the post office, that compresses letters as they flow through the system, would act as a highly efficient munition in dispersing the anthrax spore as a small particle lethal aerosol.

The perpetrator(s) responsible for the anthrax letters chose their agent carefully and with knowledge of those agent properties that are required for an effective bioagent. *Bacillus anthracis* differs significantly from all of the other potential BW agents. It stands alone in left field. The organic nutrient requirements are not complex, and processing the spore from a dry form can be done without the tender loving care that is necessary for most other bioagents. The spore has the stability to survive in a letter as it travels through the changes in temperature and humidity of the post office system. This property is truly unique and places the anthrax spore in a special category. Perhaps only *Varioli* virus (small pox) and *coxiella burnetii* (Q fever) in dry form, with a few appropriate stabilizers, would achieve the stability to withstand the rigorous environment of the postal system and arrive at the target to cause infection like the anthrax spores did.

The FBI is the lead agency responsible for capturing these bioterrorists. They have relied primarily on two respected research institutes to help them in their technical assessment of the anthrax letter. These two institutes are staffed with competent and qualified scientists; however, these professionals have no experience in the unique field of biological agent powders. Since these organizations were not particularly competent to address and characterize anthrax powders, they failed to call on a pool of expertise that still exists in the Frederick community. Who better to hunt down the perpetrators of this incident than the very men and women from the old U.S. offensive bioweapon program?

We have not called on the specialized knowledge of scientists who devoted years of their professional life to the development and manufacture of weaponized agents. Our array of ex-bioweaponeers includes scientists from the research directorates, microbiologists and engineers from the pilot plant development area, aerobiologists from Aerosol Assessment Division, and munitions development engineers from Engineering Development. I believe this group of experts stands ready and able to assist their government if called upon.

Another area where the experience derived from the former U.S. Offensive Program could have been used (and was not used) was in the decontamination of the Hart and Brentwood buildings. Forty-five years ago, Ft. Detrick safety investigators developed a highly-effective procedure for the decontamination of research laboratories and the pilot plants at Ft. Detrick, as well as the production plants at Pine Bluff Arsenal. Puraformaldehyde vapor was used often and quite successfully during our active program. When President Nixon disestablished the Offensive Program by executive order in 1969, all of the hot R&D laboratories (including the anthrax pilot plant) at Ft. Detrick and the large production facilities at Pine Bluff Arsenal were decontaminated by paraformaldehyde. All of these buildings were certified as "safe" and there have been no infections from these buildings. There also has been no increased incidence of cancer as a result of paraformaldehyde having been used. This is a decontamination procedure that simply must be used if and when another BW event occurs.

Though I am happy to see the event closed, I cannot help but fear for the future. If we can expect such panic and disorganization in response to a relatively minor incident, I shudder to think about the consequences of a *real* biological attack.

Further Reading

Leonard A. Cole, *The Anthrax Letters: A Bioterrorism Expert Investigates the Attack That Shocked America.* Reprint. New York: Skyhorse Publishing, 2009.

Jeanne Guillemin, *American Anthrax: Fear, Crime, and the Investigation of the Nation's Deadliest Bioterror Attack.* New York: Times Books, 2011.

David Willman, *The Mirage Man: Bruce Ivins, the Anthrax Attacks, and America's Rush to War.* New York: Bantham Books, 2011.

Armed Assaults

Matt Begert

Armed assaults can be defined as sudden and violent direct action employing small arms. The target: a crowd of people (usually in a public place) blissfully unaware of the carnage to come. An armed assault is, generally, the equivalent of the military tactic of an ambush, usually utilizing small arms such as pistols and automatic weapons. Like an ambush, an armed assault leverages surprise in time and place to magnify the operation's effect and increase the probability of success.

Like any other military endeavor, armed assaults require preparatory steps such as reconnaissance of place, rehearsal of events, and a logistics support plan. Armed assaults often appear chaotic and spontaneous to the observer, but they are not simple "run and guns" thrown together on the fly. Most require some degree of planning to ensure success.

A comparison to bombings, another popular form of terrorism, demonstrates the high difficulty and risk associated with armed assaults. With the exception of suicide bombers, a bombing usually involves remote or timed detonation, which takes the bomber out of the center of the area of operation. In contrast, an armed assault involves ingress or positioning to the event and direct execution of the assault, exposing the assailant to retaliation from survivors and security forces. Lastly, bombings are sudden, violent events that are impossible to stop after initiation. If security forces have failed to stop a suicide bomber from detonating himself outside of a Tel Aviv disco, the only thing they can do is collect the victims' mangled remains. However, security forces can stop an armed assailant even after his killing spree has begun. To overcome these difficulties, assailants must make use of surprise, environmental conditions, and highly lethal small arms.

Charles Whitman, known as the Texas Tower Sniper, planned and executed an armed assault, killing fourteen people and injuring thirty-two others in about 90 minutes. Surprise and a remote location contributed to the difficulty in mitigating and stopping his assault. Mir Aimal Kansi used surprise and congested traffic to kill two and injure three in an assault with an AK-47 in front of the CIA headquarters in 1993.

Certain target sets have inherent vulnerabilities that make them attractive choices for armed assaults. A particular favorite of politically-motivated assailants is civilian airports. Significant civilian airport assaults since 1969 have generally been organized attacks executed by politically motivated groups. Assaults by lone actors have occurred less often, but are not to be ruled out as a continuing threat.

Why are airports such tempting targets? The answer lies in their high importance to the global network of commerce, business, and communications. Airports are part of system of transportation that includes people, cargo, and airplanes; a hub connected to numerous far-flung destinations. Time, experience, and new technology have made this system safe, efficient, economical, accessible, precise, and dependable. As a consequence, the global financial system has become highly dependent on air travel's continued success. Long delays, interruptions, and cancellations of scheduled flights are costly in time and money, giving airlines a consistent incentive to fly precisely as scheduled with the least amount of disruption.

Inherent in the airport's efficiency, economy, and convenience are a host of vulnerabilities that assailants can exploit. The components of this system (people, facilities, and airplanes) are concentrated in time and place for maximum efficiency. While an airport administrator may look at a line of passengers stuck in the holiday rush and see a good day for business, a terrorist sees a clump of victims who can be mowed down easily.

Airport assaults leverage the density of population in controlled spaces and designated areas (lines, gate areas, coffee shops) to sudden—and lethal—effect. Airport assaults may also exploit the opportunity to attack aircraft in the most vulnerable part of the flying cycle, while closely parked on the ground. Security forces seeking to deter such incidents must deal with a basic disadvantage: airports are civilian transportation centers, not military bases. They are organized to process human traffic, not provide a multi-layered defense against multiple threats.

The most prominent example of a large-scale airport assault is the planned simultaneous assaults on the airports in Rome and Vienna in December 1985. In Rome, four assailants used guns and hand grenades to assault passengers waiting for flights to New York and Tel Aviv. The targets also included an airport coffee shop and the El Al airlines ticket counter. Fifteen passengers were killed in the attack and several were wounded. Three of the assailants died and one was wounded in the ensuing pursuit and gun battle, At the Vienna airport, three assailants armed with guns attacked waiting passengers. However, the assault was partially disrupted by an airport security guard who detected and engaged the assailants, thereby giving passengers time to seek cover. With their plan thwarted, the assailants stole a car and fled. Police pursued, killing one attacker and capturing the rest. Three passengers were killed and forty-one wounded in the Vienna attack.

Armed assaults will continue to challenge operational and functional thinking in the near term. The ability to identify, prevent, mitigate, or counter threats from armed assaults may add new dimensions to the role of public safety.

Further Reading

William H. McRaven, *Spec Ops: Case Studies in Special Operations Warfare: Theory and Practice*. New York: Presidio Press, 1996.

Joshua Sinai, *Active Shooter: A Handbook on Prevention*. Alexandria: ASIS International, 2013.

Stephen Sloan and Robert J. Bunker, *Red Teams and Counterterrorism Training*. Norman: University of Oklahoma Press, 2011.

Asymmetric Warfare

Robert J. Bunker

We are currently in a new age of conflict. It has been called many things—"fourth generation warfare," "fourth epoch war," "hybrid wars," "netwar," and even "unrestricted war." Regardless of the validity of these taxonomies, they can all be characterized as forms of asymmetric warfare.

Traditional state-on-state warfare is highly symmetric. Like combatants wage war against each other using similar weapons, battlespace parameters, targeting schemes, and rules of engagement. The biggest example of a symmetric war is World War II. Despite the vile ideologies and atrocities of the Axis powers, they fought tank against tank, airplane against airplane, and carrier against carrier. Non-state entities have in the past, at least until the recent Islamic State conventional operations in Iraq using looted divisional army depot stockpiles, had no chance of taking on states in symmetric warfare (conflict). Al Qaeda, obviously, has no armored divisions. As a result, they turn to asymmetric warfare as a means of engaging states in a 'David and Goliath' like struggle. This should not be construed as a justification for terrorist forms of warfare—it is only an observation of fact.

Asymmetric warfare has vastly different combatants, weapons, battlespace parameters, targeting schemes, and/or rules of engagement. This is natural, as asymmetric combatants will avoid the state's strong points and leverage their abilities in battlespace that the state has little to no control over. States generally have greater difficulty contending with asymmetric warfare as the level of asymmetry increases. Unfortunately for the state, the level of asymmetry inherent in any given contest is often determined by the political-military disparity between combatants.

Terrorism waged by independent non-state actors is generally more difficult to respond to than state-sponsored terrorism. States can be brought to heel using tried and true diplomatic and economic tools. If these fail, a state can resort to the threat or actual use of state-on-state warfare against the sponsor of terrorism. Non-state groups are less affected by international legal sanctions and, particularly if possessing a networked organizational structure, are very difficult for states to engage in direct warfare.

Terrorism based on conventional small arms and explosives is less severe than terrorism based on highly creative techniques which turn everyday artifacts found in modern society into deadly weapons. For example, the September 11, 2001 attacks saw our commercial airline system being turned into a weapon against us by remaking jetliners into 'flying truck bombs' and has cost our nation an immense amount of economic resources to contend with this new terrorist technique. Worse yet, non-state terrorists seek to employ Weapons of Mass Destruction (WMD) and Directed Energy Weapons (DEW) to attack the state. For example, dirty bomb scenarios based on large scale explosive dispersal of radiological devices suggest that urban area targets can be made uninhabitable for long periods of time if the right isotopes are utilized.

States seeking to combat networked non-state actors are hampered by a basic failure to recognize that the nature of the combat battlespace has changed drastically. Traditional battlespace based on four-dimensional space (x,y,z) and time (t) represents the conventional battlefield within which state-on-state warfare takes place. Warfare is now starting to expand into the dimension of cyberspace (c). This new dimension allows terrorist groups to overcome space-time limitations inherent traditional battlespace for advanced warfighting purposes. Terrorist groups are using the medium of cyberspace for recruitment, fundraising, propaganda, and command and control. They are also using cyberspace as a defensive bastion in which their stealth-masked forces operate, bypassing traditional state military defenses. In the age of Blackbeard, pirates used the vast sea to hide, operate, and trade. Now terrorists hide from the state in the oceans of megabytes and silicon.

Terrorist targeting schemes are also wholly different from those of states. States think purely in terms of objects—ground to be held, cities to be seized, or targets to be destroyed. While terrorists may destroy an object such as an airliner or symbolic building or seize a group of hostages, their inherent lack of combat potential makes this targeting scheme ineffectual. Instead, terrorism affects the 'bonds and relationships' which hold things together. Their use of Bond-Relationship Targeting (BRT) allows them to target a society with disruptive rather than destructive attacks. States have a tough time reacting against BRT because they must contend with the societal shock waves set off by an attack and not just the more limited physical destruction itself.

The rules of engagement used in terrorism are by definition 'criminal' because they violate the Western conduct of war. The killing and torture of non-combatants, especially women and children, the refusal to wear a military uniform with the proper insignia, and willingness to utilize internationally banned weapons such as poison gas are all violations of civilized warfare. Because of this, it can be said that terrorists are engaging in 'criminal warfighting.' The level of criminality is dependent on the number and severity of the international and national legal violations taking place.

The question still exists regarding at what point asymmetric warfare takes place. As has been discussed, this is very much a 'gray phenomena' which manifests lighter and darker shades depending on the level of variance to state-on-state warfare. Current thinking in the U.S. holds that once a terrorist or criminal-soldier group utilizes Weapons of Mass Destruction (WMD) then they have engaged in asymmetric warfare. It would probably be more accurate to say, however, that terrorism is itself a form of asymmetric warfare, meant to be a non-state counter to warfare conducted by the modern state, with the more sophisticated and deadlier terrorist groups adopting its darkest shades. Whatever the semantics, one thing is clear—asymmetric warfare poses a threat to democratic nation-states. Dusting off the old doctrine books won't be enough—we all have to fight and think on a higher level to defeat it.

Further Reading

Roger W. Barnett, *Asymmetrical Warfare: Today's Challenge to U.S. Military Power.* Washington, DC: Potomac Books Inc., 2003.

Robert J. Bunker and Charles "Sid" Heal, Eds., *Fifth Dimensional Operations: Space-Time-Cyber Dimensionality in Conflict and War—A Terrorism Research Center Book.* Bloomington: iUniverse, 2014.

Brian M. Jenkins, *New Modes of Conflict.* Santa Monica: RAND, June 1983.

Aviation Security

A Pilot's Eye View

Kevin R. McCarthy

In order to understand modern Aviation Security (AVSEC) in the United States, it is helpful to review some key historical events, policies, and shortcomings that enabled the unprecedented 9/11 attacks on four U.S. flights. From the 1960s through the 1980s, the principal threat to U.S. aviation was not even called terrorism. The FAA, or Federal Aviation Administration—originally an Agency, was created in 1958 and by 1961 was confronted with hijackings. President Kennedy declared hijacking or interference with flight crew a crime in September 1961, and Attorney General Robert Kennedy swore in the FAA's first "peace officers", deputy marshals in 1962. The earliest hijackers were Cubans who decided that they wanted to go home or create some sort of publicity event to highlight their cause. They hijacked commercial airliners, typically armed only with canisters of flammable liquids and a public platform to espouse their views. The preferred destination was often Havana, Cuba and the airlines handled these events as almost routine operations. The FAA was the sole U.S. Government (USG) agency responsible for oversight of all airline operations including security. The FAA promulgated a protocol that dictated how airline crews would handle a hijacking situation. The policy handed down to the airlines was called the "Common Strategy." In short, the strategy was to give the hijacker whatever transport they demanded. Protocols directed the crew to not actively confront the hijackers even if they had the capability to do so; acquiescence was determined to be the most expeditious and safest course of action. Law enforcement response to hijacking events was based on an international agreement,—the Hague Hijacking Convention, October 1971—which branded the crime "Air Piracy" and mandated that perpetrators, after arriving at their destination of choice, would be prosecuted or extradited by the host government back to the country of origin of the flight. Few, if any hijackers, were every returned to the United States to face prosecution. Most were welcomed home as "heroes of the cause" or, at minimum, granted asylum by the host country.

The hijacking of Air France Flight 139 on June 28, 1976 should have been a global wakeup call. Following on the heels of the Munich Massacre in 1972, Israel recognized the gravity of the situation and acted quickly and aggressively in response to a new global threat in which hijackers (now labeled "terrorists") were willing to kill (and die) for their cause. Flight 139 involved terrorists from the Popular Front for the Liberation of Palestine (PFLP), with aid from the German Revolutionary Cells, hijacking a flight from Athens to Paris with the intent of making a public statement through hostage taking and violence. Seven days later on July 4, 1976, coincidentally the bicentennial celebration of U.S. independence, the Israel Defense Forces (IDF) took bold action. The action, popularly known as the Raid on Entebbe, redefined the future of AVSEC for Israel. The IDF flew over 2,500 miles across the airspace of several hostile countries into central Africa and staged a spectacular rescue mission. Unfortunately, there was loss of life: three hostages and the IDF operation commander, Lt.Col. Yonatan Netanyahu were killed. The mission was subsequently renamed "Operation Jonathan" by the commander's older brother, Benjamin Netanyahu, later Prime Minister of Israel. The United States and other western countries failed to adopt Israel's analysis of the threat and bold response.

The next big wakeup call, similarly ignored by the USG, occurred on June 14, 1985. Shi'ite terrorists from Hezbollah and Islamic Jihad, seeking the release of prisoners held in Israel, commandeered TWA Flight 847 from Athens to Rome. When the hijackers' initial demands were not met during the first 3 days aboard the aircraft, U.S. Navy diver Robert Stethem was tortured and brutally murdered in a clear sign of the hijackers' commitment to using violence to achieve their objectives. The hostage crisis moved onto the ground in Beirut, continuing for 17 days during which time Israel released some prisoners before the Iranian-sponsored terrorists freed the remaining hostages from their compound.

The ingenuity, interpersonal, and language skills, and courage of a TWA flight attendant, Uli Derickson, are credited with saving many lives by defusing tense situations. The Common Strategy's shortcomings are obvious in retrospect. The hijackers succeeded in commandeering the aircraft, forced the pilots to fly to a hostile destination, killed a passenger, and escaped.

Another milestone attack was Pan Am Flight 103, December 21, 1988. All 243 passengers and 16 crew on-board and 11 people on the ground died after a bomb placed in the cargo hold by Libyan state-sponsored terrorists detonated over Lockerbie, Scotland. This was a terror attack designed to intimidate the public and influence political agendas and policies of the United States and her allies, enabling a victory for terrorists who took advantage of the lack of explosive detection or bag matching procedures. The USG did close this gap by implementing new hold baggage and passenger screening procedures, but failed to consider future "opportunities" for exploitation by those intent on causing havoc and destruction. Maintaining profits for the airlines, limiting disruption to the flying (and paying) public, underestimation of the motivation and capability of adversaries, and limited political will to change the status quo produced a culture and posture of fighting yesterday's attacks, not tomorrow's threats.

Despite these events, which clearly demonstrated that aviation threats had become increasingly more sophisticated, throughout the 1990's the U.S. airline industry and the FAA continued to adhere to the Common Strategy of passive cooperation with hijackers. Too often we are reluctant to "connect the dots" and recognize that adversaries adapt and new threats require new responses; as eloquently stated by Abraham Lincoln in an address to Congress, December 1862, "the dogmas of the quiet past are inadequate for the stormy present..." As air piracy morphed into Global Terrorism, the USG largely ignored emerging threats and the airline industry, consumed with financial bottom-lines, failed to advocate for changes in procedures that would incur costs and reduce their profit margin. One innovative action was taken during the 1990's. A nucleus of dedicated airline pilots from across the industry came together to engage the FAA Security Office and the airline industry in an ongoing dialogue to increase awareness of aviation threats and begin building a new aviation security culture. During this time, the FAA also deployed a small cadre of very well qualified Federal Air Marshals Service (FAMS) who were sent aboard international flights in response to specific threats or routes deemed high-risk for terrorist attacks. The FAMS understood the threats and vulnerabilities, but their limited deployment only allowed them to protect a couple of flights at any given time, almost exclusively to/from international destinations.

On September 11, 2001, terrorists once again took advantage of the shortcomings of the Common Strategy, infiltrating domestic flights with low probability of FAMS protection armed only with box cutters (not prohibited items), commandeering the planes, and killing the pilots trained to submit to hijackers' demands. Despite the demonstrated progression of radical Islamic terrorist tactics over the previous decade from the remote detonation of bombs to human suicide bombers, the USG was shocked that this new breed of hijackers had no intention of successfully landing the aircraft and surviving the ordeal. Their sole objective was to kill as many innocent civilians as possible and undermine America's sense of security and well being at home. Unfortunately, they did succeed in sowing fear in the hearts of the traveling public, at least initially; however, as Winston Churchill rightly remarked, "America always does the right thing, after trying everything else."

9/11 changed the lives of all Americans; 'homeland security' became both a newly minted phrase and a way of life for all. The Common Strategy had failed again. The aircrews on the 9/11 planes had the ability to resist, some more forcefully then others; they could have fought back. In compliance with the Common Strategy, they—and many of their countrymen—were murdered. For the aviation industry the Common Strategy was now not only obsolete, but also in part responsible for the deaths of nearly 3,000 Americans on U.S. soil. The new more aggressive protection and response posture adopted after 9/11 was dubbed "Aviation Security" (AVSEC). The traveling public at first willingly complied with the new world of AVSEC including long waits for enhanced passenger/baggage screening in airports, no accompanying loved-ones to departure gates, well-armed military and law enforcement officers on patrol in airports and other transportation venues, etc. They quickly became intimately familiar with the public persona of AVSEC, the Transportation Security Administration (TSA). The Department of Homeland Security (DHS) established by Congress on November 25, 2002, transferred the nascent TSA from the Department of Transportation to DHS and TSA became the nation's first agency dedicated to securing all modes of transportation used by the U.S. public and corporations worldwide, including air travel, trains, ferries, ship traffic, commercial trucks, and buses. Previously, airline passenger, baggage, and cargo screening was accomplished by airlines and private contractors.

In the hysterical frenzy post 9/11, many TSA policies and procedures were frantically put into action. Some were so intrusive and counter-productive they came close to realizing the terrorists' objective of destroying the U.S. economy by taking the United States out of the airline industry. Ever so slowly, AVSEC has evolved and many public servants stepped up, bringing years of experience form various government law enforcement and intelligence agencies to fashion AVSEC into a functional enterprise. Is it perfect? Definitely not. Is it better then it was ten years ago? Absolutely. Is it accomplishing the defined mission to protect commercial air travel? To date, since 9/11 no successful attack has been perpetrated on a U.S. airliner.

One new AVSEC action has been to substantially increase the role and responsibility of the FAMS, proactively deploying them and without specific threat requirements. These teams are now deployed everyday on numerous U.S. airline flights both domestic and international. These highly trained and qualified professionals spend their time as passengers guarding our airliners in flight. The FAMS have an auxiliary force born from that small nucleus of pre-9/11 airline pilots who were crying in the wilderness for industry and government to take AVSEC seriously. The legislation that founded DHS also established another little-known AVSEC responder, the Federal Flight Deck Officer (FFDO). U.S. airline pilots can volunteer, in addition to their duties as pilots, to become sworn, armed officers under the authority of the FAMS—and the last line of defense for the traveling public. In the words of a Washington columnist, "Sky King has now also become Wyatt Earp". The pilot/

FFDO undergoes extensive evaluation and training before becoming an officer of DHS. They have sworn a true and faithful oath to the government and Constitution of the United States of America to defend their flight and our nation from all enemies foreign and domestic. As volunteers, they receive no compensation, returning multiple times a year at their own expense to training bases in order to hone skills in fighting, shooting, and related areas. When reporting for their flights, they look and act like all the other pilots, rushing from one plane to the next, grabbing a Starbucks in passing. In fact, many thousands of pilots are involved in the program and are flying armed every day. These FFDO are fully authorized and prepared to exercise the use of deadly force to never again allow a terrorist to seize control of an airliner. Don't bother asking them, by statute and oath they are bound not to disclose the identities of any FFDO.

During the 1970s, with the Vietnam War and later the seemingly never ending Cold War, only seasoned professionals were focused on AVSEC and adversaries were considered known entities with clear goals. Now we are faced with a more amorphous threat emanating from those radical Islamists and others who want to destroy our Western way of life and everything associated with it. AVSEC is now the domain of multiple professionals dedicated to preventing attacks and building resiliency. The underlying philosophy of the new AVSEC response posture is, "We must be right 100% of the time, but the terrorists only have be right once". At least some attempted attacks by shoe, shampoo, and underwear bombers were thwarted by a more vigilant public and retrained cabin and flight crews. That said, AVSEC operations continue to be plagued by complacency about emerging threats, high costs, and the growing intolerance of the public to travel delays. Modern aviation and homeland security is a critical and intricate system of systems; it involves people, places, and things with significant coordination. An airliner full of people is an irresistible target for our adversaries; the slightest hint of an incident and the nattering nabobs of the 24/7 news broadcasts spin themselves and the public into frenzy. Our adversaries want to bring down our economy and media-driven hysteria only helps their cause.

Future effectiveness will require TSA and the airline industry to continue to adapt and implement operations focused on confounding future threats and not fighting yesterday's war. Technology will continue to evolve and TSA officers will be given better data and tools with the intent to make the whole experience more effective and less invasive. Today, there is an innovative initiative called Checkpoint of the Future, that will allow passengers to simply walk through a tunnel with all their belongings and emerge from the far end all screened and checked in for their flight. It is not science fiction. It is a vision that is being developed and tested today. Airliner systems (aircraft and other infrastructure) are also being redesigned and enhanced to build resiliency and protection into hardware, software, and operations. Almost every flight today has at least one armed and highly qualified officer aboard in either the cabin, cockpit, or both. And just like most of the operational details of air transport, the enhanced security system runs smoothly behind the scenes.

We, the traveling public, are as much a part of AVSEC now as the crews and officers who manage the security apparatus. When something doesn't feel right, doesn't look right; tell someone and keep telling him or her until they listen and do something.

Further Reading

Tomer Benito, *Rain For The Wicked*. North Charleston: BookSurge LLC, 2007.

Jeffrey Price and Jeffrey Forest, *Practical Aviation Security: Predicting and Preventing Future Threats*. Second Edition. Oxford: Butterworth-Heinemann, 2013.

Paul Wilkinson and Brian Jenkins, *Aviation Terrorism and Security*. New York: Routledge, 1999.

Beheadings

Lisa J. Campbell

One of the most famous beheadings in modern times was the videotaped and well publicized execution of Daniel Pearl, a western journalist who in 2002 was made an example of to the world by a relatively unknown terrorist group in Pakistan. This event marked the beginning of post-modern beheadings, and was followed by a large number of similar acts conducted by al Qaeda, the Taliban, and a number of lesser known groups in Iraq and Afghanistan for the next several years. Over this same period, beheadings increased in a number of other countries, primarily in several parts of Asia.

The use of beheadings by Islamist terrorist groups is not new; today's practice is a continuation of thousands of years of beheadings in warfare by their Islamist ancestors. Post-modern terrorist beheadings have a more criminal nature to them than those in previous times, which were widely accepted and even considered legitimate. Contemporary terrorist beheadings still are inspired by the Koran, tales of past Islamic battles, and the need to use excessive brutality to gain the advantage often over militarily superior opposition forces. They are also used on the civilian populace, including Westerners, Christians, and those Shia and Sunni who do not conform to a particular brand of Islam. Modern day beheadings have become a well-established tool of asymmetric warfare and have been proven effective on and off the battlefield.

Beheadings were not and are still by no means limited to Islam. Beheadings of the past were conducted by many nation states (judicial) and non-state entities (extra-judicial) and crossed many ethnic and religious backgrounds. While historical state run beheadings were primarily conducted as punishment to deter criminals, non-state beheadings were conducted for a variety of reasons, including for intimidation and to strike fear in their enemies, particularly on the battlefield. Many key historical figures were beheaded, including the grandson of the Prophet Muhammad, Husayn ibn Ali. Husayn ibn Ali's beheading, along with the beheading of 72 of his men, occurred during the Battle of Karbala in 680, which preceded the split between Sunni and Shia Muslims.

Throughout history, beheading occurrences in large numbers notably took place during times of great upheaval, including during Mahdi uprisings in the Middle East and epochal changes worldwide. Today we are once again witnessing in the Middle East a time of significant upheaval with beheadings increasingly being used by terrorists, or post-modern jihadi groups. One such group that has emerged is an offshoot of al Qaeda—the Islamic State in Iraq and al Sham (ISIS) also called the Islamic State. ISIS is fighting asymmetric jihadi-style warfare against two failing nation state armies (in Iraq and Syria) and against other opposition groups. In the same area as the historical battle of Karbala, the rift between Sunni and Shia is growing in what is largely a sectarian battle. ISIS is capitalizing on this split, and like many other jihadi groups, they very selectively use beheadings to advance their purpose.

Beheadings are circumstantial, thus the reasons for conducting them in the post-modern era vary; they can be highly spontaneous or pre-planned, staged and/or ritualistic. Reasons for beheading include for revenge as an outcome of a kidnapping—for intimidation—to make a public example of one or more individuals, for recruitment or fundraising, to strike fear and dread in the enemy, or to attempt to demoralize the enemy altogether. Most recently ISIS, with vastly smaller numbers of fighters than the Iraqi army, assisted by the use of beheadings successfully overtook Mosul, Iraq and caused thousands of Iraqi soldiers and police to flee the city and not return.

Much has been revealed about the present nature and use of beheadings since Daniel Pearl. Foremost, in order to be effective, beheadings require an audience. The audience can range from a handful of villagers to a global audience with the use of mass media. Beheading videos posted on YouTube.com can have tens of thousands to over one million views per video (the Nick Berg beheading of 2004 has been viewed over 5.5 million times). Of note, when there is an audience, captives are almost always beheaded while still alive. Modern day terrorist groups such as al Qaeda and ISIS have become highly proficient with their use of media to get their message across, and are known to bring media teams into battle along with their fighters.

Beheadings are also conducted by terrorists at the time and place of their choosing. They do not follow a specific protocol, that is, there are a number of alternative ways to punish the captive for their alleged crime. Alternatives to beheading include torture, execution-style shooting, indefinite captivity, and more recently, crucifixion. Furthermore, terrorist groups will temper or even cease their practice of beheadings in areas where they are attempting to win hearts and minds of a local population. ISIS has been shown in propaganda videos passing out food and basic supplies to local people in towns they have overtaken. Acts of goodwill such as this by terrorist groups toward a population in order to bring them into favor run counter to the harsh implementation of Sharia law that is often accompanied with beheadings. Beheadings become counterproductive when a population overwhelmingly turns against their captors; at that point, terrorist groups will cease the practice for a period of time.

The switching on and off of the use of beheadings is an effective tactic. Terrorists who use beheadings stand to gain tactically in a variety of ways. Beheadings are an enhancement to complex attacks and can have a multiplying effect on the battlefield. For example, an attack with a suicide bomber entry, followed by RPGs and gunfire can be won more quickly when captives are beheaded; remaining fighters are likely to be scared off. Similarly, beheadings can have the effect of making a small terrorist cell or unit seem far more imposing than it actually is. In areas where terrorists have established their rule with the use or threat of beheadings, citizens paralyzed with fear will flee or avoid speaking out or assisting others in need.

Short term tactical gains from beheadings can incrementally help a terrorist group achieve long term strategic goals. In Iraq, ISIS is making great progress in establishing a caliphate (a strategic objective) in part due to their use of beheadings. Similarly, in the 1990's, the Taliban took over most of Afghanistan by incrementally overtaking small villages, with the assistance of beheadings and other harsh Sharia measures.

Beheadings can come in the form of a ritual or they can be basic slaughter. In some cases, beheadings (and other executions) by terrorists are preceded by a short trial—a crude and often capricious attempt at a judicial proceeding. The weapons used to conduct beheadings can vary widely but are most commonly knives or machetes, dull or sharp, large or small. In some events, particularly for videotaped beheadings, the longer-lasting, more deliberately executed the beheading, the greater the effect on the target audience. Many victims and particularly western captives appear to be beheaded in a manner similar to how an animal is slaughtered. This type of slaughter is consistent with some jihadi rhetoric towards Westerners and Jews, which at times compares them to pigs or dogs.

There are few countermeasures for the beheadings, especially since most of the civilized world has banned the practice and has over time adopted less cruel methods of capital punishment as a gesture of its collective humanity. Terrorists, on the other hand, have reverted to the opposite, with increased brutality as optimal. Many Muslims consider beheadings to be un-Islamic. A campaign pushing the un-Islamic value of beheadings could help sway victim populations to turn on their captors and help armies/coalitions better fight against them. However, while gaining consensus among the people on what is and is not acceptable is achievable, a population overcoming its fear and taking a stand is a less likely to be accomplished. A common practice for fighters in the Middle East and in parts of Africa, however, is for opposing groups to behead in retaliation, sometimes elevating the level of brutality to regain territory or their human rights.

Terrorist use of beheadings will continue to ebb and flow as they have throughout history, and could evolve tactically in the future as warfare evolves. As groups like ISIS are allowed to grow into terrorist "armies," the opportunity for large or even massive scale beheadings increases. Large scale beheadings allow for rapid advancement on the battlefield. With the effects of beheadings well known to terrorist groups, the practice will likely continue with limited opposition.

Further Reading

Pamela L. Bunker, Lisa J. Campbell, and Robert J. Bunker, "Torture, beheadings, and narcocultos." Special Issue: Narcos Over the Border: Gangs, Cartels, Mercenaries and the Invasion of America. *Small Wars & Insurgencies*, Vol. 21, No. 1, 2010: 145-178.

Lisa J. Campbell, "The Use of Beheadings by Fundamentalist Islam." *Global Crime*, Vol.7, Iss. 3-4, 2006: 583-614.

Dawn Perlmutter, "Mujahideen Blood Rituals: The Religious and Forensic Symbolism of Al Qaeda Beheading." *Anthropoetics*, Vol. 11, No. 2, Fall 2005/Winter 2006, http://www.anthropoetics.ucla.edu/ap1102/muja.htm.

Biocrimes

Addressing the Biological Threat: Empirical Data on Bioterrorism and Biocrimes in the United States 1990-2002

Jason Pate

Following the September 11 terrorist attacks, a series of letters containing spores of *Bacillus anthacis*, the causative agent for anthrax, heightened fears of mass-casualty bioterrorism in the United States. Although hundreds of hoaxes had preceded the anthrax letters, this was the first time that anthrax had ever been used by a non-state actor, assuming that no state was involved in the attacks. In some ways, the 9/11 attacks and anthrax letters may have been irrevocably linked in public perception, in a manner not unlike the events of 1995. In March of that year, Aum Shinrikyo became the first non-state actor to use the sarin nerve agent, and a month later, the Oklahoma City bombing became the highest-fatality terrorist act on U.S. soil. Apparently linking these two events, the U.S government scrambled to prepare the country for the threat of mass-casualty terrorism involving chemical or biological weapons (CBW). Similarly, the U.S. government has again post-9/11 dramatically increased funding and developed programs to address the threat.

The threat from biological agents comes from both terrorists and individual criminals. While both are technically crimes, the nature of the motivation determines whether an incident is "terrorist." For example, the anthrax letters were sent to specifically targeted individuals, and it could be assumed that those targets were chosen for political, ideological, religious, or social reasons. From a practical preparedness and response standpoint, the differences between the threats are largely academic. However, a discussion of the differences in motivation yields some conclusions about resource allocation to address the various biological threats.

At the catastrophic end of possible biological threat scenarios is the clandestine use of smallpox against an unprotected population. Although the probability of this type of attack is very low, the potential consequences are so high that policymakers in the United States have embarked on an ambitious program to stockpile smallpox vaccine and implement rapid vaccination in the event of an outbreak. At the other end of the spectrum are incidents involving less exotic agents in low-technology attacks. These types of incidents are far more likely but would not necessarily cause many casualties. Striking the appropriate balance between these scenarios and developing policies to address the various contingencies requires fact-based analysis rather than worst-case scenario assumptions. Without such a basis, it is easy to waste valuable and limited resources.

In 1997, the Monterey Institute developed a database of worldwide incidents involving sub-state actors and chemical, biological, radiological, or nuclear materials. A review of the information in the database since 1990 reveals that 189 biological cases involved an ideological motivation, while 180 involved idiosyncratic criminal motivations, an almost even split. By far, hoaxes were the most common type of incident in both categories, with 149 ideological and 172 criminal. There were 21 terrorist uses of agent. Although this statistic sounds ominous and includes the seven fatal anthrax letter attacks, close inspection reveals that these 21 incidents include eight failed attempts by Aum Shinrikyo to spread anthrax and botulinum toxin, and a bizarre case in which an activist may have tried to infect a politician with influenza. Slightly more interesting are two cases in Israel, one of which involved the use of sewer water to ruin crops, and a second in which the perpetrators changed the labels on expired crates of eggs with the hope of causing food poisoning. Three more cases involved the deposit of containers of medical waste and anti-Semitic symbols at Jewish organizations. Of all these incidents, only the anthrax letters caused fatalities.

Among criminal cases, there were two uses of agent, one involving an American woman who used ricin to poison her spouse, and another involving the use of Salmonella to poison 60 people at a school in Russia. Neither of these cases caused fatalities.

Based on the empirical open-source data collected at the Monterey Institute, there is little difference between incidents of bioterrorism and biocrime. Both categories include diverse choices of agent and target, and both consist largely of hoaxes. On one hand, the uses of anthrax in Fall 2001 cannot be considered trivial and could arguably represent a turning point in bioterrorism. On the other hand, this is not necessarily the case, and the anthrax letters may be an aberration, a critical outlier in the data set. The 1995 Aum attack in the Tokyo subway was (and is) viewed as a turning point in CBW terrorism, but seven years later there remain very few CBW terrorist incidents, and even fewer that caused casualties. Indeed, the greatest terrorist threat still appears to come from conventional, albeit arguably innovative, means and tactics.

Further Reading

W. Seth Carus, *Bioterrorism and Biocrimes: The Illicit Use of Biological Agents Since 1900*. Amsterdam: Fredonia Books, 2002.

Peter Katona, John P. Sullivan, and Michael D. Intrilligator, Eds., *Global Biosecurity: Threats and Responses*. New York: Routledge, 2010.

Jonathan B. Tucker and Jason Pate, "The Minnesota Patriots Council" in Jonathan B. Tucker, Ed., *Toxic Terror: Assessing Terrorist Use of Chemical and Biological Weapons*. Cambridge: MIT Press, 2000: 159–183.

Biological Warfare

The History of Bioterror and Biowarfare

Peter Katona

Historically, epidemics of disease, both natural and man-made, have caused great devastation, killing tens or even hundreds of millions of people. Natural outbreaks of disease have been around since the dawn of mankind, but bioterror and biowarfare have been utilized for only about two thousand years. Even during conventional wars, infectious diseases kill more soldiers and civilians than bullets. Biological weapons are cheap, easy to use, the recipes are easy to acquire, and they cause great panic. Despite this, there are also drawbacks in using biological weapons in terror and warfare. Their effects are highly unpredictable. They depend on the cooperation of weather conditions such as temperature, wind, and inversions. They are socially unacceptable to most of us. And finally, the production of true "weaponized" biological weapons requires experienced microbiologists with knowledge of advanced "weaponization" technology.

The earliest documented use of biological warfare agents occurred in the 6th century BC, when the Assyrians poisoned their enemy's water supplies with rye ergot, a purgative. This same tactic was used by Solon of Athens during the siege of the port city of Cirrha, where skunk cabbage was dumped into the water supply. In 1346, during an outbreak of bubonic plague in Europe, a Tarter army, which was itself infected with the disease, hurled the corpses of their dead plague victims over the walls of besieged Kaffa, a seaport on the Crimean coast. Some historians feel that this may have caused the Black Death in Europe from 1347–1351 that eventually killed 25 million people or 50% of the population.

During the battle of Carolstein in 1422, Lithuanian soldiers catapulted the bodies of their slain soldiers plus 2,000 cartloads of excrement over the castle walls onto ranks of the defenders, where deadly fevers quickly broke out. Russian troops practiced similar methods in 1710 and 1718, by hurling plague-infected corpses over the city walls of Reval during their wars with Sweden.

Smallpox was brought to America by the Spaniards in the early 16th century. Once the Conquistadors Cortez and Pizarro left to conquer America, the smallpox they carried quickly spread to the local Indian population. This served initially as an unwitting, and later as a deliberate, agent of biological warfare. Hernando Cortez introduced smallpox to Mexico in 1520, and in two years it killed 3.5 million Aztecs. During the Pontiac Rebellion in 1763, the British army, under Sir Jeffrey Amhurst, provided Delaware Native Americans with blankets and handkerchiefs taken from smallpox hospitals. This "gift giving" of disease-ridden blankets was a common practice by the American military and continued into the 19th century.

The United States has had two large scale bioterror incidents in the past two decades. The first was in 1984, when the Bhagwan religious cult put *Salmonella typhimurium* into the salad bars of 10 restaurants. Their plan was to incapacitate voters in Dallas, Oregon to influence a local election. There were no deaths, but 715 people became ill with gastroenteritis. Incidentally, the Bhagwan lost the election. The four anthrax-laden letters that were sent to U.S. political and media figures following the terrorist attacks of September 11, 2001 constituted the second incident. This epidemic resulted in 22 cases and 4 deaths over a one month period. This caused great panic and anxiety, resulted in significant amounts of money spent, and left many unanswered questions about the nature of the disease. In other words, we knew much less about anthrax as a bioterror agent than we thought.

On the international level, seventeen nations are thought to have weaponized biological agents in the 20th century, and I will discuss four of the most ambitious ones. Between 1936 and 1945, the Japanese started an ambitious bioweapons program in Manchuria posing as water purification units, called Unit 731 and Unit 100. POW's were exposed to aerosolized anthrax, resulting in between 3,000 and 9,000 human deaths. By 1945, 400 kg of anthrax was designated for a specially designed fragmentation bomb. One novel Japanese tactic used was to have planes overfly areas of Manchuria and China to drop infected fleas and grain. The grain attracted rats. The rats became infected from the fleas since 24,000 organisms can be regurgitated in a single feeding. Plague could then spread to humans.

Religious groups such as Aum Shinrikyo are better known for their use of the chemical agent sarin in the Tokyo subway, but they were also very interested in the use of biological weapons such as anthrax. They invested $80 million in a biological weapons program with two biological research centers. They also purchased a 48,000 acre farm in Australia to test biological agents on livestock and sent members to Africa for Ebola samples (not understanding that the natural reservoir for Ebola is as yet unknown). They even attempted to use anthrax to kill those opposed to them, not realizing that they were using a vaccine (and thus harmless) anthrax strain.

During the Persian Gulf War, Iraq was found to have 19,000 liters of botulinum toxin and 8,500 liters of anthrax. They acknowledged filling 25 missiles and 157 bombs with anthrax and botulism toxin. Fortunately, these weapons were never fired against Israel, their intended target. The danger of a rogue state such as Iraq lies in a *sovereign state's* use of bioweapons as a *precedent*, and its capabilities as a distribution center. Iraq has far more capabilities than a very well funded terrorist organization like al-Qaeda. After the weapons inspectors were ejected, it is presumed that Iraq retained well over 2,650 gallons of liquid anthrax, and could be making more in over half a dozen facilities.

The Soviet offensive bioweapons program, called Biopreparat, employed between 32,000 and 60,000 scientists and technicians, and had 6 research labs and 5 production facilities. They developed criteria for an effective bioweapon and ranked each agent. They produced metric tons of weaponized agents. They also had at least 2 accidents: one at Aralsk in 1971 with smallpox, and another in Sverdlovsk in 1979, with anthrax. Many feel that Biopreparat, as well as another secret Russian program, are still in operation.

The United States had an offensive bioweapons program between 1943 and 1969 but only used small quantities of agents that a vaccine or antibiotic was available for. We also did several experiments with simulants such as spraying *Serratia marscens*, a tularemia simulant, and *Bacillus globigii*, an anthrax simulant over San Francisco; releasing *Bacillus globigii* in the New York City subway; and Operation "White Coat", testing Q fever on human volunteers.

International law and international agencies have banned the use of biological agents in warfare, calling them weapons of cruelty. The signing of the Geneva Protocol in 1925 made this ban official. The Biological Weapons Convention in 1972 proposed a resolution to eradicate all biological agents. This was ratified during the follow-up 1975 Convention, although the United States has refused to sign.

So, based on our history, how concerned should Americans be about the dangers of bioterrorism? Currently, we possess few large-scale defense mechanisms against a massive bioterrorism attack and are quite vulnerable. Reports from the Department of Defense have stated that a large assault against the United States is highly unlikely. Many people fear an aerosol attack, in which a biological agent would be sprayed over a densely populated area. According to the Defense Department, however, this kind of attack is quite unrealistic, being very difficult and expensive to execute. The Department warns that we should be more concerned with smaller attacks such as contamination of an enclosed space or, less likely, our food supply, as in the case of the Bhagwan episode.

Biological warfare and terror are not new. The fundamentalists, fanatics, and extremists were always around. What is new is the potential to use it on an unprecedented scale with today's technology, misinformation, religious fervor, and lack of restraints.

Further Reading

Ken Alibek, *Biohazard.* New York: Random House, 1999.

Jeanne Guillemin, *Biological Weapons: From the Invention of State-Sponsored Programs to Contemporary Bioterrorism.* New York: Columbia University Press, 2004.

Peter Katona, Michael D. Intrilligator, and John P. Sullivan, Eds., *Countering Terrorism and WMD: Creating a Global Counter-Terrorism Network.* New York: Routledge, 2006.

Black Globalization

John Robb

Twenty-first century economic globalization was the penultimate realization of the American vision for the world and a pay-off for Cold War sacrifice. Over four *billion* people are now economically interconnected and actively engaged in unconstrained commerce. The growth rate has been stunning: an increase of four times the number of a mere twenty years ago. We now all live, for better or worse, in Adam Smith's world.

However, within this success lies our ultimate failure. Governance, as a means to control the excesses of the marketplace and ensure positive societal good, has not kept up with economic expansion. In fact, it has done just the opposite. The nation-state, in every measure of power, is in deep decline; nation-states don't control borders, finances, economies, violence, and communications anymore. Further, international organizations that would allow nation-states to cooperate to control this global marketplace are weak and getting weaker.

One good explanation for this is that the expansion of the global commercial network isn't following historical models. In the historical models we commonly reference, economic expansion either into frontier areas or into new logical areas (new technology, for example) is followed by nation-state control as governments caught up with the activity (either physically or cognitively). Bit by bit, the nation-state was eventually able to increase the complexity and breadth of the rules for the new activity until it had a beneficial impact on society.

However, this new model is different. It is a network platform model, the best of example of which is the Internet. In a network platform model, expansion follows this simple process:

- The minimum rule-set required for interconnection and utilization of the network is established.
- Since interconnection with the network is fast and simple, new participants quickly join. The network effects become apparent (the value of a network increases with the square of the number of participants, also known as *Meltcalfe's Law*) and the network grows exponentially.
- Soon, the number of participants becomes so large and the amount of innovation built on the network platform becomes so complex that it becomes impossible to change the simple rules of interconnection due to a fear of damaging the system. As a result, the core rules for network interconnection freeze at the bare minimums.

This is an apt description for the situation in which we find ourselves today in global commerce. We have established the basic means of interconnection but find ourselves unable to add to those rules for fear of destroying the network itself. The system is now in control.

So far, the uncontrolled global economic system we have created has been mostly beneficial. However, there are signs that this is starting to change:

- Black market trade, from human trafficking to drugs to counterfeits to weapons, is booming on this global economic platform. It already has a value of $2-3 trillion and is growing, according to Moises Naim, at seven times the rate of "legal" trade.
- Revenue from black market activities has enabled criminal groups to build corrupt alliances with national and regional governments and thereby gain control over vast swathes of global territory.
- Any division previously seen between criminal groups and terrorists has melted away. Criminal groups are now able to fund and equip military forces on a par with the capabilities of most nations (for example, narco-terrorism). Alternatively, terrorist groups can easily enter and benefit from black market trade,

either by selling protection services or by direct involvement (for example, the Taliban with opium and the FARC with cocaine). These groups will get wealthier and more violent with each passing day.

Unfortunately, given that global commerce is a networked platform, there is very little that can be done to mitigate these trend lines on a global level. With each passing day, less and less can be done to modify or alter the standards for basic interconnectivity that are currently in place. The means that all efforts to control, regulate, and mitigate the excesses of the global economic system will likely fail. If anything, the network will get broader and less restrictive through ever more wide ranging trade agreements.

By 2025, when the global economy is approaching $150 trillion (according to Jeff Sachs, the vast majority of which will be outside the current "developed" world), it's likely that black market trade will be between $20-30 trillion, a full order of magnitude increase over what it is today.

The end result of this onrush of growth in "black globalization" will mean that law enforcement organizations, across the board, will increasingly find themselves overwhelmed—outgunned, outspent, and outmaneuvered. This is already occurring at a rapid pace in the developing world, and it will soon reach the shores of the developed world as the sources of supply continue to find ways to integrate ever more tightly with demand.

Unable to find ways to staunch global supplies of black market goods, efforts at control will increasingly focus on ways of controlling demand. In some cases, an outright embrace or legalization of demand will be tried, although this will not be widespread. In most situations, crimes associated with demand for illegal goods and services will become ever more severe. However, given the ease of interconnection with global sources of supply, this will result, particularly given the decline of the nation-state's ability to raise funds, in unsustainable burdens for enforcement.

Regional guerrilla wars, assassinations, service disruptions, and more will occur on an ever more frequent basis. Police forces, on both the local and federal levels, will be rife with corruption. Trust will dissipate. People will wax nostalgic for the days when our only worries were about attacks by random foreign terrorists. For while the acts feared were similar in kind, the reality delivered through black globalization is much more severe in frequency, intensity, and breadth.

In the long run, the bulk of the burden of protection will fall to the individual, families, and the local communities (of manageable size) to which they belong. In those areas that respond to the challenge correctly, law enforcement will increasingly localize all functions (leveraged by access to private security services) and become a shared burden between and among those that require protection. Rules of behavior will be strictly enforced and monitored for compliance. Increasingly, the ultimate punishment for a failure to adhere to the codes of conduct will be expulsion from the community rather than jail time or civil fines. Participation in a community will become a privilege and not a right.

As dystopian as this sounds, many areas will not be so lucky. In most cases, local protection rackets will arise to mitigate the spread of crime and return order to the streets. In these cases, the citizens will be trading criminals dealing drugs for militias (often composed of off-duty policemen) that fund themselves by reselling corporate/government services at a profit and charging protection fees. Justice will be informal, harsh, and without recourse.

Further Reading

Robert J. Bunker and Pamela Ligouri Bunker, Eds., *Global Criminal and Sovereign Free Economies and the Demise of the Western Democracies: Dark Renaissance*. Routledge Advances in International Political Economy. London: Routledge, 2014.

Nils Gilman, Jesse Goldhammer, and Steven Weber, Eds., *Deviant Globalization: Black Market Economy in the 21st Century*. New York: Continuum, 2011.

John Robb, *Brave New War: The Next Stage of Terrorism and the End of Globalization*. Hoboken: Wiley, 2007.

Body Cavity Bombs

Christopher Flaherty

The Body Cavity Bomb (BCB) as a IED (improvised explosive device) weapon, has a particular set of characteristics, namely:

- Low yield (and the carrier's body absorbs most of the blast power);
- Small impact area; and,
- Little likelihood of significant casualties.

This set of characteristics has a number of direct tactical outcomes. For instance, if an anally or vaginally inserted device is used, this would be equivalent of a standard U.S. Military M67 grenade, minus its fragmentation casing. It is likely, with a M67 grenade equivalent type of BCB, that the carrier will be killed outright, but leave significant detritus. This is the case, even though the explosive used will be from the family of general-purpose plastic explosives containing RDX and PETN, or possibly made from commercial C-4, and thus have a high blast yield; the loss of the bomb casing, combined with the small amounts of explosive used, results in the target/victim being significantly injured, if holding/embracing the BCB carrier, or be only lightly injured if standing more than one-meter away. The types of attack envisaged with this type of weapon, fall distinctly into 'disruptive' campaigns.

The BCB Tactical Paradigm: Disruptive Campaigns

At a theoretical level, a 'disruptive' campaign is where an adversary adopts tactics that aim to incapacitate their opponents' decision-making through shock and disruption brought about by infiltration tactics (which the BCB falls into). The aim is to commit acts that cause extensive chaos and confusion within the opponent's logistical footprint. Taking this concept into the realm of airline security, individuals with the objective of radically affecting airline transportation could either attack a departing airline or one in-flight with a more powerful BCB—such as a womb-borne device (which will be discussed below)—or the campaign could shift the centre of gravity toward the airline terminals themselves, with the use of two attackers, at a minimum, blowing themselves up with smaller anal/vaginal secreted devices. This could leave a large number of panic stricken travellers potentially being killed in crowd crushes if the emergency evacuation plan fails. An example of this situation occurred in Iraq at the 2005 Baghdad bridge stampede (31 August, 2005), wherein 953 people died following a stampede on Al-Aaimmah bridge, which crosses the Tigris river in Baghdad. At the time of the stampede, key takeaways were:

- The incident happened on a river bridge as about a million Shias marched to a shrine for a religious festival.
- Witnesses said panic spread over rumours of suicide bombers.
- People swarmed the bridge.
- There had to be a search operation at the end of the bridge, so crowds gathered there, and this created the initial crowd crush circumstances.

There had been earlier mortar attacks as well that had put crowds on edge. This type of event could easily be recreated in a busy major terminal or at global transport hubs.

The cascade impact, as many of these terminals sit directly above the city transportation network, would led to a day-long congestion and close-down of much of the city transit system, in the wake of governments trying to identify what has happened at the airport terminal. A key part of the disruption campaign is the very ambiguity of the attack—at least in the early stages—until some group come forward to claim responsibility or it can credibly be confirmed as to who was responsible.

Relationship to 2013 Boston Marathon Bombing

The 2013 Boston Marathon bombing illustrates that, in many circumstances, the reaction will be shock and confusion rather than panic. In particular, the new/future type of terrorism will be creating a spectacle which people witness in order to disrupt events or normal activities. Such was the case with the attacker's use of a claymore mine-type of weapon in the Boston bombing that created vast number of injuries with the view of leaving many survivors to witness, recount, and relive events by means of cell phone cameras and video recorders.

BCB In situ Attack

In order to be successful using a BCB, the attacker has to enact an 'in-situ' attack, physically placing their body against the target and then initiating the device. An 'in-situ' attack, occurs:

- In areas that hold large numbers of people in close proximity.
- Those people are located in physically cluttered spaces, which are optimum for producing higher than normally expected ratio of death to injury.

The other constraint is that this weapon likely decreases in effect if outdoor attacks are involved, as indoor closed environments offer the best possible physical properties, where blast-reflection is a factor in confinement. However, due to the potentially low blast yield as well as bodily absorption, blast-reflection may be a negligible factor in confinement.

Protest Horror Weapon

The BCB, as it results in the horrific death of the carriers with much less risk to surrounding people, is perfectly suited to horror displays of personnel destruction in public places. One likely future for BCB employment would be its development into a purely terror, or a 'protest horror' weapon, the effect of which has less to do with its overall effectiveness, and more to do with its grotesqueness; a weapon designed to invite horror and revulsion.

Targets

The current BCB fear is its use in an aviation attack, targeting a plane full of people rather than the assassination of an individual or a crowd atrocity. However, this is predicated on the development of a viable womb-borne BCB, as opposed to the smaller more utilitarian anally/vaginally inserted device. The targeting argument is that the airline constitutes the greater target, which seems more appropriate given the complexity of organizing such an attack. However, it is also equally likely to be an assassination of an individual or a crowd atrocity. This leads to the BCB, in the future, developing down three distinct courses:

- The mass production of modified standard-issue military grenades in a new body cavity (anal or vaginal) fitting configuration as an off-the-shelf tactical solution in basic acts of terrorism, killings, and executions.
- The development of a high explosive, barriered from human skin contact to avoid poisoning the carrier (as plastic explosives are highly toxic to human beings), anal or vaginal fitting configured IEDs to avoid airline or close personal security for specific targeting of a person. This could include targeting artwork, cultural objects, or technology in an attempt to destroy or damage these significantly.
- The high explosive womb-borne IEDs designed to specifically destroy an airplane target or a vehicle such as a school bus.

The Baby BCB

The 'Baby BCB' scenario, is the worst case (blue sky) type, which problematically raises a number of practical issues, such as what exactly would a 'fetus/unborn baby—BCB' look like? And how would it work?

The 'fetus/unborn baby—BCB' involves the removal of the fetus/unborn baby, from the woman that was carrying it, and the substitution of some type of IED. Presumably (as a 'fetus/unborn baby—BCB' has never been documented), this implanted weapon would be little different from any other type of cosmetic implant, in that its basic shape would need to replicate the object (the actual fetus/unborn baby) which had been removed, in order to effectively simulate, viewed from the outside—a pregnant woman.

It is clearly the case that a much larger IED can be implanted (the equivalent of 4.2 M67 grenades in total has been calculated), and this would make an effective IED for a close-in attack on a dignitary/VIP, or an airplane. However, it may prove dangerous or damaging to the woman, performing an extreme cervix stretch, in order to insert the said device, as any larger weapon implanted would require surgery.

Surgery used to open the womb, analogous with breast implants of a BCB offers very poor concealment, and is highly likely to be discovered with a simple body search. The surgery scars have a potentially long (one to six weeks) activity delay timeframe, which substantially increases the prospects of discovery and interdiction. The medical questions as to survivability of a human with this IED inside them, complicated by the need to maintain a drug-simulated pregnancy, remain largely unanswered.

The Mary Scenario

A proposed scenario for a 'Baby BCB', is the case of a carrier dubbed 'Mary', a woman who specifically condoned the destruction of her unborn baby with whom she had no bond. It has been suggested perhaps she might be the victim of war-rape, and the father was an 'enemy' soldier; or the father belonged to an ethnic group whom the terrorists/extremists (whom the woman will martyr herself for), are at war with and such a women could be recruited to offer her an opportunity for revenge. In this circumstance, she would likely be in a relatively stable psychological state and willing to undergo a medical procedure resulting in the destruction of the fetus/unborn baby. In terms of traditional-fundamentalist theology, a child produced under this circumstance (particularly if Mary and the medical staff belonged to the same theological group as the terrorists) would produce a construct that justified the destruction of the fetus/unborn baby.

Medico-Technology Infrastructure

The likely medico-technology infrastructure required to support and sustain the placement of an IED, disguised as a 'fetus/unborn baby—BCB' has a considerable logistical footprint, requiring at a minimum a fully serviced office-based surgical suite, with at least three qualified medical practitioners—a surgeon, *anaesthesiologist*, and a nurse; all capable of performing this type of operation. To not do so, likely increases the risk of medical complications, and therefore failure.

Tactical Aspects Using a Simulated IED Pregnancy

The tactical aspects using a 'pregnant' woman with an IED concealed inside of her are highly specific. Firstly, there is a tight 'window' of opportunity, where in a woman has to be found who is between 8 and 26 weeks pregnant, and who was in the right psychological state to operate competently. The 'attack-scenario' would need to be one where the circumstances where the dignitary/VIP was to be attacked was one where a pregnant woman was expected to be seen. That is, she was part of the narrative-scene that the security was expecting to see on the day. For example, the dignitary/VIP was to visit a pre-natal clinic and talk to pregnant women and the attacker (with her supporting husband—a second attacker who is likely to be the IED initiator) is concealed among this group.

BCB Tactical Limitations and CBRNE Potentials

The BCB can only effectively deliver a small blast yield. This dynamic, until it changes with more powerful blast materiel usable in smaller quantities (possibly developed in the future), will remain the defining operational paradigm.

The employment of a CBRNE component represents a potential 'plus-up' of effects to conventional (explosive) based BCB. This plus-up influences both point/destructive and systemic/disruptive effects [e.g. the white rectangles around the shaded regions of effect in the figure]. Thus, conceivably, a CRBNE-BCB would have an organic capacity to produce area casualties and, in so doing, would generate more 'terrorism potentials' at the systemic/disruptive level. Even with the recognition that CBRNE-BCB potentials exist, it must be realized that this does not mean that such employment is probable or even practical. Nevertheless, a biological weapon BCB is largely viewed as the most likely form of BCB upgrade. This upgrade could involve one of two scenarios. First, the bomber is sick and uses the BCB as a mechanism to dispense their disease. However, this has limitations. For example, in the case of a carrier with full-blown AIDS, the immediate risk to the victims is that they theoretically could contract HIV if they suffer cuts from the bombers' detritus; however, HIV is known to neutralize with in two seconds on exposure to the atmosphere. Second, there is a situation wherein the BCB incorporates a glass or plastic vial containing a biological substance, such as anthrax spores, and this is dispersed into a crowd upon detonation of the device.

BCB Scale of Effect and Type of Effect

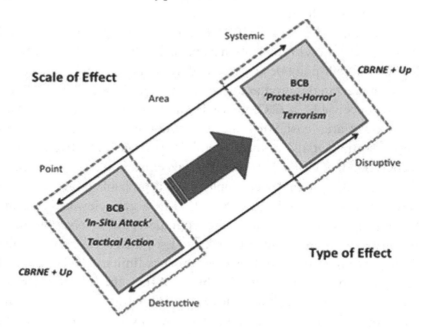

Some Concluding Remarks –
The Future Mass Production BCB

The other likely outcome of the BCB development is the mass production of modified standard-issue military grenades in a new body cavity (anal or vaginal) fitting configuration as an off-the-shelf tactical solution in basic acts of terrorism, killings, and executions, where any number of rogue states could produce this commodity for sale on the worldwide black market in weapons. This could see likely employment in a number of places worldwide—in war zones, drug cartel controlled countries, or crime zones—where security and screening is negligible.

Further Reading

Robert J. Bunker, *The Projected Al Qaeda Use of Body Cavity Suicide Bombs Against High Value Targets.* GroupIntel Occasional Paper: March 2011.

Robert J. Bunker, "Body Cavity Bombs: Fact or Fantasy?" *Aviation Security International,* Vol. 20, No. 5, October 2014: 16-18, 20, 22.

Robert J. Bunker and Christopher Flaherty, Eds., *Body Cavity Bombers: The New Martyrs—Terrorism Research Center.* Bloomington: iUniverse, 2013.

Boko Haram

Nigeria's Growing Insurgency

Caitlin Poling

The terrorist organization known as Boko Haram made front pages worldwide when it kidnapped almost 300 girls from their school in Chibok, Nigeria on April 14, 2014. However, the organization has been in existence for more than a decade and has morphed from a local insurgency into a violent militant group and major threat to Nigerian stability and the region. Boko Haram's violence has caused more than 13,000 deaths since 2009 and has displaced over a million people. The conflict is among the most deadly in the world.

Boko Haram, also known as *Jamā'atu Ahlis Sunnah Lādda'awatih wal-Jihad* (People Committed to the Propagation of the Prophet's Teachings and Jihad), is a radical Sunni Islamist sect based in northern Nigeria. The foundations of the group are murky, but Boko Haram is believed to have roots in the *Yusuifyyah* ("followers of Yusuf") sect, a group founded by Mohammed Yusuf in the mid-1990s. The name 'Boko Haram,' a mix of Hausa and Arabic means "Western education is sin," and is a derogatory nickname given to the group by the local Hausa-speaking community. Boko Haram repudiates democracy and Western governance and education. Although twelve states in northern Nigeria implemented Shari'ah law in 1999, the group views this rule as corrupt and insufficient, and has been pushing for a strict implementation of Shari'ah in all of Nigeria.

Founder Yusuf traveled to Niger Republic and Chad to study the Qu'ran. While abroad, he developed the extreme beliefs that would later be championed by Boko Haram. There are reports that Yusuf was once linked to the Afghan Taliban and has modeled aspects of Boko Haram after this group. Early on, members trained and raised funds in

Sudan, Afghanistan, and Pakistan, as well as across the Sahel. Osama bin Laden has also been linked to Boko Haram; he provided seed money to the group in 2002 and occasionally strategic direction.

Boko Haram began its offensive on December 24, 2003 when it launched attacks against public buildings and police stations in the cities of Geiam and Kanamma in Yobe State, hoisting the flag of the Afghan Taliban overhead. Until 2009, Boko Haram engaged in low-level conflict with local police forces and non-compliant civilians. These clashes escalated into a full-blown insurrection in 2009, with Boko Haram targeting police headquarters and officer's homes in the north. The government responded by launching a major crackdown on Boko Haram in Borno State. This violence culminated in a final battle in Maiduguri which ended when Nigerian forces captured and killed Boko Haram's leader extrajudicially.

Yusuf's death and the crackdown marked a turning point for Boko Haram; they were forced underground, and many leaders fled from the north. Members of the group scattered across parts of the Sahel from Chad to Sudan. While Nigerian authorities and outside observers thought that Boko Haram had dissolved, the group was actually learning new techniques and gaining resources and connections to other terrorist organizations abroad.

Following leader Yusuf's death, Imam Abubakar Shekau assumed control. In 2010, the group re-emerged significantly more violent and determined to seek revenge against the Nigerian state and security forces for executing Yusuf. A video surfaced in 2010, of Shekau announcing his new role and promising vengeance: "Do not think jihad is over. Rather, jihad has just begun. O America, die with your fury." Boko Haram's attacks intensified in size, scope, and frequency.

The group's first attack outside of the north, its traditional operating area, occurred on Christmas Eve 2010, when Boko Haram attacked the army barracks in Abuja. Previously, the Nigerian government believed the group could not operate in the capital region. The group also began targeting Christians and attacking churches in 2011, a practice that continues today. Boko Haram would frequently target Christians in divided communities, in order to spark reprisal violence from Christians onto their Muslim neighbors.

Another major turning point for Boko Haram was its attack on August 26, 2011, when the group bombed the U.N. main office in Abuja—killing 34 people and injuring more than 80 others. This was one of the deadliest attacks on a UN building in history. It was the first major signal of a shift in the group's intentions, and the first Boko Haram attack on an international, non-Nigerian target. Moreover, it demonstrated capabilities to expand beyond softer, local targets. In June 2011, for example, the group attacked the Abuja headquarters of the Nigeria Police Force. These attacks also showed a dangerous evolution of tactics. The use of a suicide car bomb on the Abuja police headquarters in June 2011 was the first recorded incident of a suicide attack in Nigeria.

In 2012, a group called Ansaru, which had a decidedly more Western focus, splintered off of Boko Haram. Ansaru's leaders, Khalid Barnawi (who was killed in August 2012) and Abubakar Adam Kambar, split off when they disagreed with Shekau's indiscriminate attacks, preferring instead to focus on high-profile killings and Western interests. To date, it is believed Boko Haram has several factions or splinter groups, with the largest led by Shekau. The most prominent faction is Ansaru.

Boko Haram has been linked to Ansar al Dine, al Qaeda in the Islamic Magreb (AQIM), al Shabaab, and the Movement for Oneness and Jihad in West Africa (MUJAO). These connections were strengthened when Boko Haram militants fought alongside these groups in Mali. On November 29, 2012, Abubakar Shekau released a video expressing Boko Haram's solidarity with al Qaeda and its leaders and saluting global jihadists. AQIM in particular provided Boko Haram with funding, weapons, and training. Many of Boko Haram's recovered weapons have been traced to Libya, as the group benefited from the arms stockpiles of fallen Libyan dictator Muammar Qadhafi.

In 2012, a Tuareg revolt began in northern Mali. Several groups of Islamist fighters came to take up arms against the Malian government. Boko Haram set up a number of bases in Mali, where they trained hundreds of recruits. Following a UN Security Council Resolution, the French and the African Union sent forces to Mali to assist the government against the rebels. The French-led mission to counter the radicals, Operation Serval, pushed Boko Haram militants back to northeast Nigeria in mid-2013.

But the group returned much more lethal, and with battlefield experience. They then launched a series of daring attacks as part of a steady campaign to seize territory in northeast Nigeria. They perpetrated risky prison breaks and engaged in battles with the Nigerian military. The militants raided an air force base in Maiduguri, destroying Nigerian aircraft and seizing weapons, and conducted other coordinated attacks on military barracks. They began massacring and overrunning towns along the border of northeast Nigeria and by mid-2013 seized power in an area the size of Maryland with a population of two million, governing as an Islamic State. Gwoza, a town of roughly half a million people, was declared its capital. As of this writing, Boko Haram continues to gain territory in Borno, Adamawa, and Yobe states.

The location of Boko Haram's stronghold along the border of Niger, Chad, and Cameroon has allowed the group to exploit weak borders and governance in the remote area. Boko Haram can easily traffic hostages and seek refuge across the border whenever the situation in Nigeria becomes too hazardous. Although official numbers are not available, it is believed that Boko Haram now has anywhere from 5,000 to 10,000 fighters in its ranks.

Today the group is more violent and ruthless than ever before. It has adopted the characteristics of an insurgency and has learned to be self-sustaining. Since Boko Haram is highly self-sufficient in funding, it is difficult to sanction. It finances its organization through kidnapping ransoms and theft. Since gaining control of towns in northeast Nigeria, Boko Haram also collects "taxes" at road blocks. In some cases, local officials pay Boko Haram in exchange for "peace." Previously, the group used bank robberies to help finance their operations, a practice that has decreased under increased security presence.

Boko Haram was launched to international infamy when they kidnapped almost 300 schoolgirls from a boarding school in Chibok, Nigeria on April 14, 2014. Once Abuakbar Shekau claimed credit in an online video, the kidnapping made front pages worldwide and sparked an international Twitter phenomenon, *#BringBackOurGirls*.

At the time of this writing, 219 of the Chibok schoolgirls remain in Boko Haram captivity, and the group continues to kidnap others. The group has used kidnappings to raise ransoms and also to negotiate prisoner exchanges with the Nigerian government. Kidnappings-for-ransom—previously a trademark of AQIM—were integrated into Boko Haram's repertoire after they went to fight alongside other extremist groups in Mali. In sum, Boko Haram has kidnapped over 500 women and girls and has claimed responsibility for numerous attacks on schools and universities.

Corruption has handicapped Nigeria's ability to respond to the threat of Boko Haram. Although Nigeria has the largest defense budget in Africa (approximately USD 6 billion), it is unable to adequately train, equip, or pay its troops due to its gross corruption. When Boko Haram's bombing campaign began in 2011, Nigerian security forces were unprepared. Although some progress has been made, Nigeria still remains ill-prepared to deal with the growing terrorist threat of Boko Haram. Their security sector has issues with inter-agency rivalries, poor intelligence sharing, and a lack of effective political leadership. On the ground, troops have low morale and are becoming increasingly hesitant to fight a well-equipped foe. In late summer 2014, reports surfaced of mutinies and desertions by Nigerian troops.

For several years, the Nigerian Army, Air Force, and police have been working together as a "Joint Task Force" (JTF) to counter Boko Haram. A group of vigilante citizens created a group known as the Civilian JTF in 2013 because they were unsatisfied with the Nigerian government's response. Initially the Civilian JTF worked in collaboration with the official JTF, but later fractured into smaller groups of vigilantes who have been criticized for human rights violations and extrajudicial killings, actions that have galvanized support among some northern Muslims for Boko Haram.

When the security forces have tried to counter Boko Haram in the northeast, their efforts have been described as heavy-handed and indiscriminate—killing suspected militants extrajudicially, detaining suspects without trial or due process, and destroying property. The Goodluck Jonathan administration has admitted that it is also riddled with Boko Haram sympathizers and enablers—including in the military.

The Nigerian government sees the Boko Haram problem as primarily a security issue, but other factors need to be considered.

Regional inequalities between Nigeria's wealthy, Christian south and the poorer, Muslim north helped give rise to Boko Haram. Three out of four residents in the northeast fall below the poverty line—twice as many as in the nation's wealthy south. The north also feels disenfranchised—the nation's presidency is set to rotate between a Christian and a Muslim leader, the result of a power-sharing agreement from 1999—yet this has not been the case. President Goodluck Jonathan, a Christian, came to power when his Muslim predecessor Umaru Musa Yar'Adua, whom he served as vice president, died while in office in 2010. Jonathan stoked outrage by seeking another term in 2011, and yet again by declaring his candidacy for the 2015 elections.

While primary responsibility for countering Boko Haram lies with the Nigerian government, the international community has been engaged in this problem as well. Nigeria's neighbors have the political will and desire to swiftly counter Boko Haram, as they have been a major destabilizing factor along the border. However, their defense budgets are markedly lower than that of Nigeria. The United States has long been engaged in countering terrorism in Africa. In 2005, the U.S. launched the U.S. Trans-Sahara Counterterrorism Partnership, a program to assist partner nations in Africa, and in 2010 established the U.S.-Nigeria Binational Commission, a strategic dialogue aimed at fostering cooperation on issues of mutual interest—including security. Other USAID programs are aimed at counter-radicalization.

The global attention brought to Boko Haram by the Twitter campaign *#BringBackOurGirls* also increased pressure on the Nigerian government to accept more international assistance. The United States, who designated Boko Haram as a Foreign Terrorist Organization in November 2013, has incrementally stepped up intelligence collection efforts and cooperation with Nigeria to counter Boko Haram since this summer. American drones are stationed in N'Djamena, Chad, along with 80 troops who are involved in the search for the missing schoolgirls abducted by Boko Haram in April. The United States has also carved out small groups of Nigerian troops that can be trained and worked with under Leahy Law requirements, which prohibit the United States from providing military assistance to foreign military units that commit gross human rights violations. The greatest obstacle to American efforts has been the Nigerian government itself. Nigeria has largely been wary of American training assistance, viewing such training as a form of subjugation or interference.

Despite the Nigerian government's claims that Boko Haram's leaders accepted a ceasefire and promised to release the 219 Chibok girls remaining in captivity, the group's violence continues. Without significant reforms in Nigeria, the threat of Boko Haram will continue to grow. With presidential elections set for 2015, the political legitimacy of the country is on the line. Should Boko Haram's control of territory in the north continue and they prevent residents from casting their ballots, chaos could certainly ensue.

Further Reading

International Crisis Group, "Curbing Violence in Nigeria (II): The Boko Haram Insurgency." Abuja: 3 April 2014.

Lauren Ploch Blanchard, "Nigeria's Boko Haram: Frequently Asked Questions." Congressional Research Service. Washington, DC: 10 June 2014.

U.S. House of Representatives Committee on Homeland Security, "Boko Haram: Growing Threat to the U.S. Homeland." Washington, DC: 13 September 2013.

Bombs

Bombs and High Explosives:
Emerging Threats for America's Bomb Squads

Ernest J. Lorelli

For supporting end note information pertaining to this essay contact the author.

America was shaken to its core by the events of 9/11. Americans woke up to the awful reality of truly international terrorism and the consequences of years of a complacent sense of security. In the wake of 9/11, President Bush declared war on international terrorism and the nation's leadership took new interest in the ability of federal, state, and local government officials to successfully manage critical incidents. More than a decade later, we see international terrorism on the rise, not in decline. What does the emergence of the Islamic State of Iraq and Syria (ISIS) mean for current and future security concerns for the United States and our Allies? The question in 2001 was "what's next?" For the nation's military explosive ordnance disposal (EOD) units and the federal, state, and local bomb squad personnel, it was a question that would change their focus for more than a decade. As we approach 2015, we're better prepared for potential threats but the question still remains: What is next?

Bomb squads have always had to be ready to successfully and safely manage and resolve a multitude of incidents involving explosive devices. However, in the wake of 9/11, they became increasingly aware that the threat was changing and that bombing scenarios never before or seldom seen on America's shores became distinct possibilities. The use of a vehicle borne improved explosive device (VBIED) in Oklahoma City carried out by Timothy McVeigh, while seen as an aberration by most Americans, is a common event in other parts of the world. What would the effect of such a bomb be in downtown Los Angeles, CA, in Orlando, FL, or in the nation's capitol? What if the bomb contained radioactive materials or chemical warfare agents? Are suicide bombers in our future? What if the bomb is on the water or underwater in one of the countries major seaports? As bomb squads focus on the various problems associated with these possibilities, four topics keep coming to the top of the list; The VBIED, the person-borne IED (PBIED) more commonly referred to as a suicide bomber, Weapons of Mass Destruction (WMD) which in this example is a device containing a nuclear, biological, or chemical material, and bombings against the nation's transportation system including commercial air, shipping, and rail systems.

A great deal of explosives can be packed into a vehicle. For example, the average four-door sedan can realistically carry 1,000 pounds of explosives. A full size commercial van can carry 4,000 pounds, and a small moving van up to 10,000 pounds of explosives. The ability of any of these to devastate a city block is now common knowledge. While much is being done to protect critical infrastructure from the massive blast effects of a vehicle bomb, we don't have the resources to turn private buildings, our market places, and city streets into blast-protected, hardened structures. Nor do we want to. Preventing the bomb from getting placed or even being built is the best defense but we need to ask what happens when the bomber does make it to the target and successfully places the bomb.

Today, security awareness is measurably better than it was before 9/11 and if someone recognizes a vehicle that "just doesn't belong there," they are more likely to take appropriate action and notify authorities. This is evident in the May 1 2010 VBIED incident in Times Square, New York City. The bomber, Mr. Faisal Shazad, a 30-year-old Pakistan-born resident of Bridgeport Connecticut had become a U.S. citizen in April 2009 but had been radicalized and used to build and deliver the device. However, citizens in NY City—having been sensitized to terrorism—spotted something was wrong and the quickly took action to get the NY City Bomb Squad to the scene, where it was successfully resolved. A key concern we should all have is if it would have been a different result elsewhere. As we get further and further from each event, and the population is war weary and security weary, will we react in time for the next one? There will be a next time.

Recognizing the threat is important because, for the bomb squad, time will be the most critical resource in any scenario. They must have time to deploy to the scene and, once on scene, have time to employ tools and tactics to disarm the device. The threat will dictate employment of diagnostics processes and dynamic procedures. The lower the threat, the more time the bomb squads will have to closely examine a vehicle to determine if it is indeed a bomb. However, if car bombs start exploding across the nation, then within minutes of arrival on the scene of a suspect vehicle, the bomb squads will need to be able to employ dynamic procedures to rapidly gain assess to the bomb inside the vehicle and separate components. Can it be done? Yes. Can it be done in time? Maybe.

The suicide bomber presents a unique problem. The idea of someone being so committed to their cause as to strap explosives to their body in order to become a living bomb is still beyond most western comprehension. The suicide bomber presents an entirely different spectrum of problems to the bomb technician.

Suicide bombs either carried on the person or loaded in a vehicle being driven by the person usually incorporate a very simple fuzing system designed not to fail.

There is significant evidence to suggest threats employing the suicide bomber tactic do not act alone. In this case, the person carrying or driving the bomb is simply the "mule" or vehicle for delivery. The person is wired with a remote control system to cause the device to function once it reaches the intended target. The person controlling the device is in a safe location watching and waiting for the right time. Any detonation of an explosive device is going to bring a response by a bomb squad. Is the problem over with the death of the bomber or his mule? No. We learned the hard way over the last decade that the threats we're up against use coordinated tactics to cause as much carnage as possible. In recognizing that fact, caution dictates that both first responders and bomb squad members have to be on guard for secondary devices intended to kill responders and on-lookers.

Weapons of Mass Destruction (WMD) are a strategic concern for the nation and the use of a WMD in an American city is every state and local government's worst nightmare. Even a small device containing nuclear, biologic, or chemical material would be a major disaster.

We've seen how a biological attack can be accomplished with the anthrax letters in the days following 9/11. The most likely nuclear threat in a terrorist attack is the use of a radiological dispersal device (RDD). In an RDD, the goal is not to obtain a nuclear detonation but to use conventional explosives to scatter nuclear material over a large area causing relatively few initial casualties but a great deal of fear and panic and a massive contamination problem. A chemical attack would be similar to the employment of an RDD, except the initial casualty count would probably be higher.

The national response to a WMD bombing scenario has been the creation of several "super teams" positioned around the country in order to allow them to respond to a WMD situation in minimal time. Most bomb technicians would agree, however, that—unless a super team is positioned in their city—any response time may be too long. As a consequence, local bomb technicians will have to execute some action to mitigate the effects of the device if it functions or make an outright attempt to disarm the device. To that end, most major city bomb squads have pursued both training and tools to deal with potential threats.

The decision to proceed or to wait for additional help may be as big a problem as the device itself. Be it a VBIED, PBIED, or a potential WMD, it will involve operational input from the bomb squad and input from political leadership from local, state, and federal government. No matter what, someone is going to second guess the decision process. Established doctrine based on a sound threat assessment, the local agencies capabilities (training, equipment, personnel), and well practiced incident task management processes will all be needed.

The most notable danger from threats using IED that we have faced in the U.S. is to the nation's commercial transportation system, including seaports, air transportation, and rail. Commercial air has been the focus of much security enhancement both after the Shoe Bomber incident in December of 2001 then again in reaction to the Underwear Bomber in 2010. Recent (2014) open source intelligence indicates that ISIS groups are plotting similar attacks in the future. Also of concern are U.S. sea ports. An incident like the one that nearly sunk the U.S.S. Cole while docked in Yemen could be carried out in a U.S. commercial seaport. Additionally, we need to be concerned with a vessel being used to smuggle a nuclear device into a seaport to be detonated at time designed to maximize damage and casualties. While many sea ports cities have stood up dive teams in their bomb squads, the ability to combat this threat is again best served by solid intelligence and prevention actions.

We need to also consider the most common of IED—the placed IED. A placed IED is one placed at the bomber's intended target in order that he can detonate it later at a time of his choosing. The Boston Marathon Bombing of 2013 is the most recent event that would come to mind of a placed IED. The terrorists, two bothers named Dzhokhar and Tamerian Tsarnaev, constructed the device using a pressure cooker and explosives gleamed from commercial fireworks. They camouflaged their device in backpacks and detonated them remotely using a radio controller from a toy car. Three people were killed outright and many were injured, including several with traumatic amputations of limbs. It can be safely assumed that similar attacks by like-minded individuals operating independently within our society are likely. Depending on their capability and motivations, the results can be expected to be much worse if we're not prepared to act.

Lastly, we should not discount the possibility of a combination of these threats into a single, terrible incident. The last time, they used airplanes. The next time may be multiple VBIED attacks carried out simultaneously in one or more cities or perhaps the use of railcars loaded with potentially explosive and toxic materials detonated while the train travels through a population center. Trains hauling literally hundreds of tons of explosive and toxic materials pass through major cities every day.

Earlier, we addressed the question of what will come next from those who pose a threat to our country and our concerns. First, we need to examine the risk that we will face this kind of attack again. We will define "risk" as the likelihood of an event happening. If we define "threat" as a person or groups of people who intend to impose their will upon us by force, then we can quickly identify the potential threats who pose the greatest risk for the foreseeable future. We must assess each threat by measuring their capability and motivation. We can assess the capability of a threat by their resources, training, and history. We can assess their motivation primarily through their stated goals, which in the case of terrorist activity is usually politically and theologically based. Al Qaeda and the various Al Qaeda-like groups have both demonstrated their capability and intention to do great harm with an end game (strategic objective) of world domination *in accordance to their rules.* They have also demonstrated their preference for weapons that cause mass casualty events and shocking destruction. To that end, we can surmise that the IED will remain their weapon of choice for a long time to come and that they will plan to use these weapons for maximum effect wherever possible.

To meet the challenges ever-evolving within our own borders, bomb squads must continue to modernize doctrine as well as their tools, tactics, and—most importantly—their training. Conducting full scale joint operations training with support assets as well as their military EOD counter-parts (when possible) is ideal but funding is and will continue to be an issue for the foreseeable future. While bomb squad funding for robotics and other technologies has vastly improved their capability, they will need to continue to fight for an equal share of the funding allocated to improve responder readiness.

An analysis of open source intelligence indicates the nation's public safety bomb squads will get an opportunity to employ their skills. It is what they do before the event that will make the difference. When the nation's public safety bomb squads get the call, they will need to be ready to respond quickly and take decisive action to protect the nation from these evolving threats.

Further Reading

TM-31-210 Improvised Munitions Handbook. Washington, DC: Department of Defense, July 2013.

IED Trigger Recognition Guide. Washington, DC: Department of Defense, July 2014.

John P. Sullivan, Robert J. Bunker, Ernest J. Lorelli, Howard Seguine, and Matt Begert, *Jane's Unconventional Weapon's Response Handbook.* London: Jane's Information Group, August 2002.

Carlos the Jackal

AKA Ilich Ramirez Sanchez, Carlos Apparat, and Organization of the Armed Arab Struggle (OAAS)

James T. Kirkhope

Even among terrorists, Carlos the Jackal is a rare breed, possessing traits of both the fictional James Bond and the very real Osama bin Laden. Although a native Spanish-speaker from Venezuela, Carlos is fluent in English, French, Russian and Arabic and lived in Jamaica, Mexico, the U.K., the Soviet Union, Jordan, Lebanon, France, Algeria, Yemen, Colombia, Hungary, Syria and Sudan. He conducted or directed operations in the Middle East, Europe, and Africa. Yet, though he participated spectacularly on behalf of the Palestinian cause, that conflict continues to rage while he languishes in a French prison serving a life sentence. Carlos, it seems—much like James Bond—was a product of the Cold War and, as communism collapsed, so did his utility to regional and global powers.

Born in Caracas, Venezuela on October 12, 1949, Ilich Ramirez Sanchez was indoctrinated in Marxist ideology from an early age by his father. Ilich was an active member of the Venezuelan Communist Youth. By age 13, Ilich's parents divorced—the boys lived with their mother, but were supported and educated by their father in Venezuela and then, by 1966, in Britain. Upon arrival in London, Ilich began circulating in high society circles and embassy parties. His father sought better schooling for his sons and, after consideration at the Sorbonne in Paris, succeeded in securing a scholarship for Ilich at the Patrice Lumumba University in Moscow—the training academy for third world revolutionaries.

Ilich studied propaganda, guerrilla warfare, and terrorism. He was trained by—and with—the very best of the best. Ilich's classmates included Palestinians with ties to Wadi Haddad and George Habash of the Popular Front for the Liberation of Palestine (PFLP). By July 1970, Ilich was invited to train with the PFLP in Jordan where he became known as "Carlos" and eventually dispatched back to London as an agent of the PFLP. There, Carlos began his reign of terror.

Carlos' first attack was an assassination attempt on a vice president for the British Zionist Federation of London in December 1973. He launched a variety of attacks in London and Paris over the next two years including bombings and rocket propelled grenade (RPG) attacks on Israeli airliners at the airport in Orly, France.

Carlos is best known for his brazen attack on the Organization of Petroleum Exporting Countries (OPEC) in December 1975. Carlos attacked the OPEC headquarters in Vienna, taking 70 people hostage. His captives included 11 high-ranking oil ministers. Carlos demanded and received access to an aircraft, securing a large ransom and freedom for himself and his colleagues. PFLP leader Haddad, however, dismissed Carlos in 1976 for failing to kill the Saudi and Iranian ministers as instructed. By the 1980s, Carlos created his own network called the Organization of the Armed Arab Struggle (OAAS) which conducted a series of bombings against France from 1982-84, including a failed RPG attack on a nuclear power plant under construction. The purpose of Carlos' one-man war was to pressure the French government to withdraw its influence from the Middle East and release his girlfriend, who had been imprisoned in the Spring of 1982.

Though Carlos was a master terrorist with few peers, it is important to recognize that state support played a crucial role in his operations. Many nations such as Algeria, Cuba, East Germany, Hungary, Iraq, Jordan, Libya, Sudan, Syria, and Yugoslavia, among others, provided Carlos with funding, safehouses, passports, transportation, weapons, and diplomatic support. He also received tactical and personnel support from other sympathetic terror groups such as the Japanese Red Army, the Basque ETA of Spain, as well as the Baader-Meinhof Gang/Red Army Faction and the Revolutionary Cells of West Germany.

In 1985, Carlos' state sponsorship and support infrastructure began to whither. By 1991, he could only find refuge in Sudan which eventually was pressured in 1994 to extradite him to France. It was a pathetic end for a master terrorist. Carlos did not go out in a blaze of glory, with AKs and Uzis spitting bullets at the "imperialist aggressors." Instead, he slowly rots in a French prison. Worse, he has become irrelevant and forgotten in today's new age of "sacred terror."

Carlos came of age in the psychedelic London of 1966, studied communism in Moscow, and matured under the influence of Marxist struggles of the Middle East throughout the 1970s. The end of the Cold War saw the death of the very Marxist ideology that Carlos had once killed for. By the mid-1990s, Carlos' compatriots in the struggle had either been co-opted or wiped out. What a sad sight, Carlos must have thought. The IRA making peace with the Ulster Loyalists, Yasir Arafat and the Yitzhak Rabin shaking hands on the White House lawn, and Coca-Cola in the Kremlin—what on Earth had gone wrong?

Terrorism hadn't totally died out, but the new hard men weren't the militant Marxists of old. Instead, they spill blood for what Carlos had always considered "the opiate of the masses." Osama Bin Laden's goal is a new Islamic caliphate, not worldwide socialism. These new terrorists are so fanatical that they think nothing of killing themselves to blow up a few Israeli teenagers. Their secular counterparts in the killing fields of Rwanda, Bosnia, and Darfur are motivated by ethnic hatred and greed, not Mao's little red book. The action has moved from the glamour of Paris, London, and Beirut to anonymous safehouses, rugged mountain bases, and Internet forums. The wars of the future are waged by cyberwarriors, jihadists, and "global guerrilas," and there is no room for playboy atheists in this new world disorder.

Further Reading

John Follain, *Jackal: The Complete Story of the Legendary Terrorist, Carlos the Jackal*. New York: Arcade Publishing, 1998.

Colin Smith, *Carlos: Portrait of a Terrorist: In Pursuit of the Jackal, 1975-2011*. New York: Penguin Books, 2012.

David Yallop, *Tracking the Jackal: The Search for Carlos, the World's Most Wanted Man*. New York: Random House, 1993.

Chemical Weapons

Twenty-first Century Terrorism

Raymond Picquet

At least since the early 1990s, a growing consensus has emerged on the importance of a new threat from weapons of mass destruction (WMD). As a result of these weapons, an increasing number of states could now inflict grievous harm on other states—and the people who inhabit them. In addition, somewhere in the middle of that decade, observers identified another more insidious threat; the emergence of non-state actors motivated to inflict large numbers of casualties through acts of terror. And, in contrast to their predecessors, these new terrorists no longer appeared to be mainly motivated with discrete political objectives, for example hijacking commercial aircraft to leverage the release of political prisoners. Now they appeared to be more interested in causing deaths and casualties for the purpose of religious-based ideological reasons and ritual. Tragically, although the U.S. government was increasingly aware of the impending threat—and trained for it, the public was not fully aware of the problem until September, 2001. Only then was it clear that the mixture of terrorist motives and WMD could cause huge numbers of casualties—in one fell swoop.

Due to popular films such as Goldfinger and various contemporary spy novels, chemical weapons (CW) were considered by the public to be highly exotic, silent killers that could exact instantaneous death and mass casualties, an ideal weapon for modern terrorists. However, fortunately for those who might face CW on the battlefield or who might be the victims of terrorist tactics using this weapon, the reality is more ambiguous. CW is now commonly considered by modern organic chemists to be a remnant of early twentieth century chemistry, neither cutting-edge nor particularly exotic technology by 21st century standards.

Paradoxically, the reality is that CW is both the most frequently used and least exotic of the WMDs. They are comparatively advantageous in terms of cost, the accessibility of common construction materials and facilities, including dual-use commercial equipment, the required technical knowledge for building and using them, and the horrible and dramatic effects of their use. Indeed, in the future, terrorists can be expected to—and probably will—use CW, because of their qualities of lethality, swiftness of effect and silence (propensity for surprise)—attributes not generally found in a single conventional weapons system.

Chemical weapons have existed in one guise or another for eons, at least since primitive tribal adversaries attempted to inflict harm on their rivals by poisoning wells or burning crops. Prior to use in World War I, CW was a product of the new science of organic chemistry. As a result of the military impasse known as trench warfare in World War I, the German chemical industry suggested the utility of a host of harmful chemicals used in a variety of industries. After World War I, commercial-industry-based research and development of insecticides and fertilizers resulted in a whole new generation of CW that was much deadlier than their forbearers.

The Weapons System

Contemporary military inventories of CW include a variety of agents derived from industrial chemicals, such as phosgene, chlorine, and hydrogen cyanide, or poisons specifically developed for use in war, such as mustard gas (HN). CW developments in the 1930s initially emerged as more or less serendipitous products of legitimate agricultural research but subsequently developed into deadly new instruments of war: nerve gases. Because chemical weapons can potentially cause large numbers of casualties over a wide area, the effects are not necessarily limited to immediate military targets, such as military personnel or facilities. Consequently, chemical weapons were defined as "weapons of mass destruction" by a United Nations statement of 1947. An important consequence of this label was to place them in a category with the world's deadliest instruments of war: nuclear and biological weapons.

Although chemical weapons are popularly perceived as "poison gas", the modern weapon involves complex manufacturing and handling processes, each of which requires specific and exacting procedures and equipment and knowledgeable personnel. In general, the weapon includes several elements: 1) the chemical agent, 2) the munitions (i.e. specialized bombs, projectiles, etc.), and 3) the delivery vehicles, such as aircraft, or artillery and critical sub-systems, such as spray tanks. For conventional military use, the CW weapon "system" includes an array of assets and activities: relevant dedicated personnel, strategic and tactical planning, logistics, and training. On the defensive side, CW is effectively protected against with adequate warning and defensive paraphernalia, such as the gas mask, protective over-garment clothing, agent antidotes, and operational environments and living spaces equipped with dedicated CW defensive configurations and specialized protective equipment. Unfortunately, protective gear is not always immediately available and its use, particularly in hot weather, invariably tends to significantly "degrade" military combat performance.

Indeed, it is because of the effectiveness of such CW protective measures that CW doctrine tends to emphasize the efficacy of surprise-attack modes and use against strong points and key points, such as behind-the-lines airfields and C^3I centers—all of which are presumably vulnerable to surprise. In addition, CW could be used to slow down an advancing conventional force by degrading combat mobility and endurance with cumbersome protective gear and complicated safety requirements.

Chemical agents are of four types: 1) nerve; 2) blister; 3) blood; and 4) choking, each of which has distinct characteristics and effects. All of these "casualty agents" are potentially fatal, depending on the toxicity of the agent, the dosage administered, and the degree and duration of exposure. Although CW is also occasionally defined to include chemical incapacitants, such as psycho-active agents (i.e., BZ) or riot control agents (RCAs e.g., CS, CN or CR), this type is not dealt with here, because they are not generally considered lethal under normal circumstances. In addition, the related topic of "toxins", a highly poisonous protein extracted from dead organisms, is more aptly considered under the topic of biological weapons.

Although all of the casualty agents have undergone extensive research since World War II, nerve agents are generally considered to be the most dangerous. They are extremely toxic and relatively quick in their devastating impact on the body's nervous system. Blister agents cause disabling burns to exposed skin surfaces, which leave tissue highly vulnerable to infection. Blood agents prevent the normal transfer of oxygen to body tissue, which often results in suffocation. Choking agents cause damage to the lungs, causing them to fill with fluids and preventing oxygen from reaching the body.

Nerve agents were initially developed in German industrial laboratories concerned with developing pesticides, soon after the emergence of organophosphorus chemistry in the 1930s. Nerve agents such as Tabun or GA (1936), Sarin or GB (1938), Soman or GD (1944), and the V agents (1952) are much more adaptable to mobile ground warfare than other types of CW agents, because of the rapidity of their action and the smallness of their effective doses.

Fortunately for the Allies, none of whom possessed nerve agents, these weapons did not become a significant factor until after World War II. They provided an exponential increase in the tactical utility of chemical warfare although they were soon overshadowed by the advent of nuclear weapons. But they were nevertheless capable of contributing a major potential offensive punch as a supplement to properly protected and trained conventional forces. The ability of CW to provide surprise, stealth and deep interdiction capabilities—as well as conventional offensive punch—also indicated that they are well suited for many of the "asymmetric" or hit-and-run tactics favored by terrorists.

Although CW incidents are currently the most common application of WMD, several structural factors have inhibited their acquisition and use by non-state actors. First, the acquisition and use of CW is illegal and international sources and cooperation is severely limited; virtually all weapons acquisition efforts are necessarily clandestine and thereby risky. CW activities, such as acquisition, possession and use violate international law, including protocols recently established in a comprehensive framework, the Chemical Weapons Convention

(CWC) which entered into force on April 29, 1997 and currently has 189 signatories. Second, CW is less costly than either nuclear weaponry or probably most types of biological weaponry, but it nevertheless involves a complex and technical set of efforts that require professional level skills and scientific competence. Although the initial costs of manufacturing or importing CW-relevant technology and materials may be relatively inexpensive relative to other WMD programs because of the overlap of CW technology to analogous commercial enterprises (e.g., fertilizer and insecticide), the clandestine nature of CW production burdens any effort to purchase materials in foreign markets or to engage in a domestic manufacturing effort. Similarly, the additional safety requirements required by CW production involves specialized training, equipment and extensive efforts to avoid harm to personnel and costly medical and decontamination efforts. Third, another important requirement is project management. In general, the effective, safe and secure production of chemical agent requires a serious management effort that would probably be difficult to obtain for a terrorist group—unless perhaps salient parts of that mission remained confidential—or effectively "outsourced" by the leadership. Although it is not inconceivable that small quantities of CW agent could be "cooked up" for limited production in temporary facilities, such improvisational "concoctions" could easily result in compromises to agent production quality (i.e., purity), safety and related security problems. In addition, the same managerial issues apply to other facets of the weapons system, such as safety training for agent handling and use.

Incidents of Use

In spite of a growing awareness of WMD as a possible source of threat, virtually none of the major terrorist incidents of the 1990s either used such weapons—or used them successfully. Indeed, based on a number of observations of failed terrorist attacks, the effective use of WMDs appears to have surpassed the capabilities of most the perpetrators. For example, Shoko Assahara's Japanese-based Aum Shin Rikyo attack on the Tokyo subway on March 20, 1995 was a largely unsuccessful effort (not including the psychological effects measured in hundreds of reported psychosomatic injuries at neighboring hospitals), because the actual dissemination of the agent (i.e., a crude procedure of piercing a plastic container with an umbrella tip) was inadequately tested and trained and the agent, Sarin, was insufficiently pure to be effective. Both Aum's grandiose ambitions and its operational incompetence are reflected in the history of its program between 1990 and 1995: it conducted 17 known CBW attacks (10 CW, including 4 GB, 4 VX, one phosgene and one hydrogen cyanide) and seven BW attacks.)—all of them were generally unsuccessful.

The Jihad organization's attack on the World Trade Center in 1993 failed because of a faulty operational planning, a lack of adequate testing, and the use of untrained personnel. An example of the incompetence was the attempt to integrate a conventional explosive device (i.e., ammonia nitrate and fuel oil or ANFO) with hydrogen cyanide. Most, if not all, of the hydrogen cyanide was effectively destroyed by the ANFO explosion. Because Ramsi Yousef, the operational leader of the attack, had hoped to see the twin towers of the World Trade Center crash down on each other with the result of tens of thousands of deaths, the terrorist attack was clearly a failure with only 6 deaths and 1,042 casualties. Another measure of incompetence was reflected in the naiveté demonstrated when Mahmoud Abouhalima, one of the terrorist group's members attempted to retrieve the deposit on the rental truck used in the bombing. Because the FBI had identified the truck from a serial number stamped on the vehicle's differential, the driver was quickly arrested. Another measure of incompetence was the ongoing audacity of Yousef Ramzi who was eventually arrested in Pakistan after the FBI placed a huge bounty on his head. Because he continued his involvement in terrorist activities in the Philippines and Malaysia after fleeing from the United States, his high profile eventually resulted in his arrest.

Another incident involving CW was fortunately still-born in the preparation phases. Jim Ellison, leader of the domestic-based religious terrorist group, the Covenant, the Sword and Arm of the Lord (CSA), expected to use hydrogen cyanide in civic water supplies, but was thwarted by a timely raid on his domicile by the FBI in 1995. CW experts generally assess the vulnerability of urban water supply systems to CW attack as relatively low for a number of reasons: the neutralization effects of chemical (chlorine), the debilitating effects of hydraulization on most agents, and the massive volume of water in most urban system. Each of these factors can be expected to flush and neutralize most agent threats.

Perhaps surprisingly, in spite of the above-referenced examples of significant technical and organizational difficulties associated with successful employment, CW appears to continue as the WMD method of choice for terrorist groups.

Motivations

Terrorist motivations range from personal psychological pathologies, such as narcissism, inclinations towards grandiose delusions, such as caused by bi-polar disorder or from other issues such as radical political ideologies or nihilism, to extremist religious orientations. But what motivates terrorist groups to acquire and use WMDs? Where do such groups fit on the above spectrum? What do recent cases of terrorist group uses of WMD suggest about their motives as a group? A case study-based research analysis of WMD at the Monterey Institute found that several such groups were characterized by charismatic leadership, an extremist-authoritarian ideology with grandiose ambitions and goals, a group culture exhibiting cult-like behavior and normative orientations and values that propagate chiliastic ideologies and reject international legal norms.

Virtually all of the WMD-relevant terrorist groups were founded by leaders with charismatic personalities with grandiose ambitions for political and social development and little regard for human life. An example par excellence of the charismatic leader beset with grandiose ambitions was Osama bin Laden. His ambitions for the re-creation of the Islamic Caliphate, and his attempt to achieve that end by destroying existing political institutions in the Middle East, in particular, the extant monarchies and the radical-modernist regimes which replaced the post-Ottoman imperial structure, was based largely on fanciful dreams.

Nonetheless, this grandiose vision has been largely frustrated—if not finally defeated—by the gradual destruction of al Qa'ida since 9/11.

Osama bin Laden announced his intention to acquire WMDs not long after he declared war on the United States in 1998. At least since that time, al Qa'ida appears to have made serious efforts to acquire WMDs on a number of levels and in a various locations. Indeed, two Pakistani nuclear scientists were reported to have offered to work on an al Qa'ida weapon soon after the invasion of Afghanistan by Coalition Forces in 2001. According to one report, they were subsequently assigned to assist in the more promising and immediate al Qa'ida effort to acquire CW. Another report indicated that al Qa'ida assigned an Egyptian chemist with the nom de guerre of Abu Khabab al-Masri to its Derunta training camp in South Waziristan, Afghanistan where experiments had been conducted on chemical weapons. According to reports, the notorious Jordanian-born terrorist, Abu Musab Zarqawi, who had formerly run a network of training camps in Afghanistan independent of al Qa'ida, provided specialized training in those camps on poisons and chemical weapons. He was subsequently involved in a plot to detonate 20 tons of chemicals and poison gas in central Amman and was also associated with the Kurdish terrorist group known as Ansar al-Islam that had established a crude CW research lab and training camp in northern Iraq. Zarqawi eventually became the brutal leader of al Qa'ida in Iraq.

At least since 9/11, the motivations of al Qa'ida are a major concern. Two theories tend to frame the issue of motivations for all contemporary terrorism: was the leadership motivated by concrete material or political goals or, conversely, were they following the dictates of a divinely inspired spiritual destiny? According to Michael Scheuer, formerly of the Central Intelligence Agency's Alec Station, an in-house research center dedicated to Osama bin Laden, al Qa'ida's leadership was largely interested in obtaining concrete objectives, such as regaining territories occupied (or dominated) by foreign powers and toppling corrupt political regimes that dominated the Middle East rather than in establishing the Caliphate for the greater glory and honor of Islam.

By contrast, political scientist and anthropologist Mark Juergensmeyer of the University California, Santa Barbara, a noted expert on terrorism with an emphasis on Sikhism, argues that contemporary terrorists are socialized by charismatic leadership into becoming fanatical believers in a religious destiny that can be directly obtained through suicidal sacrifice. Terror is incumbent in the divinely driven dynamic of good versus evil. In that context, anything imaginable can be condoned, because war is self-justifying; the enemy is by definition satanic. According to Juergensmeyer, the cosmic or divine connection between these fanatical warriors or terrorists and their mission of destiny allows for a serious and rational consideration of virtually any weaponry.

A relevant follow-up question is which of these orientations would incline a group to use WMD? The suggestion here is that a terrorist group with a more rationalist-pragmatic ideological goal set (e.g., regaining irredentist territory) would probably not want to risk using WMDs because of the complex and ambiguous implications of such use, such as the possibility of incurring large numbers of untargeted civilian casualties. On the other hand, even for such a group, the use of CW might be perceived as providing a half-measure: focused attacks with a more manageable collateral casualty problem than either nuclear or biological weapons—given the favorable environmental conditions.

CW is at once the most prevalent and most mundane of WMDs. It lacks the awesome and fascinating qualities of its nuclear and biological counterparts—and their potential for civilization-ending destruction. But, as was demonstrated at the World Trade Center in 1993 and 2001, terrorists will use what is available and effective, and they will not be necessarily daunted by western notions of what might be too commonplace to be taken seriously. Indeed, it might be well to remember the cautionary remarks of David Albright, a noted specialist on WMD proliferation, after studying captured al Qa'ida documents discovered in a house in Kabul in December, 2001: "It's not just a bunch of guys climbing along some jungle gym or shooting their guns in the air. These are people who are thinking through problems in how to cause destruction for a well thought through political strategy."

Further Reading

Anthony H. Cordesman, *Terrorism, Asymmetric Warfare, and Weapons of Mass Destruction: Defending the U.S. Homeland.* Westport: Praeger Publishers, 2002.

Eric Croddy, *Chemical and Biological Warfare: A Comprehensive Survey for the Concerned Citizen.* New York: Copernicus Books, Inc., 2002.

Jonathan B. Tucker, ed., *Toxic Terror: Assessing Terrorist Use of Chemical and Biological Weapons.* Cambridge: MIT Press, 2002.

Conditions Promoting Terrorism

Byron Ramirez

Terrorism is a complex phenomenon. Several factors have been associated with the emergence of terrorism. One factor alone does not foster terrorism. Instead, a set of dynamic variables and conditions with multiple feedback loops seem to enable its emergence. With these caveats in mind this essay will discuss the conditions promoting 'non-state based terrorism' as opposed to terrorism directly linked to states.

History

Terrorism is grounded in an evolving historical context. History delivers the context under which the resort to violence is undertaken. The historical background of a group or region may lead to the belief that new actors must break with the past and help pursue change.

Many societies around the world have experienced different forms of colonialism, invasion, and occupation which conversely have produced deep marks on those resulting cultures. A formerly colonized society may possess 'a set of memories' which in turn help to fuel its desire to reshape its identity and pursue its own goals.

Various terrorist groups have risen around the world hoping to modify an existing order that has been in place and subordinated their interests. This also has led to the emergence of ideologies, beliefs, and views that sometimes incorporate resentful and violent actions that are carried out with a sense of urgency. Most terrorist groups have justified their violence with a deep belief in the necessity and justice of their cause, and a need to amend history.

Nationalism

During the twentieth century, non-state actors with nationalist agendas emerged and challenged states through the use of terrorism. The notion of employing terrorism as a means of challenging an existing order became more prominent. In some cases, terrorism materialized into a strategic tool to express anti-colonial sentiments against the British, French and other empires.

Several terrorist organizations have centered their activities on nationalistic causes. Examples of nationalism as a contributing factor to terrorism include: Basque separatists who used violence against the Spanish state; Algerian terrorists who fought against French rule; and Irish militants who conducted actions against Great Britain.

The *Irish Republican Army (IRA)* emerged from the ideal of Irish Catholics to form an independent republic, rather than to continue to live under the control of Great Britain. The *IRA* used bombings and assassinations to oppose British rule in Ireland as well as to intimidate Protestant Irish who supported Great Britain.

Another example of nationalism playing a role in the emergence of terrorist activities is that of the *Kurdistan Worker's Party (PKK)*. This organization used terrorist tactics to pursue its intent of establishing an independent Kurdish state. In this particular case, the *Kurdistan Worker's Party* sought national autonomy from Turkey, Syria, Iran, and Iraq.

There were the *Sri Lankan Liberation Tigers of Tamil Eelam* who were members of the ethnic Tamil minority. They used suicide bombings, assassinations, and other deadly tactics to wage a fight for independence against the Sinhalese majority government. Their violent actions supported a secessionist nationalist campaign.

Another illustration is the case of the *Popular Front for the Liberation of Palestine (PFLP)*, a Palestinian Marxist-Leninist and revolutionary leftist organization which opposed the moderate stance of Fatah as well as negotiations with the Israeli government. During the late 1960s and early 1970s, *PFLP* armed-hijacked several flights and their Abu Ali Mustapha Brigades also claimed responsibility for several suicide attacks.

Culture of Violence

Some areas of the world accept violence as a legitimate means of expressing discontent or disapproval, resolving disputes, and competing with other groups for political and/or economic control.

In some cases, violence is perceived as a means of establishing political order. Hence, for some groups the use of violence is a necessity for pursuing their interests and achieving the change desired. Some regions have experienced multiple coups, insurgencies, revolutions, and conflict which have led to a cultural tolerance of violence.

Cultures where there is, or where there has been, communal conflict between competing domestic groups are at risk of seeing a rise in terrorism. Sometimes, conflict over class, ethnicity, and religion may result in violent societies that spawn terrorist organizations.

Political

Terrorism was originally used in the context of insurgency and guerrilla warfare, a type of organized political violence carried out by non-state actors. For centuries, terrorism has been used as a tool for influencing the conduct and policy of a government through intimidation and coercion.

The 20th century endured several carefully planned acts of violence orchestrated by organized terrorist groups which pursued specific political interests. Terrorist acts are used to express discontent with how society is organized and managed, as well as disapproval for those who have the power to oversee it. Unpopular regimes, tyrant governments, and dictatorships breed political instability and in turn amplify discontent and anger. There are also cases where the rule of law is weak and where there is low protection of civil and political rights. These political conditions sometimes converge and help to increase the risk of terrorism. Groups that engage in terrorism often respond to the political environment and reconcile the historical and cultural frameworks.

The acts carried out in 1972 by the *Black September Organization (BSO)*, a Palestinian non-state actor, were politically motivated. The violent acts during the 1972 Munich Olympics where *Black September* kidnapped and killed Israeli athletes had a specific political goal in mind—negotiating the release of Palestinian prisoners.

A few years later, another group, the *Palestine Liberation Organization (PLO)* placed the return of occupied lands back on the international political agenda. This move was met with resistance by the Israeli messianic, right-wing group known as *Gush Emunim* which soundly rejected the PLO's proposition as well as the position of the State of Israel during the negotiation process.

Another terrorist group, *ETA (Euskadi Ta Askatasuna)*, employed violence for political motives. This Basque nationalist and separatist movement conducted kidnappings and carried out several bombings, killing hundreds. The organization attempted to influence political affairs and drive political change. ETA's principal goal was to gain independence for the Greater Basque Country.

In the 1980s, terrorism was adopted by right-wing, neo-Nazi or neo-fascist racist groups. Similar to the terrorist actors that preceded them, these violent non-state actors pursued political interests aimed at subjugating the interests of other racial groups that had received greater political rights through constitutional reforms and civil rights reforms. Many of these neo-Nazi or neo-fascist groups grew fearful of a society that granted political and social recognition, political rights, economic franchise and freedom of movement to ethnic minorities and women.

Several groups have used violence as an instrument for coercing governments and influencing social and public policy. Fearful that some minorities would move to their neighborhoods and take their jobs, groups such as *The Popular Association—Golden Dawn* in Greece have used terrorism to intimidate and attempt to influence the political environment. In the case of *Golden Dawn,* a confluence of factors seem to drive their violent activities—anti-immigrant rhetoric, racism, xenophobia, nationalism, political views, concerns for unemployment (economic), and religious beliefs.

Socio-Economic

Socio-economic conditions play a role in the rise of terrorism. Being poor and enduring social calamities does not cause an individual to become a terrorist. However, a village or town in where there are no economic opportunities, where there is lack of education and political freedom, as well as limited choices and options to change one's personal condition may more easily enable terrorist leaders to come in and recruit disenfranchised individuals.

Poverty does not create terrorists, but, it makes many individuals susceptible to recruitment by terrorist organizations. Some terrorist groups take advantage of others' despair and desperation and provide them with an idealism that inspires recruits to join the movement with the promise of a better future. Many of these individuals who are recruited do not know how to read or write. Terrorist leaders often use religious texts and selective historical recounts of past events to persuade these individuals to join their cause.

In some cases, socialism became the seeming panacea for people to resolve the political and economic inequality they saw developing around them. Socialism provided an apparent solution through which many could enjoy greater economic justice. Seeing that there was growing inequality and a misdistribution of wealth, several terrorist groups began to use socialism as a supportive ideology.

Some economists, including Gary Becker, have suggested that there is a connection between wealth and terrorism. Becker argues that political activism, including violent activity, is less appealing to individuals who have increasing economic opportunities.

Other scholars have argued that one of the driving factors behind terrorism is income inequality which incentivizes some groups to perpetuate violence against others. Economic dislocation seems to facilitate conditions where terrorism can develop. Timothy McVeigh who bombed the Oklahoma City Federal Building has been associated with this view.

After the Gulf War, economic dislocations affected the Middle East region. Many Egyptians, Palestinians, and others working in the Persian Gulf lost their jobs due to the unstable economic climate. For many of these workers, frustration grew as they had no income to support their families. Economic disparity along with religious conservatism converged and eventually helped to propel fundamentalist movements.

Religion

Religious terrorists and violent extremists choose to interpret and use religion to justify their violence. Some argue that religious fanaticism may help to create conditions that are favorable for terrorism to surface. For instance, organizations such as *Al Qaeda, Hamas, Hezbollah,* and the *Christian Identity movement* selectively interpret and exploit religious concepts and texts to support their terrorist activities. Religions themselves do not "cause" terrorism. Instead, terrorist groups exploit religious concepts and strategically fit texts into a rhetoric that meets their interests and justifies their use of violence.

Terrorist groups inspired by religious and nationalist goals have committed violent attacks, including the assassination of Egyptian President Anwar Sadat, and suicide bombings in Israel. On the other hand, militant messianic Zionists have used religious claims to the historical land of Israel to justify their own acts of violence. According to the *Radical Messianic Zionist* perspective, the territories belong to the Jewish people by Divine decree and must be protected at all cost.

Aum Shinrikyo in Japan, *Islamic Jihadists* in Egypt, and groups such as the *Army of God* in the United States have also employed carefully selected religious language to support their respective ideologies and subsequent actions.

The increased politicization of religion and the tendency to speak politics in a religious dialect have become more common both in the mainstream as well as in violent extremist circles. This has contributed towards a greater convergence between political ideology and religious doctrine which often is manipulated by terrorist groups that seek to advance their interests.

Groups such as *Al Qaeda, Hamas,* and *Hezbollah* have used particular religious texts and conflated them with other group interests and motivations that fall under the political, economic and social realm. Many violent extremists and religious-based terrorist groups have learned to effectively manipulate religious concepts to recruit individuals and to have them carry out violent activities that satisfy the leaders' own purposes.

Group Ideology

Terrorist groups seem to embrace a mythical concept or abstract representation of an ideology. Many experts suggest that the group's collective identity is established early in the process. Usually the identity is one of 'victims of repression'. For extremist and terrorist groups, there is an existing unacceptable status quo that must be repelled in favor of an ideal towards which the group must strive. As a result, the group often seeks to develop a new found identity rooted in socio-historical contexts, experiences, and cultural factors.

The group may have members who have experience with violence. A past history of violent behavior is strongly associated with the potential use of future violence. A group's collective experience with violence may lead it to engage in violent terrorist activities.

Over time, the group's identity is transformed and no longer rooted in the specific interests and views of a certain group of individuals. Instead, the identity comes to represent an abstract figure or mythical concept that is accompanied by pseudo-mythical attributes which are not direct manifestations of the social group's original identity. The emergence of terrorist groups appears to be directly associated with a process of identity creation.

Terrorist organizations, in turn, modify an individual's or group's belief systems, values, and identity. Accordingly, they transcend the initial ideology and transform identity, ideology, and goals.

Psychological

Individual

Research into the psychological causes that take the individual terrorist as their focus began in the 1970s.

American psychiatrist David Hubbard in his influential study, *The Skyjacker* (1971), concluded that hijackers were psychically unstable, or ill, and shared a few traits including a violent, often alcoholic father, and poor social achievement. Ferracuti and Bruno conducted a study of *Psychiatric Aspects of Terrorism in Italy* (1981). Their study concluded that terrorists share some characteristics such as ambivalence toward authority, emotional detachment from the consequences of their actions, low education, and adherence to violent subcultural norms.

In 1983, the West German Interior Ministry conducted a study of 250 terrorists which revealed that thirty-three percent reported severe conflict with parents, and thirty-three percent had a history of juvenile court conviction.

Some psychologists have also presented the 'narcissistic rage hypothesis' which assumes that terrorists are filled with rage that developed because of their imperfect psychological development in childhood. According to this theory (Crayton, 1983), terrorism occurs in the context of narcissistic injury and is manifested as an attempt to acquire or maintain power or control by intimidation. Others such as Crenshaw (1981) have explained that a common emotion that seems to motivate the individual to become a terrorist is the need for vengeance on behalf of comrades. Chenshaw later notes, however, that no 'terrorist pathology' itself exists which is generally agreed upon in the literature.

Group

Recent sociological and social psychology views of terrorism suggest that groups and networks of individuals are the best way to explain social phenomena such as terrorism. This perspective also shares common ground with studies of authoritarianism and cult behavior that examine how individuals come to identify so strongly with a group that they lose individual identity.

Jerrold Post explained that terrorists have subordinated their individual identity to the collective identity, so that what serves the group, organization, or network is of primary importance.

Some scholars now agree that individual members of terrorist groups relinquish or subordinate their own identity to that of the group. Thus, to best understand how and why terrorist groups work, and how best to engage and ultimately counter them, a study of their group psychology is required.

Terrorist groups also seem to perceive a sense of imminent threat that drives them to pursue violent actions. External threats or other events that threaten the terrorist group with a possible or actual loss of control or power are greeted with intense rage, violence, and a directed effort to assert control while avoiding the shame of its loss.

Trigger Event

Some scholars have suggested that a trigger event sometimes shifts the decision making of a social group and helps turn it into a terrorist organization. These *'trigger events'* may in fact threaten the survival of the group or jeopardize its interests. As a result, trigger events effectively generate violent actions and reactions which are perceived by the terrorist group as the only available option or choice. Some underlying conditions may lead the terrorist group to believe that using violence against civilians seems like the reasonable and even necessary option.

Conclusion

Terrorism is a matter of choice and can be viewed as a tactic within a larger strategy. Terrorism is used as a tactical tool to leverage violence in order to gain specific concessions related to the group's goals.

Terrorist acts most often are rational and calculated choices that are designed to subject a government or actor to alter its decisions and policies. Groups such as *Al Qaeda* and *Hamas* use terrorist tactics as a strategy of the weak seeking to gain advantage against stronger armies or political powers.

Further Reading

James Ciment, Ed., *World Terrorism: An Encyclopedia of Political Violence from Ancient Times to the Post-9/11 Era.* Armonk: Sharpe Reference, 2011.

James J.F. Forest, Ed., *The Making of a Terrorist: Recruitment, Training, and Root Causes.* Westport: Praeger Security International, 2006.

Alex P. Schmid, Ed., *The Routledge Handbook of Terrorism Research.* New York: Routledge, 2011.

Consequence Management

Local Emergency Responders: Surviving the Rhetoric While Trying to Define Readiness

Paul M. Maniscalco and James P. Denney

Since September 11, 2001, United States national security experts and academics have forecasted the looming threat of additional large-scale terrorist attacks. Counter-terrorism experts also cite the threat of domestic terrorism and religious fundamentalists and their desire to rid the world of those that do not concur with their theological interpretations. Whether the adversaries are anti-government individuals, nation-state proxy actors, or religious zealots, it is clear that the events of the last decade have altered the global security landscape forever. Even the most jaded observer must concede that the threat of terrorism against the U.S. and its' interests has increased at an unprecedented rate.

Unfortunately, speculation regarding the capabilities and vagaries of terrorists, their various methodologies, access to weapon types, and delivery platforms has resulted in essentially an assumption that weapons of mass effect (WME) terrorism is inevitable. This translates into a sense that, while interdiction is preferable, preparing America's "first line of defense" (EMS, Fire and Police agencies) to effectively respond remains the critical step to ensuring the protection of our nation.

To date, more than a trillion dollars (USD) has been expended to identify threat mediums, determine threat sources, and in the development of a national response capability. However, how much of this funding has gotten to the local response organization? Is it being utilized effectively to achieve the stated objective of enhanced readiness? Are all emergency response disciplines receiving appropriate funds to elevate capabilities—EMS, Fire, Police, Medical, Public Health? The response sequence is multi-disciplinary and failing to fund sustainable capabilities in all functional areas creates a single point failure in the "whole of community" readiness strategy.

All incidents are local. The federal government response is significantly time-distance delayed. To wit, has this investment truly resulted in a sustainable local readiness capability or have we built an American version of the "Maginot Line," lending a false sense of security to those responsible for the nation's welfare?

The American public safety system provides high reliability and high trust to its constituency. A key point is that the public safety sector workload is not characterized solely by volume or type and is not configuration dependent. In order to maintain its robust capability, it vertically integrates multiple competencies and each individual resource is multi-task configured. However, how prepared the U.S. is has not been clearly defined or quantified. This collective effect has created a spontaneous proliferation of terrorism experts and, a deluge of new training seminars, military units to support civilian missions, and studies that allegedly solve emergency responder problems. But, has all of this resulted in solutions or has it created more confusion? We suggest that it has yielded the latter.

Understanding the Threat

With the pervasiveness of terrorist threats, confusion about what exactly is a terrorist act has materialized. For instance, the 2009 Fort Hood Shooting is labeled as work place violence by the Department of Justice while the perpetrator proclaimed it an act of jihad. The 2014 Moore, Oklahoma attack and beheading of a woman shares a similar distinction. This confusion is further exacerbated by the numerous definitions thrust upon the emergency service sector from a myriad of sources. Academia embraces one definition and various federal agencies have their own derivations.

While for the most part they all share a somewhat common theme, this diversity of definition contributes to an already complex problem when attempting to educate responders on what an "act of terrorism" really is. It is important to be cognizant that most emergency response managers are not "social scientists," they are trained consequence experts. As such, they can be easily misled by the minutia that often emerges from this discourse. The operational goals for these professionals are based on community needs and other mandates to:

- Develop an appreciation for the impact of terrorist events.
- Articulate the threat and examine the community vulnerability.
- Develop appropriate response algorithms.
- Train and equip existing resources to confront the threat.
- Exercise response plans and incorporate mutual aid assets to foster familiarity and interoperability.

The persistent use of the term "Weapon of Mass Destruction" (WMD) in many circles continues to amplify confusion to an avoidable level (*the notional term "weapon" within emergency service sector is a knife, gun, or conventional explosive device, not a jar of bacilli*). What does destruction imply? Deaths? Infrastructure crippled? Is destruction assured when employed? The answer to all is most likely no.

Perhaps broadly utilizing the term "Weapon of Mass Effect" (WME)" will realign the overarching narrative to where it should be. It sufficiently conjures up the image of an event that can be destructive but most likely will be one of complex societal disruption. It focuses pragmatically on the systemic implications not the hyperbole that accompanies destruction. This terminology emerged from spirited research discussions in 1999 with colleagues concerning how to effectively define this scenario while concurrently demystifying the event for the public safety community. For more than 15 years, this issue has been parsed and debated. Perchance it is time to embrace the simple and self-evident.

Response

Realistically, emergency responders are the only assets capable of satisfying the critical event to intervention interval. This capability helps to diminish the impact of a terrorist attack, reducing mortality and morbidity. While the federal government, in one form or another, has developed certain training and limited funding to the consequence management community, the concentration of effort has been for pre-emptive defense involving law enforcement and Pentagon assets. Initiatives such as the development of specialized military responders to seamlessly merge with local responders rather than an aggressive local consequence management effort are only effective when the local resources have robust capabilities for the initial contact with the event.

Today, American public safety system assets are precision forces that encompass the dominant body of knowledge regarding disaster response, intervention, mitigation, and acumen. Disaster Medical Assistance Teams (DMAT) and the Urban Search and Rescue system (USAR), developed by EMS & fire services, represent examples of this. These units are effectively utilized both domestically and globally because of their experience, capabilities, and knowledge of disaster consequence. While they are frequently referred to as federal assets, it is local personnel that staff these teams.

An appraisal of past U.S. disasters demonstrates that local first responders provide immediate, direct interventions which reduce mortality and morbidity while concurrently minimizing economic and infrastructure impact. The New York World Trade Center bombing (1993), Murrah Federal Building bombing (1995), Tokyo Subway Sarin incident (1995), September 11 (2001) attacks, Hurricane Katrina (2005), and Sandy (2012) are clear examples of this. They illustrate that convergent and first responders provide the majority of rescue, extrication, and emergency medical services prior to the arrival of any specialized teams or federal assets.

In order to keep within the intended context, we need to develop a full appreciation that a terrorist event is a local event. As public safety leaders, we consistently operate in environments characterized by extensive damage, human injury, and limited resources. Our knowledge of any given incident is always partial—approximate at best. Our actions are shaped by contingent, unpredictable circumstances. Local emergency response entities cannot rely upon the federal government to respond and "make everything all better." It is the responsibility of the local emergency response to ensure that existing response and mutual aid capacity are functional and effective to initiate a sustainable response.

The perceived threat of a chemical or biological incident on an American community poses serious concerns regarding the selection process to determine which communities receive training. While the federal government made obvious choices based on community size, the threat is no less significant to smaller communities. It is common knowledge that the larger cities have more capability, equipment, training, and experience than smaller ones. They are, in all likelihood, capable of absorbing the impact and managing the outcome of a terrorist incident with a modicum of federal government assistance, especially when one factors in the capacity for additional resources through regional mutual aid. What surely is not adequately addressed is the threat of additional campaign like events—coordinated, geographically-compressed events, and what those outcomes will be.

The EMS, Fire, and Police mission is save lives, protect property, and promote environmental conservation, in that order. This construct has demonstrated capability of effectively and successfully operating in ahistoric, uncontrolled, all hazards environments. This mission is accomplished daily with assets generally arriving on scene within five minutes of notification. The urgency associated with catastrophic events and the concern that problems become worse in the absence of appropriate action creates an air of uncertainty vis-à-vis what has happened or is likely to happen, coupled with a strong urge to take action "before it is too late."

It is safe to project that even with the emphasis surrounding the topic of terrorism, a WME event will be a one of a kind incident for these responders, which will contribute to the delay in actual event recognition. Regardless of whether it's urban, suburban, or rural, the effect on the American psyche will be the same. Whether the population is millions or twenty thousand, first responders will answer the call in five minutes or less. The difference is whether or not the first responder will manage or suffer the consequence of a terrorist event, adding themselves to the list of victims. The unrelenting question still remains: how do we keep responders sharp when the attack possibility exists but the frequency of events is low?

Another void that exists is mobilizing, deploying, and requisite functional exercises for EMS strike teams across jurisdictional lines. No one is responsible for this at the federal level. Presently, this has been relegated to being a private sector service contracted commodity. This ignores the inherent capacity and immediate availability of local government resources across the U.S. that can be drawn upon in a rapid fashion.

While the projected weapons of choice may be a hazardous material, the resultant effect will be that of a high impact/high yield medical disaster. Without using a self-indulgent sci-fi scenario that exploits the realm of perfection, it may be prudent to make the following assumptions regarding the occurrence likelihood and impact.

1) Container and delivery mechanism size and concealment restrict the chemical agent quantity to be deployed at an incident to a finite amount.

2) Due to technological problems experienced by even the most wealthy and sophisticated nation states, biological weapon deployment, in most instances, presently remains a hard to achieve goal of terrorist organizations.

3) The functional area that will most likely have the greatest demands in the event of a successful attack will be the medical community (EMS and in-hospital services).

4) Whereas public safety organizations have the ability to draw on rapid response mobile resources from surrounding communities, hospitals are fixed assets with limited reserve capability.

Moreover, if one were to objectively assess the readiness level for EMS and in-hospital facilities, we believe it will be found that they are the weakest links. The lack of adequate antidote stockpiles and insufficient rapid access to chemical weapon neutralization agents such as Reactive Skin Decontamination Lotion (RSDL), existing decontamination facility limitations, and the questionable availability of hospital beds and ancillary hardware such as ventilators will all contribute to increased CBRN incident lethality.

Because of the nature of biologics, the interval to intervention may preclude survival at other than the normal range for a given organism. This combination will provide significant obstacles for even the largest of communities to mount an effective response, whether or not federal assets or resources are on scene or immediately available to the community.

Education

The value of preparedness training offered by the U.S. government should not be disputed, but its global impact falls somewhat short of providing for national readiness. If the threat is as prevalent as it is portrayed, then sustainable expansion of the training initiative is required. Notwithstanding, the U.S has only funded 100 UASI cities to have this sustained capacity.

Using numbers provided by various U.S. public safety professional organizations, there are approximately 3.5 million responders that require some level of training. The existing capacity building strategy has yielded many boutique programs, a merit badge system that fails to provide for skill normalization. Additionally, there are ways to harmonize this educational obligation within existing discipline specific public safety training curriculas—but that solution has been continually dismissed. For instance, the Paramedic training curriculum is standardized through the DOT NHTSA, EMS Office. This office is the official "keeper" of the training standard that is used by the individual States. Having a mandatory training module that addresses the EMS specific issues for terrorism response institutionalized within this curriculum would promulgate a sustainable solution to skill retention. This can be employed in the Fire and Police training programs also. This just makes good sense, operationally and fiscally. But more than a decade since September 11th, this has yet to happen.

If this threat is as real as the "experts" claim, then failure to have widespread access to structured training and relevant information is reckless. When the U.S. prepared for a possible nuclear attack, we witnessed the government undertaking a massive preparedness effort that was for the most part effective. If this threat is no less real, then we need to re-evaluate the measures being instituted to ensure greater efficiency and access.

Summary

All things being equal and allegedly accurate, the information presented to emergency responders indicates that this threat is "very" real. With a greater understanding that local emergency response assets within the U.S. are in 'combat' on a daily basis (in excess of approximately 15 million times per year), a greater, more cohesive, comprehensive strategy for efficient preparation and deployment of these local resources is required if the U.S. claim of being prepared is to be more than just a good public relations campaign. The emerging strategy must appreciate that preparedness is a process and not an event. It is a continuum characterized by equipping, training, and constantly reinforcing the training through practice or drills until both individual and system performance for a given emergency is consistent, automatic, and effective.

The actions taken to date to remedy the under-prepared emergency response apparatus of the U.S. for terrorist acts are appreciated, but intelligent and defined actions based on actual threat potential are in order to remedy the prevailing deficiencies. Anything less will sustain a fragmented system struggling to survive the rhetoric while planning their response.

Further Reading

Paul M. Manilasco and Hank Christen, *Understanding Terrorism and Managing the Consequences.* Upper Saddle River: Prentice Hall, 2001.

Damon P. Coppola, *Introduction to International Disaster Management.* Boston: Elsevier/Butterworth-Heinem, 2006.

James F. Miskel, *Disaster Response and Homeland Security: What Works, What Doesn't.* Westport: Praeger Security International, 2006.

Counterinsurgency

Thomas X. Hammes

At the time of this writing, U.S. participation in Afghanistan was winding down, the American public showed no interest in putting "boots on the ground" in Iraq, and military budgets continued to fall. Thus a central question arose, "What capabilities must the United States retain in its force structure?" The rising cost of weapons systems and personnel means the nation cannot continue to do business as usual. The perceived failure of both the Afghan and Iraq campaigns means many commentators are questioning the need to maintain counterinsurgency capabilities in its national security tool kit. And, even if the United States chooses to do so, does it require a major ground force or not?

Much like after the Vietnam War, the presence of a potential peer competitor strongly reinforces the argument that counterinsurgency is not an appropriate mission for resource constrained armed forces. Many defense analysts see China as the primary threat and wish to focus U.S. defense efforts on a naval and air campaign in the Far East. Advocates for this position believe the decade of counterinsurgency operations in Afghanistan and Iraq has starved the navy and air force. Pending budget cuts mean the United States must focus its decreasing assets against China. In short, hard times mean hard choices.

Drivers of insurgency

As much as the American military would like to turn away from its bitter experiences with insurgency, the fact remains that insurgents, in a variety of forms, will threaten U.S. national interests. However, in thinking about what form a U.S. response should take, planners must understand that over the last 60 years, the primary drivers of insurgency have changed. The initial major driver—anti-colonialism—has obviously passed. Colonial powers have been driven out. However, their withdrawal led directly to the second major driver of insurgencies—conflicts over who will rule the state the colonists established and left behind. UNITA versus FAPLA's long war over who would rule Angola is a clear example of this motivation. This type of conflict continues but is less prevalent.

In its place, a third driver is emerging—the desire to change the colonial borders that were drawn without any consideration of local ethnic, cultural and religious networks. We are seeing an increase in conflicts in regions where relatively recent colonial borders artificially divided much older cultures. The current conflict in Syria and Iraq reflects this desire by pre-existing networks to reestablish themselves as the dominant political power in their regions. It has already effectively erased the Iraq-Syria border. The Pashtuns and Balouch of Afghanistan/Pakistan/Iran are also examples of older ethnic associations unhappy with their current situations. They join the Kurds of the Middle East in struggling against the colonial boundaries. We are also seeing the emergence of transborder separatist movements in several nations in Africa. At the same time, we are seeing the growth of criminal cartels who seek not to control the entire country but merely to create sanctuaries where they are free to operate. This relative new driver means these conflicts will be over the dismemberment of a state or states, rather than seizing control of a single state.

The different drivers have dramatically changed the character of the insurgencies, their organization, and their approach to gaining power. It has not changed the fact they will use force to achieve their goals.

Inevitably, whether the conflict is over the control of existing borders or the need to change borders, some of these conflicts will impact areas of strategic interest to the United States. Whether through destabilizing important allies or impinging on world energy supplies, these conflicts will be important to the United States. Some parties to the conflicts will also provide either sanctuaries or safe havens for terrorists who are focused on striking the United States or its allies. In short, U.S. interest in insurgency and, of necessity, counterinsurgency will continue.

Range of counterinsurgency approaches

However, that does not mean we should look to the Iraq or Afghan campaigns when considering the appropriate force structure. While *FM 3-24* focused on population-centric counterinsurgency, recent history shows a wide variety of approaches have been used. Some are not appropriate for use by a liberal democracy but it is important that those thinking about counterinsurgency recognize the variety of methods that exist.

Three methods not appropriate for a liberal democracy are deportation, ruthless suppression, and in-migration. In 1944, Stalin deported the entire Chechen population to Siberia. Khruschev let them return in 1956 but they did not revolt again until after the collapse of the Soviet Union. China has used economic incentives to encourage Han Chinese to migrate to Xinjian Province. By increasing the percentage of Han to Uyghurs, the Communist Party hopes to tamp down the insurgency. In 1982, Hafez Assad massacred 20,000 citizens of the city of Hama to make an example of what happens to a community that was suspected of supporting the Muslim Brotherhood. Each approach worked for that dictator.

While these methods are not palatable for democracies, others are. For insurgencies dependent on charismatic leaders, decapitation has worked. By capturing Abimael Guzman, the Peruvians crippled the Sendero Luminioso insurgency. In addition, counterinsurgency that focuses on the population has been used successfully by democracies. Britain used this approach in Malaya, Kenya, and Northern Ireland. However, in each case, they were the domestic power.

While these campaigns are obviously of interest, the most important question is what approach or approaches have worked best for the United States as an expeditionary power.

What has worked for the United States?

When discussing the future of counterinsurgency for the United States, it is absolutely essential to differentiate between those approaches that worked for domestic counterinsurgency and those that work for expeditionary counterinsurgency. *FM 3-24* drew most of its best practices from the domestic counterinsurgency efforts of the British in Malaya and Northern Ireland and the French in Algeria. In all three cases, the counterinsurgent was also the government. Thus, they could make the government legitimate by removing any person or organization what was hurting that legitimacy. This was also the approach the United States used in the Philippines between 1900 and 1902, where the United States was the domestic power.

However, in expeditionary counterinsurgency, it is much more difficult for the outside power to force the host country to make the necessary political changes. As the United States experienced in Vietnam, Iraq, and Afghanistan and the Soviets in Afghanistan, an outside power could not force the government to be legitimate. Even removing illegitimate leaders and replacing them with those picked by the expeditionary power failed. It is essentially the approach the U.S. tried in Afghanistan and Iraq. In fact, I have not found a single example where an outside power was able to apply direct, large-scale population centric counterinsurgency and succeed. By direct counterinsurgency, I mean the outside power does most of the fighting and tries to force the political changes necessary to defeat the insurgency.

And yet, the United States has been successful at expeditionary counterinsurgency. U.S. efforts to assist the Philippines in 1950s and again since 2001, Thailand in the 1960s, El Salvador in the 1980s, and Colombia against its insurgents in the 1990s and 2000s have all been successful. In each case, the United States used an indirect approach rather than a direct approach. The indirect approach meant that U.S. personnel provided advice and support to host nation forces and government as those nations fought. While this support at times even included tactical leadership, the focus was always on assisting the host nation and not on U.S. elements engaging the enemy. In addition, these efforts were kept relatively small. This had two major benefits. First, it kept the U.S. presence from distorting the local political reality too badly. Second, it prevented impatient Americans from attempting to do the job themselves when they thought the host nation lacked the resources or moved too slowly.

Strategy not Doctrine

In absence of a strategic concept for dealing with counterinsurgency, the United States has fallen back on doctrine. And unfortunately, even that doctrine has become misunderstood. Some counter-insurgency (COIN) discussions treat population centric and enemy centric counterinsurgency as separate approaches. In reality, they simply represent different ends of a spectrum of COIN actions. Even the most population focused effort still takes action against the enemy. And even the most enemy centric approach still deals with the population in one way or another. Thus, it is more accurate to think of a campaign as a mix of these approaches.

The only way to develop a strategy rather than simply trying to execute doctrine is to evaluate each conflict in terms of the interaction between the societies in conflict and develop a genuine strategy based on that understanding. That strategy must explicitly state our assumptions, bring coherence to the proposed ends, ways, and means and describe a theory of victory. Failure to do so will leave the United States in the historically disastrous position of trying to make effective tactics compensate for the lack of a strategy. Of particular importance, any strategy to intervene in an insurgency must understand the motivations and allegiances of the participants.

Implications for Force Structure

Vietnam, Iraq, and Afghanistan have demonstrated that using a direct approach to population-centric counterinsurgency is manpower intensive and actually reduces the political leverage the United States has with the host country government. In contrast, the Philippines, Thailand, El Salvador, Oman, and Colombia have demonstrated that an indirect support can develop an effective strategy that includes greater leverage over the host government than a direct campaign. If the host government refuses to make the necessary political reforms to generate popular support, the United States can disengage without a major loss of face. In these examples, the host nation politicians understood this fact and made sufficient changes to either defeat the insurgency or negotiate a settlement that left the government in charge. Each campaign was long but the United States could sustain its efforts precisely because they were relatively minor efforts that did not cause enough domestic political discontent to end U.S. involvement. In the case of Thailand and El Salvador, change in the external environment late in the campaigns allowed the government to succeed. In Thailand, the fall of Vietnam and Cambodia provided painful examples of what a Communist government would bring. In El Salvador, the fall of the Soviet Union dramatically reduced the assistance Cuba could provide to the insurgents. In only one of these cases did the United States set out to dramatically change the government or local power structures. Rather, it pushed its clients to make the adjustments necessary to reduce the appeal of the insurgency—and even to reach a negotiated agreement that allowed insurgent participation in the government.

In contrast, when the United States has made a major commitment of its own troops and prestige, the host nation politicians have repeatedly refused to modify their behavior. They seemed to believe the United States could not or would not back out of such a major commitment. And in fact, until the U.S. population tired of the commitment, the United States did not.

Thus, although the United States must maintain a capability to intervene in insurgencies that threaten its vital interests, that does not mean maintaining a major portion of its forces for that mission. Rather, it means studying the successful expeditionary counterinsurgency campaigns of the United States and other liberal democracies and developing a doctrine that uses those successful approaches. The quick analysis in this paper indicates an indirect approach with the United States limiting itself to training and advising local personnel in conducting a population focused counterinsurgency effort has the greatest potential. While further study is obviously required, this indicates future counterinsurgency efforts will rely heavily on Special Forces (not special operations), and regular forces' trainers and advisors. They must be supported by a small educational, doctrinal, and training establishment based in the United States. In addition, assignment to peacetime 'advise and assist' missions should be made an element of a successful career.

While an indirect approach creates a significant demand for more senior personnel, it does not require a major portion of U.S. force structure be dedicated to counterinsurgency.

Conclusion

While large and direct counterinsurgency efforts by an outside power have consistently failed, small and indirect efforts are not necessarily a panacea. Every counterinsurgency is unique. It is based on the economic, social, political, and technical conditions of the entities in conflict and thus requires careful study and framing of the problem one is trying to solve. The historical record shows that small and indirect provides the best and perhaps only possibility of success for an outside power. But even this approach does not assure success. This brief essay cannot begin to address the changing thinking on counterinsurgency doctrine and both the opportunities and hazards of the indirect approach. A broader and deeper understanding can be developed through study of the additional readings listed below.

Further Reading

David H. Ucko, "Counterinsurgency and its Discontents: Assessing the Value of a Divisive Concept," SWP Research Paper, Berlin, 2011, http://www.swp-berlin.org/fileadmin/contents/products/research papers/2011 RP06 uck ks.pdf.

Stephen Watts, Jason H. Campbell, Patrick B. Johnston, Sameer Lalwani, and Sarah H. Bana, "Countering Others' Insurgencies: Understanding U.S. Small-Footprint Interventions in Local Contexts," RAND, 2014, http://www.rand.org/pubs/research reports/RR513.html.

Seth Jones and Patrick B. Johnson, "The Future of Counterinsurgency." *Studies in Conflict & Terrorism*, Vol. 36, No. 1, 2013: 1–25.

Criminal Insurgency

John P. Sullivan and Adam Elkus

An earlier version of this essay, "Frontlines of Criminal Insurgency: Understanding the Plazas." was posted at the GroupIntel *Blog, 3 March 2009.*

Mexico, Central America, and the cross-border region that embraces the frontier between Mexico and the United States (known as the hyperborder), are embroiled in a series of interlocking, networked criminal insurgencies. These criminal insurgencies are essentially battles for dominance of the *plazas,* and/or corridors for the shipment of drugs into the United States. They are battles for profit and power.

Cartels battle among themselves, the police, and the military, enlisting the support of a variety of local and transnational gangs and criminal enterprises. Corrupt officials fuel the violence, communities cower in the face of it, and alternative social structures emerge. Criminal cartels, like the Sinaloa Cartel, the Arellano-Félix (Tijuana) Cartel, Gulf Cartel, and *La Familia Michoacana* and its successor *Los Caballeros Temparios* (Knights Templar). Prison gangs like *Eme,* the Mexican mafia, and—transnational street gangs—like the *maras*: MS-13, 18th Street, *Bandas Criminales Emergentes* (Bacrim) in Colombia and *Barrio Azteca,* and military bands like *Los Zetas, La Línea,* and *Los Negros* also play pivotal roles in the allocation of force and influence. These have been joined by *autodefensas* (self-defense groups or vigilantes acting as community police) that seek to stabilize or control areas suborned by the cartels and extreme cartel violence.

Collectively, the gangs and cartels are forces of instability and thuggery that act as criminal netwarriors. The *plazas* (lucrative cross-border markets) are the front lines of Mexico's drug wars. It is clear that the *plazas* are the vital terrain of the distributed criminal insurgency battles—and may even constitute certain cartels' centers of gravity. Other key nodes include transshipment points like the ports of Lázaro Cárdenas and Veracruz. These ports are key in moving drugs, precursor materials for synthetic drugs, and resources like iron ore, timber, and petroleum that have been extracted by the cartels. The cartels are strengthened by corruption and the collusion from co-opted police and political officials.

The cartels and gangs act as networks within illicit global economic flows. They control turf and territory. They both employ instrumental violence to instill fear and ward off competition and interference from the state and provide utilitarian social goods. They tax local businesses, cooperating gangs, and political officials (their extortion is known as *piso* or a *cuota*).

Journalists, mayors, judges and civil society activists are assassinated to silence scrutiny. Migrants are traded, pressed into service, and killed if they resist. Their bodies are buried in mass graves known as *narcofosas*. Barbarization helps instill fear and sustain terror. Cartel victims are beheaded and dismembered. Sometimes, they just disappear. Perhaps over 100,000 have been killed by cartel *sicarios* (hitmen) during the *sexenios* (six terms) of Felipe Calderón and his successor Enrique Peña Nieto. Many have disappeared; refugees, including unaccompanied minors, flee north to the United States; internally displaced persons (IDPs) flee failed states like Tamaulipas and Michoacán. Kidnapping and human trafficking join the *narco* trade as lucrative profit centers for the transnational criminal bands.

In addition to typical gangland murders, the cartels have embraced infantry tactics, attacking rivals with improvised infantry fighting vehicles (known as *narcotanques*), set up complex ambushes and blockades (*narcobloqueos*) in cities, and briefly embraced limited use of car bombs. Cartel actions are chronicled and broadcast via video and new media to spread the cartel's vision and threaten rivals. The cartel information operations include commissioning ballads, known as *narcocorridos* to herald the prowess and virtues of cartel capos and sicarios. This narcocultura is accompanied by the veneration of narco-saints like *Santa Muerte* (Holy Death) and *Jesus Malverde*. The cartle communiqués are augmented by corpse messaging (leaving messages attached to or carved into the bodies of victims) as well as corpses hung from bridges or, as in one case, crucified on a highway sign. Message and banners (*narcomantas*) help spread the word in this complex contest for market and power.

State response to the narco-violence has included deploying military forces to confront and contain the cartels in pacification campaigns (such as those seen in Ciudad Juárez, Tamaulipas, and Michoacán as well as in Brazil, where gangs like the *Primeiro Comando da Capital* (PCC) and *Comando Vermelho* operate in the prisons and f*avelas* of Rio de Janiero and São Paulo alike. Police reform, establishing new centrally controlled police agencies, reorganizing or re-branding existing agencies, and the development of a new gendarmerie—the *Gendarmería Mexicana*—are continuing to evolve.

Understanding the *plazas* is an essential component of addressing Mexico's drug wars. Police, military, and civilian officials can analyze the plazas as a means of gaming the "geosocial" dynamics of criminal insurgency. Looking at the influences, market imperatives, and factors that drive cartel and gang evolution, as well as the quest for dominance in the plazas helps place the violence encountered in criminal insurgency in context. In this analytical endeavor, red teaming is more than the tactical red cell penetration of vulnerable nodes. It is an adaptive exploration of the criminal enterprises and their interactions within the social and market dynamics of the plazas.

Analysts should also look at the network attributes of gangs and cartels in order to determine indicators for future activity. Which gangs or cartels are emerging in a particular area; what factors will extend their reach? Where are their new markets? What is the interaction between a specific gang or cartel? These intelligence questions can be explored through scenarios and analytical wargames. What factors are key market drivers? Where will new markets emerge? What counter-gang approaches will degrade criminal influences in failed communities? How can legitimate community political and social structures be marshaled to limit criminal reach and influence? By systematically applying adaptive, analytical red teaming, intelligence and law enforcement analysts can explore indicators of gang or cartel evolution, as well as potential courses of action to counter criminal insurgency.

Understanding criminal insurgency and criminal netwarriors is an emerging field of inquiry. Many theoretical and practical questions remain and, if answered, these questions will improve our understanding of how non-state criminal forces interact with each other and fight government power.

Perhaps the biggest question is whether the potential exists for a global insurgency to take root in failed communities in North America and how criminal actors will interface with that insurgency. To what degree will the criminal insurgency in Mexico spill over into the United States? This is not a purely academic question; nearly all observers agree that the power of criminal organizations in the Americas is rapidly increasing. Most importantly, how can domestic and foreign intelligence best be integrated to address these potentials? How can we observe the emergence of movements that can morph into insurgent or criminal insurgents within North America? How can the intelligence community work with the law enforcement community to deal with these emerging criminal insurgent security challenges?

Answering these questions is crucial to developing effective means of dealing with the problem of cartels, third generation gangs, and criminal insurgents—and the eventual goal of transforming the plazas from violent venues for criminal exploitation into *agoras* for legitimate political and social transactions.

Additional Reading

Robert J. Bunker, Ed., *Criminal Insurgencies in Mexico and the Americas: The Gangs and Cartels Wage War.* New York: Routledge, 2012.

John P. Sullivan and Robert J. Bunker, *Mexico's Criminal Insurgency: A Small Wars Journal-El Centro Anthology.* Boomington: iUniverse, 2012.

Robert J. Bunker and John P. Sullivan, Eds., *Crime Wars and Narco Terrorism in the Americas: A Small Wars Journal-El Centro Anthology,* Bloomington: iUniverse, 2014.

Critical Infrastructure Protection

Stefan Brem

Even though there have been tremendous developments in the last ten years and a thriving amount of literature, Critical Infrastructure Protection (CIP) in its basic form is actually not a new concept. It has been used for centuries—mainly in the area of the military and engineering. In those two areas, the concept has been applied particularly as a defensive or preventative tool, i.e. force protection or building reinforcements. But instead of focusing on the past, we directly turn here to the current understanding of the concept.

Figure 1: Comprehensive Risk Management Cycle

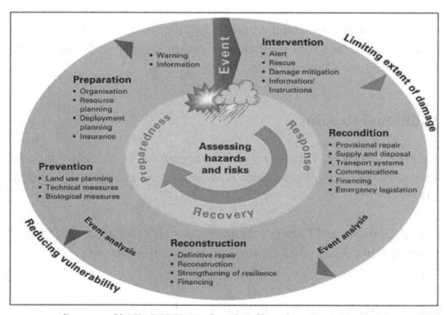

Source: KATARISK, Federal Office for Civil Protection, 2003

Today, CIP is no longer restricted to physical protection against immediate dangers, but refers increasingly to a comprehensive approach that includes a wide range of measures (see figure above). It starts with a risk and vulnerability assessment and includes measures to reduce the vulnerability [(re-) construction, prevention, preparation] and the consequences (intervention, recondition). CIP has become a truly interdisciplinary security and safety approach. It combines several scientific fields, professions, and methodologies. It is both a security and safety approach as it encompasses both active and passive protection measures as well as looks both at the threats affecting the critical infrastructures along with the risks and consequences related to them if they fail.

Usually, an all-hazard approach is applied in a CIP context—yet with different emphasis on the individual threats. In its broadest sense, the threat picture includes natural and man-made disasters, health, economic and social emergencies, espionage, organized crime, extremism and terrorism, and, finally, all out war. For reasons of simplicity, these threats are usually taken together and arranged into four main categories as listed in the table below.

Table 1: Threat and CI-Sector Matrix

Threat / CI-Sector	Natural hazard	Technical failure	Societial emergencies	Violence (below & above war)
Administration				
Chem Industry				
Energy				
Finance				
ICT				
Industrial Goods*				
Public Health				
Public Safety				
Transport				
Waste Disposal				
Water and Food				

Even though many international organizations have launched a lot of regional and global initiatives and activities over the last couple of years, so far no common standards have been established to truly identify critical infrastructures on a national or international level. However, there is a growing consensus on general definitions and common understanding of the CI sectors. This has led to the identification of up to seven or eight CI sectors that are commonly identified on a national level. Most prominently are energy, transport, and information and communication technologies (ICT). This critical trinity is accompanied by public administration, financial services, public health, water, and food.

Table 2: International Comparison of CI Sectors

CI Sector	USA	CAN	N	GER	NL	UK	EU	CH
Energy	X	X	X	X	X	X	X	X
Information & Communication Technology	X	X	X	X	X	X	X	X
Transport	X	X	X	X	X	X	X	X
Public Administration	X	X	X	X	X	X	X	X
Financial Services	X	X	X	X	X	X	X	X
Public Health	X	X	X	X	X	X	X	X
Water	X	X	X	X	X	X	X	X
Food	X	X	X	X	X	X	X	X
Emergency and Rescue Service	X	X	X	X		X	X	X
Chemical Industry	X	X		X	X	X	X	X
Postal Service	X				X		X	
Agriculture	X	X						

Welfare			X				
Defence			X	X	X		
Defence Industry	X	X					
National Monuments and Icons	X	X		X			X

Some countries, e.g. Switzerland, have introduced sub-sectors to subdivide the CI sectors. As a consequence, the energy sector is subdivided into oil, gas, and electricity supply. The actual—and socially as well as politically more challenging—identification process sets in when criteria for the definition of the critical objects and elements are specified. However, most countries, even those with advanced CIP concepts, have difficulties in actually coming up with such criticality criteria. Most remain on the level of CI sectors and sub-sectors. Those definitions are, inter alia, usually dependent on the political and cultural situations, economic development, technology, and geography of a particular country. There are also different levels of CI: from a communal well, which can be very important to a village, to the Internet and space satellites whose failure can have world-wide consequences.

Over the last ten years, the number of identified critical sectors has tremendously increased—even within the same country. The United States, as the most prominent example, has defined five CI sectors in its first CIP report. Just eight years later, an updated report specifies 17 critical sectors. And in March 2008, critical manufacturing has been added as the 18th CI sector.

The need of a coordination body for CIP activities was recognized quite early in the individual national processes and it is now commonly accepted that the CIP activities must be coordinated by a dedicated national structure. However, there are different national arrangements where and how these activities are coordinated. Early CIP activities are often performed by provisory structures like ad hoc commissions or interagency working groups. In most of the cases, especially in European countries, a special directorate, section, or center is created within existing ministries or new CIP functions are attributed to existing structures such as the ministry of defense in Sweden and Switzerland, the ministry of interior in Germany and the Netherlands, and the ministry of justice and police in Norway. In rather expectional cases, special organizations are created to have overall CIP responsibilities such as the Department of Homeland Security in the United States or the Department of Public Safety and Emergency Preparedness in Canada.

In some countries, there is an institutional division of CIP responsibilities between physical and cyber aspects. It can be found for example in Germany and the United Kingdom. There is separation between CIP and CIIP because national programs started with the protection of critical information infrastructure. Even though collaboration between these different activities has been institutionalized in the meantime, CII activities could maintain their independence which is also represented in the institutional arrangement. In other countries, there is a fully integrated approach allocating the coordination task of physical and cyber protection to the same authority. This institutional arrangement should improve the coherence and coordination of the CIP activities. The two models and exemplary countries are depicted in the figure below.

Figure 2: Institutional setup of CIP and CIIP tasks

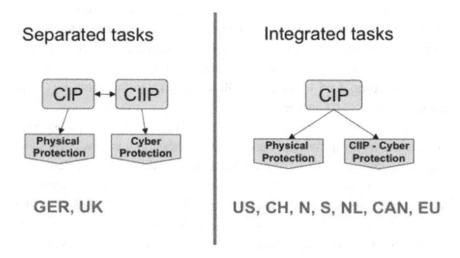

As up to 80 percent of the critical infrastructure is owned and operated by the private sector, a close cooperation between the public and private sector is indispensable. However, the depth of cooperation varies across countries. In most of the countries, the CI owners and operators are participating in the risk analysis and the elaboration and implementation of the protective measures. Usually, the public private partnership (PPP) is accompanied by legal arrangements. Yet, these provisions are not very suitable in an ever-changing environment. A general observation is that we are still lacking practical experiences and lessons learned as the CIP concepts and activities around the world are still rather new or even just emering. Yet, some sectorial approaches and selective measures have existed for quite some time but the overall framework was lacking— at least so far. In this respect, the best way to improve national CIP strategies remains to exchange information on an international level and the "second best" is to learn from major crisis and incidents. Such triggering events have been 9/11 or Hurricane Katrina.

Sharing information and experiences on an international level is crucial to improve national strategies and measures as well as to create a common understanding of the problem. The exchange can be conducted on different platforms such as international institutions and organizations or less formalized in conferences, workshops, websites etc. Additionally, some countries have established deeper bilateral collaboration, for example on cross-border risk analysis or special arrangements on security and emergency measures.

The success of the exchange depends on several factors:

- The level of confidentiality of information: sensitive information will not be shared with other countries or only with special arrangements;
- The progress of the CIP programs: obviously, you can only share the know-how that you have established yourself. As there are sometimes rather considerable differences with regard to advancement and approach, sharing of information mainly focuses on methodologies, concepts and best practices.

In the last couple of years, a consensus has emerged that it is no longer enough to (physically) protect critical infrastructures, but they must also be made more resilient. In general, resilience refers to the capacity of infrastructure, service, and social systems potentially exposed to hazards from technical, natural, or intentional events to adapt either by resisting system degradation or by readily restoring and maintaining acceptable levels of functioning, structure, and service following an event. Following Michel Bruneau's terminology, resilience for physical and social systems as well as services can be conceptualized as having four main characteristics:

- robustness describes the inherent resistance in a system to withstand external challenges without degradation or loss of functionality;
- redundancy relates to the system properties that allow for alternate options or substitutions under stress;
- resourcefulness means the capacity to mobilize needed resources and services in emergencies;
- rapidity denotes the speed with which disruption can be overcome and safety, services, and financial stability restored.

In this regard, resilience is an important part in a comprehensive CIP strategy to make them more reliable and incident-resistant.

Even though primarily designed in and for developed countries, CIP is also a relevant task in the developing world. The complexity of the system might be different, but the infrastructure might be even more prone to disruption and therefore needs to be particularly protected. Key sectors are also energy (from pipelines to refinery and electric power), communication (radio, mobile phone and internet), and transportation (mainly air and train) but a communal well might have a larger significance than the latest technical gadget.

Three developments and challenges can be identified that might shape future debates. First, there have been few binding legal terms of reference until now— particularly in the international context— governing the way critical infrastructures are to be protected. There is therefore a need for appropriate standards and agreements aimed at improving the protection and security of critical infrastructures. International agreements are also needed to limit and rectify as quickly as possible the negative consequences of damage to critical infrastructures.

This is an important consideration, particularly in the case of cross-border infrastructures (energy, communications, transportation etc.).

Second, no single entity can any longer assure the protection and security of critical infrastructures because of their complexity and mutual dependency. This requires increased cooperation between different sectors, between governmental and private actors, between the central government and its regions, between different ministries, between countries and across borders, between scientific experts and policy-makers, and between various international organizations. Terms of reference are necessary, as are incentives to promote cooperation and implement specific measures at all levels.

Third, a certain degree of conflict between values and concepts has been emerging, which has been further accentuated by the risk of terrorist attacks since 9/11. This consists of a conflict of interests between security through surveillance on the one hand and privacy on the other. Another argument exists between those who want to protect the hardware and those who prioritize the proper functioning of the service. Both are heavily interdependent and rely on each other. A further conflict is evident between the openness of western societies and their vulnerability to asymmetrical threats. Two basic considerations seem to predominate in these debates:

1) It is impossible to guarantee the absolute robustness of critical infrastructures as there will always be a certain degree of vulnerability;
2) It is important to take steps to prevent crises but also, and more importantly, to take action to manage crises and respond to them swiftly and decisively, and to make the infrastructures more resilient.

Further Reading

Ted G. Lewis, *Critical Infrastructure Protection in Homeland Security: Defending a Networked Nation.* Hoboken: John Wiley & Sons, 2006.

Tyson Macaulay, *Critical Infrastructure: Understanding Its Component Parts, Vulnerabilities, Operating Risks, and Interdependencies.* Boca Raton: CRC Press, 2008.

Robert Radvanovsky and Allan McDougall, *Critical Infrastructure: Homeland Security and Emergency Preparedness.* Boca Raton: CRC Press, 2013.

Cyberwarfare

Michael Tanji

Cyber war, information war, computer network operations, information operations; these are all variations on the common theme of using cyber space to further various military, national, or group objectives. If war is politics by other means, cyber war is simply the application of martial methodologies and tactics to accomplish in cyber space what cannot be done or is very difficult to do in the real world.

Like the word "terrorism," different government agencies have varying definitions for the offensive and defensive give and take that takes place online. This is not a paper on doctrine so, for simplicity's sake, I will use the term "cyber war" to mean any and all forms of attack and defense that occur between different parties in cyber space. Cyber space itself will be defined as the virtual environment that exists due to the interconnection and operation of hardware, software, and telecommunications systems.

For those who have experienced combat in meat-space, cyber war seems to be at least a quaint and at worst an insulting concept. No one dies in cyber space conflicts and, like a video game, recovering from all but the most devastating attacks is a matter of "rebooting" a damaged system. Sadly, medical science had not developed a parallel capability for wounded soldiers.

The tactile aspects of cyber war aside, it is still very much war in the sense that one can accomplish very significant strategic and tactical objectives by attacking or disrupting adversary activities online. In the real world, this would mean an ambush or some other kind of attack with kinetic weapons; in cyber space, it means blocking network access, preventing a piece of software from functioning properly, or preventing certain types of information from reaching its intended recipients.

Successfully executed, an offensive cyber campaign allows one side of a conflict to achieve a given goal at the expense of the other. The losing side may not physically lose life, limb, or property but, by having been denied access to certain resources or data for a given period of time, they have lost elements such as surprise, time, and information that would otherwise have been used to their advantage. Imagine, if you will, the disruption of a network that is used to process requests for military material. Delays in processing orders means troops fighting in a physical war may be denied critical supplies, the result of which is the loss of life. Cyber war may be bloodless, but it has the potential to cause casualties nonetheless.

To be successful in cyber war requires the same level of commitment, planning, preparation, and concern for accuracy and effect as in physical warfare. Understanding what your objectives are, identifying the targets that need to be destroyed in order to help achieve those objectives, understanding what it will take to neutralize opposing forces and being able to exfiltrate to safety are all subordinate missions that need to be accomplished if success on the digital battlefield is to be achieved. Cyber war is easier to execute only in the sense that issues of scale— large numbers of troops, large amounts of material—that apply in the real world do not come into play.

When computers were resources only governments and a few elite institutions had, the idea of cyber war was still thought of in the state vs. state mold. An attack from a computer in the then-Soviet Union was almost undeniably a Soviet operation. Today, just as the means of waging war have been pushed down from the state through the non-state (terrorist group, insurgency) and down to the individual level (e.g. ethnic Russian student Dmitri Galushkevich and the cyber attack that nearly crippled Estonia) so too is cyber war now capable of being waged by super-empowered individuals. Outfitted with modest equipment and with adequate but not necessarily extensive knowledge, one man with a keyboard can and has shaken the functioning capabilities of an entire society via cyber means; an impossibility in the physical world.

For all its similarities to physical war, cyber war is unlike physical war in certain ways as well. As previously noted, taking down a military network does not result in death, which tends to be a key component of war in meat-space. Cyber war is also largely a stateless activity in the sense that territory is neither lost nor gained and information— the currency of cyber space—is rarely "lost" but more often than not copied for someone else's use. At first glance, this does not seem to be a major issue until you consider that whatever advantage you had when that information was your's exclusively is now gone.

While it takes time to prepare for cyber war, executing an attack can take seconds with mission objectives over in minutes. There is no protracted occupation or risk of insurgency. In many ways, cyber war is much more "clean" than physical war, even if that is not saying much.

The effects of cyber war, like an armed conflict in real life, can also get out of hand if not executed carefully or with proper precision. The impact of unintended consequences is very real and can quickly escalate beyond the control of either attacker or defender. The cascading effects of a malicious code attack or a denial of service attack could end up negatively impacting a wide range of innocent networks and individuals. Inasmuch as there has been little "total war" being waged in recent history, an ill-controlled cyber war is probably as close as we are going to get to the wide ranging destruction (keeping issues of scope and scale into consideration) observed during the world wars.

Cyber war to date has not evolved significantly since the early writers and theorists started describing "information warfare" nearly twenty years ago. In the spring of 2007, Estonians were blaming Russia for a massive cyber attack that nearly shut down the highly wired nation; everyone covering the issue was apparently unaware that Russians had been using cyber space-based attacks against the U.S. for years. The rug was pulled out from under those who pointed the finger at Russia when it was discovered that the perpetrator was a lone Russian living in Estonia. This was good news only in the sense that it was not "cyber war"—a state vs. state conflict taking place solely in cyber space—as envisioned by so many experts.

The bad news was that an individual, in the heart of the target, was able to cause so much disruption to both private and government services, all while misleading an international cadre of experts (Estonia, as a new NATO nation, sought help from Brussels almost immediately) as to the true origin of the attacks. Galushkevich, the man convicted of the attack, drove home the point that so many network security vendors and erstwhile experts hype but fail to appreciate: the fact that where an attack appears to come from—the "last hop" in parlance—means little to nothing in and of itself.

This technical aspect of the cyber war problem is critical as we attempt to assess the capability and motivation of an attacker. A long serious of reports about Chinese hackers attacking Pentagon and other government networks serves to illustrate the point. China has tens of millions of Internet users. Despite the fact that it has something of a "great firewall" that is used to monitor Internet usage and censor certain types of content, it is largely ineffective when comes to stopping offensive activity, sanctioned or not. The thing to keep in mind is that China is an aspiring superpower with both the desire and capability to make use of every piece of information it obtains. The same cannot be said of many other countries that are labeled as the "source" of attacks against U.S. networks. Unless an alleged attack can make use of the data in some fashion, they are almost certainly not the source of the attack. This is why one worries about cyber war with China and not Indonesia or Portugal.

Answering the attack attribution question is critical because if cyber war is going to be viewed to be on par with physical war—and that is increasingly, albeit slowly, the case—then we need to be able to determine with certainty who to counterattack. Had NATO decided to counterattack in response to the attack on Estonia, and the alliance relied on the best information they had at the time, then they would have launched an attack against an innocent nation.

Attempts to control or regulate cyber war in the same fashion as traditional war have been going on for years, but to little avail. The Russians, ironically enough, have long promoted an international agreement to ban "cyber weapons;" as if a non-proliferation regime would work against such math. Establishing a legal regime—the digital equivalent to the law of war if you will—is complicated by the attribution problem, but perhaps made easier given the fact that cyber crime and cyber war share many features and national and international law dealing with cyber crimes are already on the books.

In the information age, cyber war is not inevitable: it is perpetual. Undeclared and largely invisible to most people, attacks take place every minute of every day worldwide. That cyber wars of varying sizes have largely had no effect on the vast majority of people does not necessarily detract from its seriousness, but neither does it mean that we need to over-react in a legal or technical sense. That we are able to live our lives despite a wide ranging series of cyber conflicts suggests that, at least for now, we are resilient enough as a nation and a people to deal with this type and level of conflict. How long that will last depends largely on our national leadership and the steps they take to prevent 'cyber war the nuisance' from evolving into 'cyber war the catastrophe'.

Further Reading

Jeffrey Carr, *Inside Cyber Warfare: Mapping the Cyber Underworld*. Sebastopol: O'Reilly Media, 2011.

Paul Rosenzweig, *Cyber Warfare: How Conflicts in Cyberspace Are Challenging America and Changing the World*. Santa Barbara: Praeger Security International, 2013.

Paul J. Springer, *Cyber Warfare: A Reference Handbook*. Contemporary World Issues. Santa Barbara: ABC Clio, 2015.

Deception

The Role of Deception in Terrorism and Counter-Terrorism

Scott Gerwehr

For supporting end note information pertaining to this essay, contact the editors.

Deception is the practice of *deliberately inducing disadvantageous misperception in the mind of another.* It includes a wide range of techniques, as listed in Table 1.

Table 1. Deception Techniques

Means	Definition
Disinformation	An admixture of truth plus fiction. Distortions. Can take numerous forms: memoranda, personal letters, maps or blueprints, rumors, on the record announcements, video or photos, Internet chat, etc.
Misinformation	Pure fiction. Lies. As per disinformation, can take any form.
Feints and Demonstrations	Includes diversions. *Activities* undertaken to draw the target's attention and/or resources. A feint makes contact with the enemy, while a demonstration does not.
Decoys	*Objects* meant to draw the target's attention and/or resources. Also called dummies or lures.
Disguise/Mimicry	Making one subject look like another. Also called displays or simulations.

Camouflage	The use of natural, local, or indigenous materials on a subject to conceal it from the target.
Concealment	Protection from observation. Hiding.
Low Observables/ Reduced Signatures	Structures, patterns, or materials applied to a subject, which make it more difficult to *detect*.
Disruptive Signatures	Structures, patterns, or materials applied to a subject, which make it more difficult to *identify*.
Uncertainty-Generating Techniques (UGT)	An array of techniques under one heading: they have in common the goal of creating paralyzing <u>uncertainty</u> in the mind of the target. Generating multiple or contradictory signatures are an example of this category. Firing and then quickly displacing and firing again (aka shoot-n-scoot) also falls under this heading. Some types of mis- or dis-information, which explicitly seek to promote ambiguity, also may be included here.

The practice of deception is indispensable to the terrorist; without it, the terrorist, the terrorist's organization, and the terrorist's sponsors are anemic on the offensive and vulnerable on the defensive. Irrespective of motivation—secular or sacred, separatist or revolutionary—deception is frequently employed to further or cover terrorist operations. Moreover, since deception exploits the heuristics and biases common to all human information processing, it is ubiquitous in the historical record and nearly independent of technological progress.

A Historical View of Deception in Terrorism

Deception is not the only weapon in the arsenal of the terrorist or insurgent, but it is among the most versatile; it can cause harm to the target by itself, and may also greatly increase the effectiveness and consequences of other weapons. In illustration of this latter point, for example, hostage-taking at gunpoint is a common tactic throughout the world of rebels and revolutionaries but in April 2002 members of the Colombian FARC movement managed to kidnap 13 provincial legislators by *disguising* themselves as members of a police bomb squad and penetrating the ring of security around the legislators. The ruse *facilitated or augmented* the hostage-taking tactic. There are literally centuries of precedent for such use of deception in terrorism. Terrorism by non-state actors in the second half of the 20th century demonstrates a wide variety and repeated use of deceptive techniques in furtherance of terror; some illustrative examples are listed in Table 2.

Table 2. Examples of Terrorist Use of Deception, 1944-2002

Group	Example of Deceptive Technique Used	Selected References
Irgun (Palestine)	*Misinformation and Demonstration*: Zionists effectively promulgate rumor that if British forces prevent Jews from conducting rites at the Western Wall on Yom Kippur, a violent confrontation will occur (this also served to concentrate British attention on the Wall, allowing the Irgun to attack elsewhere) (1944)	Begin (1972), Nasr (1997), Black & Morris (1991)
Viet Minh, Viet Cong (Vietnam)	*Camouflage, Concealment*: Direct action units use superb jungle camouflage (e.g., weaving together tree-tops to thwart aerial surveillance) to stage ambushes against French (and later American) patrols (1945-75)	Giap (1976), Currey and Keegan (2000)
EOKA (Cyprus)	*Camouflage, Disruptive Signatures*: Active cadre commingle with urban noncombatants (exchanging clothes, names, jobs) to evade detection and increase difficulty in identification by British (1955-59)	Grivas (1964, 1965), Alastos (1960), Holland (1994)

FLN (Algeria)	*Disguise/Mimicry*: Arab women disguised as French colonials and employed to plant bombs in Algiers (1954-58)	Crenshaw (1978), Asprey (1994)
RAF/Baader-Meinhof (Germany)	*Concealment*: Active cadre put resin on their fingertips to hide fingerprints (1968-1974)	Wright (1991), O'Neill (1980), Baumann (1975)
Red Brigades (Italy)	*Disinformation and Demonstrations*: Red Brigades leadership uses internal "sting operations" to test membership fidelity (1970-1984)	Jamieson (1992), Catanzaro (1991)
PLO/Black September (Internationally)	*Feint*: To draw attention away from the planned assassination of Israeli PM Golda Meir in Rome, Black September occupies Israeli embassy in Bangkok (1972-73)	Rubin (1994), Nassar (1991), Sayigh (1997), Thomas (1999)
PIRA (N Ireland)	*Decoys/Lures*: Active cadre emplace suspicious packages/objects to draw British first responders into ambushes, and/or observe British responses (1969-1989)	Bell (1991, 1997), Collins (1997), Coogan (1995, 1996), Adams et al (1988), Geraghty (1980, 2000), Dillon (1990, 1994)
Hezbollah (Lebanon)	*Feints/Demonstrations*: Hezbollah deliberately stages numerous false activities – sniping, movements, congregations, etc. – in order to observe Israeli responses (1985-2000)	Jaber (1997), Nasr (1997), Kifner/NYT (2000), Pelletiere (1994)
Shining Path & MRTA (Peru)	*Disguise/Mimicry*: MRTA infiltrators disguised as musicians occupy Japanese embassy (1996)	McCormick (1990, 1992), Palmer (1994)

LTTE (Sri Lanka)	*Reduced or Disruptive Signatures*: Suicide bombers (Black Tigers) employ a wide array of clothing and containers to prevent recognition in approach to target. (1990-2002)	Austin & Gupta (1988), LTTE (1984, 1984)
Chechens (Russia)	*Disinformation*: Chechens advertise capabilities meant to poison Russian intelligence analysis. For example, Khattab et al display what they claim is a Stinger missile on a web site (2000)	Thomas (1997), Gall & DeWaal (1998), Lieven (1998)

Why Terrorists Employ Deception

What do these examples have in common? Why is deception so pervasive in terrorism? What are the underlying forces or principles which motivate the terrorist to employ deception so frequently? While no formal analysis has been done to date, several reasonable hypotheses may be generated:

- *Deception is effective.* Quite simply, since the earliest recorded instance of human conflict, deception has been a staple in the arsenals of the guerrilla, insurgent, revolutionary, and terrorist. Deception has often facilitated decisive outcomes in conflict and, moreover, some of the very same techniques used thousands of years ago still work today (e.g. camouflage, diversions, lures, and disguise). The reason that deception has proven of such enduring effectiveness is that it is essentially applied psychology; while technology has changed dramatically over the years, human processes of perception and cognition have remained the same. The shortfalls in assessment and decision-making that afflicted human beings in prehistory are still very much with us today, which means that deception remains an effective instrument of conflict.

- *Deception is versatile.* The techniques of deception can be used as a force-multiplier, a force-protector, a means of manipulating the foe (e.g. into revealing a secret), or all three. Historically, it has been used to encourage an adversary to misapply their strengths; reveal or fail to shore up weaknesses; focus attention or deploy forces in the wrong place and/or at the wrong time; become paralyzed with uncertainty; and for many other reasons. This versatility is especially valuable for the weaker of combatants: it often serves to level the playing field, making it an appealing instrument for insurgents and terrorists, who are so often overmatched in manpower and materiel.

- *Deception is legion.* It is not one instrument, but a whole class of instruments meant to produce misperceptions. There are myriad techniques under the heading of deception—e.g. disguise, camouflage, hoaxes, diversions, feints, lies, and decoys—and they can all be used in a campaign of terror. Adding this to its *versatility*, it means that not only can deception be used for a variety of ends, but many different deceptions can achieve those many different ends.

- *Deception is relatively cheap and of manageable risk.* Civilian clothing is less expensive than high-quality body armor; camouflaging an arms cache is less expensive than hardening the site against bombing; infiltrating an embassy by stealth or disguise is less expensive than gathering the equipment and personnel necessary for a frontal assault; and so on. Deception is in general much more affordable than other methods for accomplishing similar ends and, moreover, is not excessively risky relative to those other methods.

As a final illustration of the power of deception when used by terrorists, there is no more salient, more dramatic example than September 11th:

- United Flight 175, American Flight 11, American Flight 77: Hijackers attempt to deceive passengers into believing that the event is a "conventional" hijacking, likely to have a negotiated and peaceful resolution if passengers comply with hijackers' instructions. While there might have been individual acts of resistance by passengers, deception succeeds and <u>hijackers' plans are successful</u>.

- United Flight 93: Hijackers attempt the same ruse, but using outside communications, the passengers unmask the deception and struggle with the hijackers, bringing down aircraft. While the ultimate target was unclear, deception fails and the <u>hijackers' plan was thwarted</u>.

As a potent weapon in the hands of terrorists, deception is not going to go away; finding ways to effectively combat it is both a daunting challenge and a clear necessity.

PART TWO: DECEPTION & COUNTER-TERRORISM

As noted above, individuals and groups who commit acts of terror often use deception for a variety of ends: in offense, defense, and as a means of collecting intelligence. This is because terrorist groups—so often out-resourced, outgunned, outnumbered, and generally existing in the margins of society—find deception crucial in attacking state authority weaknesses and avoiding direct conflict with military forces. Less prominent in the annals of terrorism are deception techniques employed by *states* against terrorist groups. In this context, deceptive measures are best understood as the methods, resources, and techniques used by states to create disadvantageous *misperceptions* in terrorist groups. When used effectively by a state—at any level of counter-terrorism, from first-responders to national command authorities—deception can undermine a terrorist group's cohesion; hinder or altogether thwart its operations; render it vulnerable and ripe for attack; discredit the terrorists' own propaganda; and accomplish many other useful ends. It should be unsurprising, therefore, that many nations faced with a campaign of terror waged by a tenacious adversary have employed deception measures in support of their counter-terror efforts.

The array of deception measures used by states against their terrorist/insurgent adversaries is very long and includes every category of technique listed in Table 1 above. The nations that have practiced deception in CT includes the United Kingdom, Israel, France, Germany (and West Germany before it), the Philippines, Peru, India, and many others. States not only use the full range of military deception measures (e.g., camouflaged uniforms and vehicles), they also use a wide array of deceptions to promote covert/clandestine activities (less charitably, these have been called 'dirty tricks'). This latter category of deception activities has included establishing false identities and organizations for operatives; the deliberate spread of lies and distortions to the international press; lures and the appearance of vulnerability to draw opportunistic attack; forged letters and electronic communications to erode trust relationships. While there have been painful and costly failures when the deception has been compromised, it remains a prized weapon in the arsenal of states engaged in protracted CT campaigns.

Interestingly, the reasons why deception is so valued in CT include the four reasons noted above explaining its value in terrorism—net effectiveness, versatility, heterogeneity, and cost/risk—but also include the following two:

- *Deception can lower the profile of a state's CT activities.* Keeping an eye on a restive population from a position of infiltration plays far better in the international and domestic press than declaring martial law and patrolling the streets with armored vehicles. Moreover, a less imperialistic approach tends to lessen the hostility of the population, in turn lowering the radicalism and resentment which feeds insurgencies.
- *Deception is particularly good at poisoning relationships among terrorists and their support.* Operating in secrecy and dispersion, insurgents rely upon trust relationships: trust in their supporters, in their comrades, in their intelligence, and in their communications. Deception—by its very definition— reduces certainty, erodes trust, sows confusion, and otherwise attacks the bonds between individuals and groups. Given the organizational and logistical burdens which terrorists bear, this is a particularly vulnerable spot for them. Witness, for example, the corrosive effects on morale, trusts, and ultimately performance, of the *pentiti* law passed by Italy as a way of

gathering intelligence. By incentivizing defection, the first wave of benefits for the Italian government came in the form of the intelligence they sought, but a secondary, powerful effect was the disruption amongst the members of the Brigades, as well as between the Brigades and their active and passive supporters.

Clearly, while government use of deception is a delicate and dangerous undertaking, it has nevertheless proved to be a very effective instrument in counter-terrorism efforts among those countries that have used it.

Further Reading

Scott Gerwehr and Russell W. Glenn, *The Art of Darkness: Deception and Urban Operations*. Santa Monica: RAND, 2000.

Scott Gerwehr and Russell W. Glenn, *Unweaving the Web: Deception and Adaptation in Future Urban Operations*. Santa Monica: RAND, 2003.

Hy Rothstein and Barton Whaley, Eds., *The Art and Science of Military Deception*. Norwood: Artech House, 2013.

Definition of Terrorism

Brian K. Houghton

The topic of definitions often arises when discussing the phenomenon of terrorism, which can often lead to frustration as the two parties involved discover that what so plainly seems to be an act of terrorism to one is not considered so by the other. Intuitively we think that terrorism is an uncomplicated topic upon which everyone agrees, but this is far from the case. Could it not be as simple as what U.S. Supreme Court Justice Potter Stewart declared about the term obscenity years ago, "I know it when I see it"? While defining terrorism may not be as easy as Justice Stewart's method, the process is not impossible.

Why is this debate necessary and is it just a pointless academic issue? Yes, the debate is necessary, and no, it is more than just an academic issue. There are several reasons why agreeing upon a definition is vital. First, having an agreed upon definition of terrorism allows us to talk coherently about this important topic. How can we have a rational discussion if one group thinks that terrorism includes despots like Hitler and Stalin with their acts of genocide while others disagree and see terrorism as a sub-state phenomenon?

Second, as we try to analyze terrorism we need to categorize the attacks, targets, methods, and perpetrators so that we can quantify the incidents and make sense of what is occurring. Without a strict definition, a database of terrorism would become either quickly corrupted with potentially non-terrorist events or have large gaps as important incidents were overlooked. Long-existing terrorism databases, like the RAND Database of Worldwide Terrorism Incidents, have precise definitions in order to preserve the integrity of their data.

Third, in order to foster international cooperation, we need to agree upon what terrorism is so that we can focus our mutual efforts on striving to reduce the occurrence of terrorism, or mitigate its affects.

Again, if we have differing definitions of terrorism, what might seem to be a terrorist to one group might not to another. This leads to the proverbial line, "one man's terrorist is another man's freedom fighter," depending on how we define terrorism.

So, what makes an incident an act of terrorism and not some other phenomenon? An incident of terrorism first and foremost needs to incorporate an act of violence. This horrific violence demands attention from the public, government, and media—as the cliché goes for the news media, "if it bleeds, it leads." However terrorism may not necessarily be just an act of violence, but might also be merely the threat of violence, which also draws the attention sought after by the terrorist.

An act of terrorism inherently needs to be political; otherwise, the act of violence might be considered an accident, merely criminal in nature, or even performed for entertainment. Terrorism is a form of political violence, on the spectrum somewhere between riots on one side and genocide and war on the other. The violence itself becomes a voice for the terrorists in expressing themselves on the political forum, often against the government, a policy, a people, or even in support of a regime. This is what makes the vast majority of school shootings a criminal act, rather than a terrorist event, since the motivation of the shooters is not political in nature.

While fear is not always used implicitly in definitions of terrorism, it is a crucial element. Violence is not the intended goal of the terrorists; rather, they hope to harness the fear created from the violence in order to motivate a people, organization, or government to make a political change (or to prevent a change). If the act of violence was not shocking or fear-inspiring, then there would be no incentive for change, no interest generated, and thus be of no value to the terrorist.

One of the elements that generates increased interest is the victim of the violence. Terrorism deliberately targets the civilian population. Some authors will use the term "innocent" as part of their definition, but often it is difficult to determine the innocence of a victim. Those perpetrating the violence often state that, by supporting a cause or government, the victims have lost their innocence. This argument over innocence makes the term problematic in nature so a better alternative is to use the term civilian. An act of political violence that generates fear can easily be defined an act of war if the intended target is a foreign government or military. This is why some terrorism databases do not consider a violent act against a military unit as an act of terrorism, even when perpetrated by a known terrorist organization. However, in the modern age, civilians are not expected to face political violence, and therefore their involvement as the intended target of the violence contributes to the act being labeled terroristic.

The last key element in the definition of terrorism is based on the perpetrators, in that they are sub-national, meaning they are not official organs of the state. The fact that they are non-state actors does not mean that a terrorist group cannot accept sponsorship or perform acts on behalf of a government; rather, it means that they are not officially part of a government. Acts performed by government organizations that are similar in nature to an act of terrorism would still be considered political violence but should be categorized as an act of war or, if targeted against its own people, an act of genocide, state terror, or crimes against humanity. In this way, historic figures such as Hitler or Stalin would be accused of mass genocide among their own people using official organs of the state to do their bidding, but they are not in the same category as an Osama bin Laden who, as the world's most notorious terrorist killed, significantly less people than the other aforementioned figures.

There are other terms often mentioned in the definitions of terrorism—such as unlawful/criminal, clandestine, coercive, premeditated, psychological impact, organized, and even group-based—but these are often less used in definitions than the previously discussed key components.

The United States definition of terrorism (Title 22 of the U.S. Code, Section 2656f(d)) states that terrorism is "premeditated, politically motivated violence perpetrated against noncombatant targets by subnational groups or clandestine agents." This definition contains most of the key elements, but does not mention fear or coercion generated by the act and leaves the possibility that terrorism can be committed by a state through its "clandestine agents." The use of "noncombatant targets" allows the United States to declare acts against off-duty military personnel or peacekeepers as terrorism. Both the clandestine agents and noncombatant terms give the United States government more latitude in declaring an incident an act of terrorism.

The Federal Bureau of Investigation used a different definition. For years, it stated that terrorism was "the unlawful use of force or violence against persons or property to intimidate or coerce a government, the civilian population, or any segment thereof, in furtherance of political or social objectives." The first noticeable difference in this definition is the act's "unlawful use." This should come as no surprise from a federal law enforcement agency, but this definition also helped to justify the Bureau taking the lead on acts of terrorism if they are indeed criminal in nature. The FBI's definition also brings up the possibility that the objective or motivation of the terrorist might not just be political, but also social in nature. Additionally, this definition makes mention that a violent act against property can also constitute an act of terrorism, and not just an incident that is intended to harm people.

Academics have also contributed countless definitions including the short definition of Alex Schmid that terrorism is the "peacetime equivalents of war crimes" or the definition by Yonah Alexander that terrorism is "the use of violence against random civilian targets in order to intimidate or to create generalized pervasive fear for the purpose of achieving political goals."

The United Nations, which encourages international cooperation in counter terrorism efforts, unfortunately does not have a formal definition of terrorism. The UN has tried on multiple occasions to produce a commonly agreed upon definition, but has failed in each of its attempts. The underlying issue is that some member states do not believe that certain acts should be categorized as terrorism if the perpetrators of the violence live in territory occupied by a foreign government. In other words, these states believe that those fighting for freedom from foreign occupation may legitimately use tactics that others would consider to be acts of terrorism.

This brings us back to the cliché of one man's terrorist as another man's freedom fighter. Yet, what is the fundamental difference between a freedom fighter and a terrorist? Do heroes kill women and children? Or more precisely, do freedom fighters use premeditated acts of violence against civilian populations in order to create an environment of fear to coerce a government to make changes towards a political goal? If the answer is yes, then those "freedom fighters" are also terrorists. Yet this might lead us to demonize some of our cherished heroes. For Americans, the revolutionary Samuel Adams and the Sons of Liberty could easily be defined as terrorists as they attacked British tax collectors, although most Americans see them as freedom fighters. Ultimately, if it looks like a duck, waddles like a duck, and sounds like a duck, it is indeed a duck. Non-state actors who use violence against civilians for political objectives are terrorists. It is that simple.

Further Reading

Bruce Hoffman, *Inside Terrorism*. New York: Columbia University Press, 2006.

Ben Saul, *Defining Terrorism in International Law*. Oxford: Oxford University Press, 2006.

Alex Schmid, *The Routledge Handbook of Terrorism Research*. New York: Routledge; Reprint edition, 2013.

Drugs

Drugs and Terrorism—TNT Intelligence

Hal Kempfer

Our world is threatened today by a shadowy spider web of interconnected criminal and terrorist organizations which can be lumped under the term Transnational Networked Threats or TNTs. With this new threat comes the now evident need for new understanding of these networks and how to best defeat them—a need met by TNT Intelligence.

What makes TNT intelligence different? I'll introduce it by relating a brief story. In September 1997, I was presenting a very "out of the box" proposal to train both military and civilian intelligence analysts working in support of counterdrug law enforcement. I was putting them through a very advanced program of instruction combining traditional criminal intelligence methods with elements of military doctrine encompassed in the term "intelligence preparation of the battlespace" (or "IPB"), M&A (mergers and acquisition) due diligence, international finance and trade, fraud examination, countertrade, competitive or business intelligence, and international money laundering analysis. Shortly after a briefing in the Pentagon, I was pulled aside by an Army Colonel who described the challenges they were having with a transnational terrorist organization, and how they desperately needed the very same operational methods we had just proposed for countering the drug cartels. Little did I know then that the terrorist group they were talking about was the al Qaeda organization. Four years later to that month, a section down the hall would be destroyed by the threat we had discussed. Ironically, the failure of the Pentagon to institutionally embrace the change needed for fighting this new threat came back to hit them directly.

What is the nature of this new threat? Why does it require a mixture of business, criminal and military "intelligence' approaches to understand it? Dr. Robert Bunker describes a new class of "criminal soldiers" working in transnational-networked organizations, or what has been referred to elsewhere as Transnational Criminal Organizations or TCOs. TCO's almost fits, for there is no doubt that Al Qaeda is conducting criminal acts in violating the laws of many nations. However, they have a fundamentally political or religiously ideological agenda, and it is not clear that the intent of the organization is truly criminal. What is clear is that this is a manifest clandestine organization with goals and objectives that works outside the law and threatens the rest of the world. The same could be said of more profit oriented networked groups like the Columbian Drug Cartels and Russian Mafia, whose very "business" poses a threat to the rest of us. Hence, hence the term TNT, and the need to develop intelligence approaches that are tailored for countering this threat.

TNTs are the future. This is 4th Generation Warfare, not 3rd Generation Mechanized Maneuver Warfare nor Second Generation Industrial Attrition Warfare. Unlike our current "physical plant" of military forces with huge specialized equipment, logistics, doctrine and structure, TNTs leverage the fabric of the global economy finding maneuver room in the seams and operating in the shadows. Their modis operandi is more akin to an international business, or more like multiple joint ventures, than some Hollywood fantasy of a band of ruthless killers. TNTs are often banking, shipping, and moving around the globe just like their legitimate business peers. Using the differences in national laws, treaties, national or regional self-interests, and societal divergence, TNTs are able to operate widely in many countries simultaneously while still usually achieving a cohesively managed program with determined objectives or outcomes. Whether this is Colombian based TNTs establishing cocaine countertrade relationships with less-sophisticated Mexican smuggling organizations as part of a risk minimization policy or al Qaeda trying explode a dirty bomb (explosive radiological device) in Chicago, TNTs are the hidden enemy, around us yet apart. The criminal-soldiers of this enemy that wants to destroy our people, nation(s) and society sit next to us on planes or across from us in restaurants. The enemy that caters to our worst social weaknesses, such as substance abuse, expertly hides its money in investments that become part of the business capital that drives the global economy.

TNT's are very much alike in what they do, whether drug or terrorism focused, in that a large part of their "value-added" is the ability to smuggle substances and arms. They move huge amounts of money and are fully integrated into a number of legitimate enterprises worldwide. In 1997, a U.S. Senate report estimated that international criminal organizations may control somewhere between $3-10 trillion dollars in wealth worldwide, and there is every indication that it could be substantially more today. Historically, the malls of America were built using Mafia money laundered through Canada. Shortly after the September 11th attack by Al Qaeda against the Pentagon and New York World Trade Center, press reports began touting the need to track the money flows of this organization; the very same problem with the very same group that was voiced in the Pentagon four years before.

The challenge for law enforcement and the military is to recognize the commonalities of TNTs and then transform their own organizations, especially the intelligence components, to meeting this new kind of threat. In the 1980s and 1990s, both law enforcement and even more so the military were very glad to take federal funds earmarked towards fighting either drugs or terrorism. However, rather than transform to best meet the threat, it became a money laundering exercise for public largess. For example, Joint Task Force Six (JTF-6), the command charged by the Department of Defense to lead this ability to interface with law enforcement against the threat of the international drug cartels, has been completely unable to meet this transformation requirement. Instead of mutually developing intelligence collection, sharing, and analysis capabilities that can effectively track and target these TNTs, they siphoned money into dead-end programs like flying military helicopters around the National Forests looking for marijuana cultivation sites. This is a relatively minor domestic drug problem by all accounts, except for maybe that of the U.S. Forest Service, but underscores the philosophical problem we face. Just as Dr. Bunker cites the inability of the knights of the Middle Ages to adapt, and how eventually musket-clad criminal soldiers ended their dominant reign, so too our military today seems unable to grasp what must be done to meet these new criminal soldiers. Many leaders in the drug enforcement community are absolutely bewildered by this completely dysfunctional and ineffective use of military support but, to the military, this is very normative in that it reinforces the internal status quo and OPTEMPO (operational tempo or business) statistics that validates existing force structure.

By the same token, many of the major shortfalls or "intelligence failures" within law enforcement were clearly highlighted in a draft White House report on Counterdrug Intelligence Architecture sponsored in 1998 by the Office of National Drug Control Policy (ONDCP) under direction of its director, then retired General Barry McCaffery. The far-reaching assessments and recommendations that were all intelligence reformation oriented that would have radically changed the landscape of how law enforcement and the military act in concert to attack the drug cartels were fought to a standstill by such agencies as the Federal Bureau of Investigation, U.S. Customs Service, the Border Patrol and others. These are the same agencies now cited for being fatally flawed in their previous approaches to intelligence in the post 9-11 aftermath. Their pyrrhic victory was finalized when a vastly watered-down version of this report was put out in 1999, and then the inherent failures of not fixing what we knew was broken visited the nation two years later.

Further Reading

Ryan Clarke, *Crime-Terror Nexus in South Asia: States, Security and Non-State Actors.* New York: Routledge, 2011.

James J.F. Forest, *Intersections of Crime and Terror.* New York: Routledge, 2012.

Frank Shanty, *The Nexus: International Terrorism and Drug Trafficking from Afghanistan.* Santa Barbara: Praeger Security International, 2011.

Event Counterterrorism

A Case Study

Thomas Greco

Preventing a terrorist attack before it occurs is obviously preferable to dealing with the bloody aftermath of an attack. Preventing an attack requires the orchestration of a directed intelligence effort that supports preemptive operations, or sets the baseline for security structures that make an attack infeasible. Additionally, while the newspapers are clogged with stories about the latest bombings, we hear little about successful *preventions* of terrorist acts. While we all have heard about infamous operations like the 1975 Munich Olympics massacre or 9/11, few are familiar with a prime example of successful preventive counter terrorism, the 1999 Balkans Summit in Sarajevo.

Securing the Summit was a short notice mission to protect leaders of forty nations from a variety of potential threats. Holding the Summit in Sarajevo, the scene of brutal fighting only a few years before, made the event a significant security challenge. Summit leaders would announce far reaching economic policies and other initiatives. The objective of these initiatives was to bolster the fragile stability in a Balkan region that had been in turmoil for most of the decade. There were still factions who stood to harvest a profit from continued instability, and such fear-reaching measures would surely threaten their power.

There was still considerable internal tension among the three entities that composed Bosnia Herzegovina despite improvements in the security situation since the arrival of several thousand NATO, Russian, and other nations' soldiers since 1995. A well-timed and targeted terrorist attack would reap a publicity bonanza, and Bosnia's powerful criminal and terrorist organizations were well-placed to deliver such a blow. Yet international leaders' demonstration of the city's return to normalcy would have great symbolic importance for the international community.

Ensuring the international leaders' personal safety would be no easy task for any single national security service, so an international task force from over twenty nations' security and military services was created to provide security. With only two week's notice, the planning for this mission was rapid but detailed. The immediate actions were to evaluate the capabilities available to conduct the mission, identify key threats and their likelihood of occurrence, and evaluate significant items that would require further consideration. Cooperation by representatives of the many participating agencies would be the key to the ultimate success of the Summit's security effort.

The situation was not totally dire, as international security forces had a wealth of resources at their disposal. Bosnia had the advantage of still having the remnants of a fairly sophisticated and professional internal security apparatus. Add to this the availability of several thousand soldiers from eighteen nations under NATO leadership, including a special force of Italian Carbinieri, and there were significant capabilities on site as planning began. Additional assets were brought in on short notice. Yet the resources alone were not enough; employing them effectively required the use of capable liaison officers with compatible communications gear, provision of maps with standardized symbols and grid systems, and rehearsals of key events. A key part of security planning was threat analysis for, with the heads of forty nations in attendance, there was no shortage of individuals and groups with enough perceived grievances to be potential attackers.

Intelligence staffs faced a daunting intellectual challenge in trying to anticipate the most likely method of attack. There were literally dozens of forms of potential attack: snipers, bombs of all types, surface to air missiles and chemical attack; to name a few. The implications of every potential attacker and form of attack had to be analyzed. The intelligence staff analyzed the intent of the potential attackers and the forms of potential attack considering the limitations or advantages afforded by the city and its surrounding area. The terrain included roads with choke points that could be easily interdicted. One main street had earned the name "sniper alley" during the siege of Sarajevo. The high ground around the airport had also been the site of anti-aircraft activity during the war. Lines of sight from the hills that encircled the city dominated the area below. Through the analysis of the terrain and integration of potential threats, the planners developed several models of potential hostile events and used those models for security rehearsals.

Some rehearsals took place on a map enlarged to cover the floor of a room the size of a volleyball court. Other rehearsals took place on the actual sites where Summit events would occur. Incoming reports confirmed or denied indicators catalogued during the rehearsals during the Summit itself. The rehearsals were essential. The clear common understanding of both the security framework and potential threats that they provided was the key to the operation's success.

Coordinating plans and the forces available was accomplished via the designation of a flexible set of "concentric bands" around the meeting site, each band having its own level of restricted access. The meeting area where the heads of state would assemble was the innermost band; it therefore had the strictest access controls. The surrounding building was next. The structure and meeting room within were primarily the responsibility of the host nation and selected security services that controlled access and monitored activity. The airport, hotels, and the routes to the meeting site were the next series of bands. The Sarajevo police, Italian Carbinieri, military police from various nations and specially trained troops secured these areas. The rest of the city was secured by military patrols working in conjunction with local police. Military forces also patrolled key terrain in the suburbs. Military aircraft with reconnaissance and precision strike capabilities patrolled the sky above the city.

Coordinating the efforts throughout the area of operations encompassing these bands of security required the use of liaison personnel (with independent communications equipment) at numerous operations centers and key coordination points. Translators bridged the many language gaps. The specially annotated maps of the city were provided to key participants, giving all elements a common reference for the operational area.

All these measures boosted the confidence of the diverse security forces to work together. And work together they did—the Sarajevo operation is a model of international cooperation

The security effort successfully deterred or neutralized numerous threats. This success was accomplished without impinging on the conduct of the event. An overly militarized atmosphere would have contradicted the mission and spirit of the Summit's peace mission. The Summit, in turn, was a successful effort in the maintenance of peace, and establishment of prosperity in the Balkans.

Further Reading

Boaz Ganor, *The Counter-Terrorism Puzzle: A Guide for Decision Makers.* Piscataway: Transaction Publishers, 2005.

Brian A. Jackson, *How Do We Know What Information Sharing Is Really Worth? Exploring Methodologies to Measure the Value of Information Sharing and Fusion Efforts.* Santa Monica: RAND, 2014.

Graeme C. S. Steven and Rohan Gunaratna, *Counter-Terrorism: A Reference Handbook.* Santa Barbara: ABC-CLIO, 2004.

Explosive Ordnance Disposal

Ernest J. Lorelli

Since the events of September 11, 2001, the importance of having a highly trained and equipped professional Explosive Ordnance Disposal (EOD) capability has become an undisputed fact. EOD units, or bomb squads in non-military organizations, are teams of men and women who disarm explosive ordnance or explosive devices in order to protect the lives and property of the people they serve. The Department of Defense (DOD) and the Department of Justice (DOJ) are responsible for the training and control of EOD units. From 2001 to today, the wars in Iraq and Afghanistan have caused some of the lines of distinction between the two groups (military EOD and public safety bomb squads) to become blurred. While the bomb squad technician still doesn't commonly resolve incidents involving military explosive ordnance, military EOD operators have become quit adept at resolving Improvised Explosive Device (IED) incidents.

Within the DOD, EOD training is the responsibility of the United States Navy. In keeping with joint service requirements for like skills, the U.S. Naval EOD School is a joint service school attended by all DOD EOD personnel. Ironically, the *Naval* EOD School is located on Eglin Air Force Base near Fort Walton Beach, FL.

Within the military, EOD School is regarded as extremely challenging, requiring mental discipline, physical conditioning, and high academic standards in order to graduate. The war forced the EOD community to change how they selected personnel applying for the program then prepared those personnel for combat operations. The washout rate is necessarily high. Trainees undergo an intensive program designed to provide "apprentice level" technicians to the military services. Those who manage to make it through the basic EOD school training course face the daunting task of getting qualified at their home unit, attending advanced schools, learning combat skills, followed by long deployments. EOD units must work in a joint environment. For example, an Air Force EOD operator may spend a deployment working with U.S. Army personnel conducting counter-IED missions along main supply routes. Navy EOD operators are frequently assigned to special operations units. They may all come together under a combined command to conduct operations to clear an airfield or a city of unexploded ordnance and IEDs.

What kind of person is selected for—and completes—training for this kind of mission? EOD School students are all volunteers, and are introduced to the career field through individual service pre-schools and indoctrination programs. "Selection" is designed to weed out persons who prove to be undesirable or incapable of successfully completing the training. Once at EOD School, the pace of the training serves as another means of eliminating those who could pose a threat to their teammates or themselves during a mission. Students must successfully pass each block of training before being allowed to move on to the next.

Students begin training by learning basic skills that will apply throughout the course of the school. They learn to safely handle demolition explosives and use specialized tools needed for disarming or "rendering safe" explosive ordnance. From there, the student will move on into specific ordnance areas for basic training. In the Ground Ordnance Division, students learn explicit processes and skills they will need to render safe projectiles, landmines, and grenades. After successfully completing this block, students move on into the Air Ordnance Division.

In Air Ordnance, students study tactical aircraft from helicopter gunships to B52 bombers loaded with explosive ordnance. They must master the explosive hazards associated with not only the bombs and missiles but also the explosive hazards of the aircraft itself.

Following Air, students spend time learning about Improvised Explosive Devices (IEDs), which are homemade bombs built by criminals and terrorists for personal and political reasons. Minimal time is spent in this division of school because the primary responsibility of the military EOD units remains the more conventional ordnance items manufactured by nations for conducting war.

Following IEDs, students move into the Nuclear Ordnance Division where they learn various aspects of nuclear physics, weapons design and effects, and, of course, EOD emergency procedures to prevent nuclear weapons accidents. This concludes the surface weapons portion of the school. While other services are graduating at this point, Navy student must complete the Underwater Ordnance Division training.

Following EOD School, students return to their parent service bases where their training becomes focused on service responsibilities and ordnance. For example, an Air Force EOD technician will master the hundreds of air-delivered weapons the Air Force employs to conduct warfare while an Army EOD technician would focus more of their training time on projectiles and mines, and a Navy technician would become an expert in underwater mines and torpedoes. All DOD technicians maintain a working knowledge of all types of ordnance.

As a result of the wars in Iraq and Afghanistan, the EOD School also houses an advanced IED course where the EOD operators return to prepare them for counter IED missions anywhere in the world. Another outgrowth of the war has been sending military EOD operators to courses in post-blast investigation and evidence preservation in order that they can collect intelligence and evidence to lead to the capture and elimination of bomb makers.

Regardless of the branch of service, all DOD EOD personnel have a similar mission. That is, the location, identification, rendering safe (disarming), removal, and disposal of conventional high explosive ordnance, chemical ordnance, incendiary ordnance, nuclear ordnance, or improvised explosive devices which pose a threat to people, the services operations or missions, and property. You will find DOD EOD units world wide, at most military installations, conducting their mission safely and effectively, anytime and everywhere they are needed.

The Federal Bureau of Investigation (FBI) is tasked to train and provide certified EOD technicians for the nation's non-military bomb squads. There are approximately 450 certified bomb squads and approximately 2,500 certified bomb technicians serving in police departments and fire departments across the nation. Unlike their military counterparts, these bomb technicians have only minimal training in military ordnance but have extensive training in the identification and rendering safe of criminal and terrorist improvised explosive devices.

Like their military cousins, bomb squad members are all volunteers. The majority are police officers and fire fighters who become familiar with the bomb squad mission and request transfer to the squad. If a position is available, and the person qualifies, they are transferred to the squad and begin training to familiarize themselves with the job. They do not become certified EOD technicians until they complete training at the FBI's Hazardous Devices School (HDS).

HDS is located on the U.S. Army's Redstone Arsenal in Huntsville, AL. Students at HDS follow a similar training regiment as the military except they do not receive the extensive training in military ordnance. Instead, their six-week training course prepares them for dealing with IEDs. Extensive training is dedicated to the use of robotic devices to conduct remote procedures against devices, which may be very sophisticated or very simple in design and function. Students learn x-ray techniques and interpretation to conduct diagnostics of a suspected bomb. They learn basic demolition techniques and learn specialized tools for disarming explosive devices. Upon graduation, students return to their police or fire departments and begin responding to bomb scares and other hazardous situations where a possible explosive device may be encountered.

The majority of bomb squad technicians are full time fire fighters and police officers and part time bomb techs. They all must complete mandatory monthly and annual training requirements to maintain their certification and must also return to the HDS every three years for refresher training. The cities and counties that have "full time" bomb squads often task the squad with additional responsibilities such as arson investigation and, in some cases, SWAT roles as well. In either case, the bomb technician's job is demanding and requires dedication, patience, professionalism, and sometimes a bit of luck.

Both DOD EOD units and public safety bomb squads have adopted a common badge that identifies them as qualified EOD/bomb squad technicians and proud professionals. Winning the right to wear the "EOD Crab" is proud moment and something that follows them the rest of their life.

The wreath symbolizes the achievements and laurels earned in minimizing accident potentials through ingenuity and devotion to duty. It memorializes those EOD Technicians who gave - or will give - their lives while performing EOD duties.

The bomb, copied from the design of the World War II Bomb Disposal Badge, represents the historic and primary objective of the EOD attack - the unexploded bomb. The three fins represent the EOD focus on conventional, nuclear, and chemical/biological ordnance.

Lightning bolts symbolize the potential destructive power of the bomb and the courage and professionalism of EOD people in their endeavors to reduce hazards as well as to render explosive ordnance harmless.

The shield represents the basic EOD mission, to prevent a detonation and to protect life, limb, and property to the utmost.

The Nation's EOD units are made up of men and women dedicated to the protecting their fellow Americans from the threat posed by explosive ordnance and explosive materials, no matter where the threat is. They train constantly to keep their skills sharp and try to stay one step ahead of the potential threat. A mistake made on the job can cost them their lives as well as the lives of those around them. The knowledge of this spawned a professional motto, which EOD technicians everywhere can identify with. That motto is, *"Initial Success or Total Failure."* Regardless of service or department, the meaning is clear for the members of any Explosive Ordnance Disposal Team.

Further Reading

U.S. Army, *ATP 4-32 Explosive Ordnance Disposal (EOD) Operations.* Washington, DC: U.S. Government, October 2013.

Richard Esposito and Ted Gerstein, *Bomb Squad: A Year Inside The Nation's Most Exclusive Police Unit.* New York: Hyperion Books, 2007.

Alain Michaux, Ed., *Explosive Ordnance Disposal: Assessment and Roles of EOD Forces.* Hauppauge: Nova Science Publishers, 2013.

Fire

Phillip Fouts and Daniel P. Heenan

People do not normally think of fire as a tool used by terrorists. However, fire is one of mankind's oldest weapons. History has repeatedly shown the use of fire by one person against another, in some cases to cause harm or death, and in other cases to terrorize one's enemy. Why has fire been frequently utilized to invoke fear or cause damage? Because it can easily cause injury or death as well as destroy property with devastating callousness.

Throughout the 20th century in the United States, fire was continuously used as a weapon of terror. In the 1920s, the 18th Amendment to the United States Constitution went into effect prohibiting the sale and consumption of alcohol. As with many illegal enterprises, rival groups fought each other to gain control of the distribution of the product. Molotov cocktails were frequently used by these groups to terrorize rivals and to pressure customers to purchase alcohol from a particular group.

After the Civil War, the Ku Klux Klan ("KKK") was formed based on the philosophy of white supremacy. The tool of choice used by the KKK to terrorize its enemies was fire. In fact, one of the most notorious symbols of hate and terror is the burning cross. In some cases, the sight of a burning cross on a lawn or in front of a church would be enough to freeze an entire community from standing up to the KKK. Further, if the presence of a burning cross did not deter a person, then a Molotov cocktail through a bedroom window would ensure compliance through devastation of personal property or even death. As recently as the 1990s, the KKK has used fire to intimidate and terrorize. There are numerous recent cases where the KKK, or people affiliated with the group, used fire to destroy churches with black congregations. In 1995, members of the KKK conspired to burn down a predominantly black church in

South Carolina and were ordered to pay approximately $38 million in damages for their actions.

In 2003, the U.S. Supreme Court heard the case of *Virginia v. Black* that dealt with the constitutionality of a statute that prohibited cross burning. Justice O'Connor stated "while a burning cross does not inevitably convey a message of intimidation, often the cross burner intends the recipients of the message fear for their lives. And when a cross burning is used to intimidate, few if any messages are more powerful."

In the last twenty years, a new type of terrorist has emerged in the United States in the form of extremist animal and environmental rights groups. It appears that fire is also the weapon of choice for this new breed of terrorist. The largest and most active of these new extremist groups are the Animal Liberation Front ("ALF") and the Environmental Liberation Front ("ELF"). Both have increasingly used fire in their fight to destroy or disrupt businesses, educational institutions, and research facilities that are acting contrary to their beliefs.

The current philosophy of both ALF and ELF is to conduct direct and major actions against government, business, and industry that they believe are responsible for animal and environmental abuses. Major actions are defined by ALF "as actions where either animals were released or rescued, fires were set, significant property damage occurred, trees spiked, or crops were destroyed." Arson is a leading activity used by ALF to further its beliefs and political agenda, and has become one of the group's most popular means of terrorizing. Numerous arsons have occurred in the last decade that have been attributed directly to either ALF or ELF through law enforcement or by a direct acknowledgement of responsibility by either ALF or ELF. The ALF Press Office claims that ALF/ELF were responsible for 18 fires in 2000 and 20 fires in 2001. The damage estimates from just four of these fires was in excess of $10 million.

In the 1998 fire of a ski resort in Vail, Colorado, for which ELF claimed responsibility, there was property loss and damage totaling $12 million. In 2006, four people were indicted for the fire that destroyed this property. Three of the suspects pleaded guilty to the crimes and received substantial prison sentences. A fourth defendant killed himself in jail prior to trial. During the sentencing portion of the trial of one of the defendants, Judge Ann L. Aiken stated, "It was your intention to scare, frighten and intimidate people and government through very dangerous acts of arson." Further, Judge Aiken ruled that some of the crimes that were committed could be subject to a terrorism enhancement which can add additional time to a prison sentence, if the actions of the defendant were intended to retaliate against, coerce, or intimidate the government. Another serious and costly fire that was claimed by ELF was set at an apartment building under construction in San Diego, CA, in 2003. Causing $50 million in damage, ELF stated that the fire was targeting rampant urban development.

The guidelines under which ALF and ELF operate are explicit in their position on and definition of "violence". The guidelines state that "no animal, human or non-human, shall be injured or killed in the course of an action" and that "all necessary precautions are taken to avoid injuring life." To date, there have been no injuries to humans in actions in which either ALF or ELF have claimed responsibility. However, the trend towards multiple ignition devices deployed by these groups suggests an increasing possibility that one of these devices will function after the arrival of firefighters or other first responders and could result in injury or death.

The actions of ALF and ELF have resulted in increased security measures by institutions that are potential targets. The Oregon Health Sciences University School of Medicine, while having never been attacked by "eco-terrorists" (as these groups are sometimes known), has spent up to $250,000 in recent years to provide extra security for its labs due to ALF arson and vandalism at other facilities on the West Coast. In his testimony before Congress, Ron Arnold, vice president of the Center for the Defense of Free Enterprise stated, "there is no region in the United States where I have not received complaints from members about being victimized by eco-terrorists. It is a broad and pervasive crime that is seriously underreported because the victims are terrorized and fear reprisals, copycat crimes, or in the case of corporations, loss of customer confidence and resulting drops in share prices." Arson has been used as a form of terrorism to affect political and other types of changes that the arsonists seek. Companies like Home Depot have begun requiring redwood vendors to place labels on boards with independent laboratory stickers informing customers they are not buying lumber from old growth trees.

While the use of fire by ALF and ELF has not yet resulted in death, fire was readily apparent in the most recent and devastating terrorist attack. On September 11, 2001, the attacks on the World Trade Center Towers were not viewed simply as arson. However, the burning jet fuel from the two aircraft that hit the towers led to the collapse of the buildings. After the first terrorist attack against the World Trade Center Towers in 1993, the terrorists realized the towers had been built to withstand an attack by an explosive device such as the truck bomb that was used. In fact, the towers had been built to withstand a direct hit from a large commercial aircraft. The two aircraft that hit the towers on September 11th caused blunt trauma to the buildings, yet the towers did indeed remain standing. However, the resulting loss of fireproofing on the metal structure and the destruction of the sprinkler system caused the fire to rage out of control at increasingly high temperatures. Further, the burning jet fuel from the aircraft quickly spread through the towers igniting all other available combustibles in the buildings, such as furnishings, fixtures, and equipment. The resulting fires caused the steel structures to lose strength. Both buildings reached the point where the steel could no longer support the weight of the structure, resulting in collapse. Unfortunately, after the complete destruction of the World Trade Center Towers due to fire, there is little doubt that terrorist groups will continue to use fire as a tool to further their agendas.

Three more recent events illustrate the grave impact that fire can have on communities and, specifically, the strain that can stretch resources to a breaking point. In 2003, there were multiple wildfires in Greece that killed 61 people and threatened to damage ancient ruins. The fires in Greece were so devastating that a top prosecutor ordered an investigation into whether the fires could be categorized as terrorism. In 2007, there were multiple wildfires in Southern California that created a burden on the law enforcement and firefighting communities. According to the California Environmental Protection Agency, these fires killed 7 people, injured 113, burned approximately 516,468 acres, damaged 436 structures, destroyed 2,772 structures and displaced 321,000 people.

While it was not determined that all of the fires in Southern California were arson, some were intentionally set. Lastly, during a four day period from the end of 2011 through early 2012, a suspect set over 50 fires in the Los Angeles Metropolitan area. The suspect primarily set fire to vehicles that were parked inside garages or underneath occupied apartment buildings. Fortunately, there were no injuries associated with this series of fires, but the residents of the affected communities were so fearful that they resorted to sleeping in shifts in an effort to not become a victim of the fires. The suspect did not use a sophisticated method to initiate the fires, but was so upset with the U.S. government that he was determined to strike fear in the heart of the victims. These examples further illustrate the high cost of the fires to communities.

Unlike other tools used by terrorists, specifically explosives, fire requires little knowledge to deliver a devastating impact on a victim. With its accessibility, affordability, and ease of use, fire will continue to be used as a criminal tool to devastating effect.

Further Reading

Robert Baird, "Profiles in pyroterrorism Convergence of crime, terrorism and wildfire unleash as a weapon on population." *The Counter Terrorist*, 2 March 2011, http://www.homeland1.com/disaster-preparedness/articles/985110-Profiles-in-pyroterrorism/.

Steven M. Chermak et al, "An Overview of Bombing and Arson Attacks by Environmental and Animal Rights Extremists in the United States, 1995-2010." Final Report to the Resilient Systems Division, Science and Technology Directorate, U.S. Department of Homeland Security. Washington, DC: May 2013, http://www.start.umd.edu/sites/default/files/files/publications/START_BombingAndArsonAttacksByEnvironmentalAndAnimalRightsExtremists_May2013.pdf

Nick Deshpande, "Pyro-Terrorism: Recent Cases and the Potential for Proliferation." *Studies in Conflict & Terrorism*, Vol. 32, No. 1, 2009: 36-44.

Force Protection

John P. Sullivan

Public safety and military personnel form the core of response to the consequences of terrorism. Yet these responders are vulnerable—as history has repeatedly shown—to acts of terrorism themselves. Recent incidents illustrate this facet of terrorist targeting. In late June 1996, Khobar Towers was the site of one such attack. At 2130 GMT, 10:30 p.m. local time, 26 June 1996 a suspicious fuel tanker pulled up to the perimeter of a military housing complex at King Abdul Aziz Air Base near Dhahran, Saudi Arabia. Seconds later, approximately 5,000 pounds of explosives detonated, ripping the face of the tower, killing 19 U.S. military personnel and injuring up to 264 others. This single bombing was the deadliest attack against Americans in the Middle East since the 1983 attack on the Marine Corps barracks in Beirut that killed 241 Americans. Naval forces were the target of the 12 October 2000 attack on the U.S.S. Cole which killed 17 U.S. sailors while the ship was refueling in Yemen's Aden harbor. Civilian public safety responders are also at risk. A suburban Atlanta abortion clinic was the site of a twin bombing in 1997. In that attack, a building housing an abortion clinic sustained severe damage from an explosion at 9:00 a.m. When local emergency responders—police fire and EMS—were on scene, a second bomb secreted in a nearby trash container exploded. The secondary blast injured 6 persons, including 3 ATF agents. The dynamics of that blast indicate that emergency responders were the intended focus of the secondary device.

Force protection—classically a military concept for protecting service members by deterring, disrupting and mitigating terrorist attacks at installations—applies equally to in-transit military forces and civilian emergency responders. Protecting responders—such as fire service decon personnel, medical providers and hazmat squads—is an important law enforcement responsibility. After the initial event, responders need to be protected from secondary attack. Force protection is an essential element of security intended to protect military service members, civilian emergency responders, their families, facilities, and equipment in all situations and locations from terrorist attack. This can be accomplished through the planned and integrated application of combating terrorism, anti-terrorism, physical security, and other means supported by intelligence, counterintelligence, operational practices, and security awareness.

Force protection is a responsibility shared by all elements and members of military and emergency response organizations. Within this general responsibility, commanders of all services bear special responsibility for protecting their subordinates so they can safely discharge both their day-to-day missions and missions directly related to terrorism response. In the civil sector, law enforcement personnel shoulder many of the incident-specific force protection tasks. But like the military, all responders and services share aspects of force protection. Threat and vulnerability assessments and organizing, training, and equipping personnel to safely conduct operations and recognize the threat of attacks (both before they occur and secondary attacks during response) are necessary elements of a comprehensive response to contemporary terrorism.

Further Reading

Defense Science Board Task Force, *Force Protection in Urban and Unconventional Environments*. Washington, DC: Defense Science Board, March 2006.

Joint Chiefs of Staff, *Joint Publication (JP) 3-10: Joint Security Operations in Theater*. Washington, DC: United States Department of Defense, 3 February 2010.

Friedrich Steinhäusler and Frances Edwards, Eds., *NATO and Terrorism: Catastrophic Terrorism and First Responders—Threats and Mitigation*. Dordrecht: Springer, 2005.

Future Conflict

Gray Area Phenomena:
Window on violence and future conflict

G.I. Wilson

In the wake of examining the changing nature of war in the 1980s and 1990s, the term "gray area phenomenon" emerged in an effort to better characterize what terrorism maven Bruce Hoffman describes "as the increasingly fluid and variable nature of sub-national conflict in the post-Cold War era." Martin van Creveld in *The Transformation of War* and John Robb in *Brave New War* call attention to how non-state actors can challenge the stability of sovereign nation states and possibly win.

Gray area phenomena (GAP) covers threats to the stability of sovereign nation states by non-state actors and non-governmental organizations. GAP provides a window on future violence, conflict, and challenges plaguing nation states. These same nation states no longer have a tightfisted monopoly on violence and waging war.

Gray area phenomena describes the overlap of crime, terrorism, and war, offering a prescient glance into future tactics, techniques, and procedures (TTPs) being embraced by non-state-actors. Many of these GAP TTPs represent creative use of the old ways of war adapted for the present and wedded to new technology. The gray area phenomenon addresses non-state violence in its regional and global impact.

These non-state and/or failed-state actors are literally citizen combatants who fill the vacuum left by the demise of a legitimate sovereign governments. GAP-like terrorism has no universally accepted definition and is considered old terminology yet has utility in developing a landscape of emerging threats.

For certain, many aspects of the gray area phenomena are not new. What is of concern is how violence and conflict are now increasingly intertwined with complex problems that include famine, disease, drug trafficking, and transnational crime. Gray area phenomenon can be thought of as conflict where one's adversary refuses to stand up and fight fair from a Western and conventional military perspective.

GAP capitalizes upon irregular adversaries and criminal enterprises that exist and operate outside the boundaries of what conventional military and law enforcement forces are accustomed to. For example, in GAP everything is targetable, ranging from non-combatants to hospitals, schools, and playgrounds. GAP operatives work outside the nation-state framework, transcending national boundaries and the law of war.

The lawless attacks on the Pentagon and World Trade Center are poignant examples of how this gray area phenomena can manifest itself. These attacks quickly dispelled the long held contention that gray area phenomenon is just "terrorism" or something like it that only happens in other countries.

GAP, in fact, encompasses indiscriminate violence and radicalization. Agendas no longer focus on the clash of opposing conventional forces. The focus is on leveraging conventional vulnerabilities. Non-state actors find low tech but sophisticated ways to take advantage of conventional forces addicted to high technology with a low tolerance for friendly casualties.

Agendas in the gray area are more political and ideological in nature coupled with indiscriminate violence and brutality. What becomes more important than finding and engaging regular conventional combatants is the development of ideological bases of popular support composed of combatant-civilians indistinguishable from the general population. This allows the self-radicalized, loners, insiders, and "soldier criminals" to plan and execute attacks against a more technologically equipped force. The idea of using of low tech to defeat high tech is not unimaginable.

In a GAP milieu, being highly successful in gathering intelligence against a foe may in fact create a backlash in the society that is being protected. The society's citizens are subjected to nation-state spying and surveillance. This culminates in the loss of privacy and individual rights. Thus, this wittingly and/or unwittingly enables our foes to not only accomplish their political-ideological goals but, in part, turn the nation-state citizenship against their own government.

The gray area phenomenon is a soup of criminality, war, and terrorism, spawning a new class of combatants. This new class of combatants has been described by Dr. Robert Bunker as "criminal soldiers," working in transnational-networked organizations, also referred to elsewhere as Transnational Criminal Organizations or TCOs. There is no doubt that groups like al-Qaeda (AQ), AQ affiliates, and AQ knockoffs, are participating in criminal endeavors violating the laws of many nation states. However, they have a fundamentally political, religious, and ideological agenda. It is clear that the intent of these organizations is not purely criminal but ideological. They will exploit criminal opportunities like black marketing of oil and blood antiquities, smuggling, and human and drug trafficking, creating revenues to support their broader regional activities.

The changing nature of war is now in our homes as brutal acts of terrorism stream across our televisions, iPads, computers, social media, and cell phones. The September 11th attack on U.S. soil suggests that there may be no safe place to hide in the world, especially if the attackers are true believers willing to die for their ideological cause. By declaring war on the al-Qaeda network of terror—a non-state phenomenon, America and the nation-state system has, for all intents and purposes, formally recognized we are in an era of GAP marked by fourth generation and hybrid warfare.

What is clear is that the GAP threat is hydra-like and capable of challenging nation states. The same could be said of networked groups like the Mexican drug cartels and outlaw motorcycle gangs (OMG), whose very "business" poses a threat. GAP actors operate in the blurred shadows, seams, and margins of a nation state's infrastructure, legal system, borders, and culture. The authors of the fourth generation warfare thesis (Lind et al) were among some of the first to address aspects of gray area phenomenon in 1989:

> The distinction between war and peace will be blurred
> to the vanishing point. It will be nonlinear, possibly to
> the point of having no definable battlefields or fronts.

The distinction between 'civilian' and 'military' may disappear.

With gray area phenomena, we can expect more high impact violence and imagery. Every aspect of the nation state is targetable not just the military. Non-state and failed-state actors will leverage terrorism and fear. Terrorism and fear have old historical roots in the history of conflict. Gray area phenomena continues to be a window on tomorrow's violence and future conflict.

Further Reading

Robert J. Bunker, Ed., *Non-State Threats and Future Wars*. London: Frank Cass, 2003.

Frans Osinga, *Science, Strategy and War*. London: Routledge, 2007.

Terry Terriff, Aaron Karp, and Regina Karp, Eds: *Global Insurgency and the Future of Armed Conflict*. London: Routledge, 2008.

Global Insurgency

David J. Kilcullen

This essay presents an overview of the "global insurgency". For those unfamiliar with this term, it is worth explaining the concept, which originated after the terrorist attacks of 11th September 2001 as a way to conceptualize Al Qaeda and as a means of distinguishing these events from traditional international terrorism.

What is Global Insurgency?

International terrorism, as conceptualized in the 1970s, was armed propaganda—an attempt to gain attention for a cause, or leverage in negotiations with a government, via relatively infrequent but high profile acts of violence. Terrorist groups tended to be small and organized in a cell structure. They had little direct contact with the population—preferring to communicate through the publicity generated by their attacks. Their center of gravity (the characteristic from which they drew their strength and freedom of action) was the ability to maintain clandestine networks that passed information, weapons, money, and equipment among cells. Thus, the center of gravity of traditional terrorists was the network itself—and hence counterterrorism (CT) strategy made that network the focus of its efforts, seeking to find, fix and destroy key nodes.

Because terrorism was the dominant paradigm for international non-state political violence at the turn of the century, the 9/11 attacks were initially characterized as terrorism. To be sure, aspects of the attacks fit the paradigm: they were high profile acts of violence, carried out by a clandestine network intent on generating maximum publicity. But analysts noted key differences. Unlike classical terrorism, the 9/11 attacks' goal was not to change government policy or highlight a cause:

these were acts of war designed to cripple the financial, political, and military power of the United States, the "far enemy" in Al Qaeda's formulation, in order to undermine U.S. support for the "near enemy"—authoritarian, apostate regimes in the Muslim world, the overthrow of which (by insurgency) was the primary AQ goal.

Moreover, AQ and its associated movements were large organizations—with tens of thousands of fighters and dozens of installations—and their strategy was mass mobilization of the world's Islamic population to overthrow the existing order. Rather than a small number of high-profile attacks, they conducted a large number of actions, big and small, to undermine the states they sought to overthrow. Thus, their actions fit better into an insurgency paradigm, albeit one of unprecedented scope, which sought to overthrow and replace the entire Western-dominated global order—a *global* insurgency.

Insurgents, unlike classical terrorists, field large organizations that may include underground resistance cells, auxiliary networks, local guerrillas, and/or a main force. There are many variations of insurgent strategy, from Mao's "people's war" through Che Guevara's "focoism"—but all seek to mobilize a mass base. Therefore, an insurgency's center of gravity is its ability to control, manipulate, and mobilize a population. Insurgents operate among the people, communicating primarily through local direct engagement rather than through the media.

These are caricatures, of course—real-world groups draw from both terrorist and insurgent repertoires, evolve over time, and differ from place to place. Yet the insurgent paradigm seemed to fit AQ better. Analysts argued that AQ sought to aggregate and mobilize local insurgencies within a global movement, and that AQ Central (centered on Osama Bin Laden and Ayman al Zawahiri in Pakistan since 2002) was an ideological, operational and propaganda hub rather than a military headquarters. Some argued that classical counterinsurgency—which focuses on strengthening governments and separating insurgents from the population, blocking their attempt to mobilize the people—was inappropriate above the national level. Instead, they argued for a "disaggregation" strategy, targeting AQ Central while cutting its links to local movements, which could then be countered with law enforcement and counterinsurgency techniques at the national level.

These ideas are now a decade old; how has AQ's global insurgency fared over that time, and what are the current trends?

Eclipse of Core Al Qaeda

The first key trend is the eclipse of AQ Central. The killing of Osama bin Laden in 2011, along with the Arab Spring (which seemed— initially—to suggest that unarmed protest could overthrow the "near enemy", something AQ had always insisted could only occur through armed struggle under its leadership), plunged the core AQ group into turbulence from which it emerged weakened, but still capable. AQ Central continues to exist, with Ayman al Zawahiri still in charge, but his authority is increasingly questioned outside the core group. AQ's role as mother-ship of the global insurgency is being eclipsed by ISIS, the Islamic State of Iraq and Syria, now known as the Islamic State. AQ's failure to mediate between ISIS and Jabhat an Nusrah (JN), its designated ally in Syria, hurt its credibility in 2012-2013.

Overall, AQ Central is suppressed, but not beaten: drone strikes, CT operations, and intelligence efforts have damaged the group but it's still a force-in-being. Events in Afghanistan in 2014-15 will determine the fate of AQ Central: the group could recover dramatically if there's a security or political collapse after international forces withdraw in December 2014. Likewise, the Pakistani and Afghan Taliban remain strong, and relatively close to AQ, and a collapse in 2015 could bring gains for the Afghan Taliban as with ISIS in 2014.

Rise of ISIS/Islamic State

This rise of ISIS is the second major trend. ISIS (now IS) is stronger militarily, and ideologically more extreme, than AQ and even more extreme than its own predecessor, Al Qaeda in Iraq (AQI). It's now the richest terrorist group in the world, with its capture of U.S. military equipment and Iraqi government treasuries giving it access to hundreds of billions of dollars, armored vehicles, heavy weapons, tanks, vast amounts of small arms and ammunition, along with extensive territory and resources.

The Islamic State is only one of 14 groups fighting to expel the Maliki regime from Western Iraq, but it's growing, already fielding more than 10,000 fighters—the size of the whole Afghan Taliban—making it a serious threat. That said, once the dust settles, IS fighters may find that they were actually the shock troops of somebody else's revolution. Baathist former regime elements under Ibrahim Izzat al Duri, Naqshbandi Sufi militias, Anbari tribes from the Dulaim confederation, and other Sunni nationalist and Baathist elements have taken significant roles in the offensive, as shown by the fact that three former Baathist generals were appointed to govern captured cities. Some Baathist leaders and tribal elders have claimed they will "clean house" against IS once they have control of key areas in Iraq; this claim is doubtful at best, since the military and political strength of IS is growing all the time.

How did this come about? There are two ways to think about it: first, we might consider the current offensive a successor conflict to the U.S. war in Iraq from 2003-2011, or secondly, we might consider it a geographical extension of the civil war in Syria since 2011. Both are valid. As a sequel to the Iraq War, the key issue is that Sunni communities, which U.S. forces won over in 2007 during the Surge (and the associated Awakening), were betrayed by the Government of Iraq (GOI) after the rapid and complete departure of the United States in 2011; these tribes and communities are now allied with IS against GOI. Simultaneously, the AQI organization U.S. forces decimated in 2007-9 displaced to Yemen and Syria, and U.S. failure to intervene in the Syrian Civil War allowed AQI to recover, gain territory and equipment, rebuild its credibility, and ultimately break out into Iraq, where Sunni grievances allowed it to find support.

ISIS has renamed itself Islamic State (IS), declared a Global Caliphate under its leader Abu Bakr al-Baghdadi (A *nom de guerre*—his real name is Ibrahim Awwad Ibrahim Ali al-Badri al-Samarrai), and quickly gained support from some elements of the broader global insurgency (including groups in Africa). But this generated pushback from AQ central, Islamic scholars, and jihadist groups. Declaration of the Caliphate brought strong condemnation from JN in Syria, and from the Islamic Front, which had been fighting ISIS in Aleppo. It's too early to tell if this is a case of extremist leaders overplaying their hand, or whether IS's success will rally other groups to support it.

Tactically, IS operates in the open, using pseudo-conventional light cavalry "swarming" tactics, with technicals (civilian all-wheel drive vehicles mounting heavy weapons and carrying a squad of fighters who dismount to fight), and increasingly employing captured tanks, Humvees, and anti-air weapons. This "war of movement" has been highly successful against a demoralized Iraqi Army, but it makes the group more vulnerable to air power or determined ground resistance than before; this methodology is the biggest difference between IS and AQI (which operated more covertly and used guerrilla methods). Operationally, some analysts believe IS is attempting to repeat the "Baghdad Belts" strategy advanced by AQI leader Abu Musab al Zarqawi, killed in 2006. But it's highly unlikely that the group can seize Baghdad or push south into majority-Shia areas of Iraq: indeed, IS is probably at its high-water mark in terms of territorial control, though it can inflict severe violence across a wider area. Administratively, IS control over Raqqa district in Syria has been tight and surprisingly effective. The group currently runs schools, hospitals, courts, taxation, road building, and infrastructure repair programs.

AQ will continue as a threat: there's no current prospect of IS *replacing* AQ. Both will continue to exist, and their rivalry for control over the global insurgency poses the risk of competition between them to damage the West and local populations and governments. That said, the combination of extreme ideology, excellent combat capability, and (newly developed) administrative and social capacity makes IS the most dangerous group in the world today.

Failure of the Arab Spring

The third trend is the failure of the Arab Spring. Instability in Libya, authoritarianism in Egypt, the Syrian Civil War, and conflict in Yemen and across North Africa have reinforced AQ's claim—at first seemingly contradicted by the success of "people power" in Tunisia, Egypt, and

Libya—that armed struggle (under AQ's leadership) was the only viable strategy.

Egypt came closest to disproving AQ's argument, with the overthrow of Hosni Mubarak by a largely unarmed, democratic movement. But this early promise dissipated, as the rush to elections favored long-established political groupings—the Muslim Brotherhood and the authoritarian parties—and sidelined the emerging secular democratic movement. The elections brought Mohammed Morsi and the Muslim Brotherhood to power, and began a drift toward sectarianism and authoritarianism, with Morsi cracking down on democracy and secular groups, and thereby alienating many Egyptians. His overthrow by the military in July 2013 prompted an even more severe crackdown on dissent. The military regime's suppression of the Brotherhood, and its general authoritarianism, is fueling a new insurgency in the Sinai and the Nile Delta, as well as an urban subversive underground—with destabilizing effects on the broader region.

In Libya, NATO intervention helped a broad-based armed uprising to overthrow Muammar Gaddafi, but the Provisional Government that succeeded Gaddafi proved unable to unify or govern the country, and necessary international support was not forthcoming. As of mid-2014, intensifying violence between Zintani and Misuratan militias at Tripoli Airport, and between jihadist groups and ex-military militias in Benghazi, underlines the functional collapse of the Libyan state. Oil production (the key to Libya's economy) has dropped off, and international companies, Western diplomats, and aid agencies are evacuating.

For its part, the Syrian War has generated ten to twelve times the number of foreign fighters as the Iraq War, and since Syria has a land border with NATO, movement for these fighters into Western countries is much easier. U.S., European, African, and Australian intelligence services all assess foreign fighters emanating from Syria as the most critical current terrorism threat. The conflict has not only produced more than a million refugees and over 100,000 casualties, it has become the proving-ground for AQI, defeated and discredited in Iraq, to achieve its spectacular recovery and to transform into the Islamic State.

In North Africa, the fall of Gaddafi released a flood of weapons and fighters into the Sahel and the Maghreb (Muslim northwest Africa). This contributed to the capture of northern Mali by Ansar el Dine and Al Qaeda in the Islamic Maghreb (AQIM), prompting the fall of Mali's government to a military coup in 2012, and a French-led intervention in 2013. AQIM has been weakened by this intervention, and expelled from parts of the region, but is now regenerating: Mauritanian leaders are replacing the original leadership, and targeting Algeria, Morocco, Tunisia, Mauritania and Mali. Algerian Mokhtar Belmokhtar, former head of AQIM, now based in Libya, has formed a new group (Al Murabitoun) that is rivalling AQ's preferred regional grouping (further evidence of franchise groups moving out from under the umbrella of AQ central as it has been eclipsed).

Meanwhile in Yemen, despite regime change in 2011, ongoing violence in the country's south—and the presence of a strong AQ affiliate, Al Qaeda in the Arabian Peninsula (AQAP)—gives little hope for future stability, while further afield, in Nigeria, AQ ally Boko Haram is literally running rings around Nigerian forces, using its kidnapping of more than 250 schoolgirls from Chibok to distract from its other operations, conducting urban attacks into Abuja and Lagos, and spreading into Cameroon. It's highly unlikely that the situation in Nigeria will improve in the medium term, and it will probably worsen in the short term.

In short, the early promise of the Arab Spring has not only failed, but the combination of state collapse, regional insurgency, and civil war that has followed in its wake is destabilizing an entire region, and creating opportunities for AQ franchise groups—formerly under control of the core group—to strike out on their own.

Conclusion: Mixed Results, At Best

These trends suggest mixed results, at best, for the "disaggregation" strategy that the author (among others) recommended a decade ago to deal with the global insurgency. Core Al Qaeda, the primary focus of western efforts for the last 14 years, is down but not out. As its influence has declined, newer, stronger, more radical groups are emerging. These groups have learned lessons from AQ's failures since 2001, and are poised to exploit opportunities created by the failure of the Arab Spring: they include the Islamic State, JN in Syria, AQIM, AQAP and others. AQ's franchise groups (the local elements of the global insurgency, which the disaggregation strategy sought to separate from AQ Central) are divided in their view of the new "Caliphate"—but we can expect them to rally to whatever group shows greater battlefield success, and at present this seems to be the Islamic State.

Perhaps the most spectacular development of the past decade has been the dramatic recovery and break-out of AQI, which was decimated, defeated, and discredited in Iraq in 2007-2009, but has bounced back, captured huge swathes of Iraq and Syria, reinvented itself as the Islamic State, and declared the Caliphate. The painful lesson is that getting into conflicts (such as Iraq) is far easier than getting out: precipitate withdrawal from Iraq, and the loss of leverage experienced by the United States as it departed, allowed a Shia sectarian Iraqi government to renege on its commitments, alienate Sunni and Kurdish populations, betray tribal leaders, and create the conditions for the re-emergence of IS. Likewise, partial international intervention in Libya, and total failure to intervene in support of a broad-based secular democratic uprising in Syria, contributed to the failure of the Arab Spring and the reinvigoration of IS.

Against this background, suppressing core Al Qaeda looks like a partial and temporary success only, especially if the international community makes the same mistake in Afghanistan—rapid and complete withdrawal before political consolidation—that it made in Iraq. AQ Central is currently eclipsed by IS, but impending withdrawal from Afghanistan could create exactly the same conditions to allow this group to revive, as U.S. withdrawal from Iraq did for IS in Iraq and Syria.

Finally, one of the enduring lessons of guerrilla war is that insurgencies can last generations, and counterinsurgency—to be effective—must be sustainable over equally long stretches of time. The global insurgency is very much alive: much as Western political leaders, public opinion, or military commanders might wish for the conflict to be over, wishing does not make it so. The challenge for the future is to find ways to counter the global insurgency that are cheap enough, effective enough, and non-intrusive enough to be sustainable for the long haul.

Further Reading

Robert J. Bunker, Ed., *Networks, Terrorism and Global Insurgency.* New York: Routledge, 2005.

David J. Kilcullen, "Countering Global Insurgency." *The Journal of Strategic Studies*, Vol. 28, No. 4, August, 2005: 597-617.

Richard H. Schultz, "Global Insurgency Strategy and the Salafi Jihad Movement." INSS Occasional Paper 66, Colorado Springs: USAF Institute for National Security Studies, USAF Academy, April 2008.

Globalization

Globalization and Anti-Globalization: The Roots of Post-Modern Terrorism

Ralph Peters

The anti-globalization protesters intent upon overturning trash barrels wherever heads of state attempt to meet offer a perfect example of reactionary conservatism faced with transcendent change. Imagining themselves as progressive leftists altering the world for the better, they would rather offer the world's poor a miserable stasis than opportunities disturbing to their own prejudices. Fundamentalists without a god, the protesters mirror religious fundamentalists in their demand for a return to a lost golden age that, in fact, never existed.

Incompetent to master the present, the foes of globalization flee into fantasies of a better yesterday. While some anti-globalization protesters do make valid points about environmental degradation, they are shamefully content with the human degradation inflicted by traditional cultures around the world. In their view, the West is always to blame, and the rest are always innocent. Born to freedom, the protesters imagine virtues for oppressors, bigots and tyrants. Psychologically speaking, one may paraphrase Tip O'Neill's comment that "all politics are local" to note that "all protests are personal." As with terrorists, it is rare to meet a happy human being committed to a life of protest. And, as with terrorists, their real discontents are not with external matters, but with their own interior devils.

The real howler about the anti-globalization movement, which substitutes passion for clarity, is that it focuses so intensely on an outmoded interpretation of tactical economics while denying globalization's evident strategic benefits. Indeed, despite undeniable economic dislocations—usually temporary—the overwhelming evidence is that globalization improves the economic situation of the majority wherever it is not stymied by local traditions of repression and corruption (and corruption in the developing world is what those brick-hurling kids *should* be protesting).

Yet, economic issues are little more than the surface effects of globalization. The deep impact comes from globalization's threat to traditional cultures that oppress women, restrict the flow of information, preach religious intolerance, practice social apartheid, and resist developing their human capital. Globalization equals liberation. While the process is sloppy and uneven, globalization is the greatest force for freedom and human rights in our new century. It is a travesty that, however thoughtlessly, anti-globalization protesters at this summit or that one are fighting for the preservation of social orders based upon intolerance, injustice, and gender oppression.

But the real stimulus underlying anti-globalization efforts is fear: Fear of change, fear of freedom, fear of equality, fear of social competition, fear of opportunities that challenge the "old ways," and fear of progress in any form that erodes the privileges of the existing elite. Utterly contrary to the accepted myths of those protesters, women and the poor are the victims of tradition, not of globalization.

Perhaps the point is best driven home by identifying the hardest of the hardcore anti-globalization protesters. They are not the vandals in the streets, and not even the incendiaries who torch new housing developments or trash research labs. The sincerest anti-globalization protesters are terrorists of the sort who crashed planes into the World Trade Center Towers and the Pentagon.

Doubtless, many in the anti-globalization movement would reject this suggestion out of hand, imaging some "fascist plot" to taint them by association. But they *are* tainted by association, at least ideologically. The extreme religious fundamentalists who turn to terror merely use more direct means and alternative language to express their rage at globalization.

Beyond the terrorists' slovenly rhetoric about purifying their sacred homelands of infidels or frustrating the "satanic" designs of the United States and Israel, what is it that really drives these men to spend their lives to kill the innocent by the thousands?

What drives them is fear, not virtue. Insisting far too vehemently upon their personal certainty of righteousness, their actions are attempts to master their own horrifying doubts. The old ways no longer work, their social orders, applied beliefs, and cherished privileges are no longer functional in a globalized world. No society that oppresses its women, while denying even males without good family connections any chance of self-betterment, can hope to compete with Western societies that have become marvels of human efficiency, ever more open to the contributions of the talented, no matter their birth, beliefs, or gender. Indeed, more than anything else, globalization is about the triumph of talent over tradition. And those who have a stake in the way things are and always have been will fight against it passionately.

My personal conviction is that the most threatening aspect of globalization to traditional societies—especially in the Muslim states of the Middle East and South Asia—is the emancipation of women. The transition of the female from the male's property to his partner is the most profound sociological development in all of recorded history. And it is a phenomenon as recent as it is dynamic—a true "shatterer of worlds." Much of the Islamic world, especially, suffers from a terror of female sexuality that would astonish even the ghost of Sigmund Freud, and the status of women is the one truly irreconcilable difference between the West and Islam. The terrorists who attacked the United States on September 11th, 2001, were afraid of the girls.

Of course, men cling to what they know, especially in times of tumult and change. Although a trip back through time might astonish us with the level of "globalization" that prevailed in the 1st century Rome world as well as far beyond the empire's borders, or in 9th century Cordoba, or along the coast of 16th century Sumatra, there never has been a period of such swift, pervasive, and fundamental change, on so many levels, as our own time. It is a tribute to our own society that we have adapted so remarkably to the flood of changes washing over us. But other less-agile and less-flexible societies are crumbling. And they see the evidence around them every day, from Cairo to Karachi, thanks to the other great current of globalization—the information revolution. Ignorance never really was bliss, but it allowed a certain contentment in threadbare cultures. The new self-awareness of one's relative deficiencies, however, has been humiliating for cultures and entire civilizations as vain as they are morally and practically inadequate. Culture is fate, and the world media rubs it in, even when they do not intend to do so.

Barring cataclysms, this will be a century of ever-accelerating change in a bewildering variety of disciplines. Organizational principles that have prevailed since the days of mythic history are crumbling all around us. The most fundamental sources of power, wealth, and authority have shifted. All this will make the 21st century one of unprecedented discontents, of volatile hatreds, of rabid jealousy, and of enduring terrorism.

We must make no mistake: we are hated by the bitterest, most reactionary, and most threatened elements of traditional societies around the world. From our freedom of speech to the freedom of a woman to decide the course of her own life, our civilization is as threatening as it is seductive. Our self-selecting enemies are not really fighting to avenge anything tangible we have done to them, despite their endless myths of victimization. They attack out of jealousy at our success, out of fear of our social fairness, and out of the twisted, peculiarly-male conviction (not unknown to our own severest fundamentalists) that God put men on earth to suffer—and to make sure that women suffer the most.

In a word, they hate our freedom.

This is not a matter of jingoism or op-ed rhetoric. I have visited country after country where the forces of reaction, of time-honored repression, and of exclusive hierarchies are struggling to secede from a global future: to quit history and make time stand still. It cannot be done, and their failures will only excite more and more disappointed men to violence and terror. The Middle Eastern male blames the West for everything from his incompetence to his impotence. It is a prescription for self-immolation of the sort we saw on September 11th, 2001.

Perhaps the gravest errors committed by Western intellectuals in the wake of the attacks of 9-11-01 were to insist that we, the citizens of the United States, were somehow at fault. Without question, our government has not always behaved wisely or even justly abroad, especially during the deformed decades of the Cold War, when the stakes were often high, while the means were frequently low. Still, we are not to blame for the rise of apocalyptic terrorists so unhappy with the world that they appoint themselves as God's avengers, with the unspoken agenda of jump-starting Armageddon.

Post-modern terrorism—the goals of which are vengeance and destruction, not practical change—is not really about us. We are merely the most psychologically-satisfying target; physical forms that substitute for the demons haunting the souls of the terrorists. This does not make the terrorists less threatening; on the contrary, it means that we hold little human reality for them. But it really is about them, not us. Their motivations are not born of our deeds, but arise from their own spiritual and practical deficiencies. They are souls adrift, gathered into the net of obsession. They can live among us and never acknowledge our human reality. We are objects, not human beings, to them. They cannot bear it otherwise. They need to dehumanize us to avoid the devastating experience of looking in the mirror, either at themselves or at their entire civilizations.

Globalization is, overwhelmingly, a force for good. It has many flaws that want correction, from the inadequate oversight of many a multinational corporation to undeniable environmental costs. Yet, no multinational entity has done as much damage to developing countries as their own corrupt elites have done, and the worst environmental damage is caused not by post-modern businesses that rely on information technologies, but by traditional economic behaviors, from slash-and-burn agriculture in the Amazon Basin to the monstrously-polluting smokestack industries of China, which are throwbacks to an earlier age of capitalism (the Age of Capitalism ended with the 20th century; we are now in the Age of Ability, in which human capital has far surpassed more tangible and traditional forms of capital in importance—anyone who protests old-school capitalism in the 21st century is simply dawdling at a funeral).

The forces of freedom and fairness unleashed by globalization—the opportunities created for the common man and woman to be heard, to find justice, and to work for a living wage—are the most promising forces to tame globalization's excesses and to improve its practices. For all its evident growing pains, globalization contains its own cures. Post-modern markets are not only self-regulating, their social environments are self-healing.

Let us make no mistake: *We* stand for the liberation of humankind from uncounted millenia of hierarchical rule and oppression. The terrorists stand for the old order. This is a war of the past against the future. The future is going to win. But the struggle will endure beyond our lifetimes. Terrorism will ebb and flow, but it will not disappear. Globalization explodes the fundamental patterns of human cultures. Ours is an age of upheavals without precedent. We have every reason to be confident, but our enemies—the enemies of the full range of human freedoms—will take every opportunity to strike back, attempting desperately to stop the clock of history.

While the most violent anti-globalization protestors are terrorists themselves, most are earnest (if sometimes loopy) young people who have not yet learned to think critically or objectively. Many mean only to do good. But good intentions do not make the world a better place by themselves. The wretched of the earth need work, not words, and only globalization can provide that work—along with opening the door to myriad new possibilities and unprecedented freedoms. It is a pity, really, that all the anti-globalization protesters' energy is spent supporting the same causes as those espoused by the worst terrorists in history.

Further Reading

Phillip Bobbitt, *Terror and Consent: The Wars for the Twenty-first Century.* New York: Knopf, 2008.

Ralph Peters, *Wars of Blood and Faith: The Conflicts that Will Shape the 21st Century.* Mechanicsburg: Stackpole Books, 2007.

Health Impacts

The "Healer-Warrior" Conundrum: Terrorism and Health Services

Fadi Essmaeel

Terrorism changes things for health professionals. Internationalism and humanitarianism are universal values that leave little room to human malevolence. Caregivers' altruistic sensitivities and routines may be challenged in ways we need to identify and prepare for.

Fundamental Challenges

Dealing with terrorism and its ramifications means introducing an adversarial component into the worldview that is used by civilian health systems for planning, training, exercising, and practice. This is a way of thinking that is completely alien to everything a caregiver has ever wanted to be and is trained for.

Operational manifestations of terrorist intent

Health officials must factor the intentional nature of terrorism into their emergency management efforts. Terrorist intent arises from a host of psychosocial, political, and religious origins and it drives and shapes planning and execution of terrorist attacks.

The physical and mental wellness of our communities and individual patients may be impacted by a deviously intelligent attacker. Raw intent becomes a realistic threat when it combines with physical capabilities available to a terrorist network. Terrorist motives, beliefs, education, training, resources, strategic goals, concerns, limitations and opportunities find outlet in the manner by which attacks are conceived, developed, executed, and dovetailed. The targets chosen, the weapon to be used, the location, timing, and dating of the attack as well as follow up actions such as media releases or additional strikes are all subject to the intent that underlies terrorist actions. In addition, terrorist intent brings into effect a series of legal ramifications pertaining to government agency authority and incident handling.

Terrorism is tailored to target our collective mind thereby facilitating a "backdoor" penetration of defense mechanisms that rely upon social inertia. Attacks are designed to deliver shock waves throughout a target society, involving jurisdictions which may not be directly attacked. The impact of each physical strike is maximized through the dynamic interconnectedness between our material and neuro-psychosocial infrastructures. This effect is accomplished through media reports, the flow of evacuees and passengers, and via critical infrastructure failures delivering their "message" far and wide.

Case Description: Knifing in Jerusalem

Here is one health system-related example of the way by which intent shapes tactics and consequences of a terrorist attack. During the late 1980's, the city of Jerusalem was terrorized by an unusual tactic: stabbing. Terrorists would emerge from alleyways and shrubbery to stab passers-by, usually older females or otherwise frail victims and proceed to attack additional victims until citizens neutralized the attacker. In addition to the injuries, the attacks had a painful economic impact since many of them were intentionally executed in shopping areas, scaring away customers and businesses.

During one of these attacks, a male attacker in his mid-twenties severely stabbed four middle-aged women in Kiryat Yovel, a blue collar neighborhood of Jerusalem. The victims of this attack were evacuated to the nearby Hadassah level-3 trauma center where this author spent most of his medical school years. Local surgeons treating these victims as well as victims of previous stabbing incidents made a striking observation: they found that the prognosis faced by terrorism victims was significantly less favorable than the one reported in the surgical literature for "ordinary" stabbing victims. Furthermore, victims of terrorist attacks fared significantly worse than other "ordinary" stabbing victims treated at the same hospital. Why?

The answer was surprisingly predictable on three accounts. Firstly, terrorists used much larger and sharper blades warranting the term "dagger" rather than "knife". Secondly, terrorist stabbings were different in the angle used to hold the weapon, the vital organs targeted by the attackers and the wide-arc leverage used by terrorists to strike the victims. In contrast, criminally-motivated stabbings tend in most cases to serve as warning-cuts rather than for murder. Thirdly, the victims of terrorist attacks were chosen from the frail, the old, and the defenseless in comparison to criminal population that tends to comprise of alert, young, and healthy males.

Mass Casualty Incidents

Mass Casualty Incidents (MCI) are situations where regular health response systems are overwhelmed by a sudden surge in the quantity or quality of injuries it needs to handle. Such critical conditions may arise due to the number of patients, the nature and extent of their injuries, and fluctuations in medical readiness.

During MCI, the medical management style must change. In routine operations, treatment of patients is prioritized so that the more severe cases warrant the fastest and highest attention; in MCI, the situation is somewhat reversed. Here, we prioritize by the likelihood of survival rather than by sheer severity of injuries. For this purpose, a standard procedure is used: "triage" (pronounced "tree-aj") literally meaning "sorting-out".

In triage, we rapidly sort out the casualties by severity of their conditions so that we are able to identify those casualties that warrant best attention. We factor in their chances of survival given their medical condition and the state of our response system. Triage standards may be done along very unrefined lines and can be as coarse as "walking" vs. "non-walking" casualties. Further resolution and refinement may be gained in different stages of incident management. Higher risk per patient is traded-off against distribution of opportunity and the risk on a wider basis. We reduce safety margins for the individual patients in favor of including as many of those who have a realistic chance of survival.

Terrorist Weapons: specific health concerns

A great deal of the information about these weapons arises from military medicine literature. As we implement military knowledge into our emergency management efforts, we do well to remember that civilian communities are more heterogeneous and less healthy than the average combat military population and therefore some adjustments may be needed.

Explosives and suicide attacks

Explosives were used for politically-motivated violence ever since they were integrated into warfare. To this day, the overwhelming majority of terrorist attacks use some form of explosives. Suicide attacks including human-borne devices and car bombs are also employed. Bombings result in trauma and blast injuries.

Bombs could be augmented with radiological, chemical, and biological agents. In some cases, the planners of these attacks deliberately choose attackers that are disease carriers. HIV, Hepatitis B, and Ebola are potential agents. This is a form of "indirect" biological attack where the body of the attacker becomes a source for penetrating shrapnel and is intended to spread these blood-carried diseases.

Chemical Agents

Poisonous chemicals were used in warfare since the dawn of time and for the most part were considered an exceptionally cowardly tool.

Chemical weapons are administered mainly by inhalation and by skin contact.

Different chemical agents attack different tissues: epithelium or skin, mucous membranes, lung tissue, and nervous tissue. Some of them act immediately while others require a few minutes to a few hours to induce symptoms. Some are lethal and some are irritants. Responders on scene may require some personal protective equipment (PPE) to defend them against contamination or infection.

Victims of chemical attacks must be decontaminated, i.e. be cleaned up. There is a well-ingrained doctrine for chemical decontamination by fire service and hazardous materials (HAZMAT) units. Decontamination facilities must be established to clean up victims using water and detergent. Water run off should be controlled if possible.

It is important to remember that all clothing items and personal effects belonging to exposed victims may be considered criminal evidence and they may be taken away by the investigative authority. This may be hard if the victim is asked to give away a sensitive property. For example, a law enforcement officer may be required to relinquish his service firearm for decontamination or as a piece of evidence.

When this author was 16 years old, he and his classmates were trained as decontamination teams for the eventuality of a chemical attack at the Hadassah tertiary medical center in Jerusalem. At that time, this scenario seemed like a distant, sci-fi type occurrence that would never materialize. Unfortunately, this esoteric scenario became a scary possibility during the U.S.-led operation Desert Storm on January 1991. Saddam Hussein's forces launched 39 scud missiles at Israel, each one of which was suspected as carrying a chemical warhead. While none of these missiles actually carried a chemical warhead, the Israeli health-response systems were stretched to their utmost preparedness potential. Hospital beds were emptied by sending patients home. Decontamination and respiratory support teams were put on alert that were mostly composed of medical students. Buses were prepared to carry patients. The Medical Corps of the IDF was closely coordinated with the rest of the national health systems. A complex command and control process was established (and revamped after the war) that involved both military and civilian authorities. The public was supplied with protective masks and auto-injectors containing nerve agent antidotes. Strategic national stockpiles of medical supplies and pharmaceuticals were stood up. Luckily, this preparedness was only partially tested during the missile strikes. It is interesting to note that the only chemical casualties resulted from erroneous antidote auto-injection by a few citizens who panicked during the attacks.

Biological Agents

These are living organisms such as bacteria, viruses, and fungi that may be used against people, animals, plants, and materiel. A growing number of countries possess biological weapons including some countries that sponsor terrorist groups. It has long been a concern within the intelligence and policymaking communities that some of these weapons may ultimately find their way into the hands of terrorists.

Biological agents may be spread from a stationary ("point") source or from a moving ("line") one. Attackers know that certain hours of the daily cycle are "preferable" for effective attack, especially when the "proper" atmospheric conditions prevail.

Many microorganisms may be used as biological agents. The CDC has designated classes of agents based upon their likelihood of deployment. The "classical" bioweapon is anthrax that is preferred by bioweaponeers due to its wide prevalence in nature and its very hardy structure. Anthrax bacteria can convert into a "spore" form that is almost totally resistant to heat, dryness, most disinfectants, sunlight etc. These spores may survive in soil for decades.

Victims exposed to a biological agent will experience clinical manifestations in due course of the disease. Biological agents multiply in the victim's body and produce toxins that generate the clinical picture. High index of suspicion is important to identify an attack. Medical staff encountering a sudden influx of patients may become suspicious of the true cause when they see identical ailments that appear out of season and/or out of geographic region where these diseases usually appear. In fact, there is a long list of "pattern breakers" in the clinical presentation that suggest a nefarious cause. Epidemiological investigation will unearth several patterns reminiscent of an intentional dissemination rather than a natural outbreak.

Toxins: are they biological agents or chemicals?

Toxins are poisons produced by living organisms. Some toxins are produced by plants, some by fungi and some by microbes. "Classical" bio-toxins considered as weapons are botulinum toxin (BTX) that is produced by Clostridium botulinum and ricin that is produced by castor beans. An age old debate is whether toxins should be listed as chemical or biological agents. It is this author's position that for the responder, including the health caregiver, toxins are a special subset of chemicals, mostly proteins that have their special properties and characteristics. For intelligence officers, toxins are biological weapons given that the processes, equipment, and facilities required for their development are similar to those required for the development of living organisms. Therefore, for the purpose of intelligence assessment, the indicators sought to identify bioweaponeering plants are the almost the same ones required to identify weaponisation of bio-toxins. In summary, we may say that until an attack takes place toxins should be approached as biological agents while during and after an attack they should be approached as chemicals. Put shortly—*they are prevented as bio-weapons and responded to as chemical weapons.*

Radio-nuclear

Radiation is the projection of particles and/or electro magnetic energy from one point in space-time ("source") to another ("target"). An example of a radiation-emitting source would be radioactive materials spread by a "dirty bomb." A great deal of analysis and planning has been dedicated to scenarios involving "dirty bombs," also known as "Radiological Dispersal Devices" (RDD). Such devices may utilize the mechanical energy released by explosion to disseminate readily-found radioisotopes such as Americium and Cobalt into key-business areas of major cities, rendering them uninhabitable for decades.

Public Information

Health sector professionals rely heavily on information flow both as consumers and as producers of intelligence. As they approach the question of terrorism preparedness, they have to become aware of existing knowledge about a wide gamut of potential terrorist threats. In a sense, they have to become something of "intelligence users" and even "intelligence producers"—a role not easily fulfilled by members of this universalistic occupation. Reality, however, leaves us little choice.

For example, some public health agencies maintain active epidemiological surveillance of certain symptoms and illnesses in the community. The intent is to monitor any unusual peaks and patterns of occurrence that may emerge from intentional spread of a bio-agent which will confirm suspicions raised by clinicians and intelligence. Epidemiological investigation that may follow such detection will look at etiology, onset, appearance, signs and symptoms, analysis of biosamples, and long-term effects of the disease. There are severe limitations and cautions that must be observed while managing health-related information in order to protect the privacy of individuals treated by caregivers. Information about casualties spread, the nature and severity of their injuries, diagnostics, and patient identities must be protected and maintained by law for both medical and other public safety reasons. The most prominent piece of legislation in this regard is the Health Insurance Portability and Accountability Act (HIPAA) that consumes inordinate amounts of administrative efforts from clinical managers.

One of the rarely discussed considerations is the need to maintain solid "operational security" or "OPSEC." OPSEC includes all the efforts we put into denying an adversary access to information that may assist them in harming us. EMS responders on scene must keep in mind that they may be watched by enemy operatives and handlers that may use the attack to collect intelligence on the EMS deployment tactics. This intelligence may be used in immediate or future sequential attacks.

Further Reading

David A. McEntire, *Introduction to Homeland Security: Understanding Terrorism With an Emergency Management Perspective*. Hoboken: John Wiley & Sons, 2008.

K. Joanne McGlown, Ed., *Terrorism and Disaster Management: Preparing Healthcare Leaders for the New Reality*. Chicago: Health Administration Press, 2004.

Randy G. Stair, Dwight A. Polk, Geoff Shapiro, and Nelson Tang, *Law Enforcement Responder: Principles of Emergency Medicine, Rescue, and Force Protection*. Burlington: Jones & Bartlett Learning, 2012.

Hezbollah

(aka Party of God, Islamic Jihad, Revolutionary Justice Organization, Organization of the Oppressed)

James T. Kirkhope

What is the most successful terrorist group of the modern era? Most people would answer "al-Qaeda" in a heartbeat. But the unsettling reality is that the Lebanese Shi'a group, Hezbollah, has achieved much more. Within the first year of its formation, Hezbollah attacked multiple UN peacekeeping forces in Beirut, killing hundreds, thus persuading President Ronald Reagan to evacuate U.S. forces from the region. With merely a handful of suicide attacks, Hezbollah humbled one of two superpowers and triggered strategic change in its Middle East policy. While the tactics introduced by the group continue to be implemented by al-Qaeda, not even Osama bin Laden has been successful in leveraging America's withdrawal from the Holy Land.

Lebanon in 1982 was one of the world's most dangerous places. A brutal multi-ethnic civil war raged, compounded by an Israeli invasion in 1981 and the subsequent deployment of United Nations peacekeepers. It was during this violent period that two fundamentalist Shi'a Muslim groups, Islamic Amal and the Da'wa Party, forged an alliance in 1982 called Hezbollah, "Party of God." Hezbollah's goals were considerably more ambitious than the myriad of other Lebanese militias. First, it sought to become Lebanon's primary Islamic party. Second, following the example of Ayatollah Khomeini's Iran, Hezbollah aspired to create a revolutionary Islamic State in Lebanon. Finally, it sought to rid the region of Western cultural, political, and military influence, including elimination of the state of Israel. These objectives held great appeal strategically for Iran and tactically for Syria—both of which provided extensive training, funding, arming, intelligence, and other logistical support. Hezbollah quickly came to represent an umbrella organization under the spiritual leadership of Muhammad Husayn Fadlallah, coordinating terrorist cells, irregular guerrilla forces, social and public service organizations, as well as political party representatives. To accomplish its grand aims, Hezbollah also built organizational structures and operations for the domestic, regional, and global arenas.

By 1983, Hezbollah was ready to take on the Western powers behind the UN peacekeeping mission. In April, a sub-group called Islamic Jihad claimed responsibility for a suicide car bomb attack on the U.S. embassy in Lebanon. Six months later, 241 U.S. Marines and 56 French soldiers serving as UN peacekeepers were killed by an Islamic Jihad truck bomb attack of their barracks in Beirut. Shortly thereafter, the U.S. withdrew its troops from Lebanon, sensing a quagmire. The civil war continued amidst the backdrop of rising Syrian and Iranian influence and a waning Israeli occupation. The success of Hezbollah's tactic certainly inspired Osama bin Laden's al-Qaeda to conduct similar operations on U.S. barracks unsuccessfully in Yemen in 1992 and spectacularly on Khobar Towers in Dhahran, Saudi Arabia in 1996.

Nonetheless, suicide car bombs represented only a fraction of Hezbollah's operational capability. In January 1984, Islamic Jihad began an assassination campaign targeting prominent Westerners such as American University of Beirut President Malcom Kerr. By February 1984, the group began kidnapping dozens of Westerners such as Associated Press journalist Terry Anderson, and later an Anglican priest Terry Waite (captured while serving as a hostage negotiator) for up to eight years. Hezbollah began an aircraft hijacking campaign in June 1985 with an attack on TWA flight 847, and later the hijackings of an Air Afrique flight in July 1987 and a Kuwaiti Airliner in April 1988. Hezbollah also extended its terrorist reach globally, bombing offices and synagogues in Copenhagen, Stockholm, Paris, Kuwait City, and even Buenos Aires through 1994. Finally, Hezbollah's regular guerrilla forces of southern Lebanon even shelled civilian targets with artillery and mortar fire.

Eventually, Israeli withdrew its last combat forces from southern Lebanon in May 2000, an event for which Hezbollah fervently claimed credit. This achievement is crucial to understand Hezbollah's appeal in the Middle East. No terrorist group—including the PLO and al-Qaeda—can claim to have driven three western powers (U.S., France, and Israel) from their country while simultaneously securing significant parliamentary representation. Perhaps that is why UN Secretary-General Kofi Anan met personally with Hezbollah leader Sheik Hassan Nasrallah in June 2000, and U.S. Secretary of State Colin Powell visited Beirut in April 2002. Hezbollah's combination of operational success and official recognition is sure to inspire future terrorists to take to battle, while al-Qaeda's flashy but strategically dubious operations may become footnotes in the history of the global jihad.

Further Reading

Judith Palmer Harik, *Hezbollah: The Changing Face of Terrorism*. New York: I. B. Tauris, 2004.

Matthew Levitt, *Hezbollah: The Global Footprint of Lebanon's Party of God*. Washington, DC: Georgetown University Press, 2013.

Augustus Richard Norton, *Hezbollah: A Short History*. Princeton Studies in Muslim Politics. Expanded Version. Princeton: Princeton University Press, 2014.

Homegrown Violent Extremism

The Threat Within and the Case for Community Engagement

Erroll G. Southers

For supporting end note information pertaining to this essay, contact the author.

In 2013, in Boston, Americans were reminded of the ever-present threat from violent extremism. Brothers Tamerlan and Dzhokhar Tsarnaev detonated bombs near the finish line of the Boston Marathon, killing three people and injuring 264 more. In the aftermath, much of the public debate focused on the fact that the brothers were ethnically Chechen and Muslim, with much speculation about links to foreign terrorist groups. The unspoken message underlying the debate was that the Tsarnaevs were not *really* American.

Yet, Dzhokhar Tsarnaev was a U.S. citizen and Tamerlan Tsarnaev was a long-time resident. The brothers grew up here, attending school, participating in sports and embracing U.S. culture. By all measures, the Tsarnaevs were American. Despite these evident facts, it still took time for the public, press and policymakers to accept that what we saw in Boston was not a foreign group penetrating America's extensive counterterrorism infrastructure. It was a homegrown attack.

Today, the public is moderately more aware that some of the gravest threats to homeland security do not come from without but from within. Yet, homegrown terrorism is a complex subject that receives overly simplistic coverage by the media and insufficient public discussion. To best address this persistent and growing threat, it is essential that we precisely define and identify what this homegrown violent extremism

(HVE) is, why it is such a substantial threat to safety and security, and, critically, what communities can do to deter it.

Much like the term "terrorism," there is no comprehensive definition for HVE; however, for the purposes of analysis, a working definition of HVE as it relates to the United States is:

> A terrorist act within the context of ideologically motivated violence or plots, perpetrated within the United States or abroad by American citizens, residents or visitors, who have embraced their legitimizing ideology largely within the United States (Southers, 2013).

Simply put, homegrown violent extremists are domestic terrorists who target members of their own country. It is important to note that the birthplace of an ideology is *not* a criterion in determining homegrown versus international extremism. For example, a Syrian national who embraces al Qaeda's violent ideology in Syria is a foreign adversary when they act against U.S. interests. An American, however, who embraces al Qaeda's ideology largely within the United States is by definition a homegrown actor. The origin of the ideology is irrelevant; what matters is where it is embraced.

Much of the public discussion on domestic and foreign terrorism focuses on extremist Islamic beliefs (what I term "Muslim Identity" ideology). Yet, in the United States, there is a complex patchwork of violent ideologies, and the majority have nothing to do with Islamic beliefs.

A Complex Extremist Landscape

The outsized focus on Muslim Identity extremism is shortsighted and insufficient to address the rampant growth of violent extremism in the United States. There are anti-government groups, neo-Nazis and white supremacists, and animal and environmental activists, to name a few. Collectively, these groups have brought far more plots and violence than homegrown jihadist extremists who have killed and injured far less U.S. citizens to date.

The U.S. HVE landscape is a messy place, and extremism cannot be neatly divided into easily identifiable groups. That said, there are three overarching ideological categories: race, religion, and issue-orientation.

With racist extremism, racial supremacy is the foundation of the ideological principles. The Ku Klux Klan is well-known for its hatred of non-Caucasian and/or non-Protestant groups, and the New Black Panther Party is equally driven by racial hatred. These kinds of racially motivated groups are perpetually and perilously operating near the threshold of violent extremism and sometimes their adherents step over the line between constitutionally protected extremist beliefs and violent action (i.e., terrorism). Take the example of Michael Wade Page, a Northern Hammerskins adherent who played in white power bands and embraced the Nazi ideology. In 2012, he walked into a Sikh temple in Wisconsin and opened fire on the congregation, killing six and wounding three, including a police officer, before killing himself.

Religion has long been a foundation for violent extremism in America and, until recently, this was largely the domain of extremist Christian ideology. For example, the United States underwent a period where "compound dwellers," largely based in the Northwest and steeped in religious hatred, grew by leaps and bounds. Groups like the Covenant, the Sword and the Arm of the Lord (CSA), The National Alliance, and Aryan Nations engaged in armed standoffs with the government. These and other groups seized on these kinds of conflicts with U.S. authorities as a way to inspire, enrage, and attract radical followers.

Issue-oriented extremists include militia and patriot groups, whose ideologies oppose the authority of the U.S. government (be it federal, state, or even local). The Sovereign Citizens movement, for example, rejects the authority of the state and advocates violence when that authority is exercised. Recent attacks on uniformed police officers show the lethality of this messaging, such as the anti-government, right-wing 2014 attack by Jared and Amanda Miller, who killed two uniformed police officers eating lunch in Las Vegas. The couple shot both officers in the head and draped one of the bodies in the Gadsden flag (i.e., the image of a coiled rattlesnake and the words "Don't Tread on Me"). The

Millers then crossed the street, killed another individual in a Walmart store and fulfilled a suicide pact.

Complicating the picture of American extremism is the increasing prevalence of hybrid ideologies. For example, anti-government extremists sometimes also embrace a racially motivated ideology. Tamerlan Tsarnaev, while a Muslim Identity extremist, also embraced decidedly anti-government, anti-Semitic conspiracy theories suggesting that the 9/11 attacks were organized by shadowy financial elites and that "the world is controlled by a Jewish cabal" (Cullison, 2013).

Hybrid ideologies underscore the knowledge that there is no such thing as a terrorist profile. Given this diversity of ideologies and factions, the growing HVE threat demands a more comprehensive, thoughtful evaluation of extremist groups in the United States.

Empowering Communities

As evidenced in comments by Homeland Security Secretary Jeh Johnson, as well as ongoing efforts within the Department of Homeland Security, the U.S. government is (appropriately) focusing increasing attention on homegrown groups. Yet, even as these government efforts are important, the public also has a role to play. We in the security community must support and collaborate with broader communities to identify people on the path to violent extremism. Indeed, working with these communities, we have the potential to disrupt the radicalization pathway altogether.

Each community in the United States faces circumstances unique to their demographic makeup and the ideological proclivities of their population. While extremist ideology is a driving HVE force, the radicalization pathway that leads to violence is fraught with grievances that make an individual receptive to violent ideology in the first place.

These grievances can include conflicted identity, perceived injustice, ethic oppression, and socioeconomic exclusion. To best meet the HVE threat, we must understand how grievances can lead to violence and develop effective strategies for preventing radicalization. This must necessarily address the specific challenges in the community.

In addition to law enforcement and intelligence work that can thwart extremist attacks, the United States can enhance its security posture by implementing strategies that work with communities to deter radicalization. This is what I have termed a Mosaic of Engagement (MoE).

The objective of MoE is to use a community-based strategy to improve community quality of life. Residents of every community want safety and security and, through consensus building and community relationships, it is possible to collectively work towards a shared commitment to public safety, by consequence reducing the potential for grievances that can lead to HVE.

Using research, data collection, and analysis, MoE can create a common ground and shared understanding via collaborative *Neighborhood Alliances*, which are comprised of community members, government agencies, academics, policymakers and leaders across different municipal sectors. Through this, MoE fosters consensus building between policymakers and community stakeholders, ensuring that both groups align their short- and long-term goals and tactics.

Participation from the adult population is critical but so too is engagement with the community's school environments. Working with young people sets the stage for lifelong learning about safety and security, while also building stronger familial bonds. Community-driven safety and security efforts that yield consensus and collaborative strategies are best suited to prevent the kinds of grievances that can lead to HVE.

Conclusions

Securing a democracy has always been a formidable challenge, balancing constitutionally guaranteed rights and protections with the need to identify and halt violent extremists. Yet, the threat from myriad extremist groups is growing fast. To be sure, the United States will see both small- and large-scale terrorist attacks in the future.

Our security programs must be based on evidence and facts. Understanding the people, processes, and outcomes associated with HVE recruitment, radicalization, and violent action empowers communities with important knowledge. Messaging—real or virtual— is the strongest weapon our adversaries possess, but words and ideas can be overcome. Terrorists do not operate in a vacuum. Every homegrown violent extremist has a family, one that can facilitate radicalization by encouragement or halt it through knowledge and public and community support. Shared information regarding groups, their ideologies, and their objectives goes a long way toward creating an environment that is more resistant to HVE.

The United States needs academics and professionals from all disciplines to take a more focused, nuanced look at violent extremism and continue to study and understand how ideology and grievances breed the potential for violence and terrorism. We must better understand how individuals traverse the radicalization pathway and develop more approaches for helping disrupt that dangerous evolution.

Further Reading

Marc Sageman, *Leaderless Jihad: Terror Networks in the Twenty-First Century*. Philadelphia: University of Pennsylvania Press, 2008.

Erroll Southers, *Homegrown Violent Extremism*. New York: Routledge, 2009.

Paul Thomas, *Responding to the Threat of Violent Extremism: Failing to Prevent*. London: Bloomsbury Academic, 2012.

Information Sharing

"Information Sharing" to Counter Terrorism

Gregory F. Treverton

This article draws on chapter seven of the author's Intelligence for an Age of Terrorism. Cambridge: Cambridge University Press, 2009. For supporting end note information pertaining to this essay, contact the author.

What the federal government calls "information sharing" in the nation's fight against terrorism isn't. Rather, the challenge is to produce and move both information and analysis across the federal government and the 18,000 states and localities—not to mention private sector managers of "public" infrastructure like information or finance. The task is better labeled "joint production," or "co-production" in the words of John Sullivan, one of this volume's editors. That joint production would be shaped by comparative advantage, that is by what the various participants are best positioned to do.

Misnaming the Challenge

The language of "information sharing" is wrong on every count. First, the language implies that agencies "own" their information, sharing it only as they see fit; in that sense, the language only reinforces the existing stovepipes. Second, the language of sharing implies that if only information could move more freely, presto, all would be well. Third, it implies that the challenge of sharing intelligence with state and local authorities, down to the cop on the beat, is technical; if enough information pipes exist to move information freely. It is not. Technology can help. But the challenge is one of policy, not hardware. Fourth, and perhaps worst, it tends to imply that the sharing goes in one direction, with the federal agencies as providers and the other as grateful recipients. Yet the new consumers are producers as well.

In fact, the heart of the issue is how intelligence does its business. Existing business practices, with each intelligence agency controlling the information it produces, make it hard enough to share across U.S. intelligence, let alone get information to state and local authorities. The problem begins with existing security procedures that are designed to limit information to those with a "need to know," not share it. Yet fresh analytic insights, to take one example, are likely to arise precisely from those who come to the information with a fresh perspective, who have *no* need to know. The fundamental challenge is reshaping how the U.S. government thinks of information, and how information should be produced, used, and controlled.

At the federal level, the simple fact of September 11th was a powerful impetus to moving information within and across agencies, and to working together. Before the attacks, very different cultures compounded the effect of the "wall" between intelligence and law enforcement. For instance, FBI agents have Top Secret clearances, but few are cleared into the Sensitive Compartmented Information (SCI) that is the woof and warp of intelligence. So, when faced by unfamiliar FBI counterparts in meetings, CIA officers might be sincerely uncertain how much they could say, and vice versa for FBI agents, who feared that inadvertent disclosures might jeopardize prosecutions. The safest course was to say nothing. If the conversation turned to matters domestic, then the CIA officials would also be uncertain how much they should *hear*.

"Coproduction," jointly producing information across the federal structure requires reshaping security to effectively confront the threats ahead—which also requires perhaps the ultimate change in culture. It will not come soon. In the meantime, a number of smaller proposals can at least ameliorate immediate problems. For instance, intelligence analysts, like other professionals, want to play at the top of their games, so their reports inevitably begin with the most classified—and thus least sharable—information. The 9/11 Commissions suggested the opposite, starting any report by separating information from sources and writing first at the level that can be most easily shared. (Some agencies, like the National Security Agency do write different versions but typically start with the most classified, then adjust it downward.) If intelligence consumers wanted more, they could query the system under whatever rules were in place, leaving an audit trail of requests. Now many, perhaps most, potential consumers would not even know what to ask for.

The military is creative during coalition operations in using "tear line" intelligence, so that information can be separated from indications about the source and transferred to non-American coalition partners. There is no reason that the FBI and Department of Homeland Security (DHS) cannot be comparably creative in thinking of ways to get information to uncleared partners. Now, the principal means the federal government has for working with state and local authorities are the FBI Joint Terrorism Task Forces. Yet those are built around FBI communications, and so require state and local participants to be cleared at the top secret level.

Taking Advantage of Comparative Advantage

Doing better starts with asking what are the comparative advantages of the different levels of government, and of the private sector, in joint production. For instance, federal authorities would naturally take the lead in intelligence gathering that is not connected to criminal investigation. The locals have neither money nor capacity for that kind of pure intelligence. So, too, that intelligence gathering would be guided by federal regulations and overseen primarily by federal courts, especially the special, secret court for national security (as opposed to criminal) surveillance established by the Federal Intelligence Surveillance Act (FISA). Ideally, the state and local authorities would conduct two kinds of information or intelligence gathering—investigation, including electronic surveillance, of possible criminal acts; and collection that is incidental to the normal activities of police officers. The latter is the eyes and ears of the cops on the beat, and the goal is domain awareness—what's going on in the jurisdiction, what's the state of possible targets, and so on.

Yet the locals get neither much guidance about what to look for nor enough intelligence that is specific enough to shape local operations. The principal information sharing mechanism, the JTTFs, is constrained by the need for security clearances, and its focus is cases and investigation; one of its key functions is "deconflicting" investigations—that is, parceling out cases to JTTF member agencies for their investigations, then making sure that the investigations don't work at cross purposes to one another. The newer "fusion centers," a DHS initiative, are meant to be complementary. If JTTFs work on cases once identified, the fusion centers are meant to assemble *strategic intelligence* at the regional level. They, too, seek to bring together federal with state and local officials, including, in principle, reaching out to the private sector. The responsibility of the centers is to fuse foreign intelligence with domestic information in order to facilitate improved policy decision-making on issues of counterterrorism, crime, and emergency response. How, exactly, to do that remains a challenge.

In practice, the fusion centers are experiencing adjustment difficulties, including poor or absent communication between centers. Not all fusion centers have state-wide intelligence systems. They also do not all have access to law enforcement data or private sector information. The problem of interoperability of systems that was widely criticized directly after 9/11 still exists. Because of the huge number of systems and the resulting duplication, reviewing incoming information is extremely time-consuming.

Moreover, as outward signs of the terrorist threat wane, many of these centers are changing their focus from a pure counterterrorism mission to an "all-hazards" approach as priorities change at the local and regional level. That reflects the simple fact that for most localities, terrorism is not a major problem. And that shift to an "all-hazards" approach may not be a bad thing as the "domestication" of the terrorist threat means that it more and more resembles organized crime.

"Coproduction" is far from a real two-way street, and reaching out to the private sector, the third frontier, is particularly troublesome. In the words of one recent assessment: "The flow of information from the private sector to fusion centers is largely sporadic, event driven, and manually facilitated." Like cops on the beat, private managers of infrastructure know their domains better than anyone. Yet interviews suggest they are triply reticent in sharing information: first, they worry about revealing gaps in security; second, they do not want proprietary information to leak to competitors; and, third, passing information risks that they will become liable for other shortcomings, such as environmental violations, for instance.

Former Secretary of Defense Donald Rumsfeld focused attention in the intelligence war on terrorism to the "known unknowns," the things we know we don't know, and, especially to the "unknown unknowns," the things we don't know we don't know. Yet much of the 9/11 failure turned on another category, the "unknown knowns," the things we didn't know or had forgotten we knew. Those are especially important given the nature of the counter-terrorism task. A traditional law enforcement investigation seeks to reconstruct the single trail from crime back to perpetrator. By contrast, the counter-terrorism task, especially prevention, needs to look at a number of paths, assembling enough information about each to know when patterns are changing or something suspicious is afoot along one of the paths. It is not only an intelligence-rich task. It is also a task rich in intelligence analysis.

Ideally, the analysis function would be split among the levels of government. The federal level has a comparative advantage in special sources, especially sources abroad. Its analysis will naturally concentrate on those and on the broad, "connect the dots" function. Sometimes, those sources and that analysis will provide warning specific enough to alert particular local authorities. In other cases, though, it will remain general and will serve mostly to tip off local officials about what they might look for—for example, a string of apparently unrelated crimes involving false identities.

The federal government is struggling, through DHS and the National Counterterrorism Center (NCTC), as well as a greatly-expanded FBI intelligence function, to do better at its part of the ideal. Yet what is still more striking is how limited the analytic capacity is at the local level. Only the very largest police departments have much of any at all, with New York in a class by itself. Yet, the local role in the division of analytic labor would be to take the general guidance provided by the feds and relate it to local domain awareness. What does new federal information or analysis add to that understanding of local circumstances?

While DHS has a legal mandate to take the lead in sharing intelligence, as a practical matter the lead in sharing is likely to continue to rest with the FBI through the JTTFs, though with the fusion centers playing more of a role. The federal, state and local authorities need to jointly develop a definition of terrorism and apply it by requiring that terrorism cases, including surveillance, be run through the JTTF. In any case, it would help if *someone* were in the lead. This is consistent with the recommendations of DHS and the Justice Department in their recent National Criminal Intelligence Sharing Plan, which lays out a number of recommendations regarding law enforcement's intelligence role in this area and how it could be improved. It is a role the Director of National Intelligence could play, as an honest broker without a direct bureaucratic stake. The DNI could develop lanes in the road for the different agencies, and standards both for producing intelligence and for sharing it— in short, for coproducing intelligence in the fight against terror.

Finally, *coproduction has to be a two-way street.* Local authorities, and especially the private sector, won't sustain the process, given their reasons for reticence, if the information they supply doesn't go anywhere, and if they don't see value in information they receive. In the end, too, expectations are critical. While the larger firms know the federal government, and many of their security managers come from careers in law enforcement and intelligence, some of the smaller local authorities still harbor grand hopes that the federal agencies can produce information magic from behind green door of classification if only they will open it.

Further Reading

John P. Sullivan and James J. Wirtz, "Terrorism Early Warning and Counterterrorism Intelligence." *International Journal of Intelligence and Counterintelligence*, Vol. 21, No. 1, 2007: 13-25.

Gregory F. Treverton, *Reshaping National Intelligence in an Age of Information.* Cambridge: Cambridge University Press, 2001.

Gregory F. Treverton, *Intelligence for an Age of Terror.* Cambridge: Cambridge University Press, 2009.

Instrumental Violence

The Purpose of Terrorism

John P. Sullivan

Terrorism is a familiar fixture in modern society yet, despite its pervasive impact on the attitudes and perceptions of society, it frequently seems incomprehensible. In the aftermath of the near-daily barrage of media images recounting terrorist atrocities—in faraway places and occasionally nearby—we ask why. Why the senseless, irrational violence; why the attacks on civilians, including women and children? Terrorism seems like it has no purpose, yet it continues. In trying to understand this dynamic, it is frequently stated that the purpose of terrorism is terror. Yet that truism oversimplifies the phenomena. Terrorism, quite simply, does have a purpose. It is violence directed to an end. Terrorism is, in short, instrumental violence.

Violence like terrorism itself is familiar yet little understood. When looking at the use of violence by individuals or groups, psychologists observe that it is either impulsive or instrumental in nature. This of course does not preclude elements of both impulse and purpose in the same act, but narrows our understanding. In most discourse, we recognize that terrorism is the use of political violence. It is often defined as the calculated threat or use of violence to cause fear, act as an instrument of coercion, or to yield intimidation. Not all violence for political ends is terrorism. States sometimes employ terror from above as an implement of social control, and war is itself the violent extension of politics as Clausewitz aptly observed.

Terrorism while sharing some of the attributes of those forms of instrumental violence distinguishes itself as a tactic (of both criminal violence and military action) and as a process to achieve an end. The key distinguishing attribute is the use of violence by the armed against the unarmed. This makes it a crime in both civil and battlefield situations—though targeting law enforcement and military personnel, who are armed, has expands the scope of this definition of a terrorist act. Terrorism uses destruction and violence to deliberately cause fear, upset and insecurity. As Hannah Arendt noted in her landmark essay *On Violence*, "the very substance of violent action is ruled by the means-end..." As such, violence is distinguished by its instrumental character. Being instrumental by nature, violence is thus, according to Arendt, rational to the extent that it is effective in reaching the end that must justify it.

In this sense, the key instrumentality of terrorism is action. Action to seize attention, send a message, elicit a response, with the end of yielding political pressure. Often the action chosen by terrorists is destruction, with the message communicated by the act itself. Thus terrorism uses the shock value of extreme violence to communicate, creating "terrorism as theatre" with the modern electronic media amplifying what the 19th Century anarchists called "propaganda by deed."

Terrorism uses violence as a means of political communication to both adversaries and supporters (current or potential). As a form of political "communication," terrorist acts possess three features. These are: 1) they contain an ideological or religious message, 2) they seek a high profile impact through a violent act; and 3) they are demonstrative in nature.

Terrorism is thus a form of deliberate collective violence. While instrumental to a goal, it must be focused to yield effect. Within that broad setting, the purpose of terrorist action may be:

- a tangential or supporting element of a broader political movement or insurgency;
- to serve limited goals, such as enforcement, revenge or propaganda, or
- to constitute a core strategy in a political campaign to seize power.

Terrorist action as the core or absolute strategy of a movement is embodied in the classic (anarchist or revolutionary) terrorist gambit. Violence is used to seize the imagination of the populace, awakening them to political issues. The state is then threatened and the destabilization of social order is possible since fear and public instability can cause a reactionary spiral where terror and counter-terror interact to erode public support. At the level of an individual terrorist act, the act can be for enforcement of internal security purposes (such as dissuading informers or solidifying group coherence) or impressive (agitational) to inspire followers and develop support for the movement. It is in this formula that apologists for revolutionary violence like Frantz Fanon felt that violence is empowering.

In this worldview, terrorism is of value due to the subjective psychological or psychosocial pressure it exerts. The actual destructive power of a single terrorist car-bombing or suicide attack is magnified to support the desired effect or political end of the terrorists. Thus deliberately focused, demonstrative violence becomes the terrorist's operational imperative. As Prince Krupotkin theorized about revolutionary terrorism, violent acts compel attention; they challenge the established order and, when the state reacts, the movement is strengthened by the public reaction to the repression.

Terrorism is used to counter a lack of power. In the earliest modern (that is post-Enlightenment) campaign of terror, Robespierre observed during Year II of the French Revolution (1794) that virtue without terror is powerless. Terror, and its variant terrorism, are applied forms of violence. According to Arendt, power and violence are opposites. Violence cannot create power. As Arendt again aptly notes, "violence can destroy power; it is utterly incapable of creating it."

This dynamic demonstrates the political calculus of terrorist attacks. The desired end is a change in the political equation. Terrorist action is far from indiscriminate; it is a rational choice to stimulate change. Yet, as such, it can only be rational in the short-term. Despite the hopes of its adherents, terrorism *itself* can't promote causes, radically alter history, or fuel revolution. While terrorism appears to work, as seen (at least at first glance) in the establishment of the state of Israel, Algeria and the revolutionary FLN, and the many chapters of the Troubles in Northern

Ireland, it does so only in conjunction with other instruments—as part of a broader insurgency, when augmented or supplanted by non-violent political process, or when accompanied by state-building efforts. Terrorism can then in a narrow sense serve to dramatize grievances and bring them to the attention of the public and civil society.

While terrorist attacks seem indiscriminate, it must be remembered that they are deliberately engineered to appear so. This illusion generates public fear and stimulates government reaction and, from a terrorist's perspective, hopefully repression. Thus, carefully chosen targets are necessary so the terrorists can express their message as meaningful political communication or in the contemporary setting as an instrument of jihad.

Terrorists across the span of time have sought to use violence as an instrument of social change. Terrorist action is designed to send a message, communicate an ideology, serve as the vanguard for a new society or lead the way to jihad. As such, terrorism is instrumental violence. But as Hannah Arendt, whose analysis continues to influence inquiries into the political philosophy of violence, as well as this essay, succinctly and rightly observed, "the practice of violence, like all action, changes the world, but the most probable change is to a more violent world." This message is particularly important with the prospect of mass casualty terrorism on the scale of September 11th or greater.

As we see the ante of terrorist action move steadily upward, with bigger, bolder, more destructive attacks needed to ensure continued media coverage and global attention, the instrumentality of violence must be countered. Contemporary terrorism is global in nature, underscoring the importance of building true political dialogue, equitable distribution of resources and power, and effective efforts to counter terrorism in both concept and practice.

Further Reading

Hannah Arendt, *On Violence*. San Diego: Harvest/Harcourt Brace Jovanovich, 1970.

Hannah Arendt, *On Revolution*. New York: Penguin Classics, 2006.

Intelligence

Frontiers of knowledge for countering terrorism

John P. Sullivan

The public and professional understanding of intelligence and its role is frequently defined by failures of intelligence. Intelligence failures—such as the failure of the U.S. Army or Naval intelligence structures to provide adequate warning and prevent the attack on Pearl Harbor by the Japanese and the failure of the contemporary U.S. intelligence and law enforcement communities to predict al-Qaeda's synchronized 9-11 attacks on the World Trade Center and Pentagon—justifiably lead to questions about the definition and role of intelligence in a democratic society. They also provide the backdrop for public and parliamentary discussions about the proper organizational architecture for intelligence services in war and peace.

The Central Intelligence Agency (CIA) and its constellation of supporting—and sometimes competing—agencies in the U.S. intelligence community were formed to correct the situation that led to Pearl Harbor. We can expect new structures to evolve to address the threat and lack of understanding of our current terrorist adversaries. Yet a lack of a basic understanding of the definition, nature, and need for intelligence is pervasive in the halls of government, among police and public safety personnel, and, ultimately, among the public for whom intelligence serves as a protection. What, in fact, is intelligence? Is it merely the province of secret agents conducting espionage against foreign governments? Is it information to support decision-making? Or is it some combination of those elements and much more?

Not surprisingly, many views about the nature and utility of intelligence color this debate. We know, at least collectively, that deception and surprise are closely related to intelligence matters. We also know that uncertainty complicates our understanding of conflict in general and terrorism specifically. Fog (unclear circumstances), friction (obstacles to action) and noise (too much information) are familiar to all decision-makers and commanders who seek to make good decisions in war and crisis. The "smog" of terrorism complicates action against terrorists due to its ambiguous and diffuse political nature.

"Know the enemy, know yourself; your victory will never be endangered." Sun Tzu

Knowing an enemy's (or opposing force's) capabilities and intentions is the foundation of intelligence. To gain this knowledge, a variety of intelligence disciplines are involved. All seek to discern several essential elements of information for a commander, decision-maker, or end user. These typically involve weather, enemy, tactics, and threat. It is not enough to know the adversary alone; knowledge of our own capabilities and needs helps define information requirements and place potential threats into an operational context.

"By 'intelligence' we mean every sort of information about the enemy and his country–the basis, in short, of our own plans and operations." Clausewitz

Much like the observation that there are several English "languages" and, as the rest of this collection demonstrates, there are different "terrorisms," there are also different forms of intelligence— "intelligences." Understanding and properly utilizing these intelligences will help address the information requirements for combating global terrorism. The first distinction is between foreign and domestic intelligence. This is particularly important as it limits or bounds the activity of intelligence agencies or practitioners.

This distinction is based in the experience of conflict among states and is designed to preserve liberties of citizens within a state and limit the abuse of secret information as a form a state coercion of its own residents. In the U.S., this is seen in the separation of the CIA's intelligence operations from the internal security and law enforcement functions of the Federal Bureau of Investigation (FBI) and state and local police agencies concerned with criminal intelligence. The same distinctions are seen in the UK's Secret Intelligence Service (SIS) and Security Service and police special branches.

As terrorists frequently operate transnationally and globally as non-state actors, the need to coordinate foreign and domestic operations becomes important to prevent terrorist acts. The distinction between law enforcement and intelligence is derived from these crucial liberty considerations. As a result, police, who often have contact with potential terrorists, are blind to threats on their own "beat." Consequently, much criminal intelligence is tactically-based investigative support lacking strategic context. A balanced approach that also preserves liberties must be struck.

Classical human intelligence (either overt or covert) known as HUMINT is another important variety of intelligence. In the recent past, however, forms of technical intelligence (*TECHNIT*) known by a number of acronyms (*IMINT* for imagery intelligence, *SIGINT* for signals intelligence, etc.) have taken front stage in western intelligence services. Sophisticated tools, super computers, intelligent software for processing information, sensors, and high-resolution satellite imagery (now commercially available along with a plethora of data-mining tools and geo-spatial information systems for terrain and data fusion) have predominated. Intelligence in its classic form—that of actionable secret information derived from human sources—became scarce.

"Secret operations are essential in war; upon them the army relies to make its every move...An army without secret intelligence is exactly like a man without eyes or ears." Sun Tzu

HUMINT is especially important in discerning terrorist threats, since technical means are a poor indicator of terrorist capabilities and an especially poor indicator of terrorist intentions. Understanding why, when, and how a group may choose to attack requires knowledge of the human and cultural dimension, an understanding of ideas. This understanding can only be gained effectively by information obtained from people in the streets, homes, and social circles of terrorist actors and their supporters—classic espionage and liaison, conducted in partnership and through alliances with police and intelligence services worldwide.

Classical human intelligence gathering is not, however, the only element needed to understand terrorism and emerging threats. All of the technical means, plus others such as open source intelligence (OSINT), *e.g.,* media reportage and public documents, and *CYBERINT* (novel means of exploiting the Internet, *e.g.,* information grid and cyber means such as data-mining and fusion) are equally important. So is incorporating disease surveillance (epidemiological intelligence: *EPI-INTEL*) and consequence management intelligence to understand the interaction between threat, vulnerability, and risk and develop appropriate response plans for civil protection. Together, these disciplines can provide indications and warning, an understanding of trends and potentials, and an assessment of capabilities and intentions to provide viable net assessment for leaders.

Virtually all agree that timely, accurate, reliable, and actionable intelligence is essential. To achieve that charge is often extremely complicated. Essentially, intelligence provides understanding. Sherman Kent, the Yale-educated theoretician and practitioner of the early U.S. intelligence community, would have termed this "knowledge," a knowledge based on an effective relationship between intelligence and its users. As Kent (an OSS veteran who shaped the early CIA and Cold War intelligence practices) noted, there is a need to evolve an understanding of intelligence. Kent viewed intelligence as an analytical discipline that resulted in "all-source" analysis. As a consequence, collection and all source assessment led to a finished product that supports decision-makers. In his view, intelligence production was more than raw collection, but included the collection, evaluation, analysis, integration, and interpretation of all available information to support planning and operations. His view serves as good guidance for negotiating current and future threats. We must also remember that classical human intelligence is a vital piece of this puzzle, one that can't be purged in favor of technical means, however attractive and risk neutral they may initially appear.

As we addressed the Cold War Threat, an understanding of the capabilities and intentions of our adversaries was pursued and largely, if sometimes imperfectly, gained. Yet during the Cold War, Soviet "capabilities" not "intentions" were decisive to Western understanding of the threat. As we enter into what appears to be the decisive conflict of the twenty-first century, a conflict against terrorists and networked global insurgents, we find a pressing need to understand *Jihadi* "intentions"—a sharp contrast to the frequently predictable adversary of the past.

Combating terrorism is the decisive conflict of our time. To succeed we will need to recognize that this conflict is largely an intelligence war. Clandestine and covert services working together with other elements of government such as the military and police will likely be at the cutting edge of domestic and international efforts to contain terrorism and forge domestic and foreign policy and response. To do so, many factors must be balanced. These include balancing foreign and domestic, the "push" and "pull" of intelligence to users, the demand for an immediate "scoop" vs. strategically relevant product, the tension between criminal and intelligence investigations, the balance between sharing and security and, finally, the most important element: the balance between intrusive protection and liberty.

We are at the frontier of this intelligence war. Like Sherman Kent at the formation of the U.S. intelligence community, we must start the dialog to build the craft, discipline, and knowledge necessary to evolve an understanding of intelligence for the conflict of our time. The sooner we resolve these issues and define intelligence for combating post-modern, networked adversaries, the sooner we can thwart the threat and preserve the liberties of Americans and other persons of good will worldwide.

Further Reading

Malcolm W. Nance, *Terrorist Recognition Handbook: A Practitioner's Guide for Predicting and Identifying Terrorist Activities*. 3rd Edition. Boca Raton: CRC Press, 2014.

John P. Sullivan and Alain Bauer, Eds., *Terrorism Early Warning: 10 Years of Achievement in Fighting Terrorism and Crime*. Los Angeles: Los Angeles County Sheriffs Department, October 2008.

Amy Zegart, *Spying Blind: The CIA, the FBI, and the Origins of 9/11*. New York: Princeton University Press, 2007.

Islamic State's Rise and Decline

Daveed Gartenstein-Ross

As of the writing of this essay, the Islamic State (IS) has somewhat passed the peak of its power, and has entered its decline phase. Following IS's remarkable offensive in June 2014 that captured Mosul, Tikrit, and other major Iraqi cities, many observers viewed the group as an unstoppable force; but IS proceeded to make a large number of errors that are now coming back to haunt it. Indeed, one of the group's critical mistakes came just after its spectacular June advance, when IS promptly declared that the longstanding jihadist goal of re-establishing the caliphate had finally been achieved. By declaring that it had established the caliphate, IS staked its legitimacy to the caliphate's continuing viability, thus limiting some of its battlefield options. IS committed a number of other costly errors thereafter, including betraying its alliance partners, constantly opening new fronts in its war, and engaging in the kind of brutal acts that may energize younger sympathizers but that can also stiffen anti-IS resistance.

This essay explores IS's early history before turning to its rise to prominence in 2014. In analyzing IS's rise, the essay examines IS's strategic weaknesses, its battlefield exploits, and its competition with al-Qaeda (AQ). The essay concludes that despite IS's tactical skill, the group is repeating—indeed, exceeding—the same mistakes that it made back when it was known as Al-Qaeda in Iraq and led by the notorious Abu Musab al-Zarqawi. Indeed, IS's extremism may have the perverse effect of allowing AQ to repair its tarnished image in the Middle East by contrasting itself with IS's more radical model. One shouldn't assume that IS will come to ruin—it may remain a significant force for years to come—but its mistakes are already beginning to diminish the organization's strength.

Table: The Islamic State's Various Names
*Adapted from Aaron Zelin, "The War Between
ISIS and al-Qaeda" (2014).*
[NOTE: Despite the group's many name changes, this essay
refers to it as "IS" throughout for ease of reading.]

Name	Dates of Use
Jamaat al-Tawhid wal-Jihad	1999-2004
Al-Qaeda in Iraq (AQI)	2004-2006
Majlis Shura al-Mujahedin	2006
Islamic State of Iraq	2006-2013
Islamic State of Iraq and al-Sham (ISIS)	2013-2014
The Islamic State	2014-present

The Islamic State's Roots

Al-Qaeda in Iraq, IS's predecessor organization, was officially established in 2004 in the midst of the U.S.-led Iraq war, but the group's organizational roots were laid earlier by Zarqawi, a Jordanian with a criminal background who would lead Iraq's first al-Qaeda franchise. Long before the onset of the Iraq war, Zarqawi led the jihadist organization Bayat al-Imam with his mentor, the famous ideologue Abu Muhammad al-Maqdisi. However, Zarqawi ended up sidelining Maqdisi when they were both incarcerated in Jordan. According to a report appearing in the *New York Times*, Zarqawi's actions toward Maqdisi while both were imprisoned "amounted to a coup," as he forced Maqdisi to "hand over control of their group" in return for a merely advisory position.

Zarqawi's early decision to push Maqdisi aside displayed a critical trait that would characterize his leadership and the personality of the organization. The move reveals a streak that is uncompromising, and believes in the inherent superiority of Zarqawi's (and later, Abu Bakr al-Baghdadi's) vision. This outlook resists both criticism and even advice, and is almost entirely unwilling to defer even to respected elders. The parallels are clear between Zarqawi's early treatment of Maqdisi and such later occurrences as his clashes with al-Qaeda's senior leadership, and later IS's military fights with al-Qaeda affiliates and unwillingness to abide by the mediation efforts ordered by the group's senior leadership.

Following Zarqawi's 1999 release from prison as part of a general amnesty, he and a number of his followers traveled to Afghanistan, where Zarqawi connected with al-Qaeda and its then-emir, Osama bin Laden. In an article appearing in *The Atlantic*, Mary Anne Weaver noted that "bin Laden distrusted and disliked al-Zarqawi immediately." There were several reasons for bin Laden's distaste for Zarqawi, including his suspicion that Zarqawi's band had been compromised by Jordanian intelligence, and also Zarqawi's personality. Zarqawi came across, Weaver writes, as "aggressively ambitious, abrasive, and overbearing," and possessed a hatred of Shias that seemed potentially divisive even for a notoriously intolerant organization like al-Qaeda. Yet Zarqawi refused to back down even to bin Laden, reportedly saying, "Shiites should be executed."

Zarqawi established a training camp in Herat, Afghanistan, and reportedly received funds from al-Qaeda during this period. Zarqawi's Herat camp had a population estimated at between 2,000 to 3,000, and was the only training camp in the country to actively recruit from the Levant region.

The U.S.'s October 2001 invasion of Afghanistan prompted Zarqawi to flee the country, but he quickly established a new base of operations in Iran and Iraqi Kurdistan. Zarqawi's forces, now operating under the banner of Jamaat al-Tawhid wal-Jihad, actively recruited and developed a logistical support infrastructure. These efforts would put Zarqawi in a strong position after the March 2003 U.S. invasion of Iraq.

IS in the Iraq War

Following the U.S. invasion, Zarqawi launched a campaign aimed at undermining U.S. reconstruction efforts and inflaming sectarian tensions. His fighters quickly became notorious, including for the highly publicized beheading of American Nicholas Berg. But one of Zarqawi's most brutal—and effective—tactics was his sectarian attacks against Shias. This targeting was designed to provoke Shias to carry out retaliatory killings against Sunnis; if sectarian killings escalated in this way, IS could insert itself as the protector of Sunnis.

IS ultimately experienced stunning success during the Iraq war, but also overplayed its hand. A critical moment in the group's sectarian campaign occurred in February 2006, when IS bombed the Askariya shrine in Samarra, which was so important to Iraq's Shias that Iraqi vice president Adel Abdul Mahdi contextualized the attack as being "as 9/11 is in the United States." Shia reprisals against Sunnis were swift, devastating, and largely indiscriminate. IS's belief that an escalation in sectarian tensions could empower it proved to be correct: The fact that IS came to the fore of the Sunni insurgency during this period of intercommunal violence was verified by insurgents who later changed sides.

Despite bin Laden's dislike of Zarqawi, the latter man deepened his relationship with al-Qaeda before and during the Iraq war, and pledged *bayat* (an oath of allegiance) to bin Laden in October 2004. However, this relationship was fraught with tension, largely caused by the manner in which Zarqawi's organization relished its brutality. Ayman al-Zawahiri, then al-Qaeda's deputy emir, reprimanded Zarqawi for the manner in which he beheaded victims in a letter urging him not to "be deceived by the praise of some of the zealous young men and their description of you as the shaykh of the slaughterers." He warned that these fanatics "do not express the general view of the admirer and the supporter of the resistance in Iraq."

Though this brutality would ultimately undermine IS's efforts in this period, it didn't stop the organization from controlling territory for a sustained period, particularly in Sunni-dominated Anbar province in western Iraq. In fact, IS's control of territory increased even after a June 2006 U.S. airstrike killed Zarqawi in a remote safe house near Baquba. A report written by Colonel Peter Devlin in August 2006 described IS as the "dominant organization of influence" in Anbar province, and said that the group had "become an integral part of the social fabric of western Iraq." Most Anbari Sunnis disliked IS but saw it as an inevitable part of their lives that would be foolish—even dangerous—to oppose.

IS's governance involved the implementation of a harsh version of *sharia* (Islamic law). In Mosul, IS's quixotic understanding of Islamic law reportedly led it to ban the side-by-side display of tomatoes and cucumbers by food vendors, in addition to banning a local bread known as *sammoun*, the use of ice, and the use of electric razors by barbers. These restrictions might be humorous, in a Monty Python-esque fashion, but the punchline was grim: Iraqis were killed or tortured for flouting these rules or defying IS.

In part due to its excesses (in addition to a U.S. troop surge and strategic adaptations on the U.S.'s part), IS's success was short-lived. The jihadist group's brutality prompted a Sunni tribal rebellion. After a few false starts in which IS's nascent opposition was crushed, in September 2006 a number of sheikhs publicly announced their plan to fight IS, calling their movement the *Sahwa*, or "Awakening." Even Sunni Islamist groups felt IS had become too inflexible, and a number of IS's former insurgent allies turned against it, sometimes being incorporated into the *Sahwa*, which was expanded throughout Iraq. At its height, more than 100,000 predominantly Sunni Iraqis participated in this program. This approach degraded IS's capabilities, and the jihadist group lost Anbar province in 2007. By June 2010, Chairman of the Joint Chiefs of Staff Admiral Michael Mullen assessed IS as "devastated."

IS's Resurgence

Although IS suffered considerable personnel losses and experienced a dramatic decline in popular support, the group was able to mount a comeback. Iraq specialist Brian Fishman noted in a 2011 study that IS switched its mode of operation as momentum swung against it, giving up "efforts to control territory and impose governance," and instead adopting "a more traditional terrorist model built on an underground organization and occasional large-scale attacks." IS also took on an increasingly indigenous identity—it was seen as basically foreign during

Zarqawi's reign of terror—and thus grew more adept at exploiting local Sunni grievances.

The group's exploitation of Sunni grievances would prove critical, as the Iraqi government remained dominated by Shias. Many Iraqi Sunnis also perceived the country's security forces as a tool of Shia domination. A further factor that helped IS's ultimate resurgence was the conflict in neighboring Syria, where IS established a reputation as one of the most virulent and capable rebel groups. The Syrian civil war gave IS the ability to control territory in another theater, and gain money and military resources there.

The combination of these two factors could be seen in a stunning offensive that IS carried out at the beginning of January 2014. Sunni dissatisfaction with that sect's treatment boiled over into the establishment of longstanding protest camps decrying sectarianism within the government of Iraq. When the Iraqi government mobilized its military at the beginning of 2014 to clear these camps out, IS mobilized also, capturing large parts of Fallujah and Ramadi. The timing of this IS offensive was significant. Not only were there tactical reasons for striking when the military was clearing Sunnis out of their protest camps—the security forces would be distracted at that moment—but this offensive also symbolically positioned IS as the protector of Iraq's Sunnis.

But in addition to strengthening IS, the Syria war also produced irresolvable tensions between IS and Jabhat al-Nusra (al-Qaeda's Syria affiliate), that would ultimately result in IS's expulsion from the al-Qaeda network. IS announced in April 2013 that it had absorbed Nusra, and Nusra emir Abu Muhammad al-Jawlani promptly issued a statement rejecting this claim. IS increasingly engaged in violent clashes with other rebel groups, including Nusra. Al-Qaeda's senior leadership attempted to foster mediation between IS and Nusra—both of which were branches of al-Qaeda at the time—and though IS paid lip service to the mediation process, in practice it ignored the senior leadership's orders. Eventually al-Qaeda assessed that the costs of maintaining IS as an affiliate outweighed the benefits, and a statement it released in February 2014 officially expelled IS from the organization.

IS's expulsion set off a fierce competition between it and al-Qaeda for supremacy over the global jihadist movement. This competition had begun even prior to IS's expulsion, as in late 2013 IS tried for the first time—while still a branch of al-Qaeda—to feel out whether other al-Qaeda branches would be willing to switch their oaths of loyalty to IS emir Abu Bakr al-Baghdadi. These entreaties became more explicit in May 2014, when IS spokesman Abu Muhammad al-Adnani publicly asked all of al-Qaeda's branches to issue "an official statement" about IS and its approach to jihad. Though none of the branches bit, IS's situation changed significantly in June 2014, when it launched an explosive military advance. IS had already controlled territory, including Raqqa in Syria, but in June IS managed to capture Mosul, Tikrit, and other territory, and then promptly declared at the end of the month that it had reestablished the caliphate. With IS's declaration of the caliphate's return, the group's calls for other jihadist groups to align with it became even more explicit: IS spokesman Abu Muhammad al-Adnani said in the declaration that "the legality of all emirates, groups, states, and organizations, becomes null by the expansion of the khilafah's authority."

The vast majority of contemporaneous public commentary on the competition between IS and AQ agreed that IS appeared to be the future of transnational jihadism, well on its way to surpassing AQ: IS had, after all, followed up on its audacious rampage through Iraq by announcing that it had achieved the dream of restoring the caliphate for which the transnational jihadist movement had long strived. Yet, although IS continued to make some gains thereafter, its continued advances also produced some of the mistakes that would ultimately weaken IS. In August 2014, IS launched a surprise attack on Iraq's Kurdish region at a time when the Kurdish Regional Government's *peshmerga* forces hadn't been fighting it, and immediately embarked on a systematic campaign of genocide against the Yazidis—a minority religious sect that posed no military threat to the self-proclaimed caliphate. This move would ultimately draw far more foes to the theater, including the United States, other Western countries, and some Sunni Arab states.

Even IS's successes provoked overreach by this organization that would eventually severely limit it.

Conclusion: The Islamic State's Errors and Decline

IS's June offensive is almost certainly the most brilliant military advance ever made by a violent non-state actor—yet, at the same time, the majority of commentators weighing in on IS's future overestimated its strengths while failing to acknowledge its significant weaknesses. Even at the apex of its power, IS's status was reminiscent of where the group stood from 2005-07, during the Zarqawi era and just after. At that time, many Western analysts thought that Zarqawi's organization had eclipsed Osama bin Laden's in power and reputation. Similar to IS today, Zarqawi was extraordinarily popular with young jihadists, and shocked the world with his brutality. Indeed, IS today parallels Zarqawi, and yet exceeds him, in virtually every way: controlling more territory and resources, and inflicting even more brutal excesses on its victims. Zarqawi's approach, as explained earlier in this essay, ultimately backfired, helping to prompt an uprising against the group— and tarnishing AQ's global brand. In addition to the potential for its brutality to backfire, IS made other errors almost from the outset.

The dangers of fighting a two-front war are fundamental to military strategy, and the Islamic State surrounded itself with enemies. It at first entered Syria, back when it was still part of AQ's network, to allegedly fight against Bashar al-Assad's regime, yet it spent more time skirmishing with other rebel groups than with Assad's forces. This didn't stop the Islamic State's June 2014 *blitzkrieg* into Iraq, which earned the group another set of formidable foes: not only the Iraqi state but also Iran and the Shia militias it supports. Despite this wide array of enemies, the Islamic State almost immediately betrayed its partners in early July by rounding up ex-Baathist leaders in Mosul who had aided their advance. And with its hands already full with opponents, the militant group's next move was to open a brand new front: attacking the Kurdish Regional Government, slaughtering the Yazidis, and drawing the United States and anti-IS coalition to the theater.

Because IS's decisions have put the group in a position where it is perpetually at war on all sides, the group needs to attract a constant flow of recruits. As such, IS needs to maintain the appearance that it has momentum. Efforts to maintain this appearance have proven costly: It poured far more resources into efforts to take the strategically insignificant city of Kobane in northern Syria, and to hold the Bayji oil refinery, than would have been justified on the merits. Despite (or perhaps because of) these maximum efforts that flew in the face of good strategy, by the beginning of December 2014 the Islamic State's loss of momentum was increasingly obvious. By that time, the group hadn't made significant territorial gains since mid-October, and was plagued by growing local resistance, defections, and loss of territory and revenue.

It is, in fact, likely that IS's power peaked in August 2014, just before the United States and coalition forces were drawn into the conflict. The group remains dangerous and, even in a weakened state, it is capable of taking thousands upon thousands of lives. IS still has a few opportunities to regain momentum, both in Iraq and also internationally. One of the main avenues the group is pursuing is attempting to harness its remaining financial might to convince regional jihadist organizations to pledge their allegiance (*bayat*) to it. Sinai-based Ansar Bayt al-Maqdis's public proclamation of *bayat* to IS on November 10, 2014 is likely the most significant success that IS has achieved in this regard to date and, if IS can move other important regional groups into its camp, that would give the caliphate a more optimistic outlook. But even if IS is unable to correct its course, its decline in no way constitutes the end of jihadism in Iraq and Syria: It seems that Iraq is still only taking half-measures to satisfy Sunni concerns, while the conflict in Syria continues to cause the loss of innocent life on a massive scale and thus provide fertile ground for jihadist groups to flourish. Other militant Islamic groups may gain as IS falters.

There are lessons in IS's rise about the immense importance of violent non-state actors to twenty-first century conflict. And, in its decline, there are lessons about how quickly strategic errors can weaken these groups.

Further Reading

Richard Barrett, *The Islamic State*. New York: The Soufan Group, November 2014.

Brian Fishman, *Redefining the Islamic State: The Fall and Rise of Al-Qaeda in Iraq*. Washington, DC: New America Foundation, 2011.

United Nations Assistance Mission for Iraq Human Rights Office, *Report on the Protection of Civilians in Armed Conflict in Iraq: 6 July – 10 September 2014*. New York, 2014.

Killing of Osama bin Laden

Robert J. Bunker

The first hint outside U.S. government circles that an effort was underway to secure Osama bin Laden was revealed as a Twitter feed by Sohaib Athar, a 33-year-old IT consultant in Abbottabad, Pakistan over the night of May 1-2, 2011. He posted, "Helicopter hovering above Abbottabad at 1AM (is a rare event)." The "tweet" appeared simultaneously all over the world with a timestamp just after 4:00 p.m. in Washington, DC. News media outlets soon picked up the live reporting of low-flying aircraft and explosions in a sleepy Pakistani military town prompting President Barack Obama to formally announce the death of Osama bin Laden a few hours later at 11:35pm on May 1.

Bin Laden had largely disappeared after the attacks of September 11, 2001. The quick U.S. response sending investigators and special forces to Afghanistan by mid-October led to the quick collapse of the government of the Taliban—his hosts in Afghanistan. Jihadist forces comprised of Taliban and al Qaida fighters were largely routed although some remaining forces protecting bin Laden were pushed to the Pakistan border. Bin Laden took advantage of an operational pause to escape from the battle of Tora Bora, Afghanistan in December 2001 and his whereabouts were largely unknown in the west thereafter.

The interdigitation of ethnic tribes straddling the Afghanistan-Pakistan border proved to be a nagging obstacle to U.S. efforts locating bin Laden and fighting a resurgent Taliban over the following decade. While U.S. and allied forces were required to recognize the international boundaries separating the two countries to maintain a productive relationship with Pakistan, militants could traverse the frontiers with impunity and the support of local populations. U.S. efforts in Afghanistan under the name Operation Enduring Freedom required close cooperation with Pakistan to ensure overflight and the use of strategically important supply routes from the key port of Karachi to reach the landlocked battlefield. Bin Laden effectively used the cover of ethnic alliances, religious fervor, and rich geographical diversity to give credence to denials by Pakistani security and political leadership of any knowledge that the 9/11 mastermind had lived in their midst for half a decade.

By August 2010, the intelligence community began to zero in on a location for bin Laden upon identification of Abu Ahmed al-Kuwaiti, bin Laden's trusted courier. They tracked al-Kuwaiti to an odd and very private residence in Abbottabad, Pakistan, approximately 70 miles north of the capitol, Islamabad. By March 14, 2011, confidence regarding the intelligence was growing and President Obama convened a National Security Council meeting to identify and discuss a range of options including capturing or even killing bin Laden. Choices ranged from close cooperation with Pakistan's intelligence and counterterrorism forces, a drone strike, a paramilitary strike, or a U.S. military special forces operation. Subsequent senior level meetings with the President narrowed the focus to a rapid military assault and extraction plan. The operational details were then finalized, the team fully trained, and the final decision made by President Obama on April 30, 2011.

The mission was given the name Operation Neptune Spear. Technically, it was designated a kill-or-capture mission since the strike team was trained and prepared to take bin Laden alive if he had raised his hands to surrender or otherwise didn't present a threat to the team. Nonetheless, under the rules of engagement, the special forces were given authority to kill him and respond to gunfire and hostile acts. The next day Central Intelligence Agency Director, Leon Panetta authorized the operational order early Sunday afternoon May 1, Washington DC time/late evening in Pakistan to launch the mission.

Soon after, a Navy team of 23 SEALs and supported by an interpreter and a dog prepared to depart from a base in Jalalabad, Afghanistan in Black Hawk helicopters to fly 150 miles east. The aircraft featured special paint and flew low to reduce their visibility to Pakistani radar. The total flight took approximately 90 minutes to reach the compound in Abbatabad. This was followed shortly by three large twin-rotor Chinook helicopters carrying support teams and refueling bladders for use by the

Black Hawks on a hilltop for the return trip. The mission was supported by an RQ-170 Sentinel stealth drone overhead, used to provide a video feed in real-time to regional commanders and the White House.

The strike team arrived at the outskirts of Abbatabad under a moonless sky to find that the electricity to much of the neighborhood surrounding the compound had been cut. The first Black Hawk crash-landed in the courtyard despite extensive training, but the crew and pilot were able to disembark without significant injuries. The second aircraft landed safely outside the walls, requiring the team to breach the gate in order to enter the compound. Meanwhile, the dog and its handler were deployed to track any inhabitants who escaped the compound, to locate hidden facilities, and to keep onlookers at bay.

The team first encountered the Kuwaiti courier who lived in a one-story residence separated by a wall from the three-story home of bin Laden and his family. The courier was armed and thus killed first while his wife was wounded. Soon after, his brother and his wife were also killed. The SEALs then entered the larger building rushing past two of bin Laden's wives and all the children on the lower floors. The assault then used explosives to breach a locked metal gate leading upstairs with explosives. Team members encountered and shot and killed bin Laden's 23 year old son Khalid. Bin Laden and SEAL members then made eye contact before bin Laden retreated to his bedroom. His wife, Amal, jumped in front of bin Laden, was pushed aside, and shot in the leg. Bin Laden was then shot in the chest and head. All told, four men including Osama bin Laden were killed, one woman was killed, and two other women injured.

Within 30 minutes of his death, bin Laden's body was brought downstairs, the helicopter was wired for destruction, and computers, cell phones, DVDs, computer disks, hard drives and thumb drives were collected for later exploitation. Throughout the mission, the compound was secured by four SEALs patrolling with the dog and overhead video-feed from the drone.

Digital photos of bin Laden were taken and sent back for digital facial recognition and tissue samples were secured for later DNA testing. One of the large Chinook helicopters then arrived and picked up the remaining SEALS, bin Laden's body, and the confiscated computer and electronic equipment. When the Chinook landed back at Jalalabad, observers noted that the full operation had taken less than four hours to complete.

Bin Laden's body was subsequently transferred to Bagram air base, approximately 65 miles away. There the body was washed, wrapped, placed in a V-22 Osprey aircraft and transported to the U.S.S. Carl Vinson in the Arabian Sea. He was buried at sea within twelve hours of his death. Pakistani officials arrived at the compound shortly after the SEAL team departed to discover surviving women and children, gunfire damage, and a remnant of the tail section of the Black Hawk helicopter which was returned to the U.S. sometime later.

The Pakistani government subsequently created the Abbottabad Commission to investigate the circumstances surrounding the death of Osama bin Laden. A formal 700-page classified report was submitted to the Pakistan Prime Minister on January 4, 2013 but eventually released by media outlet *Al Jazeera* on July 8, 2013. The Commission's report determined bin Laden had entered Pakistan in mid-2002 after narrowly escaping capture in the battle of Tora Bora in Afghanistan. It concluded that bin Laden had lived in six different locations within Pakistan over nine years. The first few years he had been in South Waziristan and northern Swat Valley, but ultimately moved to the Abbatabad compound in 2005.

Due in part to his isolation, bin Laden's al-Qaida had begun to fade from the world stage. The group had not been successful in launching a significant terror attack after the London subway and bus bombings in July 2005. Another Pakistani group, Lashkar e-Tayyiba, took credit for the complex Mumbai terrorist attack in India in 2008 which included Indian, Jewish, and American targets. The affiliate group, al-Qaida in the Arabian Peninsula, had plotted unsuccessful aviation attacks utilizing underwear explosives in 2009 and computer printer cartridges in 2010, securing and keeping the attention of Western intelligence and security officials. Finally, it seems likely that bin Laden was aware that the Arab Spring which had begun in Tunisia and Algeria in December 2010 and subsequent protests spreading to Oman, Yemen, Egypt, Syria, and Morocco in January 2011 were changing the political landscape.

In response to his death, within a week al-Qaida officially confirmed the loss of bin Laden on a jihadist website where the group's media arm had regularly posted its propaganda in the past. By mid-June 2011, the group proclaimed bin Laden's deputy, Ayman al-Zawahiri had ascended to lead the group now low in morale, gutted in manpower, and struggling to recast itself as the small corporate headquarters for the global terrorism franchise movement.

Upon reflection, the SEAL mission against Osama bin Laden turned out to last as long as the 9/11 terrorist attack. In fact, after all the international media coverage and the formal announcement by President Obama, Sohaib Athar returned to his Twitter account. Approximately eight hours after his first note, he wrote "Uh oh, now I'm the guy who live blogged the Osama raid without knowing it."

Further Reading

Peter L. Bergen, *Manhunt: The Ten-Year Search for Bin Laden from 9/11 to Abbottabad*. New York: Crown Publishers, 2012.

Mark Bowden, *The Finish: The Killing of Osama bin Laden*. New York: Atlantic Monthly Press, 2012.

Seth G. Jones, *Hunting in the Shadows: The Pursuit of al Qa'ida since 9/11*. New York: W.W. Norton & Company, New York: 2012.

Martyrdom

Rick Y. Byrum

The decision to die is both repulsive and fascinating. We judge martyrs to be superior mortal, and, in the next breath, take flight in questioning their claim to our esteem. Paradoxically, martyrs are profoundly vulnerable creatures who at the same time are in absolute control of their own existence. They look into the future and seek to influence it—either in this life or the next. Their resolve is to transform death from a final act into a new beginning, to attach substance to pure negation. Thus, the martyr facing the threshold is placed in a peculiarly exposed position. Death, like any other human endeavor, is an art, and if martyrs are to prevail as artists, they must die exceptionally well.

The concepts of martyrdom and the Holy struggle in the cause of God have their roots in various ancient writings. Out of the ideological encounter between Hellenism and Judaism emerged the concept of martyrdom as an instrument of religious warfare. The Jews may not have invented Western martyrdom—that credit goes to Socrates and Plato—but they were certainly the first to use it as a means of national inspiration and to endow its hideous suffering with eschatological purpose.

Martyr means to witness: to see the truth and be prepared to testify beyond a verbal declaration. Although we connote the word "martyr" with essentially Christian philosophies, its usage reflects the late-classical spirit of divinity, where early Christian ideas about martyrdom were heavily derivative of lessons of Judea. In early Christianity, suicide was often regarded as a virtuous act. The Romans may have fed people to the wild animals of the coliseums for sport, but they were not ready for the fact that Christians welcomed these animals as vehicles of God's glory and salvation.

The benefits of martyrdom are not restricted to the gifts attended in heaven; martyrs throughout time have become posthumous heroes on earth. Their present anguish is a dress rehearsal for their final act on earth's stage.

Today, we see too often in the media the torn and charred bits and pieces of martyrs' corpses venerated as relics more precious than jewels. The theatre of their suicidal, martyristic performance is now considered sacred ground. The moment our communities begin to classify and define its martyrs, a dilemma arises out of the ash; how do we differentiate between the contexts of religion, social justice, politics, or simply one's faith?

The concept of "martyr" within the Palestinian world established itself through the British Mandate, where Zionism began to threaten the existence of the Palestinian people in their homeland. These martyrs of today have a ready stage on which to display their self-control and superiority: the media. They thrive on publicity; it is essential to the process whereby common individuals move in the imagination of others and attract the attention of history. Human bombs are those who are more devoted to the cause of justice than they are to life.

Martyrs focus on violating the most revered and treasured abstractions that shape and create a society, the things that give soul or personality symbolic vigor. So they strike at ties of loyalty, allegiance, and sense of collective security, while at the same time they defy what the ruling class defines in society as justice, mercy, honor, love, and duty. The hallmark of the martyr is often their uncommon valor; they stand out from the others, manifesting an inner drive and conviction, which gives credence and strength to their cause. Unstable societies experiencing a process of cultural, economic, and political restructuring obviously will generate their own martyrs for a cause. Essential to martyrdom is the hallmark placed on the individual and the heroic act. If the presence of the divine is not attainable, some other secular ideology will fill the scales to substitute the two players of man and cause. The key to martyrdom is the link between life and death.

Further Reading

Mia Bloom, *Dying to Kill: The Allure of Suicide Terror*. New York: Columbia University Press, 2007.

Mohammed Hafez, *Suicide Bombers in Iraq: The Strategy and Ideology of Martyrdom*. Washington, DC: United States Institute of Peace, 2007.

Ami Pedahzur, *Root Causes of Suicide Terrorism*. London: Routledge, 2006.

Mumbai's Swarming Attack

Prem Mahadevan

What happened on the night of 26 November 2008 was unlike any terrorist attack that India's commercial capital had seen. Ten jihadists from the Pakistani group Lashkar-e-Taiba (LeT), armed with assault rifles, grenades, improvised explosive devices, and global positioning systems, landed on the city shoreline in a rubber dinghy. Dividing into 'buddy pairs', they dispersed towards their target, to begin a coordinated shooting rampage that would end 60 hours later, when the last of them were killed by Indian security forces. But within the first twelve hours of their landing over 160 civilians had been cornered and gunned down in luxury hotels, side-streets, and railway platforms.

In statistical terms, '26/11' was only the third-deadliest terrorist attack in Mumbai's history. A total of 166 civilians and 18 security forces personnel were killed and 304 persons injured. In contrast, fifteen years earlier, 257 people had died in eleven synchronized bombings (in an eerie prelude to the 2008 attack, the bombings had originally been planned to occur alongside shooting sprees, but the gunmen lost their nerve on that occasion). Then, in 2006, 181 commuters had died when bombs ripped apart seven local trains. In these two attack waves, the number of persons injured was around 700 and 900, respectively. Investigators later found strong evidence of Pakistani involvement; in the case of the 1993 bombings extending to top military officials. *Thus, high-casualty terrorism originating from Pakistani territory was not a new phenomenon as far as the Mumbai police were concerned.*

What was new was the employment of a firearms-centric attack pattern that forced the police to cope with a dynamic and fluid situation in real-time, rather than waiting until after the crisis had stabilized to begin reacting. Although bombings were not unusual in India, suicidal assaults certainly were. The country's strict gun laws had made 'active shooter' threats hypothetical—only in the disturbed northern province of Jammu and Kashmir, bordering Pakistan, did such incidents occur frequently. Elsewhere in India, terrorist incidents involving firearms would take the form of 'shoot and scoot' affairs, wherein gunmen would briefly pour automatic fire into a crowded area before fleeing. Even these were rare: out of thirty jihadist attacks during the period 2000-2008, only six (20%) had involved the use of firearms, producing a total of 73 fatalities (less than 10% of a grand total of 771).

Adaptation Failure

Seen from this perspective, one can understand why the Mumbai police were not prepared to meet a multi-pronged assault by suicidal terrorists. 26/11 was a paradigm-changing event, in which the vast bulk of civilian fatalities were caused by gunshot wounds rather than bomb fragments. The attack was not merely an incident of terrorism, but an ongoing crisis with both national and international ramifications, the likes of which the city police had never seen. As a result, they initially did not recognize it for what it was, and assumed that the shooting was part of a gang war.

When living memory does not cover a specific type of event, the possibility of its occurrence tends to be underrated in threat analysis. At Mumbai, the game-changer had been LeT's innovative use of marine infiltration to transport an attack team directly to the city shoreline, bypassing the heavily-guarded India-Pakistan land border. Although the police had received at least six intelligence alerts that an attack might be launched from the sea, they could not exploit these because there was no tactical concept from which the warnings' urgency could be gauged. Nobody knew that Israel had been similarly blindsided by a sea-borne raid in 1975, with devastating consequences. (Interestingly, Israeli police too believed at first that the firing was part of a turf war between rival gangs.)

The Mumbai police were experienced in combating organized crime (mostly through sharpshooters who would pursue and neutralize mobsters on the basis of specific intelligence). But there was no capability for urban warfare or hostage rescue. Even the 450-man Anti-Terrorist

Squad (ATS) had no expertise on these issues, being merely a subunit of the 44,000-strong civilian police force. The capability gap might be explained by the ethos of Indian policing, which has long held that 'military' firepower should not be wielded by a 'civilian' force. During the 1980s, this logic had been responsible for hundreds of fatalities in the border province of Punjab, as policemen used bolt-action rifles to confront Kalashnikov-wielding terrorists supported by Pakistan. Eventually, the police leadership in Punjab had recognized that upgrading the weaponry available to first responders was essential, if terrorist violence was to be contained. However, other provinces were slow to adapt to the threat of cross-border terrorism, because they felt that their physical distance from Pakistan obviated such a step. Maharashtra (the province of which Mumbai is the capital) was one of these.

In contrast, LeT prepared extensively for the attack. It carried out two years of preparatory reconnaissance, using an American passport holder as a scout. The ten gunmen were selected after intense physical and psychological testing at the group's training facilities across northern Pakistan. Assault tactics were taught by members of Zarrar Company, the Pakistani army's counterterrorist hostage rescue team (which had dramatically raised the operational sophistication of LeT). Communications networks extending to Europe and North America were set up to mask the origins of the attack. A boat was purchased to carry the gunmen into international waters. Lastly, a command centre was set up in the city of Karachi, from where the attack's progress could be monitored in real-time and the 'buddy pairs' directed accordingly. All told, it is estimated that 26/11 cost the group at least U.S.$ 930,000. Against this backdrop, it appears that while LeT adapted heavily to the logistics and training requirements of a sea-borne suicide raid, the Indian security apparatus did not understand the implications of its own intelligence reporting and did not prepare to meet the raid.

Outline of Events

The ten terrorists landed on the southern shoreline of Mumbai at around 2015 hours on 26th November 2008. South Mumbai is the city's business quarter. The attack planners had chosen it because massacres here would kill a large number of high-net-worth individuals and foreign tourists. Before heading off towards their respective targets, the five 'buddy pairs' agreed that they would all open fire simultaneously at 2140 hours. A healthy time buffer was allowed, to budget for any delays in traffic.

Two of the pairs hailed taxis while the others walked towards their objectives, using GPS sets for orientation. Inside the taxis, one man engaged the driver in conversation while the other placed an improvised explosive device on the car floor. The device was timed to detonate well after the terrorists had alighted at their destinations and commenced firing. It was expected that the Mumbai police would be utterly confused and demoralized when reports began pouring in about car-bombs across the city, at a time when other reports indicated firearms assaults at public locations.

Two of the gunmen were to storm a Jewish cultural centre, named Nariman House, and seize the Israeli nationals who lived there, as well as any visitors. Another two would attack the city's main railway station, gunning down as many commuters as possible and then making their way to a posh residential area nearby, where they were to seize hostages. A third pair was to attack the Oberoi-Trident Hotel, shooting anyone they initially saw and then capturing hotel guests. The fourth pair was to storm into the Taj Palace and Tower Hotel, Mumbai's most iconic building. Finally, the last pair was to open fire at a popular tourist café located close to the Taj, before running down a sidestreet to join their comrades in the hotel. All four would then proceed to shoot down hotel staff and guests and seize hostages. The teams would be in constant contact with the Karachi command centre, which would feed them tactical information about the Indian security response, based on television news reports. The command centre would also instruct all teams on what to do with their hostages.

The Initial Police Response

As agreed, all five buddy pairs opened fire roughly around 2140 hours. Each gunman carried a Kalashnikov and eight magazines (total 240 rounds), a sidearm with three magazines, eight grenades, and one improvised explosive device. Two IEDs had been planted in the taxis used to reach their targets, while the others were placed at various chokepoints that would be used by first responders.

The police reaction was prompt but uncoordinated. At the railway station, half a dozen constables and inspectors armed with revolvers and five-shot bolt-action rifles tried to face off against two expertly-trained marksmen who swiftly eliminated them. The policemen, having not fired their weapons in years (in one case, decades) could not land a single hit. Having massacred 58 people in the main arrivals hall, the two terrorists left the station and walked through the streets, shooting anyone they saw. They first entered a hospital, killed some staff and patients, and then ambushed a police vehicle that was rushing towards the scene. While doing this, they scored a massive but unexpected success: among those killed in the vehicle was the head of the Mumbai Anti-Terrorist Squad. Leaving his body on the road, they took over the vehicle and drove around, shooting at pedestrians. After a while, they switched vehicles by hijacking a private car and continued driving until finally stopped at a police roadblock. In the ensuing firefight, one terrorist was killed and the other captured.

At the Oberoi-Trident and Taj Palace and Tower Hotels, the police arrived within fifteen minutes of the first shots being fired. However, in the confusion, it took more than an hour for them to react to reports of additional firing at Nariman House, a building that few had heard of. During this time, the police control room was swamped with 'sightings' of armed terrorists on every street corner, leading to an initial estimate that as many as 60 jihadists might have invaded Mumbai. In total, 1365 emergency calls were made to the police between 2130 and 0200 hours on the night of 26-27th November. Midway through this period, at around 2235, the two taxi-borne IEDs detonated within five minutes of each other but 25 kilometres apart. Then, just past midnight, came the stunning news that the ATS chief had been killed. It was at this point that police morale collapsed totally.

Later, it would become clear to investigators that the terrorists who shot the ATS chief had no idea who he was. But at the time, through the 'fog of war' it looked as though his killing was targeted and deliberate. By 0030 hours on 27th November, it was clear that the police lacked the training and weaponry to handle such a complex crisis on their own. Only six lightly-armed policemen had entered the Taj Hotel, even as the four terrorists inside were executing staff and guests. At the Oberoi-Trident, the police had established a security perimeter but, stunned by IED and grenade explosions near the building's entrance, did not venture further. At Nariman House, they could not advance because the terrorists occupied excellent firing positions in the building's upper floors. A decision was therefore made to request immediate help from local detachments of the Indian Army and Navy. Concurrently, assistance was also sought from the National Security Guard (NSG), India's elite counterterrorist hostage rescue force, which was based near Delhi, far in the north of the country.

The Army responded by deploying several columns of infantry around the affected sites. Since these troops had no training for close-quarter battle, they could not be used to directly engage the terrorists or evacuate trapped civilians. These twin tasks fell to the Indian Navy's Marine Commandos (MARCOS). Three teams, totaling about sixty men, deployed from a naval base on the far side of Mumbai's harbour, reaching the combat zone by 0200 hours on 27th November. Without having the benefit of a floor plan or an intelligence briefing, the MARCOS rushed headlong into the two hotels towards the sound of gunfire. At Nariman House, they were ordered to assist the police in evacuating nearby apartments, whose inhabitants were being fired upon by the terrorists.

The Specialists Take Over

The MARCOS' intervention at the Taj Hotel was one of the few successes of the tragedy that had engulfed Mumbai. Twenty men, operating in near-total darkness without night-vision devices or their full complement of body armour, took on four terrorists who had by then gotten to know the layout of the hotel intimately. When the two sides first exchanged shots (around 0230 hours), the terrorists had been looking for a large banquet hall where more than 200 civilians were hiding. They had learned of its existence thanks to live telephone interviews that those inside had given to news agencies. During the subsequent firefight, the MARCOS focused on securing an evacuation route for the civilians, rather than chasing the terrorists. Meanwhile, the latter, sensing that this was the first serious counter-attack from Indian security forces, disappeared into the labyrinthine passageways of the Taj Hotel. All those trapped inside the banquet hall were moved to safety, although some were injured.

Given their limited manpower, the MARCOS could not begin a full-scale search and evacuation of the two hotels, both of which numbered approximately 650 guest bedrooms. Furthermore, the Taj Palace and Tower Hotel and Oberoi-Trident Hotel were each subdivided into two separate buildings, connected by a series of passages. Clearing them would take many days, even for a much larger force. The MARCOS therefore focused on blocking the connecting passages, to ensure that the terrorists' freedom of movement would be restricted to just one building at each site. In doing so, they contained the level of damage and casualties. At the Taj, the four terrorists were confined to the Palace wing of the hotel, while the two terrorists at the Oberoi-Trident were confined to the Oberoi. By the time the National Security Guard arrived from Delhi, the situation had partly stabilized. All guests who had not already been killed or evacuated were barricaded in their rooms, awaiting the arrival of rescue teams.

The NSG began room clearance operations at around 0900 hours on the morning of 27th November. Each guestroom took an average of five to seven minutes to sanitize, depending on whether those inside cooperated with the instructions that were shouted at them. It goes to the credit of the NSG and the hotel staff that these clearance operations, despite their nerve-wracking nature, did not produce a single civilian fatality. NSG troopers went to considerable risks to ensure that uncooperative guests were not harmed, realising that their sense of suspicion was only natural. Subsequently, several Western guests, when debriefed by the intelligence agencies of their respective countries, made a point of mentioning the professionalism with which the NSG handled evacuation efforts.

There were still mistakes made, however. At the Taj Palace, the NSG experienced difficulties with tactical coordination because the force's handheld VHF radios did not work properly within the building's thick stone walls. The standard night-vision devices issued to the troopers were of the passive variety, and could not function in complete darkness. Given that the terrorists had set fire to the hotel's upper floors and shorted the electrical system, much of the building was pitch-black. On a number of occasions, the NSG and the terrorists stumbled onto each other; the latter would immediately open fire and flee. Since the NSG operated in five-man house intervention teams (called HITs) which were dispersed throughout the hotel, it did not have enough firepower at any single time to pin down the terrorists whenever they were sighted. During one of these chance engagements the NSG lost an officer, who got separated from his men and was ambushed by the terrorists. At Nariman House, a similar loss occurred because of live broadcasting of an NSG heli-borne assault onto the building's roof. The LeT's Karachi control room immediately warned the two gunmen hiding inside about the assault and they were able to kill an NSG trooper as he attempted a dynamic entry.

Combining Success and Failure

Even today, it is hard to know for sure if Indian security forces 'succeeded' in preventing multiple hostage sieges across Mumbai, or 'failed' to prevent multiple massacres. Both possibilities might be true: barring Nariman House, at no other location did the police, MARCOS or NSG have to deal with the complicating element of human shields in a prolonged standoff. Anyone whom the terrorists came across in the hotels or on the streets was killed, either immediately or shortly after capture. An argument can be thus made that the swift initial response of the Mumbai police, coupled with the efficiency with which hotel staff alerted their guests, pre-empted other hostage-takings.

Even at Nariman House, the terrorists were not interested in negotiations. After making a brief demand for the release of their captured comrade, they killed all the hostages. Later, U.S. and Indian investigators confirmed that the executions had been carried out upon instructions from Karachi. LeT had hoped that the Indian government would be blamed internationally for the deaths of foreign nationals. In this, the group was partially successful—not until much later did it become known that the hostages' deaths had occurred *before* the Indian security forces launched their counterattack to retake the building. By the time the entire sequence of events had been reconstructed, several months later, the Indian security establishment had taken considerable criticism for alleged ineptitude.

In conclusion, it seems that 26/11 was a severe indictment of the failure of successive Indian governments at both national and provincial levels to take the threat of cross-border terrorism seriously. The biggest deficiencies were in police preparedness and crisis leadership. After the death of the ATS chief, the force was paralyzed even though it could have regained the initiative. Some junior officers, who had experience of counterinsurgency, tried to confront the terrorists. However, they were denied permission to act on fleeting tactical advantages.

In contrast, the MARCOS and NSG did as well as could be expected, given the inherent limitations that they worked under, as extraneous forces operating on a contingency basis rather than as part of a planned response. Yet, even these forces were handicapped by logistical weaknesses, which limited the number of shooters deployed at any single location, and by equipment shortages/failures. They also operated on a stand-alone basis, rather than in partnership with each other.

Since 2008, there have been substantial upgrades to the weaponry and training of Indian security forces. New NSG bases have been established to reduce reaction time. Improved liaison arrangements for calling out military commandos in aid of civil authority would ensure a faster and more aggressive counterattack to future terrorist raids. But despite all these measures, protective systems would in themselves not suffice to prevent another massacre from occurring. For that, India needs to get proactive about neutralizing terrorist planners in Pakistan.

Further Reading

Harinder Baweja, Ed., *26/11: Mumbai Attacked*. New Delhi: Roli, 2009.

The Indian Express Team, *Inside 26/11*. New Delhi: Rupa, 2009.

John Wilson, *The Caliphate's Soldiers: The Lashkar-e-Tayyeba's Long War*. New Delhi: Amaryllis, 2011.

Narcoterrorism

Irina A. Chindea

For supporting end note information pertaining to this essay, contact the author.

Narcoterrorism is an umbrella term that refers to the violent actions performed at the intersection of terrorism and drug trafficking by a variety of actors, be they state or non-state armed groups, in distinct geo-political contexts over time, and which threaten democracy and the rule of law. Many scholars and experts consider the term to be vague and unclear by nature.

The term was introduced in 1983 by Peruvian president Belaunde Terry in connection to the terrorist-like attacks that the Maoist guerrilla group, the Shining Path (Sendero Luminoso), conducted against the country's counter-narcotics police, which was investigating the group's ties to cocaine traffickers.

The term combines two threats that traditionally have been approached independently: terrorism and narco-trafficking. According to Emma Bjornehed, by bringing together two disparate concepts such as terrorism and drug trafficking, the definition of narcoterrorism ends up being "almost dual in character," and depends on where the emphasis is placed, either on the drug or the terrorism aspect of the term. While greater consensus exists on what constitutes drug trafficking (*"the illicit movement of prohibited drugs across international borders by individuals, groups or states for financial gain"*), there is less agreement on the definition of "terrorism" due to the political connotation of the term in the literature. Consequently, this ambiguity echoes into the definition of narcoterrorism. For the term to meet the definitional standards of "terrorism," it needs to refer to violence in the sense of hijacking, a bombing, or an assassination intended to induce fear in order to coerce an audience into acceding to political demands. Hence, besides a minimal definition of narcoterrorism as *"a group action that combines terrorism with some aspect of the narcotics trade,"* there is no universally accepted definition of the term.

This raises the natural question of whether narcoterrorists are drug traffickers who use terrorist tactics to advance their profit-making goals, or whether they are *"first and foremost terrorists who happen to use drug money to further their cause."* A review of the literature on the topic shows that throughout the past three decades the term has been employed when referring to both types of situations. Prior to the 9/11 attacks, references to narcoterrorism translated into the two phenomena—terrorism and drug trafficking— being mainly addressed as separate issues and through a law enforcement perspective. However, after 9/11, the two have been increasingly perceived as intertwined and approached as such.

Throughout recent history, narcoterrorism has come in different forms and has been performed by a wide range of actors with disparate goals. Authors like Vetter and Perlstein (1991) divided narcoterrorism into two parts: <u>free-lance</u> and <u>state-sponsored</u>.

- Free-lance narcoterrorism refers to the autonomous involvement of terrorist or insurgent organizations into various aspects of the drug business due to its very lucrative nature that allows them to gain financial power and further their political goals.
- State sponsored narcoterrorism refers to the overt or covert state support of revolutionary groups, illegal drug traders, and arms smugglers by governments that aim to change or destabilize the political system in a target country.

Alongside the distinction between free-lance and state-sponsored narcoterrorism, the term refers to three main types of violence that link terrorist tactics and the trafficking in narcotics:

1. The direct or indirect involvement of insurgent and terrorist organizations into the drug trade to further their political goals.

2. The use by drug trafficking organizations of terrorist tactics to protect the illicit traffic in narcotics and to further their profit-motivated goals.
3. The overt or covert support some governments may provide to non-state armed groups that engage in both terrorist tactics and the smuggling of illicit drugs to foment change in the political system of rival states.

1. The direct or indirect involvement of insurgent and terrorist organizations into the drug trade

At this point, it is necessary to point out to the distinction between insurgent and terrorist groups. The simplified definition of terrorism on which this article relies is: *"premeditated, politically motivated violence perpetrated against noncombatant targets."* This implies a distinction between terrorism and other forms of political violence such as insurgency, which may include terrorist tactics, but need not necessarily do so. This is the point where the use of the term narcoterrorism in relation to insurgent groups becomes controversial. According to certain scholars and experts, "if the distinctions between terrorism and insurgency have any meaning, [...] then whatever the term 'narcoterrorism' means it cannot be used in relation to insurgencies" unless the latter engage in terror tactics to further their political goals. Hence, the use of the term "narcoterrorism" is more appropriate in connection to those insurgent groups that use terror tactics to advance their political agenda.

This approach to narcoterrorism is the one prevailing within the United States Drug Enforcement Administration (DEA) which states that "narco-terrorism may be characterized by the participation of groups or associated individuals in taxing, providing security for, or otherwise aiding or abetting drug trafficking endeavors in an effort to further, or fund, terrorist activities." Based on this definition of narcoterrorism and on historical examples, a number of distinctions can be made within this same category:

a. The direct involvement of insurgent/terrorist groups in the drug trade.
b. The indirect involvement of insurgent/terrorist groups through taxation of the drug trade or provision of security to drug traffickers.

Traditionally, in the 1980s, leftist insurgent groups such as the Shining Path in Peru, the FARC (Fuerzas Armadas Revolucionarias de Colombia) in Colombia, and the PKK in Turkey got involved into drug trafficking in order to finance their activities, while they simultaneously made recourse to terrorist attacks to further their ideological agendas.

The Peruvian insurgent group the Shining Path was involved in the drug trade both directly and indirectly. The group was heavily directly involved in coca production in the Upper Huallaga Valley, as well as indirectly through the taxation of other producers and traffickers operating in the Valley. The group got a certain percentage of the value of all cocaine base smuggled from the region while also taxing each drug plane leaving the Valley. In this way, the group's involvement into the drug business allowed it to develop a more sophisticated arsenal to fight the Peruvian government.

In a similar vein, the FARC has been using the narcotics trade—coca crop cultivation, lab processing operations, and exportation of cocaine—in a direct manner to fund its terrorist attacks against the Colombian government. The FARC also engaged indirectly in narcoterrorism by charging protection money from growers and taxing the coca industry. Peter Lupsha called the indirect involvement of insurgent groups in narcoterrorism through the provision of security to drug traffickers, "insurgent narco-terrorism." For example, FARC guerrillas guarded the Medellin Cartel's clandestine laboratories in Yuri, Colombia.

Throughout the 1980s and 1990s, the Turkish PKK was active in almost all phases of narcotics trafficking while simultaneously being involved in urban terrorism. The group had labs in Iran, Northern Iraq, and Southeastern Turkey where they converted morphine-base to heroine, and subsequently trafficked the resulting heroine to Western Europe where the Kurdish Diaspora provided the distribution outlet for the drugs. Hence, for both the PKK and the FARC, their involvement in the drug trade and in terrorist activities provided them with the means through which they furthered their ideological goals.

Alongside the insurgent groups, traditional terrorist organizations such as Hizbullah have engaged since the 1970s into the global narcotics trade. Over time, the group expanded its historical drug trading routes and institutionalized an extensive network to traffic in narcotics and launder the corresponding illicit proceeds, to the extent to which narcotics earnings today constitute a key funding stream for the organization.

Moreover, in the post 9/11 environment, governments have faced the threat posed by terrorist groups, such as Al Qaeda and its affiliates, that are also involved in drug related activities to support their terrorist activities. The 2001 coalition intervention in Afghanistan led to a *"marriage of convenience between insurgency forces and the opium industry."* In addition to financing the insurgency in the country, the revenues from the cultivation of opium and trafficking in heroin allowed the Afghan Taliban to offer sanctuary and protection to Osama bin-Laden and various Al Qaeda elements.

The involvement of Afghan groups in opium and heroin trafficking to support their insurgent activities dated back to the Soviet invasion of Afghanistan in 1979, when the mujahidin needed *"capital to purchase weaponry that would be effective against Soviet gunships and troops."* Since the 2001 invasion and the lifting of the Taliban opium ban, opium production in Afghanistan took off and the pervasiveness of drug trafficking in the country makes it the first state in the world primarily financed through the illicit production and trafficking in opium.

2. The use by drug trafficking organizations of terrorist tactics

Another major use of the term narcoterrorism refers to the direct or indirect use by drug trafficking organizations of terrorist tactics such as assassinations, kidnappings, and bombings against civilians, government officials, or institutions in an attempt to attain limited political objectives and influence the government's anti-drug trafficking policies and their enforcement.

The main difference between an insurgent or terrorist group and a drug-trafficking organization lies in their final goal. While insurgent or

---

terrorist groups use narco-trafficking simply as a means to finance their violent political activities, drug trafficking organizations attain their final goal when narcotics and money change hands.

Although initially naroterorrism was used in connection to the involvement in the drug trade of the insurgent group the Shinning Path, the traditional use of the term mostly refers to the use of terror tactics by narco-traffickers to fight drug enforcement efforts. In Peter Lupsha's typology of narcoterrorism, *"the use of violence by drug traders to threaten governmental authority and state institutions"* is what constitutes *"true narcoterrorism."* While these narco-traffickers are not fully-fledged terrorists, their use of terror tactics aims to *"intimidate sovereign governments into weakening or abandoning their drug control policies."*

The actions of Pablo Escobar against the Colombian government in the 1980s represent a classical example of narcoterrorism. Escobar, who at the time was heading the Medellin Cartel, used terror tactics against civilians and government officials to further his political agenda of putting an end to the extradition of Colombian drug traffickers to the United States, and aimed to protect the illicit trade in cocaine that was the source of his wealth. In this regard, Pablo Escobar ordered in 1984 the assassination of the Minister of Justice Rodrigo Lara Bonilla, and of presidential candidates, politicians, police officers, and civilians.

The November 1985 assault on the Palace of Justice in downtown Bogotá by the M-19 guerillas at the orders of the narcotrafficantes was equally aimed to stop the extradition of the drug traffickers to the United States. The siege ended with the death of almost half of the 25 Supreme Court Justices. These terrorist attacks ultimately resulted in the revision of the extradition treaty between Colombia and the U.S. But the use of terrorism by the drug cartels did not stop here. In 1989, Escobar ordered the bombing of the Avianca Airlines flight #203 en route to Cali to instill fear in the civilian population and intimidate the government in order to influence the anti-narcotics policy outcomes.

There are several other relevant examples in recent history of criminal organizations involved in the trafficking of narcotics and in terror tactics to protect their trade. In the mid-1980s, the Sicilian Mafia in Italy engaged in "acts of pure terrorism" lacking any ideological objective. The use of terrorist tactics by the Mafia dates back to at least the early 1960s when, in the Ciaculli massacre of June 30, 1963, a car bomb explosion killed seven military and police officers that were sent to diffuse the bomb. The term of narcoterrorism, though, was not in use at the time as the Sicilain Mafia got into the drug business only at the end of the 1960s. However, by the mid-1980s, the Mafia was heavily involved in drug trafficking and the murder of the Italian prosecutors Giovanni Falcone and Paolo Borsellino qualifies the activities of the Sicilian Mafia as narcoterrorism that was meant to signal to other judges investigating the Mafia not to pursue such inquiries.

Similarly, in recent years in Mexico, Mafia-style attempts that were aimed to intimidate government officials carrying out their duties along with the Mexican society at large have taken place and led to the *"the transformation of narcoviolence into narcoterrorism."* The September 2008 Morelia bombings during Mexico's Independence Day, the August 2010 bombing of Televisa TV network station in Monterrey, Nuevo Leon, as well as the beheadings, summary executions, and burnings of bodies attest to the increasing use of terror tactics by the Mexican drug cartels. Given that the tactics were used in an attempt to change government policy in relation to anti-organized crime and counter-narcotics enforcement, the violence may properly fall within the category of terrorist acts. The drug gangs have adopted terrorist techniques as a systematic strategy aimed to intimidate and instill fear in a wide range of actors: their adversaries, government officials, and Mexican society. Therefore, the use of terror tactics by the Mexican drug trafficking organizations has been appropriately referred to as narcoterrorism.

3. State-sponsored Narcoterrorism

Governments may engage indirectly in narcoterrorism by providing overt or covert support to non-state armed groups engaged in both terrorism and the smuggling of illicit drugs. Very often, state-sponsored narcoterrorism takes place when some governments sponsor terrorist groups that participate in drug trafficking. The respective states do not back the terrorist organizations for financial reasons, but because they seek to change or destabilize the political system of the countries where the groups operate. State-sponsors of narcoterrorism may have a strong contribution to the establishment of terrorist organizations, which they subsequently provide with weapons and means of transportation to facilitate attacks against rival states

This approach to narcoterrorism is part of Rachel Ehrenfeld's definition as "the use of drug trafficking to advance the objectives of certain governments [and terrorist organizations]." In the context of the Cold War confrontation between the two superpowers, Ehrenfeld elaborated her thesis on narcoterrorism as a "*tactic of anti-capitalistic Marxist-Leninists who target[ed] the United States and other non-Marxist, democratic states in the Western hemisphere.*" From her perspective, besides the profit motive, another major reason behind the state-sponsored narcoterrorism was the goal to undermine Western, democratic societies, among which the U.S. was a particular target.

To conclude, a more thorough definition of narcoterrorism is needed in order to craft the appropriate tools necessary to deal in an effective manner with the combined threat of terrorism and drug trafficking. The many and often contradictory definitions of the term have prevented the creation of effective policies that would mitigate the dual threat of narcoterrorism.

Research Note

Despite the fact that the connection between drug trafficking and terrorism has become more pressing with the acceleration of globalization that has allowed both drug traffickers and terrorist groups to exploit the advances in technology, finance, communication and transportation, the topic attracts extremely few researchers. Current articles dedicated to narcoterrorism are occasional, and the key sources available are ten or even more than twenty years old.

Further Reading

Emma Bjornehed, "Narco-Terrorism: The Merger of the War on Drugs and the War on Terror." *Global Crime*, Vol. 6, No. 3 & 4., August-November 2004: 305–324.

Rachel Ehnrenfeld, *Narco-Terrorism*. New York: Basic Books, 1990.

Jonas Hartelius, "Narcoterrorism." The East-West Institute & the Swedish Carnegie Institute, February, 2008, http://www.ewi.info/pdf/Narcoterrorism%20FINAL13FEB.

Netwar and Networked Threats

Confronting the Dark Side of Networks

John Arquilla and David Ronfeldt

No word has entered our awareness more deeply over the past year than "network." It has become inextricably linked with al Qaeda and related terrorist organizations. Even now, after the fall of the Taliban, and with Osama bin Laden dead or in hiding, senior U.S. officials have made a point of reiterating their fears about continued attacks "by the network"—perhaps even with nuclear weapons. The threat persists because this shadowy, fluid use of the network form allows the enemy to operate covertly in dozens of countries around the world, swarming together only at the moment of the attack.

Beyond al-Qaeda, other insurgent and terrorist organizations have also demonstrated the power of their highly networked small units. The Chechens first demonstrated the power of networks in winning the 1994-96 war with the Russians—who fielded what was then still one of the world's better conventional armies (see Arquilla and Karasik, 1999). While the Russians have since returned to Chechnya, they continue to face stern opposition. Also in the 1990s, a sprawling network of transnational activist NGOs sided with the Zapatista National Liberation Army in developing a "social netwar" that put Mexico's government on the defensive and prevented the army from quashing the rebels (Ronfeldt *et al.*, 1998). Elsewhere, Israel faced the swarm networks of Hezbollah a few years ago, and the incomparable Israeli Defense Forces were driven from South Lebanon. Today, they confront myriad attack networks in Gaza and the West Bank, with no clear end in sight. All around the world, competent, tough militaries are having a hard time fighting terror and insurgent networks.

Transnational crime has become highly networked, too. The best example can be seen in the war on drugs, where the signal successes in killing or imprisoning the leaders of the Medellin and Cali cartels created some adverse unintended consequences. Instead of crippling drug traffickers, the end of the great cartels simply spawned a host of small networks that now export more drugs to the United States than were being shipped in the heyday of the great cartels.

Clearly, the dark-side potential of networking has been tapped; and confronting insurgents, terrorists and criminals will require substantial, sustained levels of effort. We believe that the process of countering these rising networks should begin by cultivating insights into the nature of networks—insights informed by the early studies that generally focused on the bright-side potential of networking. Starting this way, we may find ourselves in a good position to articulate effective doctrines for fighting these elusive adversaries.

The growing power and positive dynamics of networks has been on people's minds for decades. Strong early statements first appeared twenty years ago—for example, John Naisbitt (1982) and Jessica Lipnack and Jeffrey Stamps (1982) all touted this rising form of organization. Charles Perrow (1979) was also thinking about networks at that time, but had not come round to the point of view that they might outperform hierarchies. What these and other early observers did have in common was a basic belief that networks would improve efficiency and productivity in almost all commercial organizations. Much of the recent literature on organizational networks echoes and expands upon this theme (*e.g.*, Nohria and Eccles, 1992; Lipnack and Stamps, 1994, and Monge and Fulk, 1999). Until the September 2001 attacks on America, relatively few were focusing on the dark side of networking—*i.e.*, on the empowerment of terrorist and criminal organizations by means of organizational innovation.

Manuel Castells (1996) has been a particularly keen observer of both the bright and dark sides of networking, providing extensive analysis of the transnational criminal world. Phil Williams (1994, 2001) has also focused closely and insightfully on global criminal networks, while John Sullivan (2001) has looked at criminal and gang networking closer to home. Our own thoughts about the dark side of networks have addressed their use by rogues, ethnonationalists, and terrorists (Arquilla and Ronfeldt, 1996, 2001).

How can networked adversaries be defeated? Until now, our work has focused on advocating the general principle that "it takes a network to fight a network"—much as, in an earlier era, strategists recognized that it took a tank to fight a tank. While this principle seems abstract, we must note that a modicum of networking between the FBI and the CIA—i.e., sharing early warning signs of the impending attacks on America—would have made a huge difference.

9-11 was not so much an intelligence failure as an organizational failure. Despite the organizational failure that preceded 9/11, we have been pleased to see how much networking was actually going on. From highly networked intelligence organizations, like the CIA's Counterterrorism Center, to law enforcement's Terrorism Early Warning network, much progress is being made. In the military realm, "hunter networks" of special forces and CIA field agents performed, and continue to perform, at very high levels of effectiveness in Afghanistan. Solid advances are being made in terms of networking, even if much more can and must be done. But in addition to doing better at networking among ourselves and with international partners, we must learn to "disconnect the dots" (term from Garreau, 2001) of dark-side networks.

A first step in this process is to assess the strengths and weaknesses of networks along five major dimensions: the organizational, narrative, doctrinal, technological, and social levels. At the organizational level, we have emphasized the need to find out which of three basic designs—chains, hub-and-spokes, and allchannel (see Evan, 1972)—are employed or intermixed in any given network. In terms of understanding why network members are joined together—and why they Persist—we have elucidated levels of analysis that consider the common story, or narrative dimension, that guides them, and the social basis for their interactions and bonds of trust. Further, we have considered the need to understand their doctrine (e.g., are they dispersed most of the time, then pulse to the attack, like V-boat wolf packs in World War II or like al-Qaeda cells today?), particularly the idea that they might engage in omnidirectional "swarming." Finally, we see the need to consider a network's access to and reliance upon communications and other advanced technologies.

Taken together, these notions about building our own networks, then assessing enemy networks, provide a good start to the process of confronting dark-side actors. But both these notions are at a fairly high level of abstraction. Both have more to do with strategic assessments and plans. The deeper need now is to engage in some thinking that can be applied at the tactical and operational levels of what we call netwar—and to do this will require a return to and expansion upon the organizational and doctrinal levels of strategic assessment.

For as we learn more about the various forms employed by a given adversary, we must stand ready with our own concept of operations for countering a network. Three considerations in particular seem important. First, should detected cells or nodes be "taken out" or left in place and monitored? Second, should attacks, when they are warranted, be made at many points simultaneously, or should they be distributed sequentially in time and space? Third, should attacks be focused more on the nodes or on the links and flows that connect the nodes? These are the sorts of doctrinal questions that must be thought through as we contemplate strikes against various networked adversaries.

Overall operational concerns must be kept in mind when confronting terror or criminal networks. One is that the destruction of a particular node may limit one's ability to learn more about the whole network. Thus, it may prove of little consequence that one of the "spokes" in a hub-and-spokes structure is taken out. Unless the connection to the network hub is made, the enemy may simply continue ahead with his plans. This may well have been the case with the apprehension of Zecarias Moussaoui four weeks before the September 11 attacks. He was likely just one of the spokes in the attack network. On the other hand, taking out a node that is part of a communications or logistics chain might seriously impede a networked adversary—even at the price of not learning where the chain might lead. Finally, destroying nodes in an area of all-channel connectivity seems fundamentally counterproductive, as the monitoring of such a node might reap enormous gains in terms of tracking connections.

In the realm of what might be called operational tempo, there may also be a tension between simultaneous and sequential attacks upon an enemy network. Both concepts have strengths, and both have potential weaknesses. For example, simultaneous attacks may maximize the damage that can be done immediately to a network. In the war on drugs, this tactic has been used from time to time, both in the United States and in Central America. Though impressive hauls have occasionally been made, it may be that insufficient knowledge of overall network structures has vitiated the effectiveness of such all-out attacks.

Sequential operations have the virtue that they might actually "stir the pot" and provoke detectable movement among and between network nodes—thus increasing what is known about the enemy, and imposing a longer-lasting form of pressure whose psychological impact may be greater than the aforementioned short duration "smash and grab" approach. Yet, the risk of slower, sequential attacks is that the alarm is likely to be given to those not immediately under attack—and they may simply go to ground. If this happens, there is at least the benefit that the network's overall activity level has been lessened. But it does leave them in place to continue their dark work, once "the heat is off."

With the foregoing in mind, one can see that simultaneous attacks should be viewed as maximizing surprise, though sequential attacks may prove a sounder attritional tool, as it may wear down the enemy network both psychologically and physically. As to the conditions under which each tactic might be employed, we hypothesize that this choice will probably be a function of such factors as how much is known about a network, and the degree of urgency that is felt by those conducting the attack (*e.g.*, if an attack is believed to be coming, a simultaneous pre-emptive strike would seem in order).

A third operational issue area that should be considered involves analysis of whether one should strike at a network's "nodes" or at its "links." In the U.S. military today, there is a great emphasis on striking at "key nodes" of enemy systems. Much of this thinking draws its inspiration from the work of John Warden (1988), one of the military's leading strategists of the past few decades. Indeed, notions of "nodal warfare" abound today, and there is much evidence that militaries of other countries are striving mightily to create command and control systems that can function in the face of an American attack on "critical nodes." In return, American strategists, especially those concerned with homeland security, tend to think first of the need to protect critical infrastructural nodes.

Striking at nodes may well have crippling effects upon hierarchical adversaries; but to damage a network seriously may require severing the *links* between its nodes. This may be done in two basic ways. One would be to use technological means to try to disconnect nodes from each other. The other would be to undermine the terrorists' or criminals' trust in their information systems—an approach fundamentally rooted in psychological operations and deception. Both forms of attack on network links would likely employ a lot of cyberspace-based operations, though the former would emphasize hitting conduits while the latter would focus on developing the right content, inserted in the right place, to undermine trust throughout the network.

It is also entirely feasible to think in terms of using classical psychological operations and deceptions against terror and criminal networks. One effective approach was modeled by the British in the 1950s, during their struggle against the Kenyan Mau Mau gangs (which were highly networked, with splendid social and narrative ties). One way inside the network was British intelligence's creation of what they called "pseudo gangs." These looked and acted much like Mau Mau cells, but were in fact British-run forces who sometimes exploited the deception by finding out more about the Mau Mau, and sometimes by shooting up a real Mau Mau unit—in order to undermine the bonds of trust that undergirded the movement (see Corfield, 1960; Kariuki, 1963; Gann, 1970, especially pp. 74-75; and Clayton, 1976).

How is the current counternetwar against al-Qaeda going? After Afghanistan, it is hard to see the overall strategic vision in U.S.-led operations. The situation is basically one of finding evidence of al-Qaeda or Taliban presence in the field, then striking at it rather than monitoring or exploiting the initial knowledge gained about some enemy disposition. The remainder of American energy is being split between the feverish improvement of homeland defenses (which does include some network-building among and between law enforcement, intelligence, and the military) and plans to exert pressure on various nation-state "sponsors" of terror.

Some of our allies in the war on terror are developing interesting approaches to counternetwar that we should be studying and learning from. Singapore, for example, worked closely with the Philippines and Malaysia to detect, monitor, and finally destroy the apparent all-channel attack network that was planning a truck bombing campaign against Americans living there. In this case, over forty arrests were made. Spain, Italy and Germany have also been networking well, and have recently rolled up significant support elements of al-Qaeda operating in Europe. In both cases, a kind of law enforcement doctrinal paradigm has been apparent as, each time, attacks on network nodes were made simultaneously—but only at the end of long periods of monitoring.

American strategists may find they have much to learn from others' successes against al-Qaeda. There is no doubt also much to be gained from beginning to think systematically about the operational doctrines that must emerge if we are to improve our chances of winning this terror war—and the subsequent netwars that will likely bedevil us for the foreseeable future.

Further Reading

John Arquilla and David Ronfeldt, Eds., *In Athena's Camp: Preparing for Conflict in the Information Age.* Santa Monica: RAND, 1997.

John Arquilla and David Ronfeldt, Eds., *Networks and Netwars: The Future of Terror, Crime, and Militancy.* Santa Monica: RAND, 2001.

David Ronfeldt, John Arquilla, Graham E. Fuller, and Melissa Fuller, *The Zapatista "Social Netwar" in Mexico.* Santa Monica: RAND, 1999.

Nuclear Terrorism

T. Kessara Eldridge

"...the single biggest threat to U.S. security, both short term, medium term and long term, would be the possibility of a terrorist organization obtaining a nuclear weapon...If there was ever a detonation in New York City, or London, or Johannesburg, the ramifications economically, politically, and from a security perspective would be devastating..."

— President Barack Obama, April 11, 2010

According to Brian Michael Jenkins in his book *Will Terrorists Go Nuclear*:

"...two out of five Americans believe that terrorists will detonate a nuclear bomb somewhere in the United States in the next five years." In an interview, former Vice President Dick Cheney predicted that "there will be a terrorist attack on the United States within the next decade and that it will be "far deadlier" than the attacks of 9/11." "I think there will be another attack," Cheney told Hewitt, "and the next time, I think it's going to be far deadlier than the last one. Imagine what would happen if somebody could smuggle a nuclear device, put it in a shipping container, and drive it down the Beltway outside Washington, D.C." (p. 25)

To pull off a nuclear attack, a group would need to acquire nuclear materials or a weapon, build a bomb or unlock an existing one, move that weapon to its target, and detonate it. Securing nuclear weapons and materials, although critical, confronts only one part of a plot and cannot eliminate the threat entirely. We must develop a more realistic picture of nuclear terrorism that draws on a careful understanding of how terrorist groups work and how their plots can fail.

According to the 2005 RAND report *Aum Shinrikyo, Al Qaeda, and the Kinshasa Reactor,* Aum Shinrikyo, a religious cult with an apocalyptic ideology, recruited scientists and engineers to help the group acquire chemical, biological, and nuclear weapons. In the early 1990's:

> "Aum identified Russia as a potential source of nuclear weapons, and cult members made numerous overtures to senior officials and scientists. But despite these entreaties, Aum was unable to purchase a nuclear weapon. As a result, Aum chose to focus on building rather than buying a nuclear weapon. Group members investigated the mining of uranium ore in Australia and used the Internet to glean sensitive information on nuclear facilities in Russia, the People's Republic of China, South Korea, and elsewhere." [p. vii]

The study further goes on to explain that:

> "technical challenges associated with building a nuclear weapon became apparent to the group's leadership, which chose instead to devote its ample financial and other resources to acquiring chemical weapons, such as the nerve agent sarin, which Aum used in its 1995 attack on the Tokyo subway system. Second, despite the reportedly lax security in Russian nuclear facilities and Aum's high-level contacts in the government, Russian officials were unwilling to provide the cult with what it wanted." [pp. vii-viii]

Documents recovered in Kabul during and after the allied invasion in 2001 state that Al Qaeda made little progress in terms of designing or fabricating a nuclear system and failed to purchase weapons such as 'suitcase nukes'.

Recent developments with a Sunni Muslim group known as the Islamic State, show that the ideal of obtaining a nuclear weapon is still being pursued. A Reuters article of July 9, 2014 reports that "Nearly 40 kilograms (88 pounds) of uranium compounds were kept at Mosul University, Iraq's UN Ambassador Mohamed Ali Alhakim told UN Secretary-General Ban Ki-moon in the July 8 letter obtained by Reuters on Wednesday." "Terrorist groups have seized control of nuclear material at the sites that came out of the control of the state," Alhakim wrote, adding that such materials "can be used in manufacturing weapons of mass destruction." A U.S. government source familiar with the matter said the materials were not believed to be enriched uranium and therefore would be difficult to use to manufacture into a weapon.

A number of terrorist groups have actively pursued WMD acquisition. To name just a few, al-Qaeda (AQ), AQ affiliates Egyptian Islamic Jihad, Jemaah Islamiya, Lashkar al-Tayyiba, and, most recently, the Islamic State (IS/ISIS/ISIL) have all successfully acquired WMD materials/agents. While the acquisition of WMDs by terrorist groups is only occasionally an easy process for them, two factors have recently conspired to make WMD acquisition by terrorist groups much, much easier: 1) There is a tremendous amount of instability in the Middle East, and 2) Terrorist groups are in greater competition with one another than ever before.

Jenkins lays it out very clearly in his book *Will Terrorists Go Nuclear?*, "If terrorists detonated a nuclear bomb, that would, of course, create nuclear terror, but nuclear terror can be created without nuclear terrorism." In his more recent book *When Armies Divide*, he further elaborates, "Terrorists with nuclear capabilities are considered more dangerous than states with nuclear weapons, because terrorists are seen as more likely to use them" and "A nuclear weapon (or even components of one) may be of little use to rebels as a military weapon, but it could serve as an instrument of psychological warfare."

The possibility of terrorists obtaining nuclear weapons is already viewed by the U.S. government as a justification for preemptive military action. On June 30, 2014, the Department of Defense released its

Strategy for Countering Weapons of Mass Destruction (CWMD) which replaces the 2006 National Military Strategy for Combating Weapons of Mass Destruction. The strategy outlines three 'lines of effort': 1) Prevent acquisition—to ensure that those not possessing WMD do not obtain them, 2) Contain and reduce threats—to address the risks posted by existing WMD, and 3) Respond to crisis—to manage and resolve complex WMD crisis through activities and operations.

According to the U.S. Department of Defense, "nuclear security" covers procedures, facilities, and equipment designed to avoid loss of custody, theft, and diversion of nuclear weapons as well as other unauthorized actions, vandalism, and sabotage. In a book by the U.S. Army War College, editors Henry D. Sokolski and Bruno Tetrais explain further. "...each and every nuclear security crisis is and will always be driven by a unique set of human actors, individuals, or groups whose thoughts and intentions, both then and now, are largely beyond anyone's ability to precisely pin down." Furthermore, "...the history of close nuclear security calls suggests that as long as there are assets that can be diverted to make nuclear weapons or sabotaged to produce environmental disasters, there will be no absolute fix to prevent the worst."

While the possibility is out there, the likelihood is limited. It is not the reality of the situation that creates the greater threat of nuclear terror, but the psychological threat that is more damaging. Virtual terror, created using words and images spread through social and conventional media outlets without ever actually detonating a bomb, is a more active threat than the reality of an actual nuclear bomb being detonated. In his foreword to Jenkins' book *Will Terrorists Go Nuclear?*, James S. Gilmore III, the former governor of Virginia and chairman of the Advisory Panel to Assess Domestic Response Capabilities for Terrorism Involving Weapons of Mass Destruction said the following: "Nuclear terror can also have another insidious effect, one that imperils our very democracy. Terrorism does pose a terrible danger, but our fear of real and imagined threats must not persuade us to diminish our freedoms or our core values. There is no trade-off between security and liberty. One does not exist without the other."

Further Reading

Brian Michael Jenkins, *Will Terrorists Go Nuclear?* Amherst: Prometheus Books, 2008.

Brian Michael Jenkins, *When Armies Divide.* RAND Corporation commercial book series. CB-532. Brian Michael Jenkins Inc., E-Book, 2013.

Henry D. Sokolski and Bruno Tertrais. Eds., *Nuclear Weapons Security Crises: What Does History Teach?* Carlisle: Strategic Studies Institute, U.S. Army War College, 30 July 2013, http://www.strategicstudiesinstitute.army.mil/pubs/display.cfm?pubID=1156.

Oklahoma City Bombing

Brian K. Houghton

On the morning of April 19, 1995, Timothy McVeigh parked a Ryder truck in front of the Alfred P. Murrah Federal building in downtown Oklahoma City. The rented truck held approximately 4,800 pounds of the explosive mixture ammonium nitrate and fuel oil. At 9:02 a.m., the device exploded. The bomb ripped apart the lower floors and caused all nine floors of the center portion of the building to pancake upon themselves. The bomb's destruction caused multiple buildings to collapse or sustain damage, and cars parked across the street exploded into flames. In all, 167 people were killed by the explosion with hundreds injured. The shock waves from the bomb were felt many miles away.

Response to the bombing was immediate. Emergency workers and nearby citizens rushed to the scene and immediately started a vigorous yet chaotic rescue effort. A nurse rushing inside the bombed out building to assist the survivors received a blow to the head by a falling piece of concrete, becoming the 168th fatality of the bombing. In the first few minutes, duplicative staging areas were created for first responders. With no security perimeter established, a mixture of survivors, emergency workers, and volunteers swarmed inside and around the building searching for victims. Suddenly, word spread of a second explosive device in the building. While false, the immediate concern of a potential second bomb allowed the senior public safety personnel to pull the mixture of responders and public out of the building, set up a security perimeter, and establish a more organized response.

As the response took place, Timothy McVeigh raced north on the highway in a getaway vehicle he had left a few blocks away from the Murrah building. Speeding and driving a car without a license plate, he was pulled over 90 minutes later by a highway patrolman. McVeigh, who possessed no driver's license and was armed, was taken into Parry, Oklahoma to be held on minor charges.

What had prompted McVeigh to commit the worst act of domestic terrorism in American history? McVeigh, a decorated Army veteran of the first Gulf War, held extreme views on the right to bear arms which bordered on obsession. He was outraged over the attempted storming and subsequent siege of the Branch Davidian complex near Waco, Texas. Tactical units from the Bureau of Alchohol, Tobacco, and Firearms (ATF) and the Federal Bureau of Investigation (FBI) had attempted to search the compound for illegal weapons. When the Davidians resisted, a deadly siege began. McVeigh saw these horrible events as evidence of a tyrannical federal government striving to deny their second amendment right. He traveled down to Waco during the siege in support of the Branch Davidians, and he was deeply impacted when the compound went up in flames following a FBI/ATF raid. As a result of the fire, 76 men, women, and children died—and McVeigh held the federal government responsible.

McVeigh and Terry Nichols, a friend from Army basic training, believed that the federal government—especially the ATF and FBI—needed to be paid back in kind. To McVeigh, the government had declared war against the citizens and thus the citizens could be justified in declaring war against the government. Thus motivated, McVeigh and Terry Nichols made the bomb.

The bombing in Oklahoma City caused America to look inward. Immediately after the explosion, media speculation focused on Middle Eastern terrorists. Unfortunately, as a result of this erroneous speculation, mosques and "Arab-looking" individuals were targeted for harassment and violence. As soon as Timothy McVeigh was acknowledged as the chief suspect, a great shock was felt across the country as people realized that this attack came from "one of ours." McVeigh was no swarthy bomb-thrower—he was an all-American veteran from a small town in New York. This was the first major lesson of the Oklahoma City bombing—that terrorism can come from within and not only from outside—and it is a lesson that needs to be remembered. This bombing remains the largest and most destructive domestic act of terrorism in the United States.

The impact of the bombing is still felt today, even after the larger tragedy of September 11. People realized that if terrorism could strike Oklahoma City, then any city was vulnerable to terrorism, not just the major metropolitan areas of the East or West coasts. As a result of the bombing, and the earlier 1993 World Trade Center attack, the Antiterrorism and Effective Death Penalty Act of 1996 was passed in an effort to deter future terrorists. Furthermore, the bombing took place just one month after the Tokyo, Japan sarin gas attack by the apocalyptic cult Aum Shinrikyo, which led the government and terrorism experts to declare a shift in the nature of terrorism. Previously, it was believed that terrorists would use minimal damage to promote their cause so as not to alienate their base of support. The Tokyo gas attack and Oklahoma City bombings showed that the taboo of utilizing weapons of mass destruction or targeting large numbers was broken, and that terrorists in the future might have to strive for greater destruction in order to capture the desensitized attention of a world population.

While Shoko Asahara, the leader of Aum, and Timothy McVeigh did not know of each other, and while their motivations were quite different, these two individuals pushed the United States and the rest of the world into an era of terrorism preparedness and prevention. The Nunn-Lugar-Domenici Domestic Preparedness Program was created to provide funding to 120 cities for equipment and training to prevent or respond more effectively to acts of terrorism involving weapons of mass destruction. This funding for greater preparedness has continued and was greatly increased subsequent to the 9/11 terrorist attacks, but it owes its existence to Oklahoma City. The legacy of the 1995 attack also continues to provide valuable lessons learned from the bombing and collapse of the building. Examination of the bombing has led to improvements and new standards in building construction and building security, helping to ensure that countless lives might be spared the same tragedy.

Further Reading

Lou Michel and Dan Herbeck, *American Terrorist: Timothy McVeigh and the Oklahoma City Bombing.* New York: HarperCollins Publishers, 2001.

The Oklahoma Department of Civil Emergency Management After Action Report Alfred P. Murrah Federal Building Bombing 19 April 1995 in Oklahoma City, Oklahoma, nd, http://www.ok.gov/OEM/documents/Bombing%20After%20Action%20Report.pdf.

Stuart A. Wright, *Patriots, Politics, and the Oklahoma City Bombing.* New York: Cambridge University Press, 2007.

Omar Abdel Rahman

James T. Kirkhope

Sheik Omar Ahmad Ali Abdel Rahman is currently serving a life sentence (plus 65 years) in U.S. federal prison for planning what could have been the deadliest terror attack in American history. Abdel Rahman's plot, dubbed, the "Day of Terror" by prosecutors, involved a coordinated bombing attack of New York City targets including the United Nations building, the George Washington Bridge, the Lincoln and Holland Tunnels, and the FBI building in Manhattan. Following his arrest in June 1993 and subsequent trial, Sheik Abdel Rahman was convicted on October 1, 1995, on charges of seditious conspiracy, soliciting the murder of Egyptian President Hosni Mubarak, soliciting an attack on American military installations, and the bombing attack conspiracy. However, the Sheik's involvement in terrorism and violence runs much deeper. Abdel Rahman was linked to the World Trade Center bombing of February 1993, and has ties to Gama'a al-Islamiya (the Islamic Group) of Egypt and Osama bin Laden's Al Qaida terrorist network. Though Abdel Rahman is not a household name, he stands alongside Bin Laden in the pantheon of master terrorists.

Born May 3, 1938, in a small Egyptian village of Al Gamalia, Abdel Rahman suffered blindness before his first birthday. With little other opportunity for study or gainful employment, he was sent to Islamic schools. Rahman excelled at religious studies, focusing in part on the works of Ibn Taimiyya, a 14th century Islamic theorist. Taimiyya's theological tenets, which called for the death of Muslim leaders who failed to uphold traditional Islamic law, started Abdel Rahman on the path to extremist Islam—and violent terrorism. Though Abdel Rahman was blind, Ibn Taimiyya helped him to envision an Islamic society untainted by secular ways. All that was needed were strong men with the will to violently create such an Earthly paradise, and Abdel Rahman was ready to join the struggle.

After graduating from the Al Azar University of Cairo in 1965, Abdel Rahman began preaching at a mosque in Fayoum, a small town sixty miles from Cairo. The Sheik's fiery sermons soon attracted the attention of government security services, Abdel Rahman's philosophy, combined with his growing leadership role in the fundamentalist Islamic Group, prompted a brief imprisonment in the 1970s followed by a three-year self-exile to Saudi Arabia.

Abdel Rahman was arrested, tried, and acquitted for conspiracy in both President Anwar Sadat's assassination of 1981, as well as inciting later riots in which over 100 police were killed. During that decade, Abdel Rahman grew in prominence as spiritual leader of the Afghan Mujahadeen as he traveled to both Pakistan and Afghanistan, where he first met Osama bin Laden and the al Qaida network. Facing imminent additional conspiracy charges (for which he was ultimately found guilty in absentia), Abdel Rahman fled to Sudan in 1989. During his time in Sudan, he secured a U.S. visa despite his name's being on the terrorist watch list. Sheik Abdel Rahman has been linked to a variety of attacks and crimes worldwide, including assassination plots targeting Egyptian Presidents Anwar Sadat (1981) and Hosni Mubarak (1993), Muslim authors Faraj Fodha (1992) and Naguib Mahfouz (1994), and American Jewish leader Rabbi Meir Kahane (1990). He remains an unindicted conspirator in the 1993 World Trade Center bombing, but was ultimately convicted for the 1993 "Day of Terror" plot. Abdel Rahman's terrorist activities continued even after his imprisonment. By 2002, one of his attorneys, Lynn Stewart, and three others were charged with facilitating communication between the Sheik and the terrorist Islamic Group back in Egypt.

Though Abdel Rahman's dream of Islamic revolution may have failed, his sons continue his legacy of terrorism. Abdullah holds a leadership position in the Islamic Group of Egypt. Ahmed is believed to have been taken prisoner in Afghanistan. Finally, his son Mohammed (a.k.a. Assad Allah) was seen in the al Qaida videotape released on September 25, 2001, following the World Trade Center and Pentagon attacks. In the video, bin Laden vows, "We swear we will work with all-out power to free our brother, Sheik Omar Abdel Rahman and all our prisoners in America, Egypt and Riyadh." There are few images that best describe the resiliency of today's terrorism than that of Sheik Omar Abdel Rahman rotting in prison for the greatest foiled terrorist plot while his son breaks bread with the architect of 9/11.

Further Reading

John L. Esposito, *Unholy War: Terror in the Name of Islam*. Oxford: Oxford University Press, 2003.

Mitchell D. Silber, *The Al Qaeda Factor: Plots Against the West*. Philadelphia: University of Pennsylvania Press, 2011.

Camille Tawil and Robin Bray, *Brothers In Arms: The Story of al-Qa'ida and the Arab Jihadists*. London: Saqi Books, 2011.

Osama bin Laden

James T. Kirkhope

Editors' Note: This essay was written in the Spring of 2002 and has not been updated except for the further reading list. See the essay in this work on the "Killing of Osama bin Laden" concerning the eventual fate of the al Qaida leader.

Osama bin Laden was born in 1957 in Riyadh, Saudi Arabia to the large family of construction billionaire Mohammed bin Awad bin Laden who had close ties to the Saudi royal family. Bin Laden's early life was marked by privilege yet his mother died when he was young. He was raised as a devout Sunni Muslim and had some education in economics and engineering though he increasingly gravitated towards Islamic religious studies. After finishing high school in Jeddah circa 1974 Osama decided against furthering his education overseas unlike his many siblings. He sought instead to study with a group of prominent Muslim scholars in Jeddah and Mecca belonging to the "Muslim Brotherhood." Significantly, he was influenced by the recorded teachings of Abdullah Azzam, a Palestinian who played a large role in the resurgence of Islamic religiosity and a founder of the Palestinian group Hamas whom Osama later met in Pakistan and Afghanistan, as well as also meeting Islamic philosopher Mohammed Quttub.

Though he earned a civil engineering degree from King Abdul-Aziz University in 1979, ultimately it was two critical world events which left lasting impressions on bin Laden. First, radical rebels seized the grand mosque in Mecca, but were soon crushed by Saudi government troops. Bin Laden was impressed by both by their faith and action. Second, the Soviet Union invasion of Afghanistan on December 26,

1979, represented a western attack against Islam and sparked his first move to political action.

Political and Tactical Mobilization (1980-1982)

Osama bin Laden's first encounter with Afghanistan was as early as the first two weeks of Soviet invasion. During the early stages of the mujahadeen (Holy War) resistance, he traveled to Afghanistan and Pakistan to meet with scholars and leaders who had been guests at his family house. Within weeks of his first arrival in Pakistan, Osama was formally introduced to Abdullah Azzam, a charismatic mullah whose taped sermons had made an impression on bin Laden during his university days. The pair got on well. The energy, administrative talent, and contacts of the young Saudi complemented the profound Islamic knowledge and commitment of the older man. Azzam, then 38, was a founder of the Hamas guerrilla group in the occupied West Bank and Gaza and thus had the experience to run a major organization. For the next two years, bin Laden commuted between the Gulf and Pakistan. During this time, his relationship with Azzam grew stronger. He began lobbying for the mujahadeen and raised large amounts of money for their cause. He continued collecting money and also going on short trips into Afghanistan once or twice a year until 1982. From the Pakistani border, bin Laden raised funds and provided the mujahedeen with logistical and humanitarian aid.

In 1981, Osama bin Laden received a public administration degree from King Abdul-Aziz University in Jeddah, Saudi Arabia. After graduation from the university, bin Laden left Saudi Arabia for Afghanistan to join the mujahadeen. Not only did he bring with him fresh recruits, but he also brought construction machinery and large amounts of cash. According to a French journalist as provided in a PBS frontline show, bin Laden claims his desire to join the efforts of the Afghan mujahedeen dates from "the time when the Americans decided to help the Afghans fight the Russians." He stated, "To counter these atheist Russians, the Saudis chose me as their representative in Afghanistan... I did not fight against the communist threat while forgetting the peril from the West. For us, the idea was not to get involved more than necessary in the fight against the Russians, which was the business of the Americans, but rather to show our solidarity with our Islamist brothers. I discovered that it was not enough to fight in Afghanistan, but that we had to fight on all fronts against communist or Western oppression. The urgent thing was communism, but the next target was America... This is an open war up to the end, until victory."

By 1982, he decided to establish a presence inside Afghanistan. There he founded the Maktab al-Khidimat (MAK) with Abdullah Azzam, Osama's first local effort to organize an international anti-Soviet mercenary group.

Pakistan (1982-1986)

Bin Laden and Azzam established a house in a suburb of Peshawar by 1984 and coordinated the transit of hundreds if not thousands of Arab mercenaries. Since bin Laden hadn't yet participated in combat or training, he directed the newcomers to the various Afghan factions.

It is difficult to believe bin Laden did not benefit from CIA activity in the region at this time. Though both deny a connection, it is known that the CIA channeled aid through the ISI (Pakistani secret service) to Afghani factions, including the MAK. Perhaps it was his disdain for American interference that soon motivated bin Laden to sever his formal ties with the MAK. He subsequently launched the Islamic Salvation Front founded on a radical fundamentalist vision of Islam and dedicated to a broader liberation theology seeking to free Islamic nations from foreign influences, especially those of Israel, the United States, and their allies.

Afghanistan Mujahadeen (1986-1989)

Around 1986, bin Laden decided to collect documentation on the hundreds of contacts who passed through his guesthouse, his camps, and the front in Afghanistan. Bin Laden associates claim he sought to track friends and recruits as well as to foster communication with mujahadeen fighters and their families, report home on the status of missing loved ones, and reconnect friends who were out of touch. This network, which became known as "al Qaida" (or "the base"), enabled bin Laden to collect contact details of mercenaries as well as passports of fallen Afghan mujahadeen fighters which could be used in later operations.

Soon, he decided to establish his own camps inside Afghanistan and, within two years, he built more than six camps. CIA reports estimate he directed approximately $50 million a yearly to the anti-Soviet efforts. According to Islamic sources, eventually bin Laden gained command of troops and participated in a variety of engagements with the Soviet forces including the final Jalalabad battle, soon after which the Soviets withdrew. Though actively involved in these efforts, bin Laden still traveled freely to Saudi Arabia where he would stay as long as four months a year.

Saudi Arabia, Pakistan, Afghanistan (1989-1991)

Even after the Soviet departure, civil war continued. First, a relatively united mujahadeen militia struggled against the Moscow-backed government, but then the Taliban and the Ahmed Shah Massoud group factions turned on each other. In late 1989, after the Soviet withdrawal from Afghanistan, bin Laden traveled back to Saudi Arabia as he often did throughout the 1980s. However, after he gave many public speeches about the Afghan victory, the failures of the Saudi government, and an impending Iraqi invasion led the Saudi government to place a travel ban on bin Laden, effectively trapping him in the kingdom. Intelligence reports that bin Laden sought to start a new "front" of jihad in South Yemen surely also contributed to the government's action.

After the Iraqi invasion of Kuwait in August 1990, bin Laden wrote a letter to the Saudi king suggesting defense tactics and offering to raise an army of 30,000 Afghan mujahadeen veterans. Bin Laden grew incensed when the Saudis rejected the fighters that had defeated the Soviets and turned instead to the Americans. In response, bin Laden mobilized his network of religious scholars and Muslim activists to highlight the Islamic nature of the conflict and reject western intervention, resulting in the release of a fatwah emphasizing training and readiness as religious duties. Some reports suggest up to 4,000 answered the call of the fatwah and traveled to Afghanistan for training. In response, the Saudi government then chose to further limit bin Laden's movements to Jeddah only.

Despite the restrictions, bin Laden was able to permanently escape the Saudi Kingdom in April 1991. After a brief stay in Pakistan, he crossed the border into Afghanistan seeking, among other things, to broker a truce among Afghan factions. Both reconciliation efforts and attempts on bin Laden's life failed, and, thus by the end of 1991, a disguised bin Laden fled to Sudan on a private jet.

Sudan (1992-1996)

The strict and dogmatic ideology of Sudan's ruling National Islamic Front appealed to bin Laden, and so did its liberal visa policies and numerous infrastructure construction contracts. By 1992, he, his four wives, children, and staff settled in the rich Riyadh suburb of Khartoum, followed closely by hundreds of Afghan mujahedeen veterans of the al Qaida network seeking a vocation in a new world order lacking a jihad.

From this new base, bin Laden raised funds, secured weapons, and expanded a propaganda campaign against Saudi Arabia through the Advice and Reform Council's (ARC) lecturing and publishing statements condemning corrupt Muslim states and the west. Tactical alliances with Shiite dominated Iran and terrorist groups such as Hizballah were considered and a list of Saudi and American targets was circulated.

On December 29, 1992, two Yemeni Muslim militants planted a bomb that exploded in a hotel in Aden, Yemen, where U.S. troops had been staying while en route to a humanitarian mission in Somalia. The injured perpetrators were arrested and, upon learning they had trained in Afghanistan, U.S. intelligence officials soon concluded this was the first terrorist attack involving bin Laden and his associates. Bin Laden also began to train Somali gunmen in tactics learned in Afghanistan for use against US Marines.

The modus operandi of the Yemen bombing differs from the second attack attributed (at least in part) to Osama bin Laden's al Qaida. The February 26, 1993, bombing of the World Trade Center in New York City was eventually attributed to Ramzi Ahmed Yousef and Sheikh Omar Abd Al-Rahman (the Blind Sheikh) in U.S. Federal Court. Though both were linked to al-Qaida via funding, the use of safe houses in Pakistan, and Rahman's travel to Sudan, the cellular structure of the group likely limited bin Laden's foreknowledge of the operation. In short, there are some attacks that originate and are executed under the guidance of bin Laden (e.g. the Yemen hotel), and others which are merely supported and facilitated (e.g. the 1993 World Trade Center attack) much the way a venture capitalist invests seed capital to launch business enterprises, but generally avoids active executive supervision. In any event, an arrest warrant was issued by the Saudi regime on May 16, 1993, based in part on his support for fundamentalist terrorist groups in Egypt and Algeria as well as his support of radical religious groups in Saudi Arabia.

On June 25, 1993, a gunman killed 2 motorists entering the CIA headquarters. Mir Amal Kansi was eventually arrested in Pakistan on the Afghanistan border in 1997. Kansi's links to al Qaida appear to have been established after the attack. Additionally, as with the World Trade Center attack, bin Laden's al Qaida likely trained and armed the urban guerillas who killed 18 U.S. Marines on October 3-4, 1993 in Mogadishu, Somalia, but he did not have foreknowledge of the attack. But, by the end of 1993, according to U.S. government officials, bin Laden's colleagues sought nuclear weapon components and cooperated with Sudan's leadership to develop chemical weapons.

By 1994, bin Laden was funding three terrorist training camps in North Sudan and various fundamentalist Islamic movements, prompting the Saudi government to freeze his assets and revoke his citizenship. On December 24, members of the Armed Islamic Group (AIG) seized an Air France Flight on the ground in Paris bound for Algeria. AIG members in this and other attacks were later linked to al Qaida training camps. Other such camps were established in northern Yemen in 1995, according to U.S. intelligence sources.

The capture of Ramzi Yousef, mastermind of the World Trade Center bombing, in bin Laden's guesthouse in Pakistan in February

1995 and his subsequent extradition to the United States averted an elaborate plot to bomb several American airliners in East Asia. In court, it was established that Yousef met with and received funding from bin Laden associates in Manila. More AIG members trained by al Qaida failed in an assassination attempt of Egyptian President Hosni Mubarak in Addis Ababa, Ethiopia, but successfully bombed Paris targets on July 25, 1995, August 17, 1995, and December 30, 1995

More directly, bin Laden published an open letter to the royal Saudi family in August 1995 calling for the forcible expulsion of U.S troops from the kingdom. This was followed by a car bombing on November 13, 1995, targeting the U.S. military advisory group based at the Saudi National Guard training grounds in Riyadh.

By 1996, the U.S. began focusing more effort on bin Laden, resulting in increased CIA special operations against al Qaida as well as diplomatic pressure on allies to force bin Laden out of Sudan. By May, bin Laden moved with his children and wives along with dozens of his fighters to Afghanistan.

Afghanistan (1996-circa 2002)

Bin Laden arrived into an Afghanistan still split among warring factions, but soon gravitated towards the fundamentalist Taliban and he fell under the heavy influence of radical Egyptian theologians. Within weeks, he was circulating drafts of a fatwah just prior to the al Qaida bombing of June 25, 1996 targeting the Khobar Towers, a U.S. military housing facility in Dhahran and killing 19 American citizens and wounding some 500 persons. His signed, official jihad declaration was released on August 23, 1996, proclaiming the goals of toppling the existing corrupt Saudi government, ridding the holy sites of U.S. occupation, and aiding radical Islamic groups worldwide. Notably, for the first time, bin Laden mentions the struggles of Palestine and Lebanon as examples of a Judeo-Christian intervention thereby mandating resistance by all Muslims.

Mounting evidence of recent attacks as well as continued propaganda and media interviews in 1997 led to an aborted U.S. covert operation directed against bin Laden that summer. Undaunted, he forged a coalition of religious theologians and radical Islamic groups to sign and support a second fatwah titled "Jihad Against Jews and Crusaders," on February 22, 1998, targeting the American military and civilians anywhere in the world. The tone of the declaration also changed notably from a Saudi/Arabic centric perspective towards a pan-Islamic scope. Media appearances continued in April and May including an interview broadcast on ABC TV in June. Also in June 1998, in Albania, two raids on a terrorist cell called the Islamic Revival Foundation yielded hundreds of documents and computer equipment linking the four arrested Egyptian suspects to bin Laden.

In the U.S., a grand jury issued a sealed indictment, asserting that bin Laden—via financing like-minded groups as well as heading al Qaida—conspired to attack U.S. military bases worldwide. Significantly, on August 7, 1998, bombs exploded simultaneously outside U.S. embassies in Kenya and Tanzania killing 291, injuring over 5000, and causing extensive structural damage. Convictions of the participants in U.S. court confirmed the attacks were directed by al Qaida. U.S. officials had received a general warning of attack from the Egyptian Jihad two days earlier. Interestingly, the date signifies the eighth year anniversary of United Nations sanctions against Iraq and the ordering of U.S. troops into the Gulf region. In response, to the embassy attacks on August 20, the U.S. launched a cruise missile retaliation on targets in Sudan (on a chemical plant thought to be developing chemical weapons) and Afghanistan (on al Qaida camps—mostly abandoned—but previously used mostly for training Kashmiri militants). Diplomatically, the U.S. adds bin Laden and his associated companies to a Department of Treasury list prohibiting Americans from conducting business with him.

Late in the year, bin Laden begins another media campaign, giving interviews to The News of Pakistan, as well as to ABC News and Time Magazine in the U.S. Though never fully admitting responsibility for the embassy bombings, he does claim credit for instigating the attacks and menacingly describes the pursuit of chemical and nuclear weapons as a religious duty and stating that neglecting such a duty is a sin for Muslims.

By January 16, 1999, an expanded U.S. indictment holds bin Laden and al Qaida responsible for attacks in Saudi Arabia, Somalia, Kenya, and Tanzania, having also compiled as an extensive list of their conspiracy activities. Later in June, the FBI places bin Laden on the FBI's Ten Most Wanted List and offering a $5 million reward for his capture. By year's end, the threat of millennial terrorist attacks proved quite real and significant as al Qaida December bomb plots in the U.S., Israel, and Jordan as well as an October attack on the Conference on European Cooperation and Security are thwarted.

Bin Laden keep a lower profile in 2000, avoiding assassination attempts and moving his base within Afghanistan. Captured suspects in 1998 embassy bombings were tried and convicted in U.S. court, shedding much light on the modus operandi of al Qaida. Nonethelesss, subsequent investigations linked al Qaida to the suicide attack of the U.S.S. Cole in the port of Aden, Yemen, on October 12, 2000, killing 17, injuring 39 and disabling the ship. Despite increased UN Security Council sanctions imposed on Afghanistan's rogue regime, on December 19, 2000, bin Laden remained a guest of the Taliban. At this point, analysts note that over 100 al Qaida suspects in over twenty countries had been arrested since the network's founding.

By February 2001, bin Laden appears publicly at his son's wedding in Kandahar, Afghanistan, despite press reports of his failing health. A video is circulated in June of al Qaida training camps and bin Laden predicting dramatic attacks.

On September 11, 2001, four airliners were hijacked and crashed into the twin towers of the World Trade Center in New York City, the Pentagon near Washington, DC, and a field in southern Pennsylvania (suspected to be targeting another Washington, DC, building). Over 3,000 were killed and injured. President Bush linked the attack to al Qaida and, in October, launched strikes in Afghanistan, targeting known bases as well as the Taliban command, control, and fighters.

Bin Laden began another series of video appearances on October 7, 2001 when his taped message was broadcast on the Arabic-language Al-Jazeera network, just prior to the U.S. bombing attacks of Afghanistan. Al-Jazeera was then granted an interview with bin Laden, but opted not to broadcast it. By early November, CNN had obtained a copy and did air the tape in which bin Laden lashed out at the allied bombing campaign. During the ground campaign in Afghanistan, however, allied forces had discovered a video tape dated November 9—obviously not intended for media coverage—in which bin Laden brags about the September 11 events and demonstrates his foreknowledge of the attacks. The Bush administration released the tape on December 13. Finally, on December 26, Al-Jazeera aired another videotape message of bin Laden, suspected to have been recorded earlier in December.

Despite the swift and massive allied response in attacking al Qaida and Taliban forces in Afghanistan, bin Laden's global network continued planning future attacks. After September 11, U.S. intelligence discovered and thwarted bomb plots targeting American embassies in Sarajevo and Paris.

Afghanistan/Pakistan (2002-Present)

As of Spring 2002, bin Laden's whereabouts are currently unknown. Allied forces had defeated and toppled the Taliban regime of Afghanistan and patrolled significant portions of the country. Pakistani cooperation in the bin Laden manhunt had been uneven perhaps due even to limited capabilities, and thus a hidden location in Pakistan cannot be ruled out. To their credit, by early April, Pakistan had captured and handed over a top al Qaida official, Abu Zubaida, likely to provide extensive detail on the current state of bin Laden's intentions and capabilities.

Summary

Osama bin Laden began adulthood as a religiously rebellious youth looking for a cause who found it when the Soviets invaded Afghanistan. His family riches allowed him to travel to the region, enabling him to develop contacts and networks of militant Muslim clerics and fighters, radicalizing him philosophically and empowering him militarily. He began to view moderate and/or pragmatic Islamic governments (notably Egypt and especially Saudi Arabia) as failing to uphold Muslim ideals. Later, he turned violently against those regimes, the west, and especially the U.S., as he viewed the American effort to protect Saudi Arabia from Iraq in 1990 as an invasion and occupation of the Muslim holy sites. By the late 1990s, bin Laden even considered tactical alliances with the Shiite Iranian regime and other Shiite groups against the west and Israel as he finally took up the Palestinian cause. According to his current rhetoric, he can now rationalize attacks on his foes even if the U.S. departs Saudi Arabia, Afghanistan, and its presence in all Muslim countries, the Saudi government radicalizes, and Israel is destroyed, since those actions represent crimes against Islam.

Operationally, bin Laden began his political life as an information broker and fundraiser in efforts directed against the Soviet invasion of Afghanistan. Skills and contacts made during that struggle were leveraged in the 1990s as his philosophy radicalized and list of enemies grew. Functionally, he first developed two capabilities and eventually added a third. First, he served—as one analyst described—as a 'Ford Foundation' for terrorism providing primarily funding, but later arms, training, and infrastructure support to likeminded terrorist groups against targets of mutual appeal. Second, he began to build his own group of militants under his command to execute a campaign strategy of his design. Later, bin Laden began to communicate his radical Islamic political philosophy and relevant messages via fatwahs, personal interviews, and videotape messages. All activities fall under the al Qaida framework.

As a threat Assessment: Although al Qaida's infrastructure has been crippled since the U.S. attack on his facilities in Afghanistan, the loose cellular structure of his affiliated groups and their reasonably inexpensive modus operandi indicate a real and present threat remains. Notably, even after September 2001, al Qaida-linked plots against American embassies in Europe were foiled. Additionally, until the origins of the anthrax attack can be determined, al Qaida backing cannot be ruled out.

A review of the list of events attributed to bin Laden and his network reveals that significantly less than 50% are successful. He is patient, resourceful, and at times, ingenious. Additionally, he differs from many other terrorists in his acceptance and encouragement of suicide attacks. This bodes poorly for his targeted victims should he secure weapons of mass destruction (nuclear, biological, or chemical). Frequently, he has bombed significant public buildings in less secure regions and been linked to several unsuccessful assassination attempts (the pope, as well as presidents of Egypt and U.S.). His network has utilized hijackings and plotted airline bombings on numerous occasions.

To conclude, in as much as bin Laden is the greatest terrorist threat to western interests, his ability to appeal to and integrate radical Islamic militants into his operation suggests that it is among the radical transnational Muslim youth where al Qaida's latent tentacles hide. Although a large portion of attacks have occurred in Africa and the Middle East, numerous plots have been uncovered in Europe and Asia, and significant attacks have originated from these communities within North America.

Further Reading

Yonah Alexander and Michael S. Swetnam, *Usama Bin Laden's Al-Qaida: Profile of a Terrorist Network*. Terrorism Library Series. Boston: Martinus Nijhoff, 2001.

Peter Bergen, *The Osama bin Laden I Know: An Oral History of al Qaeda's Leader*. New York: The Free Press, 2006.

Michael Scheuer, *Osama Bin Laden*. Oxford: Oxford University Press, 2011.

Piracy

Piracy, Crime, and Terrorism

G.I. Wilson

Piracy is a criminal enterprise that thrives outside the context of sovereign nation states. Piracy brings with it the convergence of other global bad actors in an opportunistic-networked association (e.g. terrorists and third generation street gangs). Maritime security experts contend what makes piracy in some measure a tempting criminal enterprise is the difficulty of bringing law enforcement to bear on piracy. This jurisdictional law enforcement challenge is further compounded by the unwillingness of many sovereign nation states to prosecute pirates. This may in part help explain why we are seeing this convergence of piracy, organized crime, and terrorism. Piracy is an indicator of how criminals and terrorists are operationally flourishing on a global basis.

The *Terrorism Research and Analysis Consortium* notes, "Intelligence analysts warn that working alliances developing between traditional pirates and the global Islamic jihad make modern-day nautical terrorism a serious threat to international security." Unfortunately much of the U.S national security capabilities as well as those of other nation states, are better suited to operate within a nation-state context. Outside that nation-state construct, nation states face many challenges not least of which is adapting to emerging threats. Jonathan Boonzaier notes that a new and more dangerous type of piracy emerged in late 2010 as organized gangs attacked tankers with the sole aim of stealing their high-value cargo.

Piracy is not new, crime is not new, and terrorism is not new. All have history. What is new is an opportunistic association of piracy with terrorism, third generation street gangs, and even organized crime. In today's terms, piracy could be called maritime terrorism, although terrorism and piracy actually spawn from different motivations. According to Retired Naval Captain William Carpenter, pirates act out of greed while terrorists are out to make a political point.

Piracy is a lucrative crime and revenue generating stream in regions where states are floundering and have marginal to nonexistent law enforcement capabilities to thwart piracy. Many countries are not willing or are reluctant to aggressively prosecute pirates captured in their jurisdiction for piracy that was committed in another country's waters and jurisdiction. Modern piracy is violent, ruthless, and unconstrained by borders, thus having a lot in common with violent street gangs and terrorism.

The International Maritime Bureau (IMB) Piracy Reporting Centre (PRC) recorded 138 piracy incidents in the first six months of 2013, highlighting emerging piracy in West Africa. However, the actual number of cases of piracy are up for debate for government and non-government organizations that track piracy worldwide point out that the number of piracy cases may be underreported.

Despite the potential for underreporting, there are disturbing indicators that piracy is transforming into maritime terrorism or piracy terrorism. With greater association with sophisticated criminal enterprises and terrorists, piracy is posing a more complex threat. Piracy damages global trade, undermines sovereignty, threatens the security of nation states, and now supports broader criminal enterprises and terrorism. Today's piracy is more than a nuisance to commercial shipping. It not only affects but also significantly threatens maritime traffic in vital shipping lanes, particularly in Southeast Asia.

Attacks on oil supertankers hold the potential to ignite environmental disasters and are a consequence management problem with liability implications that could destroy major oil and shipping companies and derail economic sectors, much in the manner that the 9-11 attacks affected the airline and travel industry. Attacks by pirate craft may invite military action, as in the case of the 2009 hijacking by Somali pirates of the U.S.-flagged MV Maersk Alabama.

Because of the greater involvement of piracy in organized criminal networks, the International Chamber of Commerce (ICC) has a keen interest in hijackings. Pottengal Mukundan, Director of ICC's

Commercial Crime Services states in an International Maritime Bureau press release:

> (Piracy) typically involves a mother ship from which to launch the attacks, a supply of automatic weapons, false identity papers for the crew and vessel, fake cargo documents, and a broker network to sell the stolen goods illegally. Individual pirates don't have these resources. Hijackings are the work of organized crime rings.

However, in addition to organized crime rings, terrorist groups are also extending their capabilities to the maritime environment according to maritime security analyst, Vijay Sakhuja. He cautions that terrorist tactics involve attacking ships both in harbor and at sea. Commercial ships, liners, ferries, ports, and maritime infrastructure are vulnerable. Clearly, he feels terrorism has come to stalk the maritime environment where the perpetrators engage in violence for both political objectives and commercial profit.

This trend in piracy's hijacking tactics, techniques, and procedures (TTPs) is witnessing the expansion into kidnapping and demands for ransom. An International Chamber of Commerce report highlights the kidnap and ransom tactics observed in the Malacca Strait, a phenomenon earlier restricted to Somali waters. Piracy has spread to West Africa. Unlike Somali pirates who are often only after ransom, West Africa pirates are out to steal oil. The scenario of stealing ships brings with it added concern and trepidation when it comes to hijacking vessels containing highly flammable cargo.

Ships carrying cargos of highly flammable petroleum products hijacked by terrorists pose a gamut of threats, including being used for suicide attacks. The International Maritime Bureau's Piracy Reporting Centre cautions that forged ship and crew travel documents can be easily obtained for tankers carrying oil or liquefied gases, facilitating terrorists' suicide missions to include attacks on other vessels, ports, or infrastructure. Attacks using hijacked ships targeting such things as bridge works, vessels secured pier side, or fuel storage sites are not out of the realm of possibility. The threat to naval vessels has not been lost on maritime security analyst Vijay Sakhuja who writes:

> Terrorist tactics involve attacking ships both in harbor and at sea. They are known to use improvised explosive devices, submersibles, mini submarines and high-speed boats. Dual-use technologies such as the Global Positioning Systems (GPS), satellite communication systems, sea sport scooters and scuba diving equipment are found in their inventories. At sea, these terrorist groups have used rocket-propelled grenades, explosive-loaded speedboats and even armor piercing weapons. The terrorist networks have kept pace with changing technologies and have adapted themselves to counter maritime forces. It is therefore essential to understand the contemporary and emerging tactics and technologies employed by terrorist groups.

With the risk of attacks against ships at sea or in ports, one must consider in assessing these attacks if such acts are piracy or terrorism or perhaps both. While maritime security analysts contend piracy is committed for basically personal gains, maritime or sea terrorism is committed for ideological political purposes.

Today, there is a thinning and blurred line separating piracy from sea terrorism. With this blurring, we see piracy converging with crime, war, and terrorism in an opportunistic association. As we use maritime lanes and harvest food, water (i.e. desalination), energy (e.g. gas and oil platforms), and even habitat (i.e. waterborne populations) from the sea, we need to be aware of the impact of piracy and sea terrorism.

Further Reading

John Arquilla, *Insurgents, Raiders, and Bandits: How Masters of Irregular Warfare Have Shaped Our World*. Plymouth: Ivan R. Dee, 2011.

Robert J. Bunker, Ed., *Networks, Terrorism and Global Insurgency*. London: Routledge, 2005.

Martin N. Murphy, *Contemporary Piracy and Maritime Terrorism: The threat to international security*. Adelphi Paper 388. New York: Routledge, July 2007.

Police and Terrorism

John P. Sullivan

Terrorism involves the use of force and violence against persons or infrastructure within communities: local, national, and global. As such, terrorism is a phenomenon that entails criminal acts and conspiracies. The response to violence and criminal activities involving sub-national actors is the province of the police and law enforcement services. In broad terms, police actions to combat terrorism are organized across four general areas of police activity: Patrol, investigations, intelligence, and response.

The police service in democratic societies has the responsibility of preserving liberty and ensuring public safety and order through the rule of law. The ability of police to contain and control criminal activity, including terrorist acts and conspiracies that further terrorist activity, necessarily relies upon consent and interaction with the public, as well as coordination and cooperation with other organs of government. These include partners in the criminal justice system such as prosecutors, magistrates, and the judiciary. During extreme threats and during acute periods, the police also interact with military authorities operating in support of the civil authority. By necessity, the police operate at all phases of "response" to terrorist acts: before the event, during the incipient crisis, and in the aftermath of an attack. These phases are known, respectively, as pre-incident, trans-incident, and post incident.

Most modern nations place the police in the central role of preserving order and combating terrorism within their borders rather than relying upon military agencies. Additionally, most nations rely upon police and judicial strategies to combat terrorism that crosses borders. While direct military action and special operations forces typically augment these capabilities, police and law enforcement activity are at the forefront. Most nations rely upon a number of police agencies or specialties to address terrorist threats. These include general service police, border police, specialized police at airports, seaports, and transportation facilities, customs and immigration agencies, and investigative agencies.

In the United States, the Federal Bureau of Investigation (FBI) is the lead federal investigative agency for terrorism. The FBI is primarily an investigative agency, but also performs liaison with foreign police through its system of legal attaches (legats) throughout the world, and specialized response (such as post blast and crime scene response in support of investigations). The FBI coordinates its activities with other federal, state and local police through a network of joint terrorism task forces (JTTFs). Each JTTF has representatives of the FBI, as well as state, and local police and specialized federal law enforcement agencies. Local crime control and broader police duties are the responsibility of municipal police, county or parish sheriffs, and state police (or highway patrols) in the United States.

Patrol

Patrol is the most visible police function. Uniformed officers in marked vehicles or on foot perform this function. During their routine activities, they respond to calls for service and interact with the public. These activities place the police in an ideal position to learn about crime and potential indicators of terrorist activity in a community. Community policing and problem-solving activities ensure that community concerns and issues are addressed by the police. This interaction is essential to developing intelligence about threats and criminal activity that supports terrorists. In addition, visible police patrols help deter terrorist attacks. Because of this key role, police are sometimes targeted by terrorist groups as part of a broader insurgency (as is currently seen in Iraq and was historically seen in Northern Ireland). Police patrol often observes the "signs of crime" that serve as indicators of pending terrorist activity. Routine police activities are an important element of terrorism prevention. A classic example of this was illustrated in the 1988 arrest of Japanese Red Army terrorist Yu Kikumura during a traffic stop on the New Jersey Turnpike. A State Trooper stopped Kikumura, who was transporting explosives for use in an attack, for a traffic violation.

Investigations

Investigations bridge police patrol and community peacekeeping activities with law enforcement and judicial action. Uniformed police respond, gather facts, and then frequently pass information from the field to detectives or investigators that assemble a case for criminal prosecution before the law courts. Since terrorists need such resources as weapons, materials for constructing explosives, finances to conduct and support their activities, and false identification, they frequently interact with other criminals to further their conspiracy. As a result, organized crime (including narcotics trafficking and smuggling of all sorts) often enables terrorist activity. Since contemporary terrorism frequently operates across borders, transnational organized crime groups increasingly interact with terrorists helping to move illicit money and contraband internationally. Police investigations (locally, at the federal level, and in cooperation with police worldwide) are critical to discern these linkages and develop the intelligence necessary to combat terrorist conspiracies.

Intelligence

Intelligence provides decision-makers, investigators, and responders with the information they need to perform their respective tasks. The information that is ultimately collected, collated, assessed, and fused together to support anti- and counterterrorism operations comes from many sources. It comes from the bottom up—that is, from the public to their community police. It comes from national security entities, such as intelligence organizations and federal homeland security functions such as border and immigration enforcement, and it is derived laterally from exchanges of information among JTTFs, Terrorism Early Warning (TEW) Groups, and police to police information-sharing worldwide. Intelligence helps shape police activity of all kinds. Crime analysis and "intelligence-led policing" form the basis for resource allocation, setting priorities for response and crime control initiatives, deployment decisions, and response posture (such as heightened visibility during high threat periods). Intelligence is needed to identify threats and criminal enterprises, to prepare for potential response, and manage response activities. During the response to an attack, intelligence that includes information on the status of resources and personnel, weather, terrain, and the impact of the event as well as traditional "criminal intelligence" are essential.

Response

When terrorists strike, the police along with their partners in the fire and emergency medical services are among the first to respond. Police response, as demonstrated in the 9-11 attack on the World Trade Center which resulted in the line-of-duty deaths of 37 Port Authority Police (Port Authority of New York and Jersey) and 23 New York City Police (NYPD) officers, is multifaceted. Police officers assist the fire service in rescue, evacuate threatened persons, cordon the area (securing a perimeter and establishing a crime scene), provide traffic and crowd control, protect other responders from secondary attack (force protection), perform investigations (by interviewing witnesses and identifying potential suspects), and neutralize or apprehend terrorist suspects. Police response includes patrol officers, emergency services or rescue squads, crowd control personnel, special weapons teams, bomb squads to render safe explosive devices or perform post-blast investigations, forensic and criminalists to document the crime scene, and detectives and investigators.

Conclusion

The police are an essential element in combating and containing the threat of terrorism. The police protect the public, help preserve and restore order, investigate and support the prosecution of terrorists and participants in other criminal enterprises that facilitate terrorist activity.

The police function is central to maintaining the rule of law and ensuring public safety while preserving liberty against terrorist threats.

Further Reading

David H. Bailey and Robert M. Perito, *The Police in War: Fighting Insurgency, Terrorism, and Violent Crime.* Boulder: Lynne Rienner, 2010.

Mathieu Deflem, *The Policing of Terrorism: Organizational and Global Perspectives.* London: Routledge, 2010.

Paul M. Maniscalco and Hank T. Christen, *Terrorism Response: Field Guide for Law Enforcement.* Upper Saddle River: Prentice Hall, 2002.

Psychological Operations

A Revolution in Information Manipulation

Adam Elkus

Key to dystopian visions of the future such as *1984* and *Brave New World* has been the image of a totalitarian government manipulating the mass populace through advanced technology. Fifty years after Orwell, the information age has indeed revolutionized tactical and strategic persuasion, but the chief beneficiary has not been the massive state-controlled perception management and propaganda apparatus. Instead, non-state organizations (NGOs), criminals, and terrorists have taken advantage of increasingly advanced technologies and an almost omniscient global communications network to outmaneuver the state in the propaganda war. In order to win the digital ideological struggle, the state must embrace a different kind of persuasion.

A Short History of PSYOPS

When most think of psychological operations (PSYOPS), the images that come to mind are the familiar exhortations to surrender delivered by leaflet or loudspeaker. The more conspiratorially minded think of subliminal messages in television broadcasts, "black" propaganda, and mind-control. This view of PSYOPS is both sensationalistic and reductive. According to the Defense Department's Joint Publication 3-53, *PSYOPS* are "operations planned to convey selected information and indicators to foreign audiences to influence their emotions, motives, objective reasoning, and ultimately the behavior of foreign governments, organizations, groups, and individuals." PSYOPS is as old as war itself, with countless ancient military philosophers stressing the value of deception and sowing discord among one's enemies. However, the "golden age" of PSYOPS was the Cold War. Both the U.S. and the Soviet Union conducted large-scale strategic influence operations. A great deal of it occurred in the public sphere, with the United States utilizing radio stations like Radio Free Liberty, Radio Free Europe, TV Marti, to reach audiences inside the Communist bloc. Beneath the surface was a furious battle of "black" and "grey" propaganda, with an extensive network of covert proxies attempting to influence foreign and domestic audiences with both biased information and outright lies. This massive battle in psychological operations was made possible by advances in communications technology such as radio and television, higher levels of literacy, and the expanding reach of media coverage to the farthest corners of the world.

The United States, for many reasons, was at a steep disadvantage in this propaganda war. In an era of revolution and postcolonial change, it was largely cast in the role of backing colonial or authoritarian regimes against Soviet and Chinese-backed revolutionaries and a massive network of sympathizers who drew their ideological inspiration from Marxist-inspired New Leftism and postcolonial nationalism. Those audiences were often pre-disposed to take the worst of Soviet-inspired deceptions at face value. However, the United States did have three important advantages—an appealing popular culture, an imperfect but self-correcting democratic system, and an agency (the United States Information Agency) to coordinate public diplomacy and influence operations.

On the battlefield, tactical and operational PSYOPs involved ground teams attempting to win the "hearts and minds" of foreign civilian populations and crush the will of insurgents and terrorists. The record of tactical PSYOPS during the Cold War was mixed. Successes in counterinsurgencies such as the Philippines were offset by failures like Vietnam, where the failure of the war's greater strategic and political objectives compromised efforts of battlefield PSYOPs operators. And, as Colonel Alfred Paddock Jr. noted in his essay "US Military Psychological Operations in Transition," the military has traditionally regarded the PSYOPS community, like their cousins in the Special Operations community (SOCOM) with disdain. Despite the rising importance of "small wars" and terrorism in the 20th century, two fields of conflict heavy on political warfare and influence operations, military investment in PSYOPs has largely been episodic in nature since the second World War. PSYOPS, an unorthodox discipline that emphasizes communication and persuasion, clashes with the regular military mission of organized destruction.

Although PSYOPS itself remained a crucial part of post-Cold War humanitarian interventions such as Haiti and Bosnia, its civilian counterpart in USIA fell victim to budget cuts. An increasingly inward-leaning American public saw little need to evangelize for American interests without the Soviet menace looming. Influence operations were regarded only as a necessity on the tactical and operational levels as battlefield shaping measures. The military template for this during the 1990s to the early 2000s was an idea that came to be expressed by Harlan Ullman: "Shock and Awe"—cowing an enemy through massive network-centric air and ground operations designed to crush enemy command and control capabilities, inducing panic, paralysis, and hopefully surrender.

It is worth noting that Russia and China both made extensive innovations to their influence operations doctrine around this time, placing a greater emphasis on persuasion and information manipulation, often through exploitation of new information and communications technologies. However, these changes were barely noticed by the U.S. defense establishment, save a few intrepid military analysts like the Foreign Military Studies Office's Timothy L. Thomas.

Outgunned in the Press Room

Both the cutback of the USIA and the molding of PSYOPs into "Shock and Awe" couldn't have come at a worse time. We are currently faced with a motley array of non-state actors, ranging from well-disciplined insurgent armies to "lone wolves" who know how to leverage two important trends in modern communications: a global proliferation of easily accessible communications platforms and the increasing "realism" of the simulated reality pumped into living rooms by global

24-hour media. The U.S. diplomatic and military communities, though conscious of these trends, have not adapted to them. The consequence of this neglect has been great, ranging from a damaging inability to rebut enemy propaganda to America's increasing international isolation.

The late 20th century and early 21st century have seen a proliferation of convergent media platforms. The largest of this is the Internet, which has fulfilled H.G. Wells' prediction of a massive "Global Brain" of human knowledge. However, television and the now ubiquitous mobile communication devices such as personal digital assistants (PDAs) and cell phones are also potent weapons of strategic influence. Non-state actors have taken to these technologies, using them to influence foreign and domestic populations, demoralize their opponents, rally supporters, and recruit. The effect of this has been dramatic.

In Iraq, misinformation about American operations and gruesome images of insurgents killing American soldiers are rapidly disseminated through viral Internet video, text messaging, and satellite television. In the 2006 Israel-Lebanon war, the Israelis were confronted by a multi-pronged Hezbollah information offensive that targeted Lebanese and international audiences. Even before that, as Trinity College Professor Maura Conway notes, Hezbollah had long carried out operations to demoralize the Israeli home front by contacting nervous and bereaved parents of Israeli soldiers through the Internet to give accurate (and sometimes gruesome) information about the fates of their children, information more accurate than that of the Israeli military press office. Lastly, Al Qaeda maintains a video production unit, Al-Sahab, that distributes slickly produced media products at an astounding rate. Al-Qaeda in Iraq (AQI) was even able to fabricate a fictional Iraqi head of AQI to replace the fallen Abu Musab al-Zarqawi, a deception that was only revealed with the capture of an AQI operative.

Even criminals are beginning to develop their own PSYOP. In the Western hemisphere, gangs have also utilized the Internet to post videos of themselves executing their rivals, and are augmented by a digital network of sympathizers that "rep" their gang on an international level. In Latin America, this online propaganda is used to dissuade the people from cooperating with police and ramp up gang recruitment.

As Timothy L. Thomas and the Simon Wiesenthal Center have reported, terrorists and hate groups also use entertainment media such as video games, television dramas, web animations, and other fictional products to draw in sympathizers and propagandize. This allows them to immerse the potential recruit into a niche world where the majority of media he consumes, whether for news or entertainment purposes, reflects the organization's ideological message. Terrorist group exploitation of online virtual worlds—such as Second Life—for training purposes is regarded by spy agencies such as the Intelligence Advanced Research Projects Agency (IARPA) as increasingly likely, if not already ongoing.

The increasing realism of information media has a powerful emotional effect, shifting both public opinion and policy. Pictures of starving Somali children and dead Bosnians spurred humanitarian intervention in the 1990s. Even Americans in small towns with little to fear from potential terrorists were caught up in the nationwide epidemic of fear that occurred after the 9/11 attacks, an epidemic that was aided in part by the government's own focus on vague threat warnings. This, and the availability of relatively cheap media production tools, has resulted in the unprecedented ability of individuals to virally market themselves. This can be benign or malicious—we applaud when a Youtube poster like Lonelygirl15 manages to make herself into a celebrity but are terrified by the televised mayhem of attention-seeking mass murderers such as the 2007 Virginia Tech shooter or the 2002 DC snipers.

What's more, the increasing proliferation of information and realistic media opens it up for manipulation. Foreign special interest groups have long manipulated and distorted information to convince American audiences to support their causes, filling the Washington D.C. cocktail circuit with legions of educated press flacks—each promoting a different band of "democratic freedom fighters." Now, combatants in insurgencies such as the Israeli-Palestinian conflict, the Balkan wars, and most recently the 2006 invasion of Lebanon strive to manipulate the international media and public opinion. Palestinians have been caught attempting to provoke Israeli punitive operations for the benefit of waiting television cameras, the Serbs and Russians perpetrated a longstanding myth that the Bosnian Muslims shelled their own people and falsely blamed it on the Serbs, and the confidence man Ahmed

Chalabi managed to fool the Washington establishment into relying on his Iraqi National Congress (INC) as the main source of information about Saddam's Iraq.

Unlike Americans, insurgents and other non-state actors do not view PSYOPS and straightforward military operations as separate: they see them as one and the same in a holistic political-military struggle, something RAND Corporation social scientists John Arquilla and David Ronfeldt dub "social netwar." This doesn't entirely have to be violent in nature—witness, for example, mass activist campaigns such as the anti-globalization WTO protests in Seattle, hacker collective Anonymous' campaign against the Church of Scientology, or protests against the Revolutionary Armed Forces of Colombia (FARC) organized through the social networking application Facebook.

An Incompetent Response

The U.S. response to these operations has been wholly inadequate. For one, the U.S. suffers from a proliferation of multiple overlapping definitions for PSYOPS—such as information operations, influence operations, public affairs, and public diplomacy. The practical effect of this semantic confusion is the increasing compartmentalization of the agencies engaged in the "war of ideas" when unity is needed to successfully combat enemy propaganda. Additionally, as defense contractor and former RAND scientist Scott Gerwehr noted in a presentation for the Los Angeles Terrorism Early Warning Group, there is a lack of scientific precision and social science rigor to PSYOPS. Additionally, government agencies also suffer from a shortage of individuals able to speak important languages such as Arabic, Farsi, and Pashto.

On the strategic level, American messages are targeted to the wrong audiences, lack brand-name punch, and they frequently stand in opposition to policy. It is difficult, for example, to convince Middle Eastern audiences of American support for democracy while turning a blind eye to Egyptian and Saudi repression of pro-democracy activists. As public diplomacy specialist Matt Armstrong has reported, the U.S.

also is unaware of the symbolic impact of its institutions and actions abroad. The new fortress-like American embassy in Baghdad looks as inviting and friendly to ordinary Iraqis as Darth Vader's Death Star did to movie audiences.

Sadly enough, the U.S. has disempowered the very actors who would stand as the most credible spokespeople for its foreign policy: the military. The average Iraqi or Afghan will never meet the Secretary of State; they will interact with a Marine from Ohio manning the checkpoint. As Marine Corps General Charles C. Krulak argued, the deciding factor of future "Three Block Wars" is the "strategic corporal," whose actions can affect the operational and strategic levels of war. However, an overzealous focus on operational security (OPSEC) prevents soldiers from producing their own blogs and media products to combat insurgent propaganda and misinformation. Granted, public diplomacy is a daunting task for the ground soldier trained to pulverize, not persuade. Yet foreign audiences already see the GI as a living representation of American values, culture, and policy, and in order to win he must carry out his own battlefield diplomacy.

Until the government comes to terms with the new world of information influence, the country that gave the world Madison Avenue and Hollywood will remain outgunned by insurgents, terrorists, and criminals in the public info-sphere.

Further Reading

James J.F. Forest, Ed., *Influence Warfare: How Terrorists and Governments Fight to Shape Perceptions in a War of Ideas*. Santa Barbara: Prager Security International, 2009.

Andrew Rathmell and Kevin A. O'Brien, *Information Operations*. Surrey: Jane's Information Group, 2001.

Ron Shlaifer, *Perspectives of Psychological Operations (PSYOP) in Contemporary Conflicts*. Eastbourne: Sussex Academic Press, 2011.

Public Health and Medical Responses

Public Health in the Post-September 11 and High-Tech Era

Scott P. Layne

The public health system in the United States is a patchwork of jurisdictions and capabilities that work together on occasion. As a result, the pace in which infectious disease outbreaks are identified and investigated is variable. As seen with West Nile virus in New York City and foodborne outbreaks crossing multiple states, it sometimes takes weeks to months for health agencies to even suspect deadly outbreaks. In addition, there is no single laboratory and database system (i.e., a clearinghouse) that routinely tracks infectious disease outbreaks and organizes the information on a regional or national basis. For better or worse, the public health system is thinly distributed.

These limitations were not fully appreciated until October 2001, when a handful of anthrax letters made it apparent that Americans are vulnerable to biological attacks. The first time we were relatively lucky—five deaths, a dozen or so hospitalizations, and 30,000 people on prophylactic antibiotics. In addition, public health laboratories were overwhelmed with well over 100,000 samples to test and characterize and, to this day, they have not caught up with the post-October surge.

Whether the perpetrator, still at large, is a lone "bio Kaczynski" or an organized "bio Bin Laden" is somewhat beside the point. The primary issue is that the United States must devise a broader plan to prevent, deter, and respond to the long-term threats of biological terrorism. A central part of this plan involves upgrading the public health system and giving it the resources and tools to work with other disciplines.

Who Should Cooperate and Why?

The public health, agricultural, emergency response, law enforcement, intelligence, and national security communities must somehow find ways to work together. To this day, however, they have shown little inclination to do so. One part of the problem is due to ownership and bureaucratic turf. Another part of the problem is due to disciplinary mentality and culture clash.

The public health, agricultural, and emergency response mentalities and cultures are based on openness and lending assistance to others in large part. They want to work without hidden agendas. On the other hand, the law enforcement, intelligence, and national security cultures are based on chain of custody, due process, compartmentalization, and deadly force. Out of necessity, they have to work with hidden agendas. As a result, these two mentalities and cultures mix like oil and water. With sufficient agitation or threat, they appear to mix but separate naturally when things quiet down. This tendency is not conducive to building a legitimate bio-response capability.

Here is another part of the problem. The United States' fear of another biological attack is fading fast. Our vulnerability, however, hasn't. It costs about $1,000,000 to kill one person with a nuclear weapon, about $1,000 to kill one person with a chemical weapon, and about $1 to kill one person with a biological weapon. Radiological weapons are relatively cheap too, but they contaminate people and property rather than kill outright.

Consequently, the economy of death and potential for terrorism with biological agents (such as anthrax, smallpox, and foot-and-mouth) suggests that they will be used again by terrorist organizations. Even more alarmingly, a terrorist's personal survival may not matter and, under the right circumstances, their peoples' survival may not even matter as well. In the extreme case, an unprincipled leader of a rogue state may opt to use a "dead switch," which is set to unleash highly virulent and transmissible biological agents in the event of his overthrow.

The Role of Public Health

What should the role of public health be in response to the threats posed by biological terrorism? In broad terms, I believe that we need two kinds of undertakings as summarized below.

The more traditional undertaking involves upgrading local response capabilities and giving the public health system enough resources and tools to work with others. In somewhat progressive order, the more obvious steps are as follows. The *first* is requiring public health, emergency response, and law enforcement agencies to work together. The *second* is developing specific guidelines and operational plans against biological attacks, which should include mass vaccination and quarantine guidelines as well as emergency food and water safety guidelines. The *third* is training first responders and health care providers on how to deal with biological attacks. The *fourth* is sharpening bioattack response guidelines and plans by conducting practice exercises with public health, emergency response, and law enforcement agencies. The *fifth* is implementing an information management system that assists in all response phases. The *sixth* is creating networks for reporting infectious diseases outbreak rapidly. The *seventh* is expanding laboratory diagnostic capabilities for infectious disease outbreaks. The *eight* is establishing multi-disciplinary advisory committees that offer independent advice to local officials. These steps will lead to capabilities that are inherently dual use, meaning that they could help to save many lives and speed recovery operations in the event of naturally occurring outbreaks and/or man-made attacks.

The less traditional, yet equally important, undertaking involves engaging the public health system in national and international efforts to deter and prevent biological attacks. The 1972 Biological Weapons Convention, agreed to by 162 nations, bans the maintenance of offensive bioweapons programs but offers no provision for verification and compliance. Over the past 30 years, there have been various attempts to strengthen the BWC but none have produced tangible agreements. Today, the world still relies on the good will of nations to self-report activities and curtail offensive bioweapons programs.

What More Can Be Done?

One important way to overcome the current gap is for the United States to build a high-speed/high-volume infectious disease laboratory and information processing system that relates the molecular fingerprints of biological agents to their sources worldwide. The new system would be built on existing science and technology from the academic, industrial, and governmental sectors. It would bring together and integrate various disciplines, interests, and expertise to deal with the threat of bioterrorism in the most effective ways possible.

The high-speed/high-volume laboratory and database system would provide swift and accurate identification and attribution for effective and rapid action. It would also provide the technological foundation to develop robust national policies and take appropriate actions against those who use or might use bioweapons. Because microbial forensics can determine the origin of bioagents with a high degree of certainty, it would have a potential role in counter-terrorism and non-proliferation.

The fully operational system would be capable of handling both bacterial and viral agents. Its flexible design would make it easy to augment with new and cost-effective technologies as they become available as well as other technologies that provide more highly discriminating tests. The analysis of samples would be accomplished by integrating molecular biology, laboratory automation and robotics, and informatic capabilities into one system.

The collection of samples would be accomplished by a concerted effort worldwide. The system would also work in conjunction with outbreak investigations and syndromic surveillance efforts. Such capabilities would operate continuously, provide real-time information, and serve as a global biodefense sentinel.

The 1918 influenza pandemic killed 40 million people worldwide. And it is often been pointed out that more people will die from an unpredictable influenza pandemic than from a biological attack. This argument may be correct. Yet a well planned and implemented biological attack could have equally severe social and economic consequences. We should therefore be better prepared for both.

New Model for Public Health

Before the high-tech Internet era, public health could not be practiced on a real-time basis. Now such notions are within the realm of available science and technology. The one remaining step involves a shift in public health perspectives.

An older model of public health espoused: the spot following natural outbreaks after they begin and respond. The world can afford to wait, more or less. A newer model of public health could easily espouse: instead spot natural outbreaks immediately and respond. If possible, try to deter and prevent the man-made outbreak. Otherwise, attribute sources and respond with public health and/or national security measures. The world cannot afford to wait, because the outcome could be far too dire.

Further Reading

Girish Bobby Kapur and Jeffrey P. Smith, *Emergency Public Health: Preparedness And Response.* Sudbury: Jones & Bartlett Learning, 2011.

Barry S. Levy and Victor W. Sidel, *Terrorism and Public Health: A Balanced Approach to Strengthening Systems and Protecting People.* Second Edition. New York: Oxford University Press, 2011.

Allison M. Panzer and Lewis R, Goldfrank, Eds., *Preparing for the Psychological Consequences of Terrorism: A Public Health Strategy.* Washington, DC: National Academies Press, 2003.

Radicalization

2009 Senate Testimony—
Radicalization and the Homegrown Threat

Mitchell D. Silber

In 2007, the NYPD released a study titled, "Radicalization in the West: The Homegrown Threat." This report analyzed the process of radicalization in the West and the threat that it potentially posed to the United States. At that point, evidence of the presence of the homegrown threat in the United States was scarce. By 2010, this threat has materialized.

The Past Twenty-four Months

During the last twenty-four months, U.S. authorities have uncovered a number of radicalized clusters of individuals intent on committing violent jihad within the continental United States as well as abroad. These arrests, along with intelligence operations, indicate that radicalization to violence is taking place in the United States.

In November of 2008, the Department of Homeland Security and FBI issued a warning relating to an al Qaeda linked terrorist plot against the Long Island Railroad commuter network. The origins of the plot link directly to Bryant Neal Vinas, a New Yorker, who radicalized to violence in and around New York City before traveling to Pakistan to seek out an opportunity to participate in violent jihad.

In April of 2009, before their arrest by the Joint Terrorism Task Force, four men placed what they believed were C4 explosives outside a Jewish synagogue and community center in Riverdale, New York in an attempt to carry out a terrorist act. These men were radicalized in the United States.

In July of 2009, seven men were arrested by federal authorities in North Carolina for possessing weapons and more than 27,000 rounds of ammunition with plans to attack the Marine Base at Quantico, VA. These men, known as the Raleigh 7, were inspired by al Qaeda and radicalized in the United States.

Last September, Najibullah Zazi, age 24, was arrested as part of an al Qaeda linked conspiracy to attack locations in New York City with hydrogen peroxide based explosives. The plot has been called one of the most serious since 9/11. Zazi, who lived in Flushing, Queens during his formative years—ages 14 to 23, before departing for Pakistan, radicalized in the United States.

Later that same September, Betim Kaziu, a 21 year-old New Yorker from Brooklyn, was indicted for conspiracy to commit murder abroad and support for foreign terrorists. Arrested in Kosovo, Kaziu sought to join a foreign fighter group overseas and to "take up arms against perceived enemies of Islam," meaning American troops in Iraq or Afghanistan. He was radicalized in the United States.

And there are more—In Boston, Tarek Mehanna, age 26 and a graduate of the Massachusetts College of Pharmacy was arrested in October of 2009. Not only did he seek to fight jihad abroad, but he also is charged with conspiring to attack civilians at a shopping mall in the U.S., as well as two members of the executive branch of the federal government. He was radicalized in the U.S.

At least fifteen men of Somali descent have radicalized in Minneapolis over the last few years and left the U.S. to fight jihad in Somalia. They joined Al Shabaab, a terrorist group associated with al Qaeda and based in Somalia. Our fear is—What happens when they return to the U.S.? Australia has already thwarted a plot this year involving individuals who fought alongside al Shabaab and then returned to Melbourne seeking to carry out a plot against an Australian military base.

This past September also saw two plots involving lone wolves in both Dallas, Texas and Springfield, Illinois. In Dallas, a large office building was targeted with a vehicle borne explosive. In Springfield, a

Federal building was targeted. Though these individuals were not part of any group, much of their radicalization seems U.S. based.

There were arrests of two Chicagoans with direct links to Lashkar-e-Taiba, the group responsible for the November 2008 Mumbai terrorist attack. Though these men were involved with plotting against targets in Denmark and Mumbai, India, once again, it appears that the U.S. served as their location of radicalization.

Finally, in May and June of 2010, there was the attempted bombing attack on Time Square by Faisal Shahzad, a naturalized American citizen from Connecticut, as well as the thwarted overseas travel to join Al Shabaab in Somalia on June 5, by Carlos Almonte and Mohammed Alessa, two men from New Jersey.

Given the evidence of the past twenty-four month period, one must conclude that radicalization to violence is occurring in the U.S.

Process and Radicalization

Given what seems to be a pattern of individuals radicalizing to al Qaeda inspired violence, the NYPD has invested a substantial analytic effort in assessing the causes and process that marked the radicalization trajectory of these individuals. Among the cases previously mentioned, we saw the pattern repeating itself. It is consistent with the model from the 2007 NYPD report that identified a graduated process consisting of phases—Pre-Radicalization, Self Identification, Indoctrination and Jihadization. Driving this process is a combination of the proliferation of al Qaeda ideology in English intertwined with the real or perceived political grievances that cite a Western "war against Islam" and provide the justification for young men with unremarkable backgrounds to pursue violent extremism.

The dissection, comparison, and analysis of eleven al Qaeda like plots between 9/11 and 2006, which formed the basis of the 2007 NYPD report, led to the assessment that there is a common pathway of radicalization in the West. Each of the stages has specific cognitive and behavioral signatures associated with it. Although this model is sequential, individuals do not always follow a linear progression.

However, individuals who do pass through this entire process are quite likely to be involved in a terrorist act. The stages are as follows:

Phase 1: Pre-Radicalization

Pre-Radicalization is the point of origin or life situation for individuals before they begin this progression. Based on the original study and subsequent plots, individuals who seem to be vulnerable to radicalization to "jihadist" violence tend to be male Muslims, between the ages of 15 to 35 who are local residents and citizens from varied ethnic backgrounds. Significant proportions come from middle class backgrounds and are educated, at least high school graduates if not university students. Based on our case studies, the vast majority of individuals who end up radicalizing to violence do not start out as religiously observant or knowledgeable.

Phase 2: Self-Identification

Self-Identification is the phase where individuals, influenced by both internal and external factors, begin to explore more literal interpretations of Islam, gradually gravitate away from their old identity to a more "Islamic" identity, and begin to associate themselves with like-minded individuals who have adopted the view that, "the West is at war with Islam." The trigger for this "religious seeking" is often a catalytic event, or crisis, which challenges the individual's previously held beliefs and causes the individual to reconsider their previously held outlook and worldview.

Phase 3: Indoctrination

Indoctrination is the phase of ideological commitment in which an individual progressively intensifies his beliefs, adopts extremist ideology, and concludes that action is required to support and further the cause. That action is violence. This ideological commitment is the manifestation of accepting a religious-political ideology that justifies, legitimizes, encourages, or supports violence against the West, its citizens, its allies, or those whose opinions are contrary to his own extremist agenda.

The signatures associated with this phase include becoming an active participant in a group and simultaneously become increasingly isolated from one's former life. Gradually, the individuals begin to isolate themselves from secular society and self-radicalize. They come to believe that the world is divided between enlightened believers (themselves) and infidels (everybody else).

Phase 4: Jihadization, or the "Movement to Violence Phase"

Jihadization is a martial phase in which individuals accept their individual duty to participate in violent jihad and self-designate themselves as holy warriors or mujahedeen. Often, individuals will seek to travel abroad to participate in a field of jihad such as Afghanistan, Pakistan, Kashmir, Chechnya, Somalia or Iraq, only to be re-directed back to the West to do "something for the cause" there. Frequently, the group members participate in outdoors activities like rafting, camping, or paintball to vet, bond, and train. In addition, mental preparation commences as jihadist videos are watched. Lastly, potential targets are chosen, surveillance and reconnaissance begins, and the group weaponizes with readily available components.

New Analysis

While much of the 2007 Radicalization study remains directly applicable to the last twenty-four months' events, additional research has highlighted some new findings. The most important is that the internet has become an even more important venue and driver for radicalization. "No longer is the threat just from abroad, as was the case with the attacks of September 11, 2001; the threat is now increasingly from within, from homegrown terrorists who are inspired by violent Islamist ideology to plan and execute attacks where they live. One of the primary drivers of this new threat is the use of the Internet to enlist individuals or groups of individuals to join the cause without ever affiliating with a terrorist organization."

In 2007, we discussed the concept of a "spiritual sanctioner," an individual who lacks a formal Islamic education, yet provides religious justification for violence to individuals who are radicalizing. Within the last six months we have identified a new catalyst for radicalization—what we call the "virtual spiritual sanctioner." Although he is not the only one, Anwar al Awlaqi, based in Yemen is an exemplar of this concept.

Both Anwar al-Awlaqi's extremist ties as well as his ability to translate literature that promotes violent jihad into English have enabled his widespread radicalizing effect. Not only has Awlaqi been a religious authority cited by the convicted Fort Dix plotters, who were disrupted in a 2007 plot against Fort Dix in New Jersey, but his tapes were also played for all who attended the Toronto 18's makeshift training camp, held north of Toronto in the winter of 2005. That group plotted to explode three tons of ammonium nitrate in downtown Toronto in the fall of 2006.

Key Judgments

1) In recent years, U.S. authorities have uncovered a significant and increasing number of radicalized clusters or individuals intent on committing violent jihad either in the U.S. or abroad. These arrests confirm that radicalization is taking place in the U.S today.
2) It is also noteworthy that in the past year, there have been a half dozen cases of individuals who, instead of traveling abroad to carry out violence, have elected to attempt do it here; this is substantially greater than what we have seen in the past and may reflect an emerging pattern.
3) The al Qaeda threat to the U.S. Homeland is no longer limited to al Qaeda Core. Rather, it has decentralized and now consists of three primary elements—AQ Core, Al Qaeda allies, like Lashkar-e-Taiba, Islamic Jihad Union, and others who have begun to target the West and, most recently, the al Qaeda inspired or homegrown threat, that has no operational relationship with AQ Core, but consists of individuals radicalized in the West, who utilize al-Qaeda ideology as their inspiration for their actions.

Further Reading

Farhad Khosrokhavar, "Radicalization in Prison: The French Case." *Politics, Religion & Ideology*, Vol. 14, No. 2, 2013: 284-306.

Magnus Ranstorp, Ed., *Understanding Violent Radicalisation: Terrorist and Jihadist Movements in Europe*. New York: Routledge, 2010.

Mitchell D. Silber and Arvin Bhatt, "Radicalization in the West: The Homegrown Threat." New York: New York City Police Department, NYPD Intelligence Division, 2007, http://www.nyc.gov/html/nypd/downloads/pdf/public_information/NYPD_Report-Radicalization_in_the_West.pdf.

7/7 London Attacks

Michael Brooks

On July 7, 2005, four British Islamist radicals coordinated suicide bombings across London, killing 52 and injuring over 700 in England's first Islamist suicide attack. In many ways, the 7/7 attack served as the British version of 9/11 by prompting more comprehensive homeland security and anti-terrorism measures within the UK. It also highlighted the real threat of homegrown Islamist radicalization within Western democracies. The attack remains the second deadliest terrorist attack in the UK after the 1988 Lockerbie bombing of Pan Am Flight 103 by Libyan agents. It remains the deadliest UK bombing since World War II.

The attacks themselves were straightforward and simply coordinated. At 4:00 AM, three of the bombers left their rented flat used for bomb making and drove to the Luton train station where they were joined by the fourth bomber. With their bombs tucked away inside rucksacks, they boarded the 7:23 AM train towards London's King's Cross Thameslink. On the train, one witness described them as "smiling, laughing, and generally relaxed." Upon disembarking from the train, the bombers hugged, said cheerful farewells, and split up before continuing towards their targets. At 8:38 AM, the first bomber boarded an eastbound Circle Line train. Minutes later, the second bomber boarded the westbound train. The third bomber boarded a westbound Piccadilly Line train at 8:48 AM. These three bombs were detonated nearly simultaneously at 8:50 AM. The fourth bomber had unknown difficulties with his bomb and stopped at a shop to buy 9 volt batteries. By 9:47 AM, however, he had boarded a crowded bus, especially crowded because the other bombs had already shutdown the London Tube network. Moments later, he detonated his bomb.

The bombs threw downtown London into absolute chaos as conflicting reports kept authorities from identifying the bombs as a coordinated terrorist attack for nearly two hours. Early sources reported that the explosions came from outside the train. One Tube operator said that one of the explosions was caused by a power surge. Still others assumed that there had been a collision between trains. Once authorities sorted through the eyewitness reports and bodies strewn across the streets and Tube cars, however, the reality of something worse became obvious. Shortly after 11:00 AM, the Metropolitan Police Commissioner confirmed the fears that all four incidents were the result of a coordinated terrorist attack. An hour later, Prime Minister Tony Blair made a public statement describing the bombings as a coordinated series of barbaric attacks. Initial reports listed a death toll of around twenty. But, by the following day, the number was raised to over fifty. The three Tube bombings killed seven, twenty-six, and six, respectively, while the later bus bombing killed thirteen. In all, the four bombs claimed fifty-two lives and wounded over seven hundred.

Five days later, authorities were able to identify the bombers and began carrying out a series of raids on the apartments used for making the bombs, recovering a number of additional bombs and materials. Two weeks later, on July 21, London experienced another bomb attack, this time unsuccessful. Here, British Islamist radicals from Somalia and Ethiopia attempted to detonate four bombs on London Tubes and Buses. The bombs failed to detonate, however, and authorities arrested the would-be bombers after protracted high-profile manhunts. These attacks were originally thought to be connected to the 7/7 attacks due to their similarities but experts now suggest that they were simply copycat attacks trying to continue the terror and devastation of the earlier attacks. The 7/21 bombers are all currently serving life sentences with a minimum of forty years' imprisonment.

In the midst of the trial and investigation of the 7/21 bombing, inquiries and investigations on the 7/7 bombers and their networks continued. Three of the bombers, ages eighteen, twenty-two, and thirty, were born in England to Pakistani immigrants. The fourth, aged nineteen, emigrated from Jamaica to the UK at age five. Mohammad Sidique Khan, age thirty in 2005, was the oldest of the group and often characterized as its leader. In 1999, he developed close ties with Abdullah el-Faisal, a radical cleric who was arrested in 2003 and later deported for encouraging the murder of Jews, Hindus, Christians, and Americans. Between 1999 and 2005, Khan travelled to Afghanistan and Pakistan multiple times where he attended militant training camps and studied bomb-making. In September of 2005, Al Jazeera published a video of Khan declaring his belief in violent jihad and his self-identification as a "soldier" fighting against the Western governments for their involvement in Iraq, Afghanistan, and elsewhere. Prior to the bombings, he was working as a learning mentor for recent immigrants at a primary school, where coworkers described him as quiet and non-communicative of his religious and political beliefs. His bomb killed himself and five others.

Bomber Shehzad Tanweer was also born in England to a Pakistani immigrant family and was twenty-two when he killed himself and seven others on the Circle line near Aldgate at 8:50 AM. Known as *Kaka,* "little one," to his family, Tanweer was described as athletic and politically moderate. He frequented multiple mosques as well as a Muslim youth center used as a recruitment location by Khan. Tanweer completed the *hajj* in 2004 and then, later that year, flew to Pakistan with Khan where he attended an Islamic studies course and may have had contact with multiple terrorist organizations. In Pakistan, witnesses claimed that Tanweer had declared that he wanted to die as a holy warrior. A few days before the bombing, friends said that he had inexplicably died his hair brown. This was later explained by the strong bleaching effect of the bomb-making ingredients. After the attack, authorities recovered over a dozen other bombs of different sizes in Tanweer's car. Like Khan, Tanweer also produced a video statement that was later released by Al Jazeera. "What you have witnessed now," he states, "is only the beginning of a string of attacks that will continue and become stronger until you pull your forces out of Afghanistan and Iraq and until you stop your financial and military support to America and Israel." Tanweer left behind an estate of £121,000 after funeral and other expenses were paid off. While authorities have not been able to uncover the exact sources of these funds, they suspect that they came from a charity run in part by Khan and from terrorist networks for the purpose of recruitment and additional attacks.

Hasib Hussain was the third bomber of Pakistani descent, born in Leeds and only eighteen years old at the time of the bombing. The youngest of four children, he attended school regularly and received a vocational certificate in business in 2005. Hussain was warned by police for shoplifting in 2004 but had not fallen under any suspicion of organized terrorist activity. In 2003, Hussain met both Khan and Tanweer and the three often worshipped at the same mosque and frequented the same Muslim youth center. This timeline suggests that Hussain's period of radicalization was short—less than two years. On the day of the attack, Hussain experienced difficulties with his bomb and had to stop into a small store to buy 9 volt batteries. Almost a full hour after the other three bombs went off, Hussain detonated his on the bus in Tavistock Square, killing himself and thirteen others. His original target remains unknown.

Germaine Lindsay was the only bomber not of Pakistani origin. Having moved to the UK from Jamaica at age five, Lindsay did not convert to Islam until 2000 at the age of fifteen. He was quickly attracted, however, to its extreme forms and ran into trouble in school for distributing leaflets supporting al-Qaeda. Like Khan, Linsday was influenced by the area's extremist cleric and fellow Jamaican Abdallah al-Faisal. When Lindsay was 17, his mother moved to the U.S., leaving Lindsay alone at the family home. He dropped out of school and lived on benefits and odd jobs. Shortly afterwards, he married Samantha Lewthwaite, a white British Islamic convert he met on the internet and with whom he had two children. From this time on, more and more evidence of Lindsay's extremist views surfaced. Acquaintances reported his various acts of crime and violence as well as hateful rants against Jews and others. Lindsday was never placed on surveillance, however, for suspected terrorist activity and on 7/7 his bomb on the Piccadilly line killed himself and twenty-six others.

Lindsay's wife Samantha Lewthwaite has since become perhaps the most dangerous terrorist connected to the 7/7 bombings. Known as the "White Widow," she is wanted in connection with active involvement in numerous bomb and grenade attacks with Somalian terrorist organization Al-Shabaab. She remains at large and is suspected to be married to a senior commander within the terrorist organization.

The 7/7 attacks and the failed 7/21 London bombing attempt succeeded in their objective to terrorize the people of the UK with the prospect of continued suicide attacks. They did not, however, succeed in mobilizing more radicalized Islamists to follow their example. Besides the casualties, the greatest consequences of the attacks were a strong anti-Muslim backlash and drastic changes in UK counter-terror policy. Although homegrown radicalization remains a threat in the UK, counter-terror authorities have successfully prevented another attack of 7/7's kind.

Further Reading

David Goodhart, *The British Dream: Successes and Failures of Post-war Immigration*. London: Atlantic Books, 2013.

Steve Hewitt, The British War on Terror: Terrorism and Counter-Terrorism on the Home Front Since 9/11. London: Continuum, 2008.

London Assembly 7 July Review Committee, Volume 4: Follow-up Report. August, 2007, http://legacy.london.gov.uk/assembly/reports/7july/follow-up-report.pdf.

Sovereignty

Sovereignty, Terrorism, and the Fate of the Nation State

Martin van Creveld

The sovereign state, which since the middle of the seventeenth century has been the most important and most characteristic of all modern institutions, is in full decline. This decline is particularly evident in Western Europe. As it happens, Western Europe was the place where the adjective 'sovereign'—meaning one who, like God, has no superior and is therefore free to act according to his own interests—was first popularized in the late sixteenth century. It was in Europe, too, that the first political constructs that were known as states were created at roughly the same time; including France, Spain, and Britain.

In Europe itself, the decline of the state is mainly the result of states voluntarily coming together in order to create a larger entity of a different kind. This development has already caused them to lose some of the most important attributes of sovereignty, such as the right to create their own law without outside interference and the right to create money; nor is it likely to be reversed even by the most determined right-wing extremists. Elsewhere, as in much of Africa and Central Asia, the decline of the state was occasioned by the fact that it never succeeded in getting a hold on its own citizens, many of whom retained their allegiance to older social units such as the tribe or the extended family. Finally, everywhere, the decline of the state is very much the product of globalization. As has been said, each time another person links up with the internet the state in which he or she lives loses a little of its power—if only because the people in question are increasingly likely to receive what they need, particularly information, from abroad; and if only because, communicating with strangers, they may well end up by discovering they have more in common with those strangers than with their fellow-citizens.

Though the role that it plays differs from one region to another, globally speaking, one of the most important factors behind the decline of the state is terrorism. As authors such as Walter Laqueur remind us, terrorism is by no means a new phenomenon. Its origins go back at least as far as far as ancient Rome. At that time, groups of outlaws, known as *latrones*, would adopt some god to act as their patron and "terrorize" the populations of the districts in which they operated. Often they engaged in skirmishes with Roman units, and often they took years to put down; hardly ever *were* they put down without some other group taking over from where the last one left off. Since then, there has scarcely been a time or place which did not have their own home-grown terrorists. Meaning, in the present context, that there existed groups of people who did not accept the legitimacy of the state in whose territory they were based; and who used illegal violence not simply for personal reasons but in order to achieve wider political, or religious, or socio-economic, objectives.

In some ways, modern terrorists are the direct descendants of those groups. In other ways, they are completely new, and it is mainly their novelty that gives them their power and has turned them into the threat that we are witnessing today. The most important attribute of modern terrorism, and the one that sets it apart from most of its predecessors, is its international character. Modern means of transportation, joined with modern means of communication and data processing, often enable terrorists to run circle around states whose power is largely limited to their own sovereign territory. Conversely, should the police of any one country make life too difficult for them, then they usually find it possible to move to another and re-establish themselves there. Al Qaeda, the now infamous group responsible for the events of 9-11, represents a perfect case in point. The attacks on the Pentagon and the Twin Towers were hatched at the Hamburg Technical University, supervised and approved in some Afghan cave, financed from a banking house located in the Persian Gulf, rehearsed in a Florida flying school, and finalized between visits to the prostitutes of Las Vegas. Even now, while Afghanistan is more or less peaceful, Al Qaeda members remain at large in perhaps forty different states around the world; how long they will take to mount another more or less spectacular terrorist act is anyone's guess.

Second, the weapons terrorists may use have become incomparably more powerful. Ancient terrorists such as the *sicarii*, who according to the Jewish historian Josephus terrorized the population of the Holy Land just before the Great Revolt of 67 A.D., scarcely had weapons more dangerous than the short daggers from which they got their name. Their nineteenth-century successors used bombs full of gunpowder, occasionally killing dozens; whereas their early twenty-first century successors may soon obtain chemical, biological and nuclear weapons, if they have not done so already. With such weapons at their disposal, the destructive potential even of small groups may be immense. So immense, indeed, as to dwarf even the 3,000 or so who were killed as a result of 9-11.

The most obvious way in which terrorism threatens the modern state is by breaking its monopoly over organized violence. By doing so, it may cause the citizenry to desert the state in which they live and look for protection elsewhere; in other words, terrorism breeds more terrorism. While this is true enough, there are two other things terrorism does which may be only slightly less dangerous to the continued existence of the state. First, by provoking the authorities into over-reacting, terrorism may increase its own effects many times over; in this way, it can have its dirty work done for it by others, so to speak. Second, it is part of the very nature of modern terrorism that it does not recognize the borders separating the territory of one state from that of another. Thus it undermines what for several centuries past has been the very foundation of the state, namely, the latter's unrestricted, or sovereign, control over territory that belongs to it exclusively.

At the time of writing, the impact of terrorism varies widely in different parts of the world. Some countries, notably in Africa and Central Asia, have long lost control over their own populations and territories in favor of other groups, some large, some small. Others, particularly in Latin America, East Asia, South Asia and the Middle East, are relatively intact but engaged in a daily struggle against it. In others still, terrorism is scarcely more than a nuisance; but even in these one can see the shutters going down and the barriers going up.

That mighty symbol of open, democratic government, the United States capitol, is a perfect case in point. As this author can testify, only twenty years or so ago, the building was completely open and indeed anyone who wanted to could use the staircase leading to it to do his or her fitness training. By now, it has been turned into a virtual fortress; anyone who so much as tries to approach it without a permit and a good reason to back him up is apt to be regarded, and perhaps treated, as a criminal, a lunatic, or both.

Where all of this will take us remains to be seen. In a world where proliferating nuclear weapons threaten to turn any military adventure against a nuclear power into a form of assisted suicide, major warfare between major states seems to be on its way out. In a world that is becoming increasingly globalized, terrorism—including perhaps nuclear terrorism—appears to be on its way up. This does not necessarily mean that the entire earth will soon be awash in a mighty wave of terrorist incidents; what it does mean is that, in the future, such incidents are likely to be more numerous than major wars and may, indeed, replace them altogether. Incidents of this kind will take place now here, now there. Though some places will be much more secure than others, none will enjoy absolute immunity. Above all, terrorism will undermine states both by its own force *and* by the actions that the affected states may take in order to cope with it and put an end to it.

Along with the other factors listed above, terrorism will cause the world of sovereign states to start tottering, perhaps giving birth to a new political order whose outline cannot even be glimpsed today. In many places, the bloodshed will no doubt be massive and many innocent people will die. Yet, if the sovereign state may not necessarily survive, politics, government, and, of course, humanity will. The weapon that can put an end to the latter has yet to be invented. Once, asked what the world would look like in the aftermath of a nuclear war, Mao Tze Dong answered as follows:

> The sun will keep rising
> Trees will keep growing
> And women will keep having children.

Further Reading

Martin van Creveld, *The Rise and Decline of the State*. Cambridge: Cambridge University Press, 1999.

Martin van Creveld, *The Transformation of War*. New York: Free Press, 2001.

Suicide Bombing

Samson's Trigger: The Suicide Bomber, The Warrior, and Community Warfare

Adam Elkus

Contrary to Hollywood stereotypes, suicide bombing is not a matter of "one man, one bomb." In fact, the very term "suicide bombing" is misleading. The suicide, a desperate individual who rejects life, dies alone by his own hand. To secular morality, suicide is tragic; to religious believers, it is blasphemous. There is nothing desperate or pitiful about the modern suicide bomber. He is a fearsome weapon of war, an altruistic hero of his community, and a foot soldier in a war of total annihilation. From the bombing operation itself to the death cult that springs up in his wake, the suicide bomber is directed and exploited by the community from which he originates. In order to defeat suicide bombers, policymakers and practitioners alike cannot separate the tactical task of deterring bombers from the strategic goal of defusing the organization and ideology that gives their murderous acts meaning.

The War of Annihilation

The increasing prevalence of suicide terrorism as a tactic of war is tied to a larger trend in military affairs—the decline in interstate conflict and the new wave of crime, civil war, and terrorism. Most conflicts today are unconventional contests between a state and a sub-national actor, waged in urban environments instead of the open battlefield. Equally important is the resurgence of ferocious blood and soil nationalism, ethnic hatred, and religious fanaticism in global politics. Some experts see a looming "clash of civilizations" on the horizon, a global contest between differing cultures. While cultural identity is not the sole motivator of 21st century conflict, identity is often used to mobilize modern sub-state warriors. Ethnic and religious tensions can rally the troops even when the objectives are crassly materialistic.

Festering hatreds, maximalist goals, and a zero-sum calculus make inter-communal conflicts into wars of annihilation. The objective is not to capture the enemy's city but to murder or displace his population and give the resulting living space to one's compatriots. Momentum for slaughter is generated through the dissemination of elaborate grievance and conspiracy narratives spun out of folk history by professional propagandists. The Serbs, Croats, and Muslims of Bosnia all excused their internecine massacres during the mid-1990s by casting each other as uniformly untrustworthy, guilty of atrocities past and present, and subhuman. While greed and lust for power caused the war, it was "ancient hatreds" held as public belief that made their hateful messages so effective. In Rwanda, Kenya, and Iraq, ethnic and religious groups that co-existed for generations suddenly found themselves slitting each others' throats while authorities either watched helplessly or directed the slaughter.

Suicide bombing is a product of communal warfare—or warfare perceived by a weaker combatant as such. As Robert Pape argues in his seminal work on suicide terror, *Dying to Win*, suicide bombings occur when these sub-national actors are unable to military defeat an overwhelming, culturally alien force. The source of the threat—real or perceived—is often a foreign occupier, ethnic group, or sectarian rival. The sub-state actor employing suicide attacks perceives the cost of defeat as more than just subservience. At best, erasure of the actor's cultural and religious traditions and imposition of the enemy's is presumed. At worst, sub-state actors rightly or wrongly fear annihilation. Whether or not the aggressor really intends such measures is irrelevant. While American troops occupying Iraq do not intend to erase Sunni Islam and impose their own values, some Sunni suicide bombers certainly believe they do.

Analysts must guard against the false conclusion that suicide bombing is somehow intrinsic to Islam. In truth, suicide bombers spring from a melding of two traditions common to all cultures: the warrior and the martyr.

Soldiers and Warriors

As military historian John Keegan noted in his *History of Warfare*, warriors have long predated soldiers. Although all militaries pride themselves for having "warrior' instincts, there are real—and crucial—differences between the soldier and the warrior. The soldier—career or conscript—is a disciplined fighter accountable to a hierarchal organization. In all Western militaries, the principles of civilian control and the laws of land warfare are drilled into the soldier from boot camp onwards. He does not target civilians and ceases action against a disarmed enemy. The institutional culture of the modern military emphasizes duty and self-sacrifice, rewarding those who risk or give their lives for others. Navy SEAL Mike Mansoor, who fell on a grenade to save the lives of his men, is a prime example of the kind of soldier that the Pentagon wishes new recruits to emulate.

The warrior, a creature of pride and violence, has no such scruples. Instead of the state, he serves more traditional entities such as the gang, the clan, or the tribe. Whereas the soldier is tightly controlled, the warrior operates with a great deal of autonomy. With very few exceptions, the warrior does not fight for country, duty, or his compatriots. The warrior fights for personal gain, religious rapture, blood feud, or the sheer rush of violence. Easily defeated by conventional forces with superior discipline, numbers, and firepower, the warrior utilizes deception and trickery to gain the advantage. While the warrior has a moral code, it does not correspond to traditional Western laws of armed conflict. He will mistreat and kill prisoners, terrorize civilians, loot with abandon, and utilize forbidden weapons and tactics. The classic warrior is the *Illiad's* Achilles, a celebrity figure who fights for his own glory, refuses to engage in battle when his favorite concubine is taken, and desecrates his opponent Hector's dead body. The military writer Ralph Peters notes that warriors pose the chief threat to peace in the developing world, and can be found ravaging a number of third world battlefields.

Warriors are revered by societies caught in the grip of communal warfare. The Serbian warlords and politicians responsible for the Bosnian war's worst excesses enjoyed enormous public adulation and the amorous attentions of numerous beautiful women. Samir Kuntar, a Hezbollah operative responsible for the death of a small Israeli child, was welcomed home to Lebanon by cheering crowds and his nation's Presidential cabinet. The inconvenient fact that Kuntar dashed an Israeli child's brains against the rocks was either dismissed as a false accusation or justified by Israel's occupation of the Palestinians.

There is no place for intellectuals, businessmen, or public servants in the hyper-masculine world of the warrior. All men must fulfill their duty to fight or be shamed in front of their women and children. Women's bodies are possessed—either for the warrior's comfort or as factories for more fighters. It is also the woman's duty to instill warrior virtues in her children and cheer on her men from the sidelines. "Come back with your shield or on it," Spartan mothers famously told their sons and husbands. At best, educated men who do not contribute to the battle are considered effete cowards. At worst, they are traitors to be exterminated.

Just as the gun allowed the lowly foot soldier to be the equal of the knight, the backpack bomb allows ordinary men to become warriors. With it, they can strike terror into even the most technologically advanced and militarily superior enemies. Al-Qaeda's videos are replete with the paramilitary cool of the warrior. Men in camouflage fatigues march across the screen, American armored vehicles disappear into pillars of flame, and the suicide bomber detonates his deadly cargo in the midst of a group of clueless "Zionist lackeys." What these images—set to stirring martial music—promise the average recruit is power, authority, and agency. Cosmopolitan intellectuals who view war, nationalism, and tribal tradition as anachronisms cannot begin to appreciate how such paramilitary imagery plays to the most basic of human emotional needs. Human beings of all cultures and creeds indulge in the fantasy of regeneration through violence, and revolutionary theorists from Frantz Fanon to Bin Laden have proscribed murder and mayhem as a means of moral recovery and advancement.

Killer Martyrs

The figure of the martyr is just as central to understanding the suicide bomber as that of the warrior. In times of war, soldiers who sacrifice their lives to destroy the enemy become secular saints, central figures in the war's grand pageant of grievance, conspiracy, and nationalism. The Serbs valorize the fallen army that lost the titular Battle of Kosovo against the Turks, seeing meaning in their resistance rather than the battle's ultimate outcome. The word *"kamikaze"*—"divine wind" in Japanese—refers to the storm that wrecked an invading Chinese-Mongolese navy off the coast of Japan. In World War II, Japanese pilots crashing their explosive payloads into American ships were cast as the saviors of a Japan under threat from a similar invading armada. Every country has a similar story of sacrifice and a national myth built around it. The military martyr dies to save the nation, and his body becomes a symbol of community sacrifice and resistance.

The suicide bomber, however, differs from the military martyr of old in that his target is the whole of the enemy society. To the suicide bomber, blowing up a busload of children is just as honorable as a raid on an enemy platoon. He is feted by his compatriots as a great hero, and his family may receive a financial reward for their loss. In Israel's occupied territories, a death cult has sprung up around the "martyrs" who kill Israeli civilians in crowded public places. As in the warrior society, women's bodies are commandeered as vehicles for the creation of more killers, and mothers are quoted telling international news agencies that they too desire their children will one day grow up to detonate a backpack bomb loaded with nails and ball-bearings.

For low-status individuals such as women and the poor, suicide bombing can be a means of achieving a higher community status. Israeli political scientists Mira Tzoreff and Yoram Shweitzer argue that the data shows that Palestinian female suicide bombers are often individuals whose personal difficulties (including one woman who was caught sleeping with married Hamas operative) led them to become objects of communal sacrifice so they could be remembered as "martyrs," avoiding familial shame. This often flies in the face of opposition by Palestinian groups appalled by the thought of delicate women leveling discos and pizza parlors. Prospective female terrorists have even petitioned Al Qaeda, arguing that they too deserve the right to kill infidels. However, demonstrating once again that terrorist groups are by no means monolithic, female suicide bombers are widely utilized by the Chechen guerrillas and the Tamil Tigers. Even children have attempted or carried out suicide bombing, though the vast majority—like most child soldiers—are coerced into doing so.

Cogs in the Murder Machine

The bomber himself is nothing but a vessel for his weapon. Most effective suicide bombings are the product of a team. The suicide bomber requires (obviously) a bomb, pre-operational selection and surveillance of the target, and guidance to his destination. If the bomber cannot or will not overcome his selfish love of life, an operative hiding in the crowd with a remote detonator will push the button for him. Insurgent infrastructure for suicide bombing ranges in size and scope from the clandestine bombing workshops of Al Qaeda in Iraq to the Tamil Tigers' regimented suicide bombing corps. Nor is the suicide bomber restricted to any one weapon or delivery method. While the classic suicide bomber utilizes a bomb vest or backpack bomb, bombers have utilized cars, boats, and, most recently, planes.

The suicide bomber's method of targeting can be explained by Robert J. Bunker's concept of "Bond-Relationship Targeting" (BRT). Targeting of symbolic or economic nodes creates concentric waves of psychological and economic damage. Thus, the greater damage inflicted by the suicide bomber is extended far beyond the original target. As community warfare is fueled by epic symbols of violence, BRT provides both strategic gain and emotional sustenance to terrorists and their admirers. Osama Bin Laden, for example, preached that America and the West was engaged in a war of annihilation against the greater Muslim *umma*. The bombing of the World Trade Center, a key symbol of American wealth and national power, was greeted with widespread joy in the Middle East.

Suicide bombing can also stimulate the growth of *foco* insurgencies by casting the body of the martyr as a tool to raise the consciousness of the masses. BRT demonstrates to both the insurgents' potential supporters and victims that the opposing force, despite its conventional superiority, is weak at its core. Naturally, suicide bombing often provokes brutal reprisals by security forces seeking to prove their strength. As repression is answered with bigger body counts, security forces sometimes turn to collective punishment of the population. Such tactics can alienate the very people security forces need to stop the insurgents—and swell their numbers. Nevertheless, weak-minded politicians find repression an easy way to ingratiate themselves with their fearful electorates. More authoritarian states do not tolerate any threat to their rule and respond by unleashing their worst thugs, torturers, and assassins on those who cannot fight back.

The city is the suicide bomber's main target. Utilizing swarming tactics, suicide bombers can besiege cities from within. Masked by the vastness of the mega-city, suicide bombers appear out of nowhere to strike a target. Sadly, the accumulated economic and psychological effect of bombing transportation infrastructure, markets, and communal landmarks can reduce cities to shells of their former selves. People learn to avoid open-air markets, buses, and nightclubs. Suspicious or unfamiliar vehicles provoke panic and paranoia. And as Mike Davis notes in his history of the car bomb, walls, "rings of steel," and other mobility-constricting structures quickly become features of the urban landscape. The whole of Israel, for example, has been walled off from the Palestinian territories to constrict the flow of suicide bombers into Israel proper. Baghdad, a city relentlessly targeted by Sunni suicide bombers, divided Sunni and Shi'ia with multiple blast walls.

Defeating the Suicide Bomber

Suicide bombers defy easy solutions. Target hardening can only go so far, as it is impossible to bomber-proof every civilian target. Another impediment to static defense is the bomber's mobility and anonymity—once the bomber reaches his target it is nearly impossible to identify and

---

neutralize him. Rather, police and security units must take the offensive by targeting the suicide bomber's support apparatus, most notably the bombmaker. Otherwise, stopping of individual bombers is worthless.

For the United States and Europe, defusing diaspora terrorism through networked police intelligence is the key to success. In California, the Los Angeles County Sheriff's Department and the LAPD have implemented counter-terrorism training for patrolmen (the first line of defense), trained terrorism liaison officers (TLOs) to interface with national intelligence agencies, and created both informal and formal intelligence networks such as the Terrorism Early Warning Group (TEW) and the Joint Regional Intelligence Center (JRIC). While such networks utilize an extensive array of technological sensors, the key is human intelligence—provided both from patrol personnel and a network of cultivated community informants. Only through aggressive (but, it must emphasized, *legal)* intelligence gathering can police construct models of terrorist cells that can be used to thwart suicide bombings.

In environments where a state of general war exists, cutting off the enemy's mobility through checkpoints, blast walls, and grid systems is a starting point, though not a cure-all as bomber mobility can proceed through deception. In this extreme environment, targeted operations aimed at wiping out bomb cells may also prove useful. If the mission is foreign internal defense, the quicker indigenous forces can mount these kinds of operations, the better. The sight of natives dismantling the suicide bomber networks will have a greater civil affairs effect. Yet while these kinetic operations against the insurgent are important, they must not be utilized on an ad-hoc basis. Rather, they must serve a holistic—and political—strategy. A purely military response will have a neglible—or even detrimental—effect on the overall conflict.

As Dr. Sergio Catignani argues in his article "The Israel Defense Forces And the *Al-Aqsa Intifada*," the Israeli IDF's tactical and operational focus on degrading Palestinian infrastructure and decapitating the Palestinian leadership may have achieved a temporary reduction in suicide violence but paved the way for Hamas' 2006 rise to power. The response was heavy-handed as it lacked a strategic focus and only alienated the Palestinian population. It was the Israeli withdrawal from Gaza and the West Bank and the sealing of the wall that finally stemmed the tide of suicide bombings, but they were merely traded for the equally deadly and no less terrifying mobile rocket attacks. One can also observe that, though the increase of American troops and the co-opting of Sunni insurgents has lowered the level of sectarian violence in Iraq, suicide bombings still continue to kill dozens in major urban centers.

Policymakers must also resist the temptation to utilize means that will heighten the violence of the community war. Collective punishment, massive security sweeps, and torture will only reinforce the adversary's narrative of a grand, inter-communal struggle. While the tactical and operational objectives are certainly the deterrence and neutralization of the suicide-bomber apparatus, the strategic objective must be the isolation of the suicide bomber from the community which he claims to serve. In order to do so, the community must come to view the killing of innocents as abhorrent. It is not necessary to make the community love the government or even give up their sympathies for insurgent forces aligned against the authorities or their allies. But it must come to see those who target innocents as murderers and charlatans.

This is admittedly a difficult task, but it is made easier by our common humanity. The deliberate killing of innocents is repulsive to most cultural and religious traditions. It can only be tolerated when the community sees itself as under extreme threat. If authorities work to address community grievances, refrain from repressive measures, and cultivate contacts with community leaders, they can contain the threat. Sometimes, such an understanding can be reached even in the midst of strategic mistakes. Few would judge the United States' public diplomacy in the Muslim world to be a success, but overwhelming majorities polled in the Middle East reject suicide bombing and the important Deobandi Muslim sect (one of the largest in the world) have declared it to be sinful. The best defense against suicide bombing is ultimately the firm establishment of community norms against wanton bloodshed. With such an understanding, suicide bombing will be limited to a tiny death cult easily mopped up by law enforcement. Without it, they will continue to thrive amid the chaos and bloodshed of community warfare.

Further Reading

Mia Bloom, *Dying to Kill: The Allure of Suicide Terror.* New York: Columbia, 2005.

Mohammed Hafez, *Suicide Bombers in Iraq: The Strategy and Ideology of Martyrdom.* Washington, DC: United States Institute of Peace, 2007.

Robert A. Pape, *Dying to Win: The Strategic Logic of Suicide Terrorism.* New York: Random House, 2005.

Super-Empowered Individuals

Night of the Lone Wolves

Adam Elkus

The end of the Cold War and beginning of the War on Terrorism has given rise to a number of revolutionary concepts in the study of unconventional warfare. In only 17 years, a vibrant alternative defense community has produced innovative operational and strategic concepts such as fourth generation warfare, netwar, non-trinitarian warfare, Thomas P.M. Barnett's SysAdmin, and John Robb's global guerrillas. The latest in this distinguished intellectual line is the concept of the "super-empowered individual" drawn from Thomas L. Friedman's 1998 characterization of 'super-empowered angry men'. When theorists like Robb, Barnett, Col. T.X. Hammes, and Fred Ikle weigh in on this ominous figure, they are not talking about The Hulk, Magneto, or Professor X. Instead, defense thinkers warn that technology and the increasing vulnerability of modern globalized society could one day allow a single man to "take on the world."

Super-Empowered Individuals

Who is the "super-empowered individual?" He is talented, alienated from society, and willing to kill large numbers of people. The technological revolution has given him destructive tools unimaginable to the anarchists and terrorists of old. He is an innovator—he creates new doctrines, tactics, and operations. A "brittle" infrastructure that lacks redundancy and resiliency gives him a perfect target. Living off the grid, he is invisible to authorities. The unprecedented nature of his attack ensures that no counter-measures are in place to prevent it. And when he strikes, his attack will not only kill massive amounts of people, but also profoundly change the financial, political, and social systems that govern modern life.

This is a frighteningly plausible vision. As blogger and futurist Mark Safranski gloomily noted, "the world is but one self-sacrificing genetic microbiologist away from a super-empowered suicide bomber riding international air routes to a new black plague." That being said, many scientists and security experts note the immense difficulty involved in acquiring, maintaining, and deploying weapons of mass destruction. One expert, Bruce Schneier, is especially vehement in deriding what he calls "movie-plot" threats.

Who is right? Both sides. For now, the probability that a super-empowered individual will trigger a extreme mass casualty event is extremely low. But the high odds against such a catastrophe occurring will ensure that, when it happens, we will be taken totally by surprise. If a mass-murdering microbiologist is indeed preparing to make engineered smallpox complimentary to the in-flight meal, there is little we can do to stop him. Confused? With apologies to The Matrix, it's time to take the red pill.

The Black Swan

Safranski's bioterrorism scenario is what mathematician Nassim Nicholas Taleb calls a "Black Swan," an event [whose] very unexpectedness helps create the conditions for it to occur. The very unlikeness of such events prevents us from taking them seriously which, in turn, enables them to happen. One can retroactively implement security measures that would have prevented the event from occurring, but it unlikely that such an event would happen again.

The immediate alternative is what journalist Ron Suskind calls the "1% doctrine," an attempt to investigate or prepare for every threat, even one that has only 1% chance of occurring. Such an overreach weakens overall preparedness and makes the public more likely to disbelieve government warnings of a credible threat. The only thing we can do, as Robb eloquently argues in *Brave New War*, is to increase our own societal resilience to these threats, and build redundancies into our complex and fragile systems. If we cannot predict or prevent a Black Swan, we can at least lessen its damage.

The Lone Wolf

The biggest problem, however, with analysis of super-empowered individuals in the defense community is that it sets the entry level for a super-empowered individual too high and misses what truly makes them super-empowered. One does not have to have a suitcase nuke to be super-empowered, although it certainly helps. Super-empowered individuals are able to change systems not because of the magnitude of their attacks, but because those attacks effect us on Boyd's moral/mental level. Bin Laden's biggest achievement on 9/11 was not the scale of the destruction, but that the attacks disrupted American life enough to alter our entire grand strategy in response.

While Col. Hammes uses the 2002 Anthrax attacks as a model for how the super-empowered individual can take on the state, a closer model can be found in another attack that occurred that year: the Beltway sniper attacks. Two alienated loners shot and killed ten people. Their message to the media was crude and simple: "Your children are not safe, anywhere, at any time." Needless to say, the media was transfixed by the case, and it dominated the news cycle. The fear that the snipers spread was disproportionate to the actual casualties they inflicted.

There have always been alienated and sociopathic individuals who have sought—and succeeded—to make a name for themselves through violence. From the early anarchists of the late 19th and 20th centuries to today's serial killers, the media has consistently amplified and exaggerated the threat posed by lone killers, terrorists, and other malcontents. Many explicitly seek this attention, as evidenced by the flood of manifestos, messages sent to the media, and sensationalistic crimes. This desire for attention is frequently reciprocated with heavy coverage and breathless media pseudo-psychology designed to uncover (on camera) what "drove" these individuals to kill.

However, what makes these individuals "super-empowered" today is the way that their acts of terror are magnified by the power of electronic media to involve us in that violence. It is not completely accurate to state that those acts are wide-ranging because of the attention they receive. It is because that attention, and the realism and immediacy of electronic media, makes us experience fear of them as if we were there ourselves. It is a manufactured experience.

In the aftermath of 9/11, countless news stories featured individuals in small towns across America's heartland expressing fear over terrorism, despite the extremely low probability that Bin Laden would care about the town rec center in Peoria. The true innovation represented by the advent of super-empowered individuals is the blurring of the tactical and strategic levels. An individual's actions, with or without a weapon of mass destruction, can disrupt our society's moral cohesion. The entry cost for this disruption is very low—all one needs is a cheap weapon and a sense of theater.

Given the continuing transfer of technological and social power to the individual, the future of super-empowered individuals may be the megalomaniacal super-terrorist. But today's super-empowered individual is not the scowling jihadist with the suitcase nuke. It is the school shooter, the office shooter, the serial killer, the anarchist and survivalist. The nihilistic, televised face of today's super-empowered actor is Seung-Hui Cho, the Virginia Tech shooter. Armed with commercially available small arms, Cho killed dozens, publicizing his efforts with a video sent to NBC News (which was promptly broadcasted). It is also Theodore Kaczynski, the Unabomber, who waged a one-man crusade against industrial society with the aid of letter bombs and rambling manifestos distributed by the New York Times. And it is also Timothy McVeigh, who drove a Ryder truck packed with explosives into the Alfred P. Murrah Federal Building in Oklahoma City.

An Appetite for Apocalypse

Against this, what can be done? There are a couple of obvious tactical steps—better preparing police and first responders for these kinds of scenarios. The larger problem, however, lies in the way we react to such violence. One can blame the media for amplifying acts of violence by lone wolf killers and terrorists, but such amplification would not sell unless there was a demand for it.

Perhaps, as European philosopher Slavoj Zizek theorized, we are unwittingly addicted to images of our own destruction. We eagerly devour disaster movies and thrillers that prominently feature events that range from catastrophic to world-ending. In a time of global terrorism and insurgency, one of the most popular television shows is Fox's *24*, which regularly shows fictionalized usage of biological, chemical, and even nuclear weapons. Disturbingly enough, before 9/11 several popular thrillers had plotlines featuring planes being flown into buildings.

Why do we vicariously crave these experiences? Zizek himself echoes Freud in claiming that they tap into deep anxieties and fears we unconsciously hold about modernity—that we fear that underneath the edifice of ordered, secure civilization is little more than raw savagery that threatens to consume us at any given moment. One can also point to the long tradition of apocalyptic literature and mythology, common to all faiths and cultures, and note that these media displays tap into a deep, subconscious cultural nerve honed over the centuries.

They Don't Have to Win

In any event, we have always lived with danger and always will. And the threat posed by murderous, alienated individuals, with or without weapons of mass destruction, will also always be with us. But the good news is that the key to overcoming these threats lies in two bedrock American values--hope and pragmatism: hope for a better world and the determination to create such a world; and the pragmatism that has helped us continuously innovate to overcome seemingly insurmountable challenges.

What is needed is leadership at the top level that encourages and channels those values within the American people, instead of leadership that burdens them with fear. True leadership will recognize that strategy is not just protection against wanton destruction—it is also, as John

Boyd stated, a "pattern for vitality and growth." If we recognize this, we can all be "super-empowered individuals" instead of victims huddling in fear of the sound of anything beyond the campfire.

Further Reading

Thomas L. Friedman, "Foreign Affairs; Angry, Wired and Deadly." *The New York Times*. 22 August 1998, http://www.nytimes.com/1998/08/22/opinion/foreign-affairs-angry-wired-and-deadly.html.

T.X. Hammes, "Fourth Generation Warfare Evolves, Fifth Emerges." *Military Review,* Vol. 87, No. 3, May/June 2007: 14-23.

John Rob, *Brave New War: The Next Stage of Terrorism and the End of Globalization.* Hoboken: John Wiley & Sons, 2007.

Surface Transportation Security

Brian Michael Jenkins

The discovery of notes in Osma bin Laden's compound indicating that the terrorist leader was contemplating attacking trains in the United States on the tenth anniversary of September 11 underscores the continuing terrorist threat to public surface transportation and the enormous challenges of securing these targets.

Public surface transportation—particularly trains, buses, stations, and even groups of people waiting at bus stops—offers terrorists an attractive target: easy access and easy escape; concentrations of people in confined environments that enable an attack to achieve the high body counts terrorists seek; confined environments that can enhance the effects of explosives; and unconventional weapons.

While terrorists remain obsessed with attacking commercial aviation, they regard surface transportation as a killing field. Since September 11, 2001, terrorists have carried out 75 attacks on airliners and airports worldwide, causing 157 deaths. During the same period, terrorists carried out nearly 1,804 attacks on surface transportation, most of them against bus and train targets, killing more than 3,900 people (per the Mineta Transportation Institute).

The enormous investment in aviation security seems to have worked, at least as a deterrent to many terrorist attacks. Between the late 1960s and the late 1970s, an average of nine to ten terrorist airplane hijackings occurred each year. This dropped to an average of six a year in the 1980s, and to three a year between 1987 and 1996. In the past 15 years, there have been only six airplane hijackings, including the four successful hijackings on 9/11.

Several factors in addition to aviation security contributed to this decline, including the elimination of some terrorist groups and international agreements to prosecute or extradite hijackers. Increased security after 9/11 and, more importantly, a fundamental change in passenger reactions—from passive acceptance to defiant action—oblige terrorists to think twice before attempting a hijacking today.

Terrorist attempts to sabotage airliners also have declined over time, from three to four attempts a year in the 1960s and 1970s to less than two a year in the late 1980s and 1990s. In the past decade, only six attempts have been made to smuggle bombs onto passenger planes and only two onto cargo planes. Unfortunately, the terrorists succeeded in placing their devices on board all eight planes, although they brought down only two of the passenger planes, both in Russia.

While terrorists have been attacking aviation targets less often, they have been attacking surface transportation more frequently. Between 1970 and 1979, terrorists carried out a total of 15 surface transportation attacks that caused fatalities. (We include only incidents with fatalities to avoid counting apparent increases due solely to better reporting.) The number grew to 43 attacks with fatalities in the 1980s, 281 in the 1990s, and 465 between 2000 and 2009.

Many of the attacks involved only a few fatalities and did not make headline news, but 11 of them since 9/11 resulted in 50 or more deaths, and three of the attacks killed nearly 200 people. The total number of fatalities in these 14 attacks is the approximate equivalent of the fatalities in seven or eight airline crashes. One can imagine the furor that would have resulted if eight commercial airliners had been brought down by terrorists after 9/11.

The West is not immune. Most of the attacks have occurred in developing countries like India, but there have been attacks on trains in France, Spain, the United Kingdom, Russia, and Japan. Further terrorist attacks have been uncovered and foiled in the United Kingdom, Germany, Spain, Italy, and Australia.

Attacks on surface transportation can happen in the United States. Since 9/11, there have been seven reported terrorist plots involving attacks on trains in the United States. Authorities reportedly uncovered a plot in 2003 to release poison gas in New York's subways. In 2004, New York police infiltrated a plot by two men to bomb a mid-Manhattan subway station. In 2006, a plot was uncovered in Lebanon to blow up train tunnels under the Hudson River. Bryant Vinas, a homegrown recruit to al Qaeda, offered terrorists his assistance in attacking the Long Island Railroad and, in 2009, authorities uncovered a mature plant to bomb New York's subways. Faisal Shazad, the Time Square bomber, initially planned to follow up that attack with a bombing at New York's Grand Central Station. Later, in 2010, Farooque Ahmed was arrested in an FBI sting operation for planning to bomb Washington's Metro stations.

The aviation security model will not work for public trains, given the current and even near-term limits of technology. Screening of all train passengers would be nearly impossible. Even before airline screening was initiated, passengers boarded airliners in single lines on the tarmac, a dangerous place to wander. But trains and their stations use multiple, simultaneous access points. Moreover, the difference in the volume of air and train passengers is staggering. New York's Penn Station alone handles in each morning's rush hours the same number of passengers that O'Hare International Airport in Chicago handles in 60 hours.

While airline passengers may be willing to wait 15-20 minutes to be screened for a flight to a distant city, train passengers would not be willing to add that time to their daily commute each way. Also, train systems and stations tend to be more diverse than their airline counterparts, making a uniform approach less likely to work.

Moreover, the cost of screening would be prohibitive. Staffing a force of TSA officers to screen subway and commuter train passengers would require adding $7 to $8 to each fare, which would destroy public surface transportation.

Finally, the waiting lines at the security checkpoints themselves would make tempting targets, easy for terrorists to access. The bottom line is that security that shuts down the public surface transportation system—as airline-style screening would—or even makes it more vulnerable is not acceptable. However, measures can be taken to make terrorist planning more difficult, to increase deterrence, and to make responses to terrorist threats rapid and flexible, as well as to improve the effectiveness of responses to attacks.

Rail operators and transit systems have increased the presence of security personnel. They have added cameras to improve surveillance, assist in rapid diagnosis if an event occurs, and deter terrorists who want to avoid capture. Smarter camera systems alert monitors to objects that do not move when they should or to movement where there should be none. Some transportation systems have implemented random passenger screening, which introduces uncertainty for attackers and therefore has deterrent value. Explosives-sniffing dogs are increasingly being used to search for bombs and detect vapor trails left by explosives. Remote explosives-detection technologies are being deployed on an experimental basis, but there is no near-term technological solution.

All of these measures enhance security, but local governments and operators—strapped for cash—can do only so much. Whatever security measures are put into place must be sufficient to handle the huge volumes of passengers, must not trample civil liberties, must be economically sustainable, and must offer a net security benefit. Implementing such measures will require intelligence and imagination. The answer is not merely implementing more security, but implementing smart security.

Employee and passenger awareness counts. Just as airline passengers have become the last line of defense against terrorists on airplanes, rail passengers can become the first line of defense in ensuring their own security. Daily riders know the environment intimately and are most able to identify suspicious objects or behavior. During the Irish Republican Army's bombing campaign, British authorities depended on alert passengers, already sensitized by IRA bombings, to report suspicious objects within minutes of their being placed. Reports were followed up with visual diagnosis through cameras and personnel on scene. This made London's tubes and trains a hostile environment for terrorist operatives. One can see the results over time, as the terrorists gradually edged away from their preferred targets in crowded central London to more remote venues.

The failure of the British public to detect the al Qaeda-inspired terrorist bombers who killed 52 people on subway trains and a bus in 2005 was due to the fact that the terrorists did not leave their backpacks unattended, but remained attached to them when they detonated.

Passengers can be enlisted as partners in their own security. Current "see something, say something" campaigns are a first step. They need to be evaluated to see if the message is getting through and how better to engage the public. Communications have to be facilitated. Procedures have to be established to ensure rapid diagnosis and response. Callers need to be acknowledged, for their efforts, even when it turns out to be a false alarm. Disruptions must be minimized.

Further Reading

Annabelle M. Boyd and John P. Sullivan, "Emergency Preparedness for Transit Terrorism." TCRP Synthesis 27, Transit Cooperative Research Board, National Research Board, 1997.

Frances L. Edwards and Daniel C. Goodrich, *Introduction to Transportation Security.* Boca Raton: CRC Press, 2012.

Brian Michael Jenkins and Joseph Trella, "Carnage Interrupted: An Analysis of Fifteen Terrorist Plots Against Public Surface Transportation." Mineta Transportation Institute, San Jose State University MTI Report 11-20, April 2012.

Tactics, Techniques, and Procedures (TTPs)

Christopher Flaherty

Role in Terrorism Analysis

The role of TTPs in terrorism analysis is that this concept is used to identify individual patterns of behavior of a particular terrorist activity, or a particular terrorist organisation. The concept of TTPs helps examine and categorize more general tactics, and weapons used by a particular terrorist activity, or a particular terrorist organisation.

Requirement to Identify Individual Terrorism TTPs

The current approach to terrorism analysis involves an examination of the behaviour of a individual terrorist, or that of a terrorist organisations—in particular their use of specific weapons, used in specific ways, and which may included different tactics and strategies being exhibited. This approach also recognises that, historically, a wide range of TTPs have been exhibited by individual terrorists or terrorist organisations worldwide.

Key TTP Concepts

Underpinning our understanding of TTPs, is that terrorism, like all forms of warfare, has undergone changes and continues to evolve. All terrorists or terrorist organisations worldwide, historically, have exhibited an evolution in TTPs. These can be as a result of any number of factors, or a combination of these, such as the response to changing circumstances, resources availability, changing ideologies, or a change in 'war-focus'. For example, in the case of the Taliban, their tactics have consisted primarily of guerrilla-style attacks using a range of improvised explosive device (IED), as well as attacks and small-arms ambushes against international and state-level security forces and interests, such as police checkpoints and military supply convoys. However, more recently, Taliban TTPs have expanded to include mass casualty attacks by suicide bombers and other suicide attacks in order to undermine the current government.

The Kill-Chain Model

The 'Kill-Chain Model' is a conceptual tool used in terrorism analysis. Broadly, this involves describing the 'hierarchy of tasks and sub-tasks that may be involved in the execution' of a terrorist act. These involve the arrangement and sequence of activities a lone terrorist, or any number of terrorist organisations, uses in planning, organizing, mobilizing, training, equipping and staging resources and/or operatives. These activities make up the terrorist, or terrorist organisations', modus operandi or what is known as 'its attack system'.

Figure 1 Illustrates the Kill-Chain Model (KCM), and Kill-Chain Model Variations. All terrorists' or terrorist organisations' TTPs form part of understanding their kill chain; which is the pattern of transactional activities that are linked together in order for a terrorist act to take place. Four sets of steps make-up the full Kill-Chain Model (KCM).

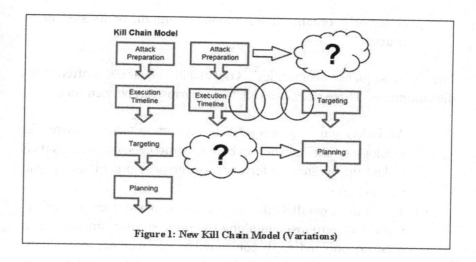

Figure 1: New Kill Chain Model (Variations)

- The first set of activities identified in the KCM are the 'Attack Preparation Steps'. In terms of terrorism analysis, individual transactions, such as acquiring finances, acquiring expertise, acquiring materiel, munitions or capability, recruiting members, conducting reconnaissance, mission rehearsal, conducting an attack, etc., have signatures that identify them as terrorist or criminal acts; or are consistent with the operations of a specific individual, cell, or group.

- The second set of activities identified in the KCM are called the 'Execution Timeline'. This identifies the timeline along which the terrorist or terrorist organisations various activities leading up to an attack process flow time-wise.

- The third set of activities identified in the KCM is identified as 'Targeting'. An individual or group would carry out some form of dedicated reconnaissance with the aim of identifying weaknesses in the site or operation and, with that information, determine the best method of attack.

- The fourth set of activities identified in the KCM is identified as the 'Planning Stages'. These involve some type of planning activity embedded into the 'kill-chain', and is part of the process of organizing, mobilizing, training, equipping, staging, and collecting resources and operatives. These make up the terrorist' or terrorist organisations' modus operandi, or its system of attack.

The KCM 'sequence of activities', is not usually linear but is often more discontinuous. Three additional KCM scenarios can be identified.

- An individual or group actively promote a terrorist/extremist ideology on the internet, in books, pamphlets, etc. This is then picked up by another terrorist, or terrorist organisation, who then act on it.
- Two or more parallel kill chain sequence of activities (by various individuals/groups) run along the same/similar timelines; and these are only indirectly connected by intermediary individuals/ groups sharing similar beliefs, but cross over into complementary beliefs/ideologies. Many such intermediaries can operate in this space, passing ideas and resources and even recruits between the various terrorist or between terrorist organisations' groups and cells.
- A terrorist or terrorist organisation picks-up ideas or knowledge and jump-starts into various places along the 'standard' concept of the KCM (in such circumstances, they are using someone else's 'kill chain').

The fact that terrorist(s)/terrorist organisations 'jump' between various stages in the KCM presents a fundamental challenge to counter-terrorism activities, as it can be difficult to track such individuals, as well as distinguish between real and false threats.

Transfer of Terrorist Tactics, Techniques and Procedures

Terrorist Tactics, Techniques and Procedures (TTPs), are often transferred between various terrorists, or terrorist organisations, and they often learn from each other. The degree to which the transfer of TTPs occurs depends on their relative success when transferred to a different conflict, and a different environment. The similarities in TTPs between various terrorists or terrorist organisations across conflicts and periods suggest a transfer of information in two particular forms:

- Explicit Knowledge: This is the theoretical information which is often stored in hard copies, such as textbooks, manuals and on computers through PDF and video files. These are extremely easy to get hold of but, without the appropriate teaching or experience, this easy access information is commonly not effectively used.
- Tactical Knowledge: Most commonly taught or learnt through experience and hands-on teaching. This requires training establishments to be organised. For terrorists or terrorist organisations, acquiring this information is more difficult, however, it is seen as a more effective transfer of knowledge.

The Link Between Beliefs – Behaviours – Tactics

Ideology plays a crucial role in an attacker's target selection, and this is always a significant part of understanding TTPs. Ideology supplies the initial motive for action and provides a prism through which a terrorist(s)/terrorist organisation(s) view events and the actions of other people. Additionally, the manner in which the enemy is attacked is important in itself. For example, the 9/11 operation was designed not only to inflict mass casualties, but to create a spectacle of violence so dramatic and unprecedented that the entire world would be compelled to watch, polarising audiences by their reaction: horror or jubilation.

Understanding the link between beliefs, behaviours, and tactics requires a judgement to be made. This involves identifying the particular behaviour leading to tactical elements which underpin a terrorist(s)/terrorist organisation(s)' attack. For example, in order to achieve surprise, the attacker may alter their methods to ensure surprise, panic, and genuine disruption. This also involves identifying exactly what makes one attack different from others. This is so much in the sense that the particular terrorist(s) involved were clearly different in terms of background and ideology, but that certain personnel and group characteristics exhibit very different patterns of conflict.

From a TTPs view, a terrorist(s)'/terrorist organisation(s)' behaviour is a combination of personal and situational factors, including the setting and potential target. Other factors 'shaping' the TTPs are the degree of security or target hardening that exists. However, target vulnerability and access aside, tactics and targets come from the particular behaviours and beliefs of the attacker.

Patterns of Conflict

The 'patterns of conflict' thesis, embedded in the analysis of TTPs essentially draws a functional distinction between various forms of warfare. The approach adopted here is to continue with this thesis but reducing it to a micro-level analysis identifying various archetype 'families' of terrorist tactics. Adopting this approach is also in keeping with identification of terrorism and terrorism tactics as a fourth generation mode of warfare, namely seeking to further differentiate functionally terrorism into its micro-component parts. Figure 2 illustrates the micro-components of terrorism. This model seeks to draw together three elements:

- Various archetypes;
- Followed by identifying relevant attributes (A1-A2-A3); and,
- Some identifiable tactics (T1-T2).

The argument presented here, is that the mode of tactics used is an outcome from the influence of politics, ideology, or belief systems. These could be indirectly linked (i.e. a few of the attributes lead to a particular type of tactic being adopted). Thus 'A1-A2 = T1'. Alternatively, these could be directly an outcome of a particular attribute, thus 'A3 = T2'.

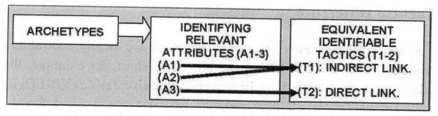

Figure 2: Micro-Components of Terrorism

It can also be argued that seemingly similar or even the same tactics can in fact be realised in very different ways which again can be linked back to individuals' attributes. For instance, it could be argued that elemental tactics such as the use of 'extreme brutality' (as opposed to force moderation or restraint of violence) could be expressed in two very different modes:

Terrorist A:	• Uses extreme brutality to kill his/her target, but will avoid harm to a bystander as the reason for the attack is to eliminate a political figure and this is part of a campaign for political change. • The terrorists act this way because they do not want to alienate public opinion.

Terrorist B:	• Uses extreme brutality to kill his/her target, and indiscriminately kills and injures many other bystanders. • The reason for the attack is to eliminate a political figure, who is seen as evil, and other people are punished because they are 'perceived' as somehow complicit in the 'evil' the terrorist is fighting.

Tactical Difference

The conventional view of tactics is that these are largely neutral and irrespective of the attacker's motivations. In short, for example, the adage about the vehicle-born improvised explosive device (VBIED) is:

- If a capability has been identified in any potential opponent's tool box, it must be mitigated against. Therefor—*a VBIED is a VBIED, wherever it originated.*
- This view is simple and incorrect. Even in the cases of McVeigh and Breivik both used the same attack mode—a VBIED loaded with similar charge weights in ANFO—and used these weapons in the same type of locations near multi-story office buildings, however, the results differed greatly.

The adage—*a VBIED is a VBIED, wherever it originated* becomes doubtful if it is taken into account that the design will vary significantly in terms of blast size and weight intended, its weaponisation and fragmentation, its placement in the environment, and its component additions (i.e. will it be used to spread a pathogen or poison such as radioactive material?). Other factors making one VBIED very different to another is the intended target and the degree of collateral damage desired or anticipated, or whether the VBIED is designed to specifically achieve a single kill or injury, to kill a large group, to only cause multiple casualties or to act as a 'deterrent' (i.e. a demonstration of power). In each case, the tactical outcome is directly linked to the attributes of the attacker type. Finally, issues such a competence effects the design. For example, it appears that the mixture Breivik produced for his IED was only approximately 20% efficient (TNT equivalence was about 80 kg even if larger quantities of ANFO were involved).

Conclusion

TTPs are an essential part of the terrorism studies tool kit and are significant in understanding the evolving tactical and strategic threats represented by various terrorist(s)/terrorist organisation(s)' over time.

Further Reading

Randy Borum, *Psychology of Terrorism*. Tampa: University of South Florida, 2004, https://www.ncjrs.gov/pdffiles1/nij/grants/208552.pdf?q=psychology-of-terrorism.

Christopher Flaherty, *Dangerous Minds: A Monograph on the Relationship Between Beliefs—Behaviours—Tactics*. OODA LOOP. 7 September 2102, http://www.oodaloop.com/security/2012/09/07/dangerous-minds-the-relationship-between-beliefs-behaviors-and-tactics/.

Matthew Hedges and Theodore Karasik, *Evolving Terrorist Tactics, Techniques, and Procedures (TTP) Migration Across South Asia, Caucasus, and the Middle East*. INEGMA Special Report No. 7, 2010.

Taliban

Anti-Modernism in the Name of Religion: The Rise and Fall of the Taliban

Ali A. Jalali and Lester W. Grau

Editors' Note: This article was written in late 2001. The further reading section was updated prior to this book going to press.

The Taliban were not the Mujahideen that fought the Soviets. Rather, the Taliban commanders were former Mujahideen. The Taliban fighters were most often the children of the refugee camps who had grown up without the benefit of the traditional structure and social discipline of their villages and tribes. The Taliban were not guerrillas. Rather, they were semi-conventional forces armed with a variety of modern and older weapons. The Taliban were a motorized light force tailored to fast-paced combat against a loose coalition of dissimilar armed groups. Various foreign "volunteers" from Pakistan, Saudi Arabia, Yemen, Chechnya and other countries joined the Taliban ranks. The bulk came from Pakistani religious parties, religious schools, and militant groups.

However, the Taliban movement was soon hijacked by the Pakistani Inter Service Intelligence Directorate (ISI) and infiltrated by extremist Deobandi Islamists from Pakistan and by Arab militants, including Osama bin Laden's terrorist Al-Qaeda organization.

The late and generally-unmourned Taliban was the bogey man of the West and drew wide-spread condemnation for its repressive, rigid orthodoxy. However, when it came into being, many people welcomed it as the best hope for peace in Afghanistan. Its rapid rise and ignominious fall leaves Afghanistan neither better nor worse and the only apparent gain is hope.

Following nine-plus years of bloody, inconclusive warfare, the Soviets completed their withdrawal from Afghanistan on 15 February 1989. Each of the Mujahideen factions began jockeying for power, despite the fact that the Afghan communist government was still holding on in the main cities. The Mujahideen also had difficulty in switching from guerrilla tactics to conventional tactics and fielding a conventional force against the communists. In 1992, the Afghan communist government finally collapsed and the factions battled for who would control the successor government. Some refugees returned to their rural homes, but the pre-war hierarchy and social order was shattered. The Mujahideen changed from unpaid volunteers to armed members of warlords' gangs. These gangs raped and pillaged unchecked while the factions continued to quarrel over who was in charge in Kabul. Many Afghans, and their neighbors, looked to the United States for help in restoring order and the economy in Afghanistan. They felt that Afghanistan had fought America's war with the Soviet Union and defeated a super power at the cost of over 1.3 million people. Consequently, Afghanistan was in a shambles and America ought to help put it right. The United States asserted that they lacked the money, that domestic problems had priority and thus refused to play a significant role in settling the region.

Anarchy stalked the Afghan countryside. The emergence of the Taliban was initially a popular reaction to a state of lawlessness and chaos. The sudden appearance of the Islamic student movement of the Taliban in September 1994, and its swift development into a viable military force in Afghanistan has been the subject of different interpretations, speculations, and conspiracy theories. Whether Pakistani intelligence had a role in its creation or it evolved from a local vigilante group challenging the corrupt warlords, the puritanical Sunni militia found extensive support among the masses that had been victimized by continued infighting and lawlessness. Riding a wave of public discontent, the Taliban, led by a village cleric and former Mujahideen fighter—Mullah Omar, embarked on a major drive aimed at unifying the country and disarming the warring factions. The Taliban's stated commitment to a popular mission of fighting corruption and chaos won enormous support. Thousands of young recruits from the refugee *madrasas* (religious schools) across the border in Pakistan swelled their ranks. Many ex-army officers and dissatisfied former Mujahideen commanders who resented the continued infighting among the Mujahideen groups also joined the emerging force.

In a northward movement from their birthplace of Kandahar, Taliban forces made a lightning advance reaching the gates of Kabul by mid February 1995. The move broke former Prime Minister Golbuddin Hekmatyar's three-year military siege of Kabul and dislodged the Iranian-backed *Wahdat* faction from the southwest precincts of Kabul after the Taliban killed the *Wahdat* leader Abdul Ali Mazari. The Taliban's military victories had far-reaching political consequences. They intensified ethnic polarization within Afghan factional politics and moved Iran and Pakistan further apart as their Afghan policies gradually diverged.

The Taliban movement found extensive support among the Pashtuns, the largest ethnic community in the country. Domination of the government by the Tajik-led coalition of President Burhanuddin Rabbani, who unilaterally extended his mandate several times, had caused discontent and a sense of diminution among the Pashtuns who have been the traditional ruling group in Afghanistan since 1747. Even Pashtun intellectuals in the West, who seriously differed with the Taliban on many issues, expressed support for the movement on ethnic grounds. On the other hand, fears of Pashtun political and cultural hegemony through the Taliban, particularly after the fall of Kabul to the students' militia in September 1996, precipitated a political alliance of Tajik, Uzbek, and Shia factions in an anti-Taliban coalition.

Who were the Taliban?

As noted earlier, while the Taliban commanders were former Mujahideen, the Taliban fighters were most often the children of the refugee camps removed from traditional village life. Under-educated, with no real skills or prospects, and full of testosterone with little available sexual outlet, these young men were willing disciples of a cause that would use them and give them meaning and status. The Taliban provided this cause and accepted them into the ranks of various armed groups headed by clerics and former warlords who had joined the Taliban cause.

They Taliban had tanks, artillery, armored personnel carriers and some combat aircraft. Their tactics were not guerrilla tactics. Rather, they used a variation of light cavalry or mounted rifle tactics in the flat lands of the north where pickup trucks and left-over Soviet armored vehicles substituted for horses. The pickup truck was the all-purpose combat and combat support vehicle. Combatants could readily fire from it as it moved, it had a tactical "lightness," and excellent cross-country maneuverability. The pickup truck was the primary troop carrier, transporting ten or more combatants, who fought both mounted and dismounted. This light cavalry pickup force was very effective in exploiting tactical success.

In the mountains, the Taliban used conventional light infantry mountain tactics. However, they were not a conventional force since they lacked the organization and discipline affiliated with a conventional force. There was no standard Table of Organization and Equipment (TO&E) and there was no standard squad, platoon, or company formation. Units ranged from a few dozen combatants to several hundred, depending on the charisma, political influence, and resources available to the commander. Larger units might have organic artillery, armored vehicles, and support systems. Commanders led their followers, often without an internal system of subordinate leaders and chain of command. The Taliban, like the Mujahideen, were warriors, not soldiers. They fought for the glory of battle and the loot and booty that are a warrior's due. They were loyal to their leader and responsible to their leader for their behavior. They were not bound by a soldier's code, discipline, or obedience.

There were elite Taliban militia units who were loyal to factional leaders and played pivotal roles in combat. They usually spearheaded the attack. Several units would group together for major combat under a temporary command. Former army officers and pilots operated the complex systems—aircraft, armored vehicles, artillery and air defense. Senior command positions were the realm of the clergy, not the military professional.

The Taliban's enforcement of a rigid and pre-modern interpretation of Islam clashed with the accepted norms of Afghanistan—moderate norms of Islamic behavior that Afghans had practiced for centuries. In the areas under their control, the Taliban enforced a rigorous Islamic social order including a religious dress code for both men and women, which prescribed full beards for men and complete veiling for women. The Taliban barred women from work outside the home and closed girls' schools. It also banned listening to music and watching TV and videos, and some other forms of entertainment. Over time, the Taliban leadership was isolated from the international community. This was due to their extensive links to Pakistan's ISI and the Deobandi *madrasas* as well as their links to foreign extremist networks and wanted terrorists. Furthermore, the Taliban leadership condoned massive drug production and exhibited a poor human rights record. The Taliban imposition of far-reaching social restrictions and the country's economic failure caused increasing domestic disapproval.

The more the Taliban movement became isolated, the more it became dependent on foreign fighters including extremists from Arab countries, Pakistan, Uzbekistan, and Chechnya.

The Taliban factor impaired the spirit of cooperation between Pakistan and Iran in finding a solution to the Afghan crisis. Inspired by competing interests in the Afghan conflict, the two countries backed rival factions in the war. Pakistan hoped that the Taliban's military victory would lead to restoration of Pashtun preeminence in Afghanistan and the security of trade routes to Central Asia. Both would support Islamabad's long-term geopolitical goals. Consequently, Pakistan patronized the religious militia from the early days of its inception, providing it with organizational and logistical support and "volunteers."

Iran viewed the Taliban as an anti-Shia and anti-Iranian fundamentalist Sunni movement supported by hostile foreign forces. The movement's close ties with Pakistani anti-Shia groups, its links with Saudi *Wahabis,* and the alleged Washington backing of the Taliban in support of its anti-Iranian policy were the source of Iran's distrust and fear. The Taliban's sectarian and ethnic parochialism coupled with its tendency to marginalize Iran-backed non-Pashtun factions and their ouster of the Rabbani government added to the distrust. Iran saw the victory of the Taliban as part of a plot by Sunnis and the United States to isolate Iran. Iran improved the logistical infrastructure of anti-Taliban forces and set up five training camps near the Afghan border for thousands of pro-Rabbani troops. After the fall of Kabul, Iran continued to send supplies to the Rabbani-led anti-Taliban alliance through Central Asia.

In 1996, the Taliban movement took Jalalabad and Kabul. The nature of the Taliban changed with their occupation of Kabul. They changed from a stabilizing element, bringing law and order to an ethnic Pashtun movement fighting the minority Tajik, Uzbek, and Hazara populations, which grouped to form the Northern Alliance. Soon, this fighting evolved beyond an ethnic civil war to a transnational conflict with Iran, Russia, India, Tajikistan, and Uzbekistan backing the Northern Alliance and Pakistan, Saudi Arabia, and the United Arab Emirates backing the Taliban.

The Taliban was the antithesis of modernization and secular government. For the past one hundred years, modernist elites had sought to bring stability to the country. The build up of the traditional anti-modernist clerical class, embodied by the Taliban movement, weakened and marginalized the efforts of a century of Afghan government. The Taliban ideal is to return the country to the way it was when the prophet walked the earth. Man should tend his herds during the day and read the Koran at night. Secular pastimes, such as television, VCRs, kite flying, chess, and music distract from the study of the Koran and, consequently, were banned. Secular government was suspect and the Taliban did little to restore Kabul as the effective seat of government. Rather, Mullah Omar ruled by edict and cash outlays from Kandahar. Schooled in the religious institutions (*madrasas*) during the war, thousands of Afghan refugee students in Pakistan, mullahs, and their supporters coalesced in 1994 into the major political/religious Taliban movement. They declared the Islamic Emirate of Afghanistan.

The Taliban movement has been a popular reaction to prevailing chaos in a broken state. Its commitment to fighting corruption and lawlessness won the movement massive popular support. But, this radical Islamic militia, which established control over 90 percent of the country in less than five years, failed to stabilize the country and create an effective government system. The Taliban's heavy dependence on foreign fighters, their imposition of far-reaching social restrictions, their poor human rights record and economic failure, made them a reactionary and anachronistic force incapable of meeting the challenges of modern life. It became internationally isolated over the refusal to extradite suspected terrorist Osama bin Laden. The country became the largest producer of opium in the world.

The Taliban was neither a monolithic force nor a government. It was a coalition of Pushtun warlords, which generally subscribed to the moral regimen prescribed by Mullah Omar. Mullah Omar's cash box often created more compliance among distant cadres than his edicts. There were also rifts within this Pashtun alliance, particularly between the northern Ghilzai and southern Durrani Pashtun tribes. Mullah Omar's continued defense of Usama bin Laden and defiance of world opinion further prompted Taliban commanders to look for a way to distance themselves from Mullah Omar and withdraw from the Pashtun alliance or realign themselves with the Pashtun element within the Northern Alliance. Faced with reinvigorated Northern Afghan ground forces, backed by United States and British aircraft directed by coalition special forces, the Taliban finally disintegrated along its many fracture lines.

The fall of the Taliban opened a new era in Afghanistan's turbulent political history. The emerging post-Taliban government faces enormous challenges of stabilizing the country, unifying the fragmented society, reconstructing the devastated economy, building the state institutions, and strengthening the civil society. These are no easy tasks. The source of hope is the pledge by the international community that it will not walk away from Afghanistan until peace and stability returns to the war-torn nation.

Further Reading

Hasan Abbas, *The Taliban Revival: Violence and Extremism on the Pakistan/Afghanistan Frontier.* London: Yale University Press, 2014.

Ali A. Jalali, *A Military History of Afghanistan.* Santa Barbara: Praeger, 2015.

Ahmed Rashid, Taliban: *Militant Islam, Oil and Fundamentalism.* London: L. B. Tauris & Co Ltd, 2000.

Terrorist Mindset

Crawling into the Terrorist's Head: Finding Utility in Terrorist Mind-Sets

Jeffrey A. Baxter and Daniel S. Gressang IV

Propaganda by the deed. The phrase has been used to describe terrorism ever since Paul Brousse first used the phrase in August 1877's *Bulletin de la Féderation Jurassienne.* The phrase denotes a sophisticated understanding of the dynamics of terrorism and expressed that understanding very simply. It suggests that terrorist violence is, first and foremost, an integral part of a contest to shape and manipulate perceptions. Terror, by definition, plays upon its audience's fears and uncertainties through the mechanisms of violence and the threat of violence.

Terrorists of all stripes seek to use this dynamic to their advantage, although their perception and understanding of their audience can differ markedly. Authorities at all levels of government, in turn, have sought to use an understanding of the terrorists' mindset to craft effective and efficient counter- and anti-terrorism policies and practices. Achieving this goal, however, has been easier in the abstract. Much of the difficulty has been the result of competing perceptions and theories of terrorist motivations and objectives. For some analysts, the terrorist is driven by a rational cost-benefit calculation centered on expected or desired social and political outcomes while others see a pattern of behavior tied to mental pathology and development, or ideologically or theologically driven. Reading available biographical and autobiographical works, such as those by or about Leila Khaled, Sean MacStiofain, Timothy McVeigh, Kerry Noble, Michael "Bommi" Baumman, and an otherwise forgettable group of Detroit skinheads, reveals a much more complex mosaic of motivations, individual perceptions, and world-views within the radical world. Teasing out the nuances and unique qualities of the terrorist mind can, as a result, easily become an exercise in futility.

Despite the complexities of terrorist mind-sets, several salient areas exist which can be better understood and exploited by the counter-terrorist and law enforcement communities. In general terms, analysis can distinguish between two basic types of terrorist groups, divided on the basis of the group's broader conceptualization of its role and "struggle." One type can be characterized as instrumental in outlook. These terrorists and terrorist groups see a quantifiable social or political goal they seek to attain. Most well-known terrorists in this category seek to reorder social and political institutions and practices to suit their particular vision of the future. Commonly referred to as "political" terrorists, the instrumental terrorist seeks power, control, and standing, often desiring change in accordance with an identifiable *political* ideology. Communist and communist- or anarchist-inspired groups such as the Red Army Faction, the Symbionese Liberation Army, and Sendero Luminoso are well known examples. Similarly, far-right and fascist groups, such as the Ku Klux Klan and neo-Nazis, also seek a political and social reordering. Separatists and idea-driven terrorists, like the Republic of New Africa, the Order, and Ted Kascinski are also driven by a desire to affect vast and sweeping societal change.

More difficult to understand and effectively counter are the visionary terrorist. Often associated with a religious motivation and imperative, the visionary terrorist also holds goals and perspectives which drive and inform his actions, yet these goals and ideals are not easily identified and associated with the temporal world. The visionary terrorist seeks a place in history, seeks to change the course of human evolution, or seeks to achieve some theologically-based end state. He is, in a very real sense, seeking to interact with, and act for, an audience which does not exist outside his own mental capacity. He believes he is speaking for God, Allah, Jehovah, or other deity and acting in accordance with the wishes and dictates of that other-worldly audience. His motives, and justifications, are grounded in his understanding of the deity's plans and purposes, making his actions in the temporal world of man always justifiable. He is driven by higher purpose, associated with a theological belief set or by his own megalomania. Usama bin Laden,

Timothy McVeigh, Aum Shinrikyo's Shoko Asahara, and Ygal Amir, the assassin of Israeli Prime Minister Ytzhak Rabin, all illustrate the visionary terrorist. His motives and goals may be so self-specific that they almost impossible to fathom or find a familiar thread to which they might be connected.

Regardless of type, instrumental or visionary, those who engage in political violence are rational in their choices and actions. They have goals and objectives, grounded in the temporal and affixed to the ephemeral that they hope to attain. The terrorist's specific set of preferences and the order in which those preferences are arranged in the terrorist mind may differ quite markedly from what we are familiar and comfortable with, particularly in the case of the visionary terrorist. Terrorists tend to be preference maximizers, acting in ways they expect to lead to the realization of their greatest and highest preferences given existing circumstances. This is not to say that terrorists will adhere rigidly and blindly to their preference set and order but that, given the choice and the opportunity, they will act in ways consistent with their belief system.

The counterterrorism and law enforcement communities can, by paying close attention to the rhetorical messages of the terrorists, gain at least some understanding of their adversary's perceptions, world-view, and objectives, and structure countermeasures accordingly. But it is difficult, since paying attention to gain this level of understanding requires analysis of both the rhetorical message of the terrorist—his "propaganda"—and the symbolic message inherent in his actions. It cannot be over-emphasized, however, that anyone who is trying to understand how the terrorist thinks and acts, must first try and free him or herself from the mindset of the "normal" and "rational," as they are typically defined, and strive to comprehend and apply a "logic" that by most definitions, is not "logical" or "rational." Understanding the terrorist's cultural roots, his environment, how he was and is influenced by philosophies, beliefs, other people, and institutions is critical to understanding the terrorist mindset. The analyst must de-construct his own belief "set" and re-build it piece by piece using as much information gleaned from analyzing the terrorist, and "getting into his head." The resulting, "template" could differ from the original in anything from a small detail to a completely different set of values. By both word and deed, the terrorist identifies for us his vision and expectations. By striving to understand his message, as well as his logic "template," the counterterrorism and law enforcement communities can gain a greater appreciation for his motives, for the most likely effective countermeasures suitable for employment in each particular case, and for the nature and extent of the real, rather than perceived or expected, threat.

Further Reading

Daniel S. Gressang IV, "Audience and Message: Assessing Terrorist WMD Potential." *Terrorism and Political Violence*, Vol. 13, Iss. 3, Summer 2001: 83-106.

Brian Michael Jenkins, "The Terrorist Mindset and Terrorist Decisionmaking: Two Areas of Ignorance." RAND Paper Series. Santa Monica: RAND, 1979.

Jerrold M. Post, *The Mind of the Terrorist: The Psychology of Terrorism from the IRA to al-Qaeda*. New York: Palgrave Macmillan, 2007.

Threat Analysis

Emerging Threats

Robert J. Bunker

Flip on CNN any day of the week and you'll see a story about a looming threat—be it a new gang, terrorist group, or weapon of mass destruction. The ceaseless repetition of new threats on the 10'clock news blurs together into a confusing, amorphous mass. The purpose of this essay is to give the layperson a context and criteria to examine the real strategic threats on the horizon—and how they will affect our society.

Emerging threats can be viewed from tactical, operational, and strategic perspectives. Tactical level emerging threats are based on the weaponry, techniques, and targeting schemes employed by an opposing terrorist group or criminal-soldier force. Criminal-soldiers are networked guerrilla/terrorist groups such as the Revolutionary Armed Forces of Colombia whose aims have shifted from straightforward political overthrow to leveraging illicit contraband within lawless state and nonstate territories. Such tactics would include the application of CBRNE (Chemical Biological Radiological Nuclear and High Order Explosives), DEW (Directed Energy Weapons), and IW (Information Warfare) against designated targets. Tactical-level emerging threats are more likely to be known to the general public because they are tailor-made for media coverage. Understanding of tactical-level threats does not require a background in counter-terrorism or intelligence—only the knowledge that there are bad people with deadly weapons out to kill you. Rarer (yet equally, if not more important) is understanding of the operational and strategic perspective on emerging threats.

Operational level emerging threats are based on criminal-soldier coordination of varying forms of destructive and disruptive weaponry and techniques. Operational-level attacks can range from car bombs to cyber-terrorism—and sometimes both at the same time. Non-state actors can combine humanspace and cyberspace operations for hybrid attacks, creating a lethal synergy. Criminal-soldiers could also engage in 'combined arms' cyber-operations which draw upon varying IW techniques (firewall penetration, denial of services, data warping, etc.) much in same way that traditional armor, artillery, and infantry attacks can be combined in physical based operations. Asymmetric warfare, which represents a non-state counter to traditional state-on-state warfare waged by the West, also falls within this level of emerging threats.

Emergent tactical and operational level threats are of less significance than strategic level emerging threats. This level of emerging threats is based on the type of threat entity and its sophistication. Great concern exists that violent non-state actors are becoming more of a threat to democratic nation-states than traditional totalitarian nation-state opponents. Non-state threat groups of concern include terrorist organizations, drug cartels, street gangs, organized crime, religious cults, private armies, and freelance mercenary groups. All of these organizations are gaining increasing combat (terrorist) potentials.

The sophistication of these groups vary greatly. Recent generational/phase research suggests that many of these entities are undergoing rapid organizational evolution. As they come in conflict with democratic nation-states, an action-reaction process takes place, resulting in a shift to more sophisticated and dangerous forms of organization. In the case of street gangs, the first generation turf gang type has evolved into the drug (cartel) based gang type in some instances. The latter draws upon a more sophisticated gang organizational form with increasing levels of politicization and internationalization. Current trends suggest that a third generation mercenary gang type may at some point appear. This gang type could leverage its skills to cooperate with terrorist groups and other state actors, far outclassing the response capabilities of traditional law enforcement groups.

Drug cartel research suggests that two phases of evolution have taken place. The first phase (aggressive competitor) based on the Medellín model has transitioned over to the second phase (subtle co-opter) represented by the Cali model. This newer cartel phase is more successful when engaged in conflict with democratic nation-states than its predecessor form. The Mexican Federation of cartels has been able, to a limited extent, to graft itself onto the Mexican state—something a first phase cartel is not capable of doing. Such state co-option represents a highly sophisticated evolutionary adaptation to the conflict environment. Concern over a third phase (criminal state successor) cartel form, derived from the Ciudad del Este model, has been discussed. This would allow for the capture of the institutions of the state and its full blurring with a drug based criminal entity.

Unpublished guerilla and terrorist research suggests that, since World War II, defined periods of criminal-soldier evolution have taken place. For guerrilla forces, the operational environment has shifted from rural areas to urban centers. The 'urban guerilla' of the late 1960s, in turn, evolved into the 'political terrorist.' The milieu shifted from that of the "Battle of Algiers" to Carlos the Jackal, and live TV coverage became a more potent weapon than the AK-47. This, however, was not the end of terror's evolution.

With the fall of the Soviet bloc, the jet-setting, Marxist playboy terrorists of the1960s/early 1970s faded into the background. The new terrorists that replaced them were more fanatical, deadly, and willing to slaughter. The 1990s and early 2000s saw the rise of 'ethnic/religious' terrorists who were less constrained in their application of violence and willingness to create great amounts of casualties. The structure of the new insurgent forces was also wholly original. Organizational changes saw the emergence of flatter and more networked command, control, and communications (C^3) structures for these groups.

Two emergent trends are now taking place which suggests that what could be considered second generation (ethnic/religious) terrorists are also undergoing their own evolutionary process. With cyberspace becoming an increasingly important operational environment, terrorist group organizational adaptation to this environment is highly likely. In addition, a true transnational threat entity such as the *al Qaeda* represents a magnitude shift in the network capability of second generation (ethnic/religious) terrorists. A good argument may be made that *al Qaeda* represents a third generation terrorist group and/or first generation warmaking entity capable of engaging and defeating very weak nation-states.

Organized crime, religious cults, private armies, and freelance mercenary groups also appear to be evolving, however, due to lack of published generational/phase research, the rate and type of this change is unknown. Much of the research on strategic level emerging threats has benefited from the writings of military historian Martin van Creveld and 'netwar' theorists David Ronfeldt and John Arquilla. Current concerns focus on the increasing interaction of non-state threat entities with each other and their continuing evolution. While no one has a crystal ball, its clear that non-state threats will continue to evolve—and so must the security agencies charged with combating them.

Further Reading

Robert J. Bunker and John P. Sullivan, *Studies in Gangs and Cartels*. London: Routledge, 2014.

Martin van Creveld, *The Transformation of War*. New York: The Free Press, 1991.

John P. Sullivan, Robert J. Bunker, Ernest J. Lorelli, Howard Seguine, and Matt Begert, *Jane's Unconventional Weapons*. London: Jane's Information Group, 2002.

Threat Convergence

A New and More Lethal Category of Terrorist Warfare

Joshua Sinai

A new category of terrorist warfare has emerged that is exponentially greater in the magnitude of its operational activities, areas of operation, political impact, and attack lethality than heretofore because it has converged across multiple threat dimensions that previously were largely singular in nature. These converging threat dimensions—some of which are mature while others are still nascent—consist of the following:

(1) Terrorist groups that seek to conduct 'world class' catastrophic warfare against their adversaries;

(2) Organized criminal groups that seek to expand their spheres of activity by cooperating with terrorist groups or adopting terrorist warfare themselves;

(3) Increasing availability to terrorist groups of weapons of mass destruction (WMD) (particularly rockets and mortars), as well as rogue scientists and engineers with WMD proficiency;

(4) Increasing availability to terrorist groups of social media instruments with which to conduct propaganda, radicalization, and recruitment activities that enable them to reach ever larger audiences, as well as funding and command and control functions that expand the geographical range of their activities;

(5) Increasing availability to terrorist groups of new technologies to conduct cyber-warfare;

(6) State sponsors that seek to exploit their terrorist proxies to inflict greater lethality attacks against their adversaries;

(7) Anarchic conditions in weak and failed states that provide safe havens to terrorist groups; and

(8) Enabling conditions in strong states, particularly the proliferation of radical subcultures in Diaspora communities, that provide constituencies and 'no go' areas in Western states that provide recruits and safe havens to foreign terrorist groups.

Converging Threat Dimensions

Each of the eight converging threat dimensions discussed in this section are dangerous by themselves, but when they are linked and intertwined, the terrorists' position is substantially strengthened in their asymmetric warfare vis-à-vis their state adversaries.

TC#1: Terrorist Groups Seeking 'World Class' Warfare Capability

As some of today's terrorists go about converging their capabilities and linkages into a new category of exponentially upgraded warfare, they do not seek to use violence only in the conventional definition of inflicting casualties and physical damages that are still calibrated in order to coerce their adversary governments to give in to their demands. In this new paradigm, such terrorist groups view themselves as 'world class' destroyers who seek to inflict against their adversaries catastrophic casualties and physical and economic destruction without regard to whether or not such attacks will prevent the targeted governments from giving in to their demands. This category was introduced by al Qaida's 9/11 attacks in which multiple airliners were employed in coordinated attacks as weapons of mass destruction to cause more than 3,000 fatalities and billions of dollars in economic damages—the first time in the history of terrorist warfare that such catastrophic casualties had been inflicted by a single terrorist group.

Seeking to inflict such 'world class' catastrophic warfare against their adversaries is also due to their apocalyptic ideology that provides their objectives with a transcendental dimension that is unconstrained by any political and moral constraints, since the catastrophic devastation caused by their warfare is expected to usher in an apocalyptic 'new order.'

TC#2: Organized Criminal Groups Seeking to Expand Spheres of Activity

A second dimension of threat convergence is the opportunistic cooperation between terrorist groups and criminal networks, with the criminal elements providing terrorist groups the means for profit maximization and organizational/cell maintenance through their expertise in illicit services such as document forging, logistics and human smuggling across borders, money laundering, illicit drug trafficking, and arms trafficking.

With this 'conventional' model continuing, however, three new developments in the convergence between terrorist and criminal groups appear to be emerging. In the first development, terrorist groups could potentially use their criminal network counterparts to escalate the lethality of their warfare against their adversaries by using them to illicitly acquire CBRN/cyber weapons from rogue elements, including the logistical support in delivering them to their intended targets. In the second development, terrorist groups might adopt criminal techniques in their own modus operandi, for instance, by organizing their own drug trafficking enterprises to raise funds for their organizational maintenance. In the final development, criminal organizations, particularly those that primarily engage in narco-trafficking operations, are adopting terrorist techniques in their own operations, such as assassinating their political and law enforcement adversaries in order to punish them and deter others from interfering with their illicit activities.

Examples of 'conventional' convergence between terrorist groups that collaborate with criminal organizations include Hizballah, which has a long history of involvement in criminal enterprises, whether illicit drug trafficking, diamond smuggling in West Africa, or petty crimes in the United States. The Afghan Taliban and Colombian FARC are noted examples of terrorist organizations with a long history of engaging in illicit drug trafficking. Moreover, examples of terrorist operatives that engage in criminal activities prior to executing their attacks include the cell that carried out the Madrid train bombings in March 2003, which financed its operation with funds earned from trafficking in hashish and Ecstasy.

The involvement of terrorist groups in criminal enterprises, however, may also be calibrated at times by their operational cells' need to avoid engaging in illicit activities that may attract the attention of law enforcement authorities. This could jeopardize an imminent terrorist attack, so not all terrorist groups are likely to risk a potential attack's operational security by involving criminal elements in its execution.

TC#3: Proliferation of WMD Weapons and Rogue Scientists/ Engineers

The third converging component represents the most significant threat in the form of the potential acquisition by terrorist groups of weapons of mass destruction (i.e., chemical, biological, radiological or nuclear weapons), whose employment in an attack would result in catastrophic casualties and physical damages against their adversaries. It is also the least developed warfare capability by terrorist groups, although several terrorist groups and lone wolves have either launched or attempted to launch attacks using chemical weapons.

Unlike the steps involved in the acquisition of a chemical (or biological) weapon, terrorist groups' acquisition of a nuclear weapon would require access to highly specialized material and a high level of technical expertise that historically has been beyond their reach. Nevertheless, the political and security upheavals in countries that possess nuclear arsenals, such as Pakistan, are a reminder of how precarious the security of nuclear weapons facilities can be in weak states where terrorist groups such as al Qaida operate.

TC#4: Proliferation of Social Media Cyber Instruments

The increasing availability to terrorist groups of social media instruments, such as Twitter, Facebook and YouTube, to conduct propaganda, radicalization, and recruitment activities has enabled them to expand such activities into the virtual world of cyberspace, where they are able to reach ever larger audiences, as well as 'narrowcast' their messages to specific audiences such as women and children. By utilizing various encryption technologies, cyberspace has also enabled such technologically capable terrorist groups to conduct crucial operational functions (especially between operational managers and local operatives) such as communications, funding, and command and control—the types of functions that enable them to significantly expand the geographical range of their activities as well as avoid the surveillance of their activities by their counterterrorist adversaries.

TC#5: Proliferation of New Technologies in Cyber-Warfare

Cyber weapons have become an important component of modern warfare. Thus, while terrorist groups have long exploited social media's instruments, in this new converging trend they may have acquired or are in the process of acquiring cyber weapons in order to significantly upgrade the lethality of their overall warfare capability.

As a component of their new category of terrorist warfare, cyber terrorism is defined as the premeditated, politically motivated warfare by sub-state groups that engage in terrorist violence against an adversary's IT infrastructure's computer systems, software programs and data, which is designed to inflict physical disruption, destruction, as well as economic damage. Cyber terrorism would be conducted on its own or in conjunction with a group's conventional attacks.

To develop a cyber-warfare capability would require not only an intention but the resources and trained personnel to achieve such an objective. A terrorist group's personnel would have to possess a technical knowledge of hacking and an adversary's information technology vulnerabilities, as well as the funds to employ specialized cyber warriors in those areas. To acquire such cyber warfare capabilities—which already form a component in states' warfare arsenals—terrorist groups would have to develop it, for instance, by recruiting radicalized IT engineers and technicians, pay mercenary hacktivists to conduct such warfare on their behalf, or obtain such a capability from a state sponsor.

Types of cyber warfare that would be conducted by terrorist groups that would exponentially upgrade their military capability might include a Stuxnet-like virus in the form of a highly specialized malware coded to attack Supervisory Control and Data Acquisition (SCADA) systems that control and monitor specific industrial processes in critical infrastructural targets such as nuclear power plants (for example, to force changes in the rotor speeds of centrifuges), electricity grids, water plants, telecommunication networks, or transportation systems (including traffic lights).

TC#6: State Sponsors

A state sponsor of terrorism is a designation given to governments that provide support to terrorist groups that engage in such activities on their behalf. The incentives for governments to support terrorist proxies include the ability of the terrorist proxy to advance that government's ideological and foreign policy and national security objectives in their targeted countries and, especially when such support is covert, deniability and absence of attribution and retribution when an attack against the state's adversary takes place. For terrorist groups that ally themselves with their state sponsors, such state support is crucial because without it they would have difficulty in funding and conducting their operations. Such support can be active (i.e., direct) or passive (i.e., providing political support and tolerating the presence of a terrorist group on its territory). Types of active support include arms procurement and supplies, funding, training and training facilities, diplomatic cover (including false travel documentation, diplomatic pouches to transport weapons and explosives, and immunity from extradition), logistical assistance, safe haven, and headquarters for a group's organization. A state with CBRN weapons of mass destruction capability and facilities (for instance, Iran, North Korea or Pakistan) could also provide its terrorist proxy such weapons and devices, as well as expertise in launching such WMD warfare.

TC#7: Weak and Failed States

Weak and failed states provide conditions that enable terrorist groups to establish safe havens in their ungoverned or poorly-governed regions. It is in such safe havens that terrorist groups are able to establish areas where they can freely operate, including the ability to manufacture weapons and devices and plan terrorist attacks around the world. In this converging component, the proliferation of such anarchic conditions has enabled terrorist groups such as al Qaida and its affiliates to establish safe havens in territories' ungoverned spaces, such as exist in Afghanistan, Pakistan, Iraq, Nigeria, Somalia, Syria and Yemen. The political and security turbulence in parts of Egypt, for example has allowed al Qaida affiliates safe haven in the anarchic and lawless Sinai Peninsula, from which they have carried out direct attacks against Egyptian forces and launched rockets and mortars against Israel's southern tourist city of Eilat. Although they were reported to be small in number, al Qaida adherents were active even the weakly governed Palestinian Gaza Strip, in control by Hamas since 2007, as well as parts of the West Bank, also weakly controlled by the Palestinian Authority.

TC#8: Enabling Conditions in Strong States

Enabling conditions in what are considered 'strong states,' such as Western Europe and the United States and Canada, in which radical subcultures' "no-go" areas provide safe haven to terrorist operatives and their cells, constitute the final component of threat convergence. This component is characterized by states that—even though they are considered as 'strong'—still experience problems controlling portions of their own territories, whether through weak border controls (for instance, within the European Union or along the American-Mexican border), or in the form of "no-go" enclaves in certain Diaspora minority-dominated communities, where local police forces exert little authority. Such 'no-go' neighborhoods also serve as facilitating environments for the spread of extremist ideologies among increasingly radicalized individuals in those communities, some of whom have turned to terrorist violence to achieve their objectives. The failure to fully integrate such minority communities into their larger societies, whether due to discrimination problems or resistance by some among those communities to integrate, is a significant contributor to the convergence of this component to form the new threat category.

Conclusion

As demonstrated by the preceding discussion and cases, the convergence of significant threat dimensions appears to be growing, not diminishing (even if some of these dimensions are still nascent). This has produced new categories of terrorist warfare that are potentially more dangerous and pose a higher level of threat to regional and international stability than heretofore. In response, equally multi-dimensional and comprehensive counter-measures will be required, whether by single governments or multilaterally.

Focusing on the convergences of such threat dimensions that are usually perceived individually, and determining whether such convergences are fully mature or are in the early stages of coalescing, is not intended to imply that each of these specific threat dimensions no longer requires tailored and customized responses. Rather, we need to broaden our thinking and conceptual approaches to effectively address the evolving intersections where these multiple threats are in the process of converging.

The converging threat dimensions, whether nascent or current, present problems as well as opportunities for the counterterrorism community. On the one hand, a multitude of facilitating conditions, whether in weak or strong states, are attracting different terrorist groups to different regions, resulting in the convergence of such threats and the overlapping of their networks. As a result of the emergent confluence of such threats and networks, counterterrorism planners now need to anticipate which emerging failed state is likely to become the next attractive safe haven for a transnational terrorist group to set up bases, training facilities, and, in a worst-case scenario, laboratories for the development of WMD-related CBRN weapons and devices. Similarly, a new and previously unknown illicit trafficking network may emerge either in a weak state or in a strong state to provide opportunities for a terrorist group to acquire WMD through illicit means. As mentioned earlier, in a worst-case scenario, certain nuclear states, such as Pakistan, may fall into the hands of terrorist groups.

Understanding how these different threats are converging also provides valuable early warning indicators of emerging vulnerabilities that may result in new categories of threats. To improve our understanding of how to respond to the challenges being generated by threat convergences, we need a comprehensive inventory of the problem areas, whether in weak, failing, or even strong states, in order to identify the threat dimensions that have the potential to converge into new categories of threats. This also provides us with the opportunity to understand which capacities need to be improved in weak states as well as strong states, such as effective governance (including opportunities for wider political participation), control over a nation's territory, provision of socioeconomic benefits to solve social ills and employment opportunities for aggrieved communities, strengthening of education to improve a population's skills to advance in society, and countering of the spread and appeal of extremist ideologies that have the potential to escalate into violence.

Further Reading

James J.F. Forest, Ed., *Intersections of Crime and Terror*. New York: Routledge, 2013.

Joshua Sinai, "The Evolving Terrorist Threat: The Convergence of Terrorism, Proliferation of WMD, and Enabling Conditions in Weak and Strong States." *The Journal of Counterterrorism and Homeland Security International*, Vol. 13, No. 2, Summer 2007: 10-16.

Joshua Sinai and James J.F. Forest, "Threat Convergence: A Framework for Analyzing the Potential for WMD Terrorism," in James J.F. Forest and Russell D. Howard, Eds., *Weapons of Mass Destruction and Terrorism*. New York: McGraw-Hill, 2013: 725-737.

The Unabomber

Theodore John Kaczynski

James T. Kirkhope

On May 25, 1978, a Northwestern university campus security officer was injured by a mailbomb meant for a professor. Another act of counterculture terrorism? Hardly. This seemingly minor incident was the start of 18-year terror campaign which was to stretch until the arrest of Theodore John Kaczynski on April 3, 1996, near Lincoln, Montana. After the mailbombing of a United Airlines executive in June 1980 was linked to three previous attacks, law enforcement officials labeled the investigation the UNABOM case – an acronym for the two *UN*iversity and two *A*irline *BOM*bings already under review. Kaczynski had already launched 12 attacks by 1987; the year that authorities circulated the famous drawing of the "Unabomber." Kaczynski was not deterred by his newfound notoriety—he stepped up his bombing campaign, expanding his list of targets to include the computer industry.

By the 1990s, the Unabomber was being hunted by a multi-agency task force comprised of the Bureau of Alcohol, Tobacco, and Firearms, Postal Inspectors, local police departments, and led by the Federal Bureau of Investigation (FBI). However, the massive law enforcement manhunt was largely a failure: the Unabomber was still at large. After four more bombings in the 1990s, targeting geneticists and forestry executives, as well as the threat of a continued campaign, the FBI approved the Unabomber's request to publish his essay "Industrial Society And Its Future" in the *Washington Post* and the *New York Times* on September 19, 1995. The questionable decision to release the document generated a strong lead for the multi-agency task force: Kaczynski's own brother. By February 1996, David Kaczynski had read the manifesto, recognized numerous phrases often used by his brother, and subsequently notified authorities. Soon after, agents surrounded a small cabin in Montana, and arrested Ted Kaczynski. On the day the often-delayed trial was about to begin, prosecutors and the defense struck a plea agreement despite lingering concerns about Kaczynski's sanity. On January 22, 1998, Theodore Kaczynski pleaded guilty to 13 charges, ensuring a life sentence in prison but avoiding the death penalty. Like the similar case of Oklahoma City Bomber Timothy McVeigh, the Unabomber defies the terrorist stereotype of the swarthy, bomb-throwing foreigner. His paranoia, zealousness, and sociopathic nature is entirely all-American.

Born May 22, 1942, in Chicago, Kaczynski was briefly but severely ill as an infant. Court ordered psychiatric profiles suggest that extended isolation from his mother and family as well as possible injury or psychological damage resulting from the illness may have inhibited his social development. Whatever Kaczynski lacked in physical strength or social skills, he more than made up in intelligence, skipping a grade in both elementary and high school prior to entering Harvard at age 16. By 25, Kaczynski had earned a Ph.D. in mathematics from the University of Michigan and secured a tenure-track appointment at University of California, Berkeley. Less than two years later, Kaczynski left his position, moved home, and worked odd jobs until 1971. He then relocated to the now-infamous rural shack in Montana where he lived until his arrest.

Many consider Kaczynski the prototype for "lone wolf" terrorism, but can we really label the "Unabomber" a terrorist? Though Kaczynski's 18-year bomb campaign directed against industrial and scientific targets generated terror, the Unabomber case does not easily lend itself as a useful example of terrorism. The FBI suggests, "Terrorism is the unlawful use of force or violence against persons or property to intimidate or coerce a government, the civilian population, or any segment thereof, in furtherance of political or social objectives." Although the Unabomber campaign can be characterized as such, it lacked evidence of a conspiracy common to most definitions of political terrorism.

Additionally, Kaczynski failed at the outset to communicate a social or political agenda. Once formulated, Kaczynski's goals were vague and unreasonable, if not irrational. More directly, the case of the Unabomber follows the pattern of a serial killer with paranoid schizophrenic tendencies—making him more Ted Bundy than Osama. However, while Ted Kaczynski's philosophies harken back to a simpler appealing agrarian utopia of America's past and holds a certain appeal, his anti-technology and anti-industry rage instilled a fear and terror across the country not soon forgotten.

Further Reading

John Douglas and Mark Olshaker, *Unabomber: On the Trail of America's Most-Wanted Serial Killer.* New York: Pocket Books, 1996.

Jim Freeman, Terry Turchie and Max Noel, *UNABOMBER: How the FBI Broke Its Own Rules to Capture the Terrorist Ted Kaczynski.* Palisades: History Publishing Co, 2014.

Theodore J. Kaczynski and David Skrbina, *Technological Slavery: The Collected Writings of Theodore J. Kaczynski, a.k.a. "The Unabomber."* Port Townsend: Feral House, 2010.

Urban Terrorism

Cleansing the Polluted Urban Seas

Russell W. Glenn

Most attempts to categorize terrorist threats focus on the nature of the terrorist groups themselves: member motivations, ends sought, demographic characteristics, or tactics employed. It is perhaps more revealing to consider an alternative perspective, one that looks at the nature of the urban populations in which the terrorists operate.

Terrorist and other insurgent groups often require support from their environments to a greater extent than do regular military forces. Mao Tse-Tung aptly characterized this relationship of dependence on the general population by his revolutionary guerrillas: "The former may be likened to water and the latter to the fish who inhabit it." No less than with Mao's revolutionaries, terrorist successes are functions of the seas in which the individuals operate.

From organized criminal elements to urban gangs to terrorist groups, all of these organizations rely on the acceptance or tolerance of those who share their operating areas. Both the Irish Republican Army (IRA) and the Palestinian Liberation Organization, for example, operate in areas where subsets of the population are sympathetic to their goals, while the greater population is either: apathetic, uncooperative, or antipathetic. In many other urban areas, the sea is predisposed toward tolerance as long as its members believe that dissident groups are merely exercising legitimate rights.

Even if the urban sea is universally hostile to a group's intentions, the waters are nevertheless dense and heterogeneous, making it fairly easy for attackers to conceal themselves. Unlike in rural areas, those speaking a foreign language and unfamiliar with local customs are commonplace. Daily contacts are typically superficial. Unusual behaviors may go undetected due to the high density of activities. The "hum" of urban daily life veils what would immediately attract attention in less frenetic domains. Uncovering a planned attack may be virtually impossible barring infiltration of the organization itself or a mistake on the part of the perpetrators.

Thus, even the most hostile waters are in some ways hospitable. At a minimum, the indigenous population provides concealment merely by virtue of its considerable numbers. It likely provides sustenance through routine commercial exchange. The residents of most cities are little concerned and receive at best limited guidance as to how to detect threats from unfriendly individuals. Most residents are therefore unlikely to take action when they see unattended articles, marginally unusual behaviors, or other signs that would signal potential danger to the better informed. The sea may be overwhelmingly antagonistic in intent, but it is benign, even supportive, in effect.

To mitigate the dangers it is necessary to treat the waters on which the threats depend. Removal of oxygen from a river causes its fish to die. Likewise, public officials can stunt or kill the undesirable elements in their troublesome seas, pools, ponds, or puddles. But the remedy must be tailored. A reckless poisoning will destroy legitimate and illegitimate enterprises alike. Effective treatment will vary depending on the nature of the threat and the sea in which it swims.

Two recent examples illustrate successful, yet completely different, kinds of treatments. In Northern Ireland, dissatisfied members of the Catholic community have for decades provided a haven for the IRA. Long-standing antipathies, such as those between Protestants and Catholics, may be immune to rapid treatment. However, the British have demonstrated considerable patience in improving the economic and political status of Northern Ireland's Catholic population despite the resistance from Unionists. Living standards, education levels, and other measures of basic well being are slowly improving through mutually supportive economic, social, political, and military efforts. There is now evidence that the IRA is being deprived of its oxygen. The once-friendly pool shows signs of desiring to purge itself of the group's violence.

On the other side of the world, in San Diego, the city successfully contained demonstrators who were attempting to disrupt the 2001

Biotechnology Industry Organization tradeshow. City officials recognized that the key target group was the sea at large (the general population) in which the demonstrators had chosen to operate. A preemptive educational campaign directed toward the urban area's residents undermined support for the demonstrators prior to the event. An informed, law-abiding citizenry and city police force together refused to tolerate incursions onto the property and rights of fellow residents, choosing instead to support law enforcement efforts to restrict the activities of demonstrators who had other than legitimate agendas.

Eliminating sources of popular discontent, encouraging public intolerance of illegal acts, increasing public awareness of criminal methods—such initiatives make the seas unwelcome for dangerous interlopers and unsavory indigenous elements. These groups must then seek support from the shrinking segments of the population who remain willing to be of assistance. Sources of provisions shrink accordingly. Further actions taken by the authorities to limit the freedom of movement—monitoring explosive materials, imposing curfews, and restricting travel routes—force those with ill intentions ever further into the shallow waters where they are more readily detected and removed.

The final step is to throw a net around these exposed threats. Ultimate success depends on considerable cooperation between disparate governmental and sometimes nongovernmental agencies. Other nongovernmental elements, most notably the public itself, should also be invited to play a role. The greater the collective support to limit the activities of urban threats, the tighter the weave on the net woven to sweep the threats from their supporting seas.

Further Reading

Russell W. Glenn, "'Cleansing Polluted Seas: Non-State Threats and the Urban Environment." Robert J. Bunker, Ed., *Non-State Threats and Future Wars.* London: Frank Cass, 2003: 109-120.

Jamison Jo Medby and Russell W. Glenn, *Street Smart: Intelligence Preparation of the Battlefield for Urban Operations.* Santa Monica: RAND, October 2002.

Contributors

Dr. John Arquilla is Professor and Chair in the Department of Defense Analysis at the United States Naval Postgraduate School. He is best known for his work with David Ronfeldt on cyberwar, netwar, and swarm tactics. Over the past two decades, they have served as principal interpreters of the strategic implications of the information revolution. Dr. Arquilla's other books include *The Reagan Imprint* (Ivan R. Dee 2006), *Worst Enemy* (Ivan R. Dee 2008), *Insurgents, Raiders, and Bandits* (Ivan R. Dee 2011), and *Afghan Endgames* (Georgetown University Press 2012). His work as an advisor to senior leaders on matters of strategy and policy has extended from Operation Desert Storm to the Kosovo War, and on to the various campaigns that have comprised the ongoing conflict with terrorist networks.

Jeffrey A. "Skunk" Baxter is currently a consultant/contractor for a number of U.S. government agencies and advises top military, government and civilian groups on missile defense, terrorism and counter-terrorism, cyber-warfare, intelligence, virtual reality, next-generation technology and unconventional strategies. He currently holds consulting agreements with the NRO, NGA, OUSD/I and the ODNI, among others. He is also a Senior Fellow and member of the Board of Regents at the Potomac Institute for Policy Studies, a member of the Director's Strategic Red Team at MIT/Lincoln Laboratories and holds consulting agreements with LEIDOS, Defense Group Inc., Northrop-Grumman, Logos Technologies, Decisive Analytics Corp and Sierra Nevada Corp. He was a Specialist Reserve Officer with the Anti-Terrorist Division of the Los Angeles Police Department for 15 years, a founding member of the Terrorism Early Warning Group, Los Angeles Sheriff's Department and an advisor to Mr. Charlie Allen, Under Secretary for Intelligence and Analysis at DHS.

Matt Begert currently works for The Aerospace Corporation and is tasked to adopt advanced technology into first response organizations and nongovernment organizations involved in humanitarian assistance and disaster relief. He is also a member of Team Rubicon and an adjunct member of the Coast Guard. He is a 25-year veteran of the U.S. Marine Corps, retiring as a Lt.Col., with operational experience in infantry, aviation, and intelligence. He holds undergraduate degrees in anthropology and journalism from the University of Kansas, and completed both the Naval War College senior officers' course, and an executive seminar at the Kennedy School at Harvard. He has researched and written works on intelligence and operations for the Terrorism Research Center (TRC) as well as having advised and instructed immersion courses created and delivered by the TRC between 2004 and 2009. This "Mirror Image" training created in situ conditions mimicking Jihadist training and indoctrination in remote sites.

Dr. Stefan Brem holds a Ph.D. in Political Science from the University of Zurich and specializes in critical infrastructure protection. He joined the Federal Office for Civil Protection within the Swiss Federal Department of Defence, Civil Protection and Sport in March 2007, where he leads a section on Risk Analysis and Research Coordination. Prior to this, he served for four years at the Federal Department of Foreign Affairs' Centre for International Security Policy where he was responsible *inter alia* for Critical Infrastructure Protection (CIP), Security Sector Reform, Border Security and Private Military Companies. He has contributed to *The Politics of Positive Incentives in Arms Control* (University of South Carolina Press, 1999) and co-edited and contributed to *Reframing the Agenda* (Greenwood 2003), along with a special issue on *Intelligence and Counter-Terrorism* in the *Journal of Policing, Intelligence and Counter Terrorism* (2007) and *Cooperating without America* (Routledge 2008). He has also published on various security issues in other publications.

Michael Brooks graduated with honors from Patrick Henry College with a B.A. degree in International Policy and Politics and is fluent in French. As a foreign affairs and security analyst, he has contributed to a variety of intelligence journals and private business projects. He has written original analysis for the OODA Loop project since its creation by Matthew Devost in 2012 and manages the company's daily report on international security issues. His areas of interest include security and international development across North, Central, and Eastern Africa. He currently works for LifeNet International, a health care conversion franchise operating in Burundi and Uganda.

Dr. Robert J. Bunker attended California State Polytechnic University, Pomona and the Claremont Graduate University. He holds a Ph.D. in Political Science and an M.A. in Government and bachelors' degrees in Anthropology/Geography, Social Science, Behavioral Science, and History. Dr. Bunker is an Adjunct Research Professor, Strategic Studies Institute, U.S. Army War College and adjunct faculty, Division of Politics and Economics, Claremont Graduate University. Past positions include Minerva Chair, Strategic Studies Institute, U.S. Army War College; Futurist in Residence, Behavioral Science Unit, FBI Academy; and CEO, Counter-OPFOR Corporation. He has delivered over 200 presentations, including papers and training, to military, law enforcement, and academic and policy audiences, including U.S. congressional testimony. He has hundreds of publications, including over two dozen edited books and booklets, along with numerous reports, chapters, articles/essays, response guidance, subject bibliographies, and encyclopedia entries in academic, policy, military, and law enforcement venues.

Rick Y. Byrum entered theological studies and formational seminary training in the early 1970s, earning his Bachelor's degree at Divine Word College in Ethnology, with an emphasis in African Studies, followed by three years in Ghana, West Africa, designing and building schools, medical clinics, and the rebuilding of war torn villages. He continued graduate studies at the Chicago Theological Union, earning his Masters of Divinity. He currently lives in Los Angeles, serving the community over 20 years as a Reserve Captain of the Los Angeles County Sheriff's Department, with over 2,500 hours of government training in Homeland Security, Search and Rescue, and Disaster Management. As a priest, Father Byrum continues his religious commitment by way of International Inter-religious Dialogue, and pastoral work with Hospice

Care and Gerontology at the Covington, as well as other medical facilities in Orange County.

Lisa J. Campbell is a Lt.Col. with the California Air National Guard specializing in predictive threat analysis, force protection, and wartime air base operability. She holds a B.S. in Geology from Cornell College, and graduated from the USAF Intelligence Officer Course at Goodfellow Air Force Base, TX. She has been a Red Team analyst supporting U.S. Africa Command in Stuttgart, Germany. Past written works include articles and chapter contributions on topics covering operational and order-of-battle assessments of Los Zetas and al Qaeda, Islamic fundamentalist use of beheadings and beheadings in Mexico, and the effects of lasers on aviation. She was a member of the Los Angeles Terrorism Early Warning (TEW) Group and a contributor to a law enforcement webbase on suicide bombings coordinated by a national law enforcement center.

Irina A. Chindea is a Ph.D. candidate in the International Security Studies Program at the Fletcher School, Tufts University. For her doctoral research, she is investigating the patterns of cooperation and conflict among organized criminal groups in weak and strong states. More specifically, her dissertation focuses on the shifts in alliances among the main Mexican and Colombian drug cartels, gangs of Salvadorian-origin operating in the United States and Central America, as well as Canadian Mafia groups. In this regard, in 2012, she conducted extensive field research on the U.S.–Mexico border, in Colombia, El Salvador, Canada, and in gang infested areas of Los Angeles. Ms. Chindea received her B.S. in 2003 from the Academy of Economics in Bucharest, Romania. Prior to completing her Master's at the Fletcher School in 2008, she worked as a senior analyst for the investment-arm of Raiffeisen Bank and for the Financial Advisory Services unit of KPMG Romania.

Dr. Martin van Creveld is Professor Emeritus at the Hebrew University of Jerusalem and is one of the world's best-known experts on military history and strategy. Born in the Netherlands, he has an M.A. from the Hebrew University of Jerusalem and a Ph.D. in History from the London

School of Economics and is fluent in Hebrew, English, German, and Dutch. He is the author of twenty-five books. Most are about military history and strategy; these include *The Transformation of War* (The Free Press 1991) and *The Rise and Decline of the State* (Cambridge University Press 1999) and his most recent, *Wargames: From Gladiators to Gigabytes* (Cambridge University Press 2013). Others deal with a broad range of subjects, such as political history, women's history, American history, and Israeli history. Between them, these works have now been published in twenty different languages, including Russian.

James P. Denney, deceased, managed operations and led personnel in emergency environments of all types throughout his 40+ year public service career spanning all branches of the Public Safety Emergency Services System. He retired from the Los Angeles City Fire Department. He was an adjunct faculty member of Loma Linda University, EMS Bachelor Program, instructor/controller for the Department of Homeland Security Health Care Leadership program, and instructor with the LSU National Center for Biomedical Research and Training Academy of Counter-Terrorist Education. He was a member of the U.S. Maritime Advisory Committee and a member of the Department of Defense, Defense Science Board (DSB) Civil Integration and Response Panel for Transnational Threats. Mr. Denney served as an advisor to the Defense Advanced Research Project Agency (DARPA), the Defense Science Research Council (DSRC) and the RAND Advisory Panel to Assess Domestic Response Capabilities for Terrorism Involving Weapons of Mass Destruction. He also served as a member of the Mount San Antonio College Paramedic Advisory Committee. He received his B.A. in Business and an M.S. in Health from Emerson College, Ontario, Canada.

Matthew G. Devost holds a B.A. degree from St. Michael's College and a M.A. in Political Science from the University of Vermont. He is currently the President & CEO of FusionX, LLC, a global cybersecurity consultancy. He is also the Founder of OODA LLC, (OODA.COM) and co-founded the Terrorism Research Center, Inc. (TRC) in 1996, where he served as President and CEO until November 2008. He has been an

Adjunct Professor at Georgetown University since 2002, teaching a flagship graduate course entitled "Information Warfare and Security", and is a Founding Director of the Cyberconflict Studies Association. In 2004, he was appointed to the Defense Science Board Task Force on Critical Homeland Infrastructure Protection. He has co-written or authored chapters for several books including *Cyberadversary Characterization, Threats in the Age of Obama, Information Warfare Vol. 2, Sun Tzu Art of War in Information Warfare*, and was the technical editor for *Hacking a Terror Network*.

T. Kessara Eldridge holds a B.A. in Business Administration, a M.S.I in Strategic Intelligence and a M.A. in Criminal Justice from American Military University. Over the past 12 years, she has provided research and analysis to U.S. government agencies and commercial financial organizations. Ms. Eldridge is a subject matter expert in the areas of threat finance, money laundering, Hawala, and terrorism (such as Burmese import/export regimes); Iranian economic and military infrastructure; and criminal use of Internet online gaming sites. Additionally, through her 20 years of experience in the government and private sectors, Ms. Eldridge has conducted numerous studies that utilized all-source intelligence and information to analyze various aspects of economic, political, and military infrastructure. She was a contributing reviewer for *Exploring the Literary Landscape: Resources for Teaching Intelligence* (International Association for Intelligence Education—IAFIE 2009) and author of *Social Networking: Threats & Risks* (Helios Global 2010).

Adam Elkus is a Ph.D. student at George Mason University, studying computer simulation of strategy in the department of Computational Social Science. He has written on conflict, security, and technology in *War on the Rocks, Foreign Policy, The Huffington Post, Slate, Small Wars Journal, SWAT Digest*, and other publications and has spoken to defense and technology audiences at conferences, ranging from the annual John Boyd conference at Marine Corps Base, Quantico to the U.S. Geospatial Foundation's AnalystOne government technology summit. Mr. Elkus has worked as a civilian open-source researcher in the Los Angeles County Sheriff's Department and is an Associate

Editor with *Red Team Journal*. He holds a B.A. in Diplomacy and International Affairs from Occidental College and a M.A. in Security Studies from Georgetown University.

Dr. Fadi Essmaeel, a physician and emergency manager, grew up in Jerusalem where exposure to hate crimes motivated him to join conflict-resolution initiatives and become a member of Amnesty International. He was first trained in WMD response at the age of 15 as member of a hospital decontamination team and again during operations Desert Shield and Desert Storm as a medical student. As a Medical Corps officer, he responded to numerous incidents in various operational settings and against the backdrop of historical events including the Lebanon War, the Oslo peace process and the ensuing waves of violence. Since 1999, Dr. Essmaeel has served as Homeland Security Director for US Congressman Dana Rohrabacher of California's 48th Congressional District. He designed and has overseen the delivery of 120,000 training hours on a myriad of HS/EM subjects for first responders via a nation-wide educational online information-sharing network.

Dr. Christopher Flaherty has a Ph.D. in Economic Relations from the University of Melbourne with a focus on networking. Following this, he pursued a career in defence and security research in the Australian Department of Defence. He has been based in London since 2008. He is a Senior Research Associate of the Terrorism Research Center (TRC) and the primary co-author of *Body Cavity Bombers: The New Martyrs* (iUniverse 2013). Two essays of his from 2003 and 2010 were reprinted in the TRC book *Fifth Dimensional Operations* (iUniverse 2014). He is also the author of *Australian Manoeuvrist Strategy* (Seaview Press 1996). Dr. Flaherty has been an active contributor on security, terrorism early warning, and related international intelligence issues, including on tactics, techniques and procedures analysis, published in the TRC report 'Dangerous Minds' (2012). He has a long-term involvement in the development of a 'Scripted Agent Based Microsimulation Project', at the University of Wollongong (NSW, Australia).

Phillip W. Fouts holds a B.A in Psychology from Southern Methodist University and a J.D. from South Texas College of Law. As a Special Agent for over 15 years with the Bureau of Alcohol, Tobacco, Firearms and Explosives (ATF), he worked as a Certified Fire Investigator. He also served as a full-time member of ATF's prestigious National Response Team (NRT), where he was also assigned to the International Response Team. With expertise investigating over 250 fire scenes, he recently formed The Fouts Group, based in Austin, TX. Some high profile cases he has worked on include the East Texas Church Fires in 2010, the Los Angeles Serial Arson Case in 2011, and the fire and explosion in West, Texas in 2013. Mr. Fouts regularly instructed at the National Fire Academy and the Federal Law Enforcement Training Center. He also taught at the International Law Enforcement Academy in Bangkok, Thailand.

Dr. Daveed Gartenstein-Ross holds a Ph.D. in World Politics from the Catholic University of America and a J.D. from the New York University School of Law. He is a senior fellow at the Foundation for Defense of Democracies and an adjunct assistant professor in Georgetown University's security studies program. He is the author or volume editor of fifteen books and monographs. He frequently conducts field research in relevant regions, including North Africa, the Persian Gulf, and South Asia, and he has been to the Guantánamo Bay detention facility on two separate occasions. Dr. Gartenstein-Ross also consults for clients who need to understand violent non-state actors and twenty-first century conflict, including working on hostage negotiations in the Middle East, risk assessments for oil and gas companies, border security refinements in Europe, and serving as an expert witness for asylum seekers from the Horn of Africa.

Dr. Russell W. Glenn has a B.S. degree from the United States Military Academy and Masters degrees from the University of Southern California (M.S., Systems Management), Stanford University (M.S., Civil Engineering and M.S., Operations Research), and the School of Advanced Military Studies (Master of Military Art and Science). His Ph.D. in American History with secondary fields of military history and political science is from the University of Kansas. Past research includes studies on counterinsurgency, urban operations, military and police training, and intelligence operations. His *Rethinking Western Approaches to Counter-Insurgency* was published in spring 2015. His military assignments included service in Korea, Germany, United Kingdom, and a combat tour in Iraq during Operations Desert Shield and Desert Storm. He was a senior defense analyst with RAND from 1997 to 2009 and is currently on the faculty of the Strategic and Defence Studies Centre at The Australian National University.

Scott Gerwehr was a pioneer in understanding deception in conflict. He died in a motorcycle accident in May 2008. He specialized in the study of deception and influence across many areas of national security. These include computer network operations, low-intensity conflict and terrorism, aerospace operations, espionage, confidence artistry, strategic denial and deception, public and covert diplomacy, and advertising/marketing. On the topic of deception, he led projects for RAND, Defense Group International, Inc., the CIA, the National Security Agency (NSA), Defense Advanced Research Projects Agency (DARPA), Joint Task Force-Computer Network Operations (JTF-CNO), U.S. Army Training and Doctrine Command (TRADOC), and the U.S. Marine Corps Warfighting Laboratories.

Dr. Lester W. Grau, Research Director for the Foreign Military Studies Office at Fort Leavenworth, Kansas, is a retired infantry Lieutenant Colonel. His service spanned from the Vietnam War to Cold War assignments in Europe, Korea, and the Soviet Union to the wars in Afghanistan and Iraq. He has conducted collaborative research in Russia, Afghanistan, Pakistan, and with numerous organizations in Europe. Dr. Grau has authored 14 books and over 200 articles and studies on tactical, operational, and geopolitical subjects, translated into several languages. *The Bear Went Over the Mountain: Soviet Combat Tactics in Afghanistan* (NDU Press 1996) and *The Other Side of the Mountain: Mujahideen Tactics in the Soviet-Afghan War* (USMC Studies and Analysis Division 1999), co-authored with former Afghan Minister of Security Ali Jalali, remain the most widely distributed, U.S.

government-published books throughout the conflict in Afghanistan. He holds a Ph.D. in History from the University of Kansas. His advanced military education includes the Army Command and General Staff College and the Air Force War College.

Thomas Greco is a member of the Defense Intelligence Senior Executive Service, and currently serves as the G2 (Intelligence Officer) at the U.S. Army's Training and Doctrine Command (TRADOC) where he is responsible for identifying the future operational conditions that drive Army training, leader development, and capability development. Prior to his current assignment, he served as the Senior Intelligence Officer at U.S. Army Europe, coordinating counter terrorism efforts with 20 nations around the world, and served a one year detail as the senior civilian intelligence advisor during the surge with Multinational Forces-Iraq Headquarters. He is a retired Army officer who was chosen five times to lead U.S. intelligence operations during contingency deployments. He is a graduate of Hunter College of the City University of New York; the School of Advanced Military Studies; executive programs at Northwestern University and the University of Virginia; and has held an intelligence community fellowship.

Dr. Daniel S. Gressang IV is a Strategy and Engagement Lead for the U.S. Department of Defense and an Adjunct Professor for the University of Maryland University College. He has previously served as visiting professor at the National Intelligence University, curriculum manager for the National Cryptologic School's analytic skills curriculum, and in a variety of analytic and managerial positions. His research centers on the interaction between terrorists and their audiences, terrorist and insurgent strategies, intelligence analysis, and critical thinking. He holds an A.B. and M.A. in Political Science, both from the University of Alabama, an M.S. in Strategic Intelligence from the National Intelligence University, and a Ph.D. in Government and Politics from the University of Maryland.

Dr. Rohan Gunaratna is Professor of Security Studies and head of the International Centre for Political Violence and Terrorism Research at

Nanyang Technological University in Singapore. He is also a member of the Steering Committee of George Washington University's Homeland Security Policy Institute and serves on the Advisory Board of the International Centre for Counter-Terrorism, The Hague. He was senior fellow at the United States Military Academy at West Point and at the Fletcher School of Law and Diplomacy. Invited to testify before the 9/11 Commission, he interviewed terrorists detainees in Iraq, Afghanistan, Pakistan, Libya, and in other countries. He is the author and editor of 15 books including *Inside Al Qaeda: Global Network of Terror* (Columbia University Press 2002). Admiral William McRaven appointed him to the International Senior Advisory Panel of the U.S. Special Operations Command in 2013. For advancing international security cooperation, he received the Major General Ralph H. Van Deman Award in 2014.

Dr. Thomas X. Hammes is a retired U.S. Marine Colonel and counterinsurgency specialist. He has a M.A. in Historical Research and a Ph.D. in Modern History from Oxford University. He is currently a Distinguished Research Fellow at the Institute for National Strategic Studies, National Defense University and an Adjunct Professor at Georgetown University and has lectured widely at U.S. and International Staff and War Colleges. In his thirty years in the Marine Corps, he served at all levels in the operating forces to include command of an intelligence battalion, an infantry battalion, and the Chemical Biological Incident Response Force (CBIRF). He participated in stabilization operations in Somalia and Iraq as well as training insurgents in various places. He has over 150 publications including *The Sling and the Stone: On War on the 21ˢᵗ Century* (Zenith Press 2006) and *Forgotten Warriors: The 1st Provisional Marine Brigade, the Corps Ethos, and the Korean War* (University Press of Kansas 2010).

Jennifer (Demmert) Hardwick has been a consultant for the Department of State's Overseas Security Advisory Council (OSAC) since January 2011, filling various roles including analytic senior editor; the Regional Analyst for Europe, Western Hemisphere, and West/Central Africa; and, soon, transnational safety and security concerns, to include pandemic outbreaks. Prior to OSAC, Jennifer joined the start-up

Terrorism Research Center, where she helped create their geo-political risk analysis service and was the Vice President of Client Management before it was purchased by The Prince Group. Prior to that, she took on many roles to stand up fee-based, private geo-political risk consulting services for Pinkerton, Inc., and Kroll, Inc. She lived overseas for seven years as a child and speaks German fluently. She graduated from The George Washington University with a B.A. in International Relations with double concentration in cross-cultural understanding and Western Europe and double minors in Political Science and German.

Daniel P. Heenan has been employed as a special agent (SA) with ATF since 1988. He began his career in San Francisco where he worked firearms, narcotics, explosives and arson investigations for nine years. During this time, SA Heenan was a member of the ATF Special Response Team for seven years, the last four of which were as the team sniper. For the past eighteen years, he has worked in the Las Vegas office where he is ATF's Certified Fire Investigator for the State of Nevada. He travels throughout the United States and foreign countries assisting in the origin and cause determination of fires as well as teaching the fire investigation community regarding origin and cause. He has been a member of the ATF National Response Team for the past twelve years and served as a full time member of the team for four years. He was selected as the Team Leader for the NRT in 2013. SA Heenan is currently the Vice-President for the International Association of Arson Investigators, has served as Chairman of the IAAI Training and Education Committee for six years and serves as a member on the NFPA 1033 committee. He is an IAAI-CFI as well as a Member of the Forensic Science Society. He is a graduate of the University of Nevada where he obtained a degree in Criminal Justice.

Dr. Brian K. Houghton is a Professor and the Associate Dean of the College of Business, Computing, and Government at Brigham Young University-Hawaii, where he teaches courses on crisis management, international relations, and terrorism. He regularly provides support for the U.S. State Department Antiterrorism Assistance Program. Prior to joining the BYU-H faculty, Dr. Houghton spent over five years as the Director of Research at the National Memorial Institute for the Prevention of Terrorism (MIPT) in Oklahoma City. Dr. Houghton was also a founding director of the Terrorism Research Center and a research analyst at the Strategic Assessment Center. He has a Ph.D. in Policy Analysis from the RAND Graduate School.

Ali A. Jalali, former Interior Minister of Afghanistan (January 2003-October 2005), is currently serving as both a Distinguished Professor at the Near East South Asia Center for Strategic Studies (NESA) and as a researcher at the Institute for National Strategic Studies (INSS) at NDU. He has served as the Director of Afghanistan National Radio Network Initiative and Chief of the Pashto and Persian Services at the Voice of America in Washington D.C. A reputed multi-lingual military and political analyst, Ali Ahmad Jalali has extensive academic, managerial, journalistic, and writing experience. During his VOA employment from 1982 to 2003, Mr. Jalali has directed broadcasts in Pashto, Dari, and Farsi (Persian) languages to Afghanistan, Iran, and Central Asia. As journalist, he has covered the war in Afghanistan (1982-1993) and the former Soviet Central Asia (1993-2000). A former officer in the Afghan Army, Col. Jalali served as a top military planner with the Afghan Resistance following the Soviet invasion of Afghanistan. He graduated from high command and staff colleges in Afghanistan, United Kingdom, and the United States. A published writer in three languages (English, Pashto, and Dari/Farsi), Mr. Jalali is the author of numerous books and articles on political, military and security issues in Afghanistan, Iran and Central Asia including topics related to Islamic movements in the region. His works are published in the United States, Britain, Afghanistan, Pakistan, and Iran. He has taught at higher education institutions of Afghanistan and extensively lectured at U.S. National Defense University, U.S. Army War College, U.S. Naval Postgraduate School, Monterey, and other defense institutions.

Brian Michael Jenkins is the senior advisor to the president of the RAND Corporation. He also directs the Mineta Transportation Institute's research on protecting surface transportation against terrorist attacks. From 1989-1998, he was deputy chairman of Kroll Associates and prior to that he was chairman of RAND's Political Science Department. He holds a B.A. in fine arts and a Masters degree in history, both from UCLA. He also studied in Mexico and was a Fulbright Fellow in Guatemala, where he received an additional fellowship from the Organization of American States. A Captain in the Army Special Forces, Jenkins is a decorated combat veteran with service in both Latin America and Vietnam. He has authored numerous articles, reports, and books, including *Will Terrorists Go Nuclear?* (Prometheus Books 2008) and *The Long Shadow of 9/11* (RAND 2011).

Dr. Peter Katona is Clinical Professor of Medicine in Infectious Diseases at the David Geffen School of Medicine at UCLA and Adjunct Professor of Public Health at the UCLA Fielding School of Public Health. He has worked at the Centers for Disease Control and Prevention (CDC) as an EIS Officer studying viral diseases and doing epidemic investigation; and at Apria/Corum Healthcare as their Corporate Medical Director. He has held appointments at Louisiana State University's National Center for Biomedical Research and Training and the Los Angeles County Emergency Management Services (EMS) Agency. He teaches a yearly Honors course at UCLA on terrorism, and has co-edited *Countering Terrorism and WMD: Creating a Global Counter-Terrorism Network* (Routledge 2006) and *Global Biosecurity: Threats and Responses* (Routledge 2010). He also maintains a private practice in infectious diseases and internal medicine in Los Angeles.

Hal Kempfer is the CEO/Founder of Knowledge & Intelligence Program Professionals (KIPP), Inc., in Long Beach, CA, and a retired Marine Reserve Lt.Col., with a long history of working on counterdrug intelligence both in the United States and overseas, including working in undercover task forces, regional intelligence centers and even the Plans section of the U.S. Southern Command's Intelligence Directorate. Under KIPP, he has conducted training and exercises as one of the most widely used trainers in intelligence and Homeland Security supporting the DHS sponsored fusion centers across the country. He has taught for the Naval Postgraduate School, National Guard's Civil-Military Interagency Training Institute and Joint Interagency Training

Center-West, and approximately fourteen DHS sponsored fusion centers along with various state and local entities. He has also been a featured expert on Southern California National Public Radio (KPCC 89.3 FM) and KABC-7 on Homeland Security, terrorism and military affairs, going back to 2002.

Dr. David J. Kilcullen served 24 years as an army officer, diplomat, and policy advisor for the Australian and United States governments. He has engaged in peacekeeping, counterinsurgency, and military advisor missions in Southeast Asia, the Middle East and the Pacific. After retiring as a Lt.Col., he was selected to become Chief Strategist in the U.S. State Department's Counterterrorism Bureau, serving in Afghanistan, Pakistan, Iraq, Southeast Asia, and the Horn of Africa, before deploying to Iraq as Senior Counterinsurgency Advisor, Multinational Force—Iraq during the 2007 Surge. He served as Special Advisor for Counterinsurgency to the U.S. Secretary of State in 2008-2009. He founded Caerus Associates, a research and design firm, in 2010, and launched First Mile Geo, a geospatial analysis startup, in 2014. His works include *The Accidental Guerrilla* (Oxford University Press 2009) and *Out of the Mountains* (Oxford University Press 2013). Dr. Kilcullen was named one of the *Foreign Policy* Top 100 Global Thinkers in 2009.

James T. Kirkhope possesses over 25 years experience delivering a broad array of consulting and research projects on counterterrorism, international affairs, and homeland security. Currently, he serves as the Counterterrorism Coordinator for the United States Transportation Command of the Department of Defense. In 2008, he was appointed Executive Director for the Council for Emerging National Security Affairs (CENSA). In 2006, he joined the Editorial Board of the international *Journal of Business Continuity and Emergency Planning*, published in London. Mr. Kirkhope founded both the Terrorism Studies Network and Terrorism Studies Group in 2002. He has published widely in academic journals, books, and electronic media on political violence and domestic security issues since 1989. He holds a B.A. in History and Psychology from Bowling Green State University, an M.A. in

International Affairs from The George Washington University, and an M.A. in Political Science from Columbia University.

Dr. Scott P. Layne, MD, is a recognized expert in the field of infectious diseases. He is a board-certified specialist in infectious diseases, Fellow of the American College of Physicians, and Fellow of the Infectious Diseases Society of America. He practices medicine at several major Los Angeles hospitals and is a Professor Emeritus at UCLA. As a Professor at the UCLA School of Public Health, he taught ground-breaking courses on responses to disease outbreaks including bioterrorism. He also served at the Los Alamos National Laboratory, where he worked on predicting the devastating growth of AIDS in Africa. Dr. Layne organized an AIDS epidemiology workshop for the White House Science Office under President Ronald Regan. He organized a forward-looking meeting at the Institute of Medicine and edited its instrumental proceedings *Firepower in the Lab* (2001). He served on the National Biosurveillance Advisory Sub-Committee created by President George W. Bush. Dr. Layne is an editor of *Jane's Chem-Bio Handbook* (2005), a definitive reference for emergency responders. He has published in *Nature, Science,* and *Proceedings of the National Academy of Sciences.* He presents talks to scientific and public audiences nationally and internationally.

Ernest (Ernie) J. Lorelli is the President and CEO of RDX, Inc, a Service Disabled Veteran Owned Small Business based in Henderson Nevada with core competencies in education, training, and program management. Mr. Lorelli is a retired Air Force Chief Master Sergeant with 25 years experience in Explosive Ordnance Disposal operations and was decorated for heroism for saving the life of a police officer. He is a national expert in directed energy effects and has worked on classified projects for Joint Improvised Device Defeat Office. An expert in the CARVER Risk, Threat and Vulnerability Assessment Model, Mr. Lorelli developed and implemented a unique CARVER program for the Department of Homeland Security, Transportation Security Agency for assessing the security infrastructure of the nations' 35 category X airports and the national transportation infrastructure. He holds a

Masters Degree in Education from Boston University and is a licensed teacher in the state of Nevada.

Dr. Prem Mahadevan is a Senior Researcher with the Center for Security Studies at ETH Zürich, where he specialises in the study of intelligence systems and international terrorism. He has completed a B.A., M.A., and Ph.D. in War Studies and Intelligence Studies from King's College London. His doctoral thesis examined Indian strategic responses to cross-border terrorism. He has briefed NATO Headquarters and European government agencies on contemporary jihadist threats, and advised Indian security agencies on counterterrorist operational management. Besides authoring more than 70 publications on international security, he has completed Hostile Environment Awareness Training (HEAT) with the Swiss Army and also trained as a foreign correspondent and political risk analyst in the Czech Republic and United Kingdom.

Paul M. Maniscalco has over 35 years of Public Safety and Emergency Management Response, Supervisory, Management, and Executive service and presently serves as a senior executive policy consultant to several governmental bodies and private sector organizations. He is a faculty member and subject matter expert to the Louisiana State University-National Center for Biomedical Research and Training-Academy of Counter-Terrorism Education. He is President Emeritus of the International Association of Emergency Medical Service Chiefs and is also a former President of the National Association of Emergency Medical Technicians and a member of the InterAgency Board (IAB). He served on the Advisory Panel to Assess Domestic Response Capabilities for Terrorism Involving Weapons of Mass Destruction (Gilmore Commission). Maniscalco earned his Bachelors in Public Administration—Public Health & Safety from the City University of New York, a Master of Public Administration—Foreign Policy and National Security from the NYU Wagner Graduate School of Public Service, and a Master of Science in Emergency Services Management from The George Washington University.

Kevin R. McCarthy is a Delta Air Lines Captain (retired) and founder, MoonRaker Associates and COO, MoonRaker Aviation Services Inc., two firms delivering global transportation and logistics expert advise, cutting edge technology enhancements, and hands-on operations guidance. He has over 33 years experience flying commercial and military aircraft worldwide. A B777 captain and acknowledged aviation security expert, in response to 9/11 he was appointed founding Director, Intelligence and Emerging Threats, Air Line Pilots Association. At the request of the Pentagon, he led a team of experts to develop operational procedures to reopen Baghdad International Airport to civilian aircraft. He has served as an advisor to The White House, U.S. House of Representatives, and senior officials in DHS on matters related to commercial aviation operations and the protection of airliners. He is active on several private sector advisory boards and resides in Park City, Utah.

Jason Pate holds an A.B. in International Relations and National Security Studies from Stanford University and a M.P.M. in International Security and Economic Policy from the School of Public Affairs at the University of Maryland. He is a Senior Research Associate and Manager of the Weapons of Mass Destruction (WMD) Terrorism Project for the Chemical and Biological Weapons Nonproliferation Program, at the Center for Nonproliferation Studies (CNS), Monterey Institute of International Studies (MIIS). A certified Emergency Medical Technician (EMT), his primary interest is law enforcement/first responder response to and emergency planning for terrorist incidents. His research focuses on understanding motivations and patterns of behavior associated with terrorism involving weapons of mass destruction, the militia and Christian Identify phenomenon in the United States, and the causes of violence. Mr. Pate is co-author of "The Minnesota Patriots Council," in Jonathan B. Tucker, Ed., *Toxic Terror* (MIT Press 2000).

William C. Patrick III, deceased, was president of BioThreats Assessment, a biological warfare and terrorism consultancy whose clients included the FBI, CIA, and U.S. military. He was a chief scientist at the Army Biological Warfare Laboratories at Fort Detrick, Maryland for much of the Cold War where he was involved with the military's top-secret weaponization of anthrax, tularemia, and other deadly pathogens. As a former bioweaponeer, he held five classified U.S. patents for the process of weaponizing anthrax. He served in the U.S. Army in World War II and later obtained a B.S. in Biology from the University of South Carolina and a M.S. in Microbiology from the University of Tennessee. He was a contributing author of *Jane's Chem-Bio Handbook* (2005).

Ralph Peters is a writer, strategist, Fox News commentator, and retired military officer. He is the author of 27 books and more than seven hundred columns, articles, essays, and reviews. Uniformed service, personal interests, and research have taken him to 70 countries and six continents. He served in the U.S. Army for 22 years, retiring shortly after his promotion to Lt.Col. to write with greater freedom. He served in Infantry and Military Intelligence units before becoming a Foreign Area Officer specializing in Russia and surrounding states. His commentaries, essays, and reviews have appeared in *The New York Post, The Washington Post, The Wall Street Journal, USA Today, The Atlanta Journal- Constitution, The Los Angeles Times, Newsday,* the *Frankfurter Allgemeine Zeitung, Newsweek, Harpers, The Weekly Standard, The National Review, The Washington Monthly, Wired, Parameters, Armed Forces Journal, Strategic Review, Armchair General, Military Review, Maclean's* and a wide range of other domestic and foreign publications.

Dr. Raymond Picquet has worked as a defense analyst for over thirty years. He has specialized in two major areas, the proliferation of weapons of mass destruction and international terrorism, with an emphasis on regional aspects of both those issues in the Middle East, Africa, and Central Asia. In the 1990s, he leveraged his in-depth knowledge of WMD proliferation to contribute to the development of emerging arms control efforts that culminated in the Chemical Weapons Convention in 1996. Over the next ten years, he worked in various capacities in Iraq and Afghanistan as both an intelligence analyst and as a cultural affairs advisor to the Coalition Forces in both of those countries. Dr. Picquet has written several books on international terrorism and recently completed a Ph.D. dissertation on chemical weapons acquisition in the Middle East at the Claremont Graduate University.

Caitlin Poling serves as the director of government relations at the Foreign Policy Initiative (FPI). Prior to joining FPI, she worked in the House of Representatives, most recently serving as a legislative assistant to Congressman Mike Pompeo (R-KS), focusing on foreign affairs, human rights, homeland security, and immigration. In this capacity, she led initiatives with the International Religious Freedom Caucus for the rights of persecuted religious minorities in Hungary and Nigeria. She writes on Africa and counterterrorism issues, and her work has been published in *U.S. News and World Report, e-International Relations,* and *The Huffington Post.* She holds a B.A. (summa cum laude) in Political Science, International Studies, and French from Ashland University and an M.A. in Security Studies (with honors) from Georgetown University. She wrote her master's thesis on Boko Haram and affiliated terrorist groups in the Sahel.

Byron Ramirez is a researcher and analyst who specializes in economic and international political affairs. He is a Ph.D. Candidate in Economics and Political Science at Claremont Graduate University and holds an M.A. in Economics, a M.S. in Management, and an MBA. He has worked for Wikistrat as a geopolitical analyst focused on macroeconomic and globalization issues, and collaborated with *Small Wars Journal—El Centro* on topics related to Latin America's criminal groups. His areas of research include economic and social development, geopolitics, sustainable development, domestic security, illicit trade, and illegal economies. Some of his past publications include: "The Evolution of 'Narco-Submarines' Engineering", "Narco-Submarines: Applying Advanced Technologies to Drug Smuggling", and the co-edited book titled: 'Narco Armor: Improvised Armored Fighting Vehicles in Mexico" (U.S. Army Foreign Military Studies Office 2013).

John Robb is a former special operations pilot, technology entrepreneur, and military futurist. He is a graduate of the U.S. Air Force Academy and Yale University. While in the military, he served in a tier one unit assigned to the counter-terrorist mission working with Delta and Seal Team 6. After military service, he became the world's leading technology analyst with numerous quotes in the *New York Times, Wall Street Journal*, BBC, *The Economist*, CNBC, and Fox. John's entrepreneurial career led to the founding of a $300 million financial company and running a company that pioneered the social media technology currently used in Facebook and Twitter. Over the last decade, he successfully developed a theory of modern warfare called "open source warfare" that led to consultations with the DOD, NSA, JCS, CIA, and testimony for the House Armed Services Committee. This warfare theory has also become extremely popular with guerrillas and terrorists all over the world, from Nigeria's MEND to *Inspire Magazine*.

Dr. David Ronfeldt has a B.A. in International Relations from Pomona College, M.A. in Latin American Studies from Stanford University, and Ph.D. in Political Science from Stanford University. He worked for the RAND Corporation from 1971 until retiring in 2008. During the first fifteen+ years, he worked mostly on U.S.-Latin American security issues (esp. Mexico, Cuba) and, during the next fifteen+ years, he worked on worldwide implications of the information revolution (e.g., cyberocracy, cyberwar, netwar, swarming, noöpolitik) plus episodically on other matters (e.g., terrorism, hubris-nemesis complex). Now, via blogging, he continues working on two theories: one on how and why four forms of organization (tribes, institutions, markets, networks) shape social evolution; the other on how and why people's space-time-action orientations shape their mindsets and cultures. Dr. Ronfeldt is the author of many monographs on network and tribal warfare, including *Networks and Netwars* (RAND 2001), *In Athena's Camp* (RAND 1997), and *Cyberwar is Coming!* (RAND 1993).

Mitchell D. Silber received his B.A. in Economics and European History from the University of Pennsylvania and his M.A. in International Security Policy at Columbia. He is the Executive Managing Director at K2 Intelligence for Intelligence and Analytic Solutions. He is the former Director of Intelligence Analysis for the New York City Police Department (NYPD) where he supervised the Intelligence Division's entire portfolio of ongoing terrorism-related investigations. He also built and managed both the Analytic and Cyber Intelligence Units. Mr. Silber has presented on behalf of the NYPD at the White House, National Security Council, CIA, FBI, and National Counter Terrorism Center and testified before the U.S. Senate and House of Representatives. He was a co-author of the 2007 NYPD report *Radicalization in the West: The Homegrown Threat*, the author of *The Al Qaeda Factor: Plots Against the West* (University of Pennsylvania Press 2012), and co-author of *Cyberwarfare and the Law* (Thomson Reuters–West 2014).

Dr. Joshua Sinai is a Director of Analytics and Business Intelligence at the Resilient Corporation and at its wholly-owned subsidiary, CRA, where he specializes in terrorism, counterterrorism, and homeland security studies. He has worked as an Associate Professor/Research at VT Research Center–Arlington, Virginia Tech (National Capital Region), which he joined in April 2010. Dr. Sinai's specializations include methodologies to forecast terrorist warfare, root cause analysis, and performance metrics in counterterrorism. He has more than 25 years of experience in government (including working at Department of Homeland Security's Science and Technology Directorate and, as a contractor, at an FBI counterterrorism operations center). Dr. Sinai has published a pocket handbook on active shooter prevention and more than 80 articles and book reviews on terrorism and counterterrorism related topics in academic publications, magazines, and newspapers. He holds a Ph.D. in Political Science, with a specialization in Comparative Politics and the Middle East, from Columbia University.

Dr. Erroll G. Southers is the Director of Transition and Research Deployment at the National Center for Risk and Economic Analysis of Terrorism Events (CREATE) at the University of Southern California (USC). He was California Governor Arnold Schwarzenegger's Deputy Director for Critical Infrastructure of the California Office of Homeland Security. He has served as Assistant Chief of Homeland Security and Intelligence at the Los Angeles World Airports Police, as an FBI Special Agent, and as a Santa Monica Police Officer. He is also a Visiting Fellow and member of the Professional Advisory Board of the International Institute of Counter-Terrorism in Herzliya, Israel. He developed CREATE's Executive Program in Counterterrorism and is adjunct professor of Homeland Security and Public Policy in the Sol Price School of Public Policy, where he received the *2014 Outstanding Doctoral Project Award* and was named the *2013 and 2014 Outstanding Adjunct Professor of the Year*. He is author of *Homegrown Violent Extremism* (Routledge 2009).

Dr. John P. Sullivan is a career police officer. He currently serves as a lieutenant with the Los Angeles County Sheriff's Department. He is also an adjunct researcher at the Vortex Foundation in Bogotá, Colombia; a senior fellow at the Stephenson Disaster Management Institute (SDMI) at Louisiana State University; senior research fellow at the Center for Advanced Studies on Terrorism (CAST); and a senior fellow at *Small Wars Journal-El Centro*. He completed the CREATE Executive Program in Counter-Terrorism at the University of Southern California and holds a B.A. in Government from the College of William and Mary, a M.A. in Urban Affairs and Policy Analysis from the New School for Social Research, and a Ph.D. in Information and Knowledge Society, from the Internet Interdisciplinary Institute (IN3) at the Open University of Catalonia (Universitat Oberta de Catalunya) in Barcelona.

Michael Tanji holds a B.S. in Computer Science from Hawaii Pacific University, an M.A. in Computer Forensics from The George Washington University, and is a 2007 Claremont Institute Lincoln Fellow. He is presently Chief Security Officer, Kyrus Tech, Inc., after having had spent nearly 20 years in the U.S. intelligence community. Trained in both SIGINT and HUMINT, he has worked at the Defense Intelligence Agency, the National Security Agency, and the National Reconnaissance Office. A veteran of the U.S. Army, he has served in both strategic and tactical assignments in the Pacific Theater, the Balkans, and the Middle East. He lectures on intelligence issues at The George Washington University and has also been a contributor to the *Weekly Standard* and *Wired Danger Room*. He is also the editor of *Threats in the Age of Obama* (Nimble Books 2009).

Dr. **Gregory F. Treverton** is chairman of the U.S. National Intelligence Council (NIC). In nearly two decades as a senior analyst at the RAND Corporation, he also directed the Centers for International Security and Defense Policy, Intelligence and Policy, and Global Risk and Security. Earlier service in government included staffing the first Senate Select Committee on Intelligence, handling Western Europe for the National Security Council, and serving as vice chairman of the NIC. His latest book is *National Intelligence and Science: Beyond the Great Divide in Analysis and Policy* with Wilhelm Agrell (Oxford University Press 2014). He holds an A.B. summa cum laude from Princeton University and an M.P.P. and Ph.D. in Economics and Politics from Harvard University.

Donald E. Vandergriff, U.S. Army retired, is currently a consultant for numerous Western militaries and law enforcement agencies. He spent two years in Afghanistan working for NATO on Afghanistan National Security Forces development. He also served for 24 years of active duty as an enlisted Marine and Army officer. He is a recognized authority on the U.S. Army personnel system, Army culture, leadership development, Soldier/Marine training and, in the early 21st century, the emergence of asymmetric warfare, also known as 4th generation warfare (4GW). He has authored over 60 articles, numerous briefings, and six books. His forthcoming book is on how to develop leaders to operate under the command culture of Mission Command.

G.I. Wilson is a Marine Corps combat veteran, retiring as a Colonel, with over 40 years of combined experience in military operations and law enforcement. He is a board certified protection professional (CPP) and certified forensic consultant (CFC). He has published in professional journals, appears on national TV and radio, and has contributed to several books regarding national security. He teaches at the college level concordant with serving as a North San Diego County Gang Commissioner. G.I. Wilson is a recognized civilian and military subject matter expert regarding maneuver warfare, fourth generation warfare, and emerging threats that include non-state and failed state actors. His particular areas of interest are criminal behavior associated with gangs, psychopathy, criminal enterprises, and terrorism. He holds an undergraduate degree in psychology from State University of New York at Albany and master's degrees in Security Management from Webster University, and Forensic Psychology from Argosy University.